Events Management

Contemporary events management is a diverse and challenging field. This introductory textbook fully explores the multidisciplinary nature of events management and provides the student with all the practical skills and professional knowledge they need to succeed in the events industry.

It introduces every core functional area of events management, such as marketing, finance, project management, strategy, operations, event design and human resources, in a vast array of different event settings from sport to political events. This new edition has been updated to include:

- New and updated content on technological developments in events such as virtual/hybrid events, artificial intelligence, virtual/augmented reality, holograms in music events, software for event planning and projection mapping.
- New content on eSports, the sustainability sector, employability skills, policy changes, diversity and inclusion, ethics and responsibility in events, and contemporary event safety and security issues including the threat of terrorism.
- New and updated case studies that cover a wider range of regions.
- A fully updated and extended companion website that includes web and video links, quizzes and a case study archive for students, as well as PowerPoint slides for instructors and a brand-new instructor manual full of teaching strategy ideas.

Every topic is brought to life through vivid case studies, personal biographies and examples of best practice from the real world of events management. Written by a team of authors with many years' experience of working in the events industry, *Events Management: An Introduction* is the essential course text for any events management programme.

Charles Bladen is an international academic, researcher and business consultant specialising in customer experience design.

James Kennell is Reader in Events and Hospitality at the University of Surrey, UK.

Emma Abson is Senior Lecturer on the Events Management courses at Sheffield Hallam University, UK.

Nick Wilde is Dean of Sports Business Management at the Global Institute of Sport in London, and a Visiting Professor at the Real Madrid Business School.

Events Management

An Introduction

Third Edition

Charles Bladen, James Kennell,
Emma Abson and Nick Wilde

Routledge
Taylor & Francis Group

LONDON AND NEW YORK

Designed cover image: © Getty Images

Third edition published 2023
by Routledge
4 Park Square, Milton Park, Abingdon, Oxon, OX14 4RN

and by Routledge
605 Third Avenue, New York, NY 10158

Routledge is an imprint of the Taylor & Francis Group, an informa business

First edition published by Routledge 2012
Second edition published by Routledge 2018

British Library Cataloguing-in-Publication Data
A catalogue record for this book is available from the British Library

Library of Congress Cataloging-in-Publication Data
Names: Bladen, Charles, author. | Kennell, James, author. |
    Abson, Emma, author. | Wilde, Nick, author.
Title: Events management : an introduction / Charles Bladen, James Kennell,
    Emma Abson and Nick Wilde.
Identifiers: LCCN 2021057868 (print) | LCCN 2021057869 (ebook)
Subjects: LCSH: Special events—Management.
Classification: LCC GT3405 .B63 2022 (print) | LCC GT3405 (ebook) |
    DDC 394.2068—dc23
LC record available at https://lccn.loc.gov/2021057868
LC ebook record available at https://lccn.loc.gov/2021057869

ISBN: 978-0-367-61014-2 (hbk)
ISBN: 978-0-367-61004-3 (pbk)
ISBN: 978-1-003-10287-8 (ebk)

DOI: 10.4324/9781003102878

Typeset in Sabon and Frutiger
by Apex CoVantage, LLC

Access the companion website: www.routledge.com/cw/bladen

Contents

Contents

Contents

Images

Figures

Tables

Tables

Case studies

Acknowledgements

Charles Bladen
Dedicated to Freya

James Kennell
Thanks to Lyra, Aphra and Evie for the inspiration

Emma Abson
Thanks to Andrew, for all the coffee

Nick Wilde
To Max and Honey and all my students

Guided tour

A visual tour of *Events Management: An Introduction*.

Pedagogical features

Events Management: An Introduction offers a variety of ways to help lecturers introduce this exciting discipline, and to engage students and help them understand key concepts and issues.

CHAPTER AIMS
Each chapter opens with a series of key learning outcomes that students will be able to attain after reading the chapter. They serve to ensure more focused learning and teaching.

1.2 Aims of the second edition
By the end of this chapter the student will be able to:

- describe ... aracteristics of events;
  ... n and history of events;
  ... e of the contemporary events industry;
- expla ... tionships between the events industry and the education sector; and
  ... k in order to develop their knowledge of event management.

FIGURES, TABLES AND IMAGES
The text uses a rich mix of figures, tables and images to represent important concepts and issues, creating an inviting visual design.

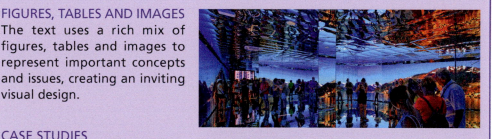

CASE STUDIES
International case studies are included in each chapter, illustrating the chapter topic area through a focused presentation of events management on the ground. Case studies are supplemented by study activities asking students to engage actively with the material. See 'List of case studies' for full details.

CASE STUDY 1.1

Good Food & Wine Show Gauteng, South ... rica

... ican annual food event of its kind, The Good Food & Wine ... the latest food and beverage products, innovations, lifestyle ... d appliances. The events have been held at various South African ... g Johannesburg, with more recent event extensions in Cape Town ... ban.

The prosperity of economy and image experienced by South Africa in the post-Mandela era has arguably been tarnished by what many regard as misgovernment, leading in particular to a devalued currency and falling wine sales. This festival has therefore been heralded as one of the important avenues by which these deficits might be corrected.

The core concepts of the show include themes, such as 'Eat Well, Live Well', 'Fresh', 'lifestyle' and 'baking'. The live theatre includes sessions on wine and

STUDY ACTIVITIES

The book fosters an active learning approach through discussion points and activities interspersed throughout each chapter. These can be used as the basis for class discussion, or developed into essay questions or research projects.

Study activity

1 In you~~r opinion~~, to what extent is events management a profession? Use ~~~~port your answer.
~~present approach of defining the attributes of the events~~ ~~pro~~fession resemble the various approaches presented in
~~~~gest event professionalism can be more effectively

INDUSTRY VOICES

Voices come from a range of companies, organisations and individuals, from sponsorship consultants to security advisers, communication executives to mega-event programmers.

Industry voice

Joanna Griffith

~~~~he British Council as an events officer, just after they had ~~~~ning the launch of a series of seminars to commemorate the ~~anniv~~ersary of world-famous playwright William Shakespeare's

~~~~g interviewed, the initial plan was that the event, based ~~~~play Twelfth Night, was to take place on the twelfth day ~~However~~, by the time I commenced employment, the event ~~~~cheduled for performance on its original date, 2 February, at its original venue, Middle Temple, in London.

As a fairly recent graduate of Events Management, I was so excited to join the British Council team and the launch of the 'Shakespeare Lives Seminar Series' on such a significant date and venue.

CHAPTER SUMMARIES

A concise overview of each chapter – perfect to consolidate learning, or as a useful tool for student revision.

4.8 Summary

T~~his chapter has high~~lighted the importance of events operations. Throughout the chapter, it ~~~~at every event is different and individually complex, so there is no set ~~~~. The legislation relating to health, safety and risk changes regularly ~~~~event managers keep abreast of the current legalities and regulations. ~~~~cused on two key operational aspects of events: the consideration of ~~~~ences, permits and contracts involved when managing an event; and ~~~~g logistical planning for customers and on-site at venues.

~~~~ent operations to decide which resources, skills and equipment will be re~~quired... ~~ess~~ential part of the events management process and needs to be considered fully within the context of both the event planning process and health, safety and risk analysis.

FURTHER READING

Each chapter concludes with a list of key scholarly books and articles that will provide additional treatment of the theories and concepts covered. Students will find this list particularly helpful for developing and researching papers and other assignments.

Further reading

~~~~lago, L. K. and Veal, A. J. (eds) (2000) *Events beyond 2000: Setting the* ~~~~*of the Conference on Evaluation, Research and Education, Sydney* ~~~~ustralian Centre for Event Management, University of Technology. ~~~~s on event operations, including the Abbott and Abbott paper on ~~~~nd control. These proceedings also cover many fundamental issues ~~~~t studies and are thoroughly recommended.
~~~~porate Manslaughter Law: No Place to Hide, *Personnel Today*, 17 ~~~~at: www.personneltoday.com/articles/2008/03/17/44774/corporate-~~~~aw-no-place-to-hide.html. Accessed 28 December 2010. An interesting article that offers a useful checklist for event managers operating within the regulations of the Corporate Manslaughter and Corporate Homicide Act 2007.
BSI ISO20121 Sustainability in Event Management Available at: www.bsigroup.com/en-GB/iso-20121-sustainable-events-management/. Full details on the ISO20121 standard can be found here.

REVIEW QUESTIONS

Chapters include review questions – ideal for students to test their knowledge and ensure they have fully understood the content of each chapter.

Review questions

~~~~tions management important to the success of an event
~~~~ave a leading role in determining the strategic direction
~~~~ns between cost minimisation and quality maximisation
~~~~ustry. Why do they occur, and what can be done about
~~~~rying to offer the best event at the cheapest cost?
4. D~~iscuss the~~ use of the IPO model as applied to event operations.
5. Read Olly Galvin's industry voice – were you surprised by the number of things he suggests you need to consider when thinking about site management? What was the most interesting point that Olly made?

Companion website

 www.routledge.com/cw/bladen

The third edition of *Events Management: An Introduction* also includes an updated, comprehensive companion website of online resources for both students and lecturers. These include:

Student resources

- Annotated further reading for each chapter to provide an accessible gateway to in-depth information on key issues highlighted.
- Various tools used by events management professionals to provide further insight into the realities of the industry.
- Multiple-choice questions for each chapter for students to test their understanding.
- Further discussion questions for each chapter, which can be set as assessment tasks or used to prompt seminar or in-class discussions.

Lecturer resources

- PowerPoint presentations for each chapter to provide lecturers with a ready-made foundation for their lecture preparation. The files can be downloaded and annotated.

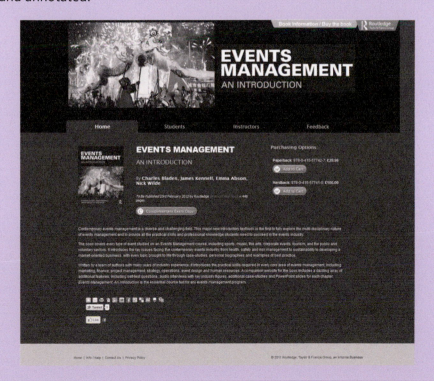

Chapter 1

Introduction to events management

Contents

DOI: 10.4324/9781003102878-1

1.1 Introduction to the third edition

Many changes have transpired since we wrote the first edition of this book. The events sector and the profession have greatly developed, as have the geopolitical and economic environments surrounding them. In particular, we publish this volume in the shadow of a world ravaged by the Covid-19 pandemic, which has wreaked havoc on the events sector, along with the rest of the world's societies and economies. This chapter, in addition to introducing the rest of the book, is intended to 'set the scene' for the reader in terms of the crucial role of events in human history through to the present day. The emphasis here is on events as an artefact of human culture that has developed into a fast-growing industry, which has recently and increasingly established itself as central to local and global strategies for many kinds of change, in local, national, international and digital realms. At the time of the publication of this third edition, the authors have endeavoured to incorporate key changes to the events sector by advances in technology, cultural and geopolitical changes and world health issues. The book also attempts to address other contemporary questions that are raised by the continued development of the events sector, and the education provisions designed to serve it.

1.2 Aims of the third edition

By the end of this chapter, students will be able to:

- describe the main characteristics of events
- explain the evolution and history of events
- analyse the structure of the contemporary events industry
- understand the relationships between the events industry and the education sector
- navigate this book to develop their knowledge of events management.

1.3 What is an event?

There are various answers to this question, depending on the viewpoint of the person defining it. Many definitions of 'events' have evolved in recent decades from various academic writers such as Getz (2019) and Goldblatt (2014). As such definitions become more detailed, their 'real-world' application becomes more problematic. Thus, this book provides a general definition as follows:

Events are temporary and purposive gatherings of people.

It follows that 'events management' as a field of industrial practice should be defined as:

The organisation and coordination of the activities required to achieve the objectives of events.

The aims of this text are to discuss and evaluate the management of these activities in the context of various and common types of events within their wider industrial and societal context. To do this, a clearer discussion of the features of events, which make them distinct from more general business activities, is required.

Events generally possess the following characteristics:

- They are temporary in nature.
- They are gatherings of people, either 'physically' or online.
- They are often displays of ritual.
- They are, in some sense, unique occurrences.

Though these points may seem obvious, the more we observe the phenomenon of events in our society, and its influence on our business and social lives, the more we could be forgiven for finding inconsistencies between these basic descriptors and that which we witness daily in the media, our neighbourhoods or even our own social networks.

1.3.1 Events are temporary

Events differ from other, more common, organisational activities because they possess a finite beginning and end. Managers and students probably agree that most events have a start time, a programme and a finishing time. Though this is certainly true of managed events, it is generally not the case with 'spontaneous events' which generally take place without much specific planning.

It is necessary to plan times and programmes for the successful delivery of a planned event yet these 'spontaneous' displays of ritual, events that take place without much specific planning, can be wide-ranging in nature and expression. For example, there has been much publicity in the media about the governmental changes that have taken place due to various Covid-19 pandemic lockdowns across the globe, illicit events that have been publicised in the media to have broken these restrictions, and events to protest that 'Black Lives Matter'. Informal events have continued to accompany more formal, programmed events in all parts of the world, such as protest events surrounding the 2020 US Presidential election.

There are also important differences between events and the attractions in or around which they are held. Getz (2007) focused on differences between events and permanent attractions such as historical venues; though many events take place for a pre-planned period at such venues. For example, in previous years, permanent art galleries, such as the Thyssen-Bornemisza Museum in Madrid, regularly hold events within their venues to display works by artists for a limited period only. Such events can last for several weeks, and while their attraction to tourists is clear, their limited duration still places them in the category of events.

1.3.2 Events are gatherings of people

So far, we have established that events are comprised of people, although numbers of such attendees may vary considerably. A clear definition of an event attendee is often easier to define in certain situations than in others. Somebody attending a sports or music event is unlikely to be allowed to enter without a ticket, whether paid for or not. However, as will be discussed in Chapter 10, mega-events include in their scope entire locations, destinations and even the whole world in the form of international media coverage.

Events can involve single people as the focus, as in the case of concerts by solo music celebrities, or whole groups, such as those who attended the event discussed in the following case study.

CASE STUDY 1.1

Electric Medway Digital Arts Festival

Aiming to showcase 60 miles of North Kent and South Essex as one of the most creative areas in the whole of the UK, Electric Medway 2021 was organised by Sparked Echo, a sound-based organisation. The extensive ten-day hybrid programme of events included both physical and digital arts presentations. Multiple sites and virtual locations, which included five virtual zones, hosted a diverse array of events including Railing, a set of dance films created by Harriet Parker-Beldeau, and Medway Megaliths, a five-part sci-fi drama. The event received a successful debut in 2020 and the 2021 programme supports the development of Medway's bid for UK City of Culture 2025. The government-organised UK City of Culture competition take place every four years and winning bids result in the creation of a national year-long cultural event focused on that city. This important programme has the potential to encourage new partnerships, innovation and inspiration in terms of cultural and creative activity. The programme is proposed to leave a lasting legacy in terms of visitors and sustainability and act as a supporting mechanism for regeneration in local communities. The event was supported by leading sponsors and partnerships with Medway Council, Arts Council England and a Creative Estuary Commission. Councillor Doe (Medway Council) proposed this was a 'wonderful opportunity . . . for young people to get experiences that they wouldn't get anywhere else', whilst the co-director of the event suggested that 'with the arts I think we've still proven it's a powerful way to bring people together and inspire people even if it's all digital and online' (Kevin Grist, Artistic Director, Electric Medway). The programme supports pathways into creative industries for young people and showcases work in the local area through interaction with over 450 people of all ages including the 70 artists directly involved. A robust social media presence through Facebook, Twitter (@ElectricMedway) and Instagram (@electricmedway) supports dissemination which works in collaboration with other local events.

Source: Electric Medway (2021a, 2021b)

Study activity

1 Which are the main groups of people being gathered by this event?
2 What do you think are some of the possible event planning aspects that need to be considered for this event?
3 What are your ideas about potential future developments of the event concept?

As can be seen from this example, events (including hybrid events) can comprise both planned staging elements and unplanned spontaneity. The scale and formality of events can vary considerably as can the levels of ritual display.

When considering such events as gatherings, we should also consider the impacts of more recent technologies on these otherwise age-old practices. Certainly, web conferencing – the ability through media to share information from widespread geographic locations – has progressed in terms of effectiveness and popularity in recent years. In a sense, the participants gather without travelling.

Applications of web conferencing include meetings, training events, lectures or presentations and have the advantage of being real-time, and carry the facility to be recorded, which is a valuable service for many businesses. Downsides of web conferencing include technological failure, which can fast make a promising event a complete non-event. This is particularly frustrating for organisers of larger web conferences as the technology is rarely under their direct control.

Webinars or webcasts have been born of these technologies, making one-way mass-presentations possible to international audiences, with webinars tending to be more interactive than webcasts. Workshops can also be effectively held by organisers using online tools.

Despite certain suggestions at one time about the possibility that web conferencing would end 'real' conferencing completely, it has proven to be used as a supplement to face-to-face contact rather than its replacement. One of the main limitations of web conferencing is that it cannot replace the richness of face-to-face interactions.

1.3.3 Events are often displays of ritual

Humans are the most socially evolved species on the planet. As such, we develop social interactions beyond our family structures which facilitate the need for events. According to Maslow (1943), human social needs are related to each other, as shown in Figure 1.1.

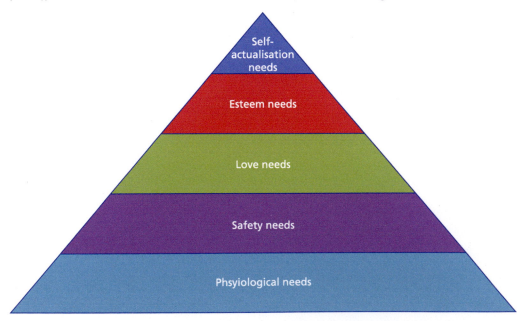

Figure 1.1 Maslow's hierarchy of needs
Source: Adapted from Maslow (1943)

As this early model suggests, humans are on a journey to the achievement of self-actualisation, which relates to the ultimate fulfilment of one's potential. Initially, physiological needs, followed by safety needs should be satisfied before a person can go about satisfying their needs for love and belonging to a social group. Clearly these latter needs are partially fulfilled through family ties and social relationships, but they could also be said to form the main motivating factor behind the age-old practice of holding events.

Events are characterised by rituals, symbols and artefacts, which themselves denote meaning. For example, one has only to consider the average wedding event, which will likely be comprised of various costumes, food and drink, speeches and behaviours, which denote the meanings of the culture in question. More discussion of how these meanings can be designed is provided in Chapter 3.

1.3.4 Events are unique occurrences

Events, because they are not permanent, are held at different times, in different locations for different reasons. Even the same event held annually can differ considerably in its characteristics. These features make every event, in a sense, unique. As will be discussed in Chapter 14, this makes planning for event legacy particularly challenging, as the enduring things left over after the event are often very difficult to predict.

1.4 Events management challenges

The previous discussion raises some important challenges for anybody seeking to manage the delivery of an event. Whether the reader is an event professional or a student, they could be forgiven for concluding that a coherent understanding of the events industry and its effective 'management' is almost impossible due to its very breadth, complexity and fast-moving nature. A definition and categorisation of different events has been attempted and results in some common labels, which include mega-events, cultural events, special events, corporate events, sporting events and so on.

Although such a clean categorisation of events should enable their management requirements to be easily communicated, in practice it seems that these labels are often too broad and unclear to be useful. For example, many of the special events upon which Goldblatt (2010) based his discussions could also be categorised by several other classifications. While clearly recognising such problems, it was decided to use many of these classifications as chapter headings. Industry professionals do still use many classifications, such as 'special events', to define certain event concepts, but terms such as 'corporate events' are widely recognised to encompass a variety of concepts, such as conferences, exhibitions or brand experience events, which are generally more useful in conveying their ideas.

However, the aims of this book focus on the systematic management of these practices involved in the delivery of events as formal projects on a variety of scales. As discussed in Chapter 2, the origination, planning and delivery of events, regardless of their classifications, tend to require similar frameworks, based upon the events management theory accumulated.

1.5 Events, human history and culture

Despite the obvious advantages of clear and definite information, particularly to those embarking on new study of this exciting and fast-evolving field, it should be worth remembering that events management is largely the modern-day practice of age-old expressions of human social interactions and activities. Before commencing an understanding of some of the mechanics of modern-day events management, a more historical view of their development throughout the ages may enable the reader to put contemporary events management into the context of its origins.

Ancient texts, such as those used to translate the Christian and Jewish scriptures, record the early practice of festivals. These were enshrined in law and primarily took the form of the seven feasts of Israel, where the people of the nation gathered seven times throughout the year in religious celebration and remembrance. Such records show various customs and rituals were carried out, from the eating of the Passover feast through to the offering of various sacrifices. Variations of these different feasts are still carried out today. World religions, such as Islam, later developed their own annual pilgrimages, like the one to Mecca, which in the present day has led to a number of significant crowd safety challenges. Indeed, it was religious observance to the gods of Greece that birthed the first ancient Olympic Games. Modern-day festivals such as Christmas and Halloween also find their roots in such observances, whether pagan or otherwise. The development of modern-day events from their origins is illustrated in the following case study.

CASE STUDY 1.2

The Kentucky Derby, USA

The Kentucky Derby was first held in 1875 in Louisville. Inspired by the British Epsom Derby, its founder Meriwether Lewis Clark acquired land to build the USA's first competitive racetrack. Many changes have occurred to this prestigious event since the first 10,000 spectators arrived at the Louisville Jockey Club to watch 15 horses race. The first jockeys were mainly African American, who mostly left the sport due to racial discrimination. The track was shortened due to spectator complaints it was too long. Media coverage also developed from radio to television to its present-day digital delivery. The $100,000 purse of 1954 is now $3 million. Traditions that remain are the mint julep beverage and the Burgoo, which is a stew of beef, chicken, pork and vegetables. Women still generally wear traditional, floppy hats and the crowd enjoys the song 'My Old Kentucky Home'. 159,070 spectators and $32 million in bets were recorded in 2017. The Kentucky Derby has been written about in classic American literature (Thompson, 1970) and has never missed a year, including during the recent pandemic, and continues to encapsulate classic Southern culture in its traditional food, drink and clothing, as a hallmark of American history.

1.6 The events 'business'

In the previous case study, one of the reasons for the modernisation of the event from its traditional origins was the changing culture and other aspects of the way people live as members of a fast-developing, global economy.

Festivals are generally common forms of cultural practice and, although many have long histories, the majority have been founded in the much more recent past (Getz 2005). The International Festivals and Events Association estimates that there are over 4.5 million recurring festivals worldwide per year (IFEA 2009: 1).

The influence on the UK national economy alone of all types of events is clearly substantial.

In a 2014 report entitled *Events Are GREAT Britain*, compiled on behalf of the Business Visits and Events Partnership (BVEP) about the presence of events in UK industry, many useful conclusions were reached, including:

● The sector is worth £39.1 billion per annum to the national economy.
● Leisure visitors spend £583 per visit while visitors to UK exhibitions from overseas spend £611 per visit, worth £4.4 billion annually, and the spend by those accompanying attendees at business events is worth an additional £7.7 billion.
● Events account for 35% of the UK visitor economy.
● Trade transacted at exhibitions and other business events held in the UK is conservatively estimated to be worth over £100 billion.
● There are more than 25,000 businesses in the sector, which sustain at least 530,000 full-time equivalent (FTE) jobs.
● Inbound business visits to Britain equate to 23.5% of all visits and, at £4.4 billion, 24.4% of the total spend.
● Business events account for 30% of the UK visitor economy.

The economic influence of the industry alone is substantial, and Figure 1.2 illustrates this with a breakdown according to many of the different types of events discussed in our later chapters.

Total value £36.1bn			
Corporate events £30.3bn	Cultural events and festivals £2.3bn	Sports events £2.3bn	Outdoor events £1bn

Figure 1.2 The value of Britain's events industry by sector

Source: Adapted from *Events Are GREAT Britain Report* (2014)

1.7 Role of events managers

Such a presence and development of just one nation's events industry as part of the overall international and global picture has prompted a greater need for trained specialists to plan, organise and deliver such events. Such undertakings, often mammoth in scope, have raised new requirements of those tasked with them. As with most professionalising fields, there has been some discussion of the most suitable traits, attributes and skills needed by the modern-day events manager. Their leadership style and qualities are discussed further in Chapter 2, and the skills they need to be able to apply are touched upon in each of the relevant, subsequent chapters. These newer industry requirements logically present questions about how such skills are acquired and the role of events management education in the professionalisation of future events managers.

CASE STUDY 1.3

Events management as a profession

Most readers and practitioners in the field would likely confirm events management as a profession. However, events are seldom compared to more traditional examples of professions, such as healthcare, law or education. Part of the problem in referring to the events field as 'a profession', and its managers as 'professionals', lies in the historical definitions of such terms, which are probably now quite outdated, and have become even more so during the last pandemic, because of the well-publicised notion of 'key workers' as professionals.

Professional visibility

There has been much progress since our initial discussion about events management professionalism (Bladen and Kennel 2014; Bladen, *et al.* 2012). Our discussion focused on the events sector lacking a coherent professional body and the provision of undergraduate education to students who eventually intended to enter a career in events management. Since then, greater prominence of organisations such as the Institute of Event Management has helped to promote visibility of this burgeoning field. There has also been a plethora of new short courses designed to support professional practice in the field.

These developments stemmed in part from the issues highlighted by Bladen and Kennell (2014), who discussed whether the traditional university model of academic education was fit for purpose, the extent to which events is actually a profession, rather than merely a service industry, and how professionalism can be developed to serve such an important vision and can be more effectively tailored to serve such an important and diverse global sector.

Wilensky's (1964) model of a profession concluded that it must have:

1 The emergence of a full-time occupation.
2 The establishment of a training school.
3 The founding of a professional association.
4 Political agitation directed towards the protection of the association by law.
5 The adoption of a formal code.

Following this discussion, there appears to have been progress made in some of the above qualifiers. Recent global events in particular have sought to emphasise the extent of employment flexibility and insecurity present in the events industries that make up the sector. There is likewise a series of different pathways in events education and training, still with many successful events managers foregoing any formal events education whatsoever, often preferring to cite their own personal experiences as an adequate foundation for their own industry practice. There still exists an array of events-related professional bodies, which tend to represent only their own industries. Many events employees still have no formal professional, legal or collective representation. Also, outside the areas already legislated, or general quality management or environmental initiatives, there is still no formal events code of practice, mainly because of the diverse activities of the sector.

Though useful for academic programme development (Barron and Leask 2012), criticisms of the Events Management Body of Knowledge continue, mainly due to its static nature and limited breadth of use for educators and industry specialists. A variety of certification programmes still await wider and more universal adoption.

As events management develops as a profession, the sector requires increasing numbers of appropriately skilled workers. This need has bcome even more acute following the attrition that occurred throughout the pandemic-related lockdowns, which saw events in most countries curtailed, if not halted, traditional revenue models disrupted and swathes of industry talent seeking gainful employment elsewhere.

As far as events management graduates are concerned, there continues to be a need for them to gain employment and for events industry organisations to acquire large amounts of cost-effective, skilled labour. However, the skills required have changed and there needs to be continued discussion about the future shapes that events education, training and the related certifications take, in order that recent gains in professionalisation continue.

> ## Study activity
>
> 1 In your opinion, to what extent is events management a profession? Use evidence to support your answer.
> 2 How far does the present approach of defining the attributes of the events management profession resemble the various approaches presented in this case?
> 3 How can you suggest event professionalism can be more effectively achieved?

1.8 About this book

As previously stated, the overarching aim of this book is to provide a working knowledge of the field of events management. Following our general review of the development of the present-day industry, and some of the fundamental questions raised for both students and practitioners of the field, a review of the key debates which this book attempts to facilitate in the chapters which follow should be noted.

This book has been designed to cover the wide variety of events that make up the subject matter of most events management courses, as well as to provide practical event planning and events management skills and knowledge. There follows a brief outline of each chapter.

To support students in developing their understanding of the topics covered in each section, a number of features have been included in each chapter:

- clearly stated aims at the start of each chapter
- international case studies
- student activities
- further reading suggestions.

There are also a variety of industry-focused features available on the book's companion website.

1.8.1 Chapter 1 Introduction to events management

This first chapter analyses the role and significance of events from historical times until the present day. It sets out how events have evolved and describes the current state of the events industry. Importantly, it contains this summary section, setting out the book's structure. When researching any aspect of events management, this chapter will provide a key starting point from which the rest of the text can be navigated.

1.8.2 Chapter 2 Event project management

This chapter analyses events as projects, with specific features that need to be planned, managed and evaluated in order for a successful event project to be delivered. As projects, events generally have fixed budgets, precise timelines and limited resources, including employees, suppliers, venues and volunteers. In this chapter, students will be introduced to the principles of project management and shown how these principles can be applied to events. This chapter discusses these techniques outside the simple application of limited, functional management theories and argues that, when applied correctly, event project management can produce better and faster results to plan and deliver events.

1.8.3 Chapter 3 Event design and production

Event design, as a core process in events management, is rarely covered outside logistical considerations in the events literature. This chapter evaluates the value of a range of social and psychological approaches to understanding the event experience and explores how these can be applied in the design of events to produce authentic and exciting attendee experiences. Working through this chapter will support event managers to design events from the initial event concept through to design development and production considerations.

1.8.4 Chapter 4 Event operations

Operational planning begins once the event concept has been decided upon, a venue has been chosen, the event has been designed and a project plan put in place. To deliver an event successfully, event managers must consider all of its elements and decide the resources, skills and equipment needed to deliver them. This chapter covers all aspects of operational planning and management, including the legal external environment – the consideration of legalities, regulations, licences, permits and contracts involved when managing an event – and the event logistics – including the logistical planning for customers and on-site at venues or event sites.

1.8.5 Chapter 5 Event human resource management

This chapter provides an overview and analysis of core human resource management issues in the events industry, including recruiting, motivating and rewarding staff, the role of volunteers in events and the requirements of key legislation affecting the human resources function of events management. The relationship between event organisations and their staff will be considered from the perspective of the 'pulsating organisation'. Finally, the issues of professionalism in the contemporary events industry will be evaluated.

1.8.6 Chapter 6 Event finance

Financial management is vital to the success of an event and forms a core area of competence for any event manager. This chapter examines the key aspects of event finance, at a variety of scales, supporting students to develop their knowledge of important financial terms and methods. The chapter has been written to provide event managers with the ability to write, interpret and present financial documents that will be required by colleagues, internal and external stakeholders and clients.

1.8.7 Chapter 7 Event marketing

As the events industry has grown, so has the wealth of research and practical guidance on how to market events. This chapter sets out the key areas of marketing, such as market analysis, marketing planning, marketing techniques, control methods and evaluation. As well as these established areas of event marketing, this chapter also explores the role of sponsorship within the events industry and the advantages and challenges that this presents to event managers. Connections are made between the development of the marketing function for modern events, the scope for communication of sponsorship messages to specific audiences and the significant cost-recovery potential to event managers of developing relationships with sponsors.

1.8.8 Chapter 8 Event law, health, safety and risk management

Historically, issues of health and safety have been perceived as a bureaucratic burden on event managers and event organisations. In recent years, however, a number of high-profile accidents and disasters have occurred that have focused the industry on the importance of developing excellence in the management of health, safety and risk for organisations, their staff and event attendees. As well as this focus from within the industry, governments and other regulatory agencies have promoted and enforced new legislation and standards on the events industry that organisations must comply with or face hefty financial and criminal penalties. Individual event managers have a significant responsibility to deliver events that reflect this new reality and this chapter evaluates key areas of risk facing event managers and supplies important techniques for managing these.

1.8.9 Chapter 9 Sporting events

In this chapter, the specific characteristics of sporting events are analysed. They have been hugely significant in the development of the events industry and continue to feature prominently on the events landscape, from the smallest community competition to mega-events responsible for billions of dollars of turnover. The chapter considers the factors affecting attendance at sporting events, and the behaviour of these spectators, as well as how this sector has developed to meet the changing profile of sporting events audiences – who may attend in person or form part of the huge global sports media audience. Issues of crowd management and venue design are explored in detail, enabling readers to learn about these cutting-edge aspects of events management in which sporting events lead the field.

1.8.10 Chapter 10 Mega-events

Mega-events such as the Olympic Games and the World Expositions have become features of the global economic and cultural landscape. Governments compete to bring them to their cities to catalyse economic, social and cultural change. This chapter analyses the rise of the mega-event as an instrumental device for promoting development and regeneration, and also examines vital aspects of the management of these global media events, including the bidding process, resourcing, media, security and event tourism.

1.8.11 Chapter 11 Events in the public and third sectors

In this chapter, the differences between the private, public and third sectors of event organisations are explained. The public and third sectors operate in a different context to the profit-seeking private sector, which has been the focus of the majority of events management texts. Building on the material elsewhere in this book on key aspects of events management that are applicable to events in all sectors of the economy, this chapter attempts to highlight the particular characteristics of the third sector and public sector events and the different nature and style of managing their success. Forms of event that are unique to these sectors are analysed, including consultations, fundraising events, political events and faith events, along with issues such as the political impacts of public sector events and the funding challenges facing third sector event organisations.

1.8.12 Chapter 12 Business events

The corporate events sector is extremely broad and diverse. This chapter introduces readers to this complexity, exploring the success factors and challenges for meetings and conferences, incentives, networking events, corporate hospitality and exhibitions and trade shows. As well as analysing the different forms of corporate events, this chapter also presents an analysis of the corporate event consumer and looks at the influences on the contemporary corporate events industry from the perspectives of both suppliers and consumers.

1.8.13 Chapter 13 Cultural events and festivals

This chapter provides an overview of the cultural events and festival sector of the events industry. Cultural events and festivals can often only be understood by reference to the relationship that they have to the expressions of individual and group identities and cultures, and this chapter provides a categorisation of cultural events from this perspective, as well as an overview of arts and entertainment events. In addition to this categorisation, management approaches for cultural events are also introduced that are specific to this sector, including audience development and specialised marketing techniques.

1.8.14 Chapter 14 Event impacts and sustainability

The issue of the impact of events is central to both events management education and the sustainable management of the events industry. This chapter analyses the economic, environmental and social impacts of events and provides techniques for the management and evaluation of these impacts. The concepts of sustainability and sustainable events are introduced in this chapter and these are put into the context of the changing global climate and the global economic crisis. In this chapter, a new model of sustainable economic development is put forward that offers a novel perspective on the future growth of the events industry.

1.8.15 Chapter 15 Events and the media

The relationship between events and the media is critical, both in terms of how events are represented in the media and how event managers make use of the media to communicate with their stakeholders. Media coverage of an event can shape how that event is perceived, with positive and negative implications for how those events are managed. This chapter explores the ways in which event managers can obtain and shape media messages – understanding how the media operates and how to develop positive relationships with journalists and editors and work with new forms of social media can be vital in delivering a successful event.

All these chapters have been updated to incorporate viewpoints which have developed due to recent occurrences, including the more popular emergence of particular protests, the effects of the Covid-19 pandemic and technology innovations, which are showcased in each chapter.

Industry voice

Paul Cook, International Hybrid Event Specialist

 The events sector is fascinating. There is always something new to learn. The sector is never boring and never stands still. And it is a sector that is positive and creative. Every year there are thousands of events that take place across the globe, and every year a new bunch of event planners join at the start of their career in events.

One of the key issues that the events sector must embed in its DNA is the capability of dealing with constant change. Change has always been at the heart of the events sector. Yes, ROI returns, making clients happy and embracing new technology are all important. But they are also timeless. I am pretty sure they were among the key concerns when the first Great Exhibition took place from May to October in 1851. These issues are always going to be the issues that people question year on year, event on event. But change comes from all directions and the savvy event professional is always aware that it could arrive from any point.

As an example, let's look at the three Ds (as I have just named them) that have affected the events sector over the last few years. First, there was disability discrimination legislation that required venues and planners to review how they were making events accessible to all. Then there were changes to data security and how personal data was looked after. This had a massive impact in the events sector as data was largely floating around any number of suppliers without much control before European legislation came in. My third D is connected to the issue of diets. There is now a higher proportion of attendees that have specific dietary requirements than in years gone past. It is another challenge for planners, but I know they will put it on their list and deal with it.

However, beyond the three Ds, the one big issue that no one can avoid is the Covid-19 global pandemic. This has led to an explosion of virtual events, which was not a surprise as countries entered into lockdowns and travel beyond borders was largely prohibited. In-person events came to an abrupt halt and this caused a shockwave in the events sector.

What the coronavirus pandemic has done is to level the playing field of experience. In the past, if you were an in-person event planner and you had years of experience, you were likely to win more work than new entrants. But now, that has changed. Whilst a lot of event experience is still valuable, roles and responsibilities have changed, which means new opportunities emerge. Opportunities for new entrants abound.

One thing is crystal clear, event planners cannot go back to the way things were.

And for companies that use events, what do they want from events now? Are they going to be happy to encourage their staff to travel around the globe? What the pandemic has done is to save organisations thousands of dollars, euros or sterling in terms of expenses that were no longer needed. I wonder how they may rethink their policies on travel and entertainment expenses in the future.

And if we think about the impact on carbon pollution, which has been dramatically reduced by virtual events, then are we going to carry on that trend, knowing that climate change is a key issue? And when it comes to diversity and inclusion, are we going to shut the door on people who have been with us at the virtual events just because in-person events have come back or are coming back? As I mentioned earlier, change is the key constant and it isn't ever going to go away.

I believe that the events sector is on the cusp of being in a pretty optimistic stage. It is a stage where, in many respects, we have been forced to investigate and explore new technology. We have people that are hungry to make things work and we also know that governments around the world now understand, or understand more clearly, where events fit. And that can only be a good thing for the people who are coming into this profession.

My journey in the events sector is an unlikely one. I came into events following a career in insurance. Today I work as a creative event producer and strategic consultant. I guess this shows that we create our own career path and in events there is bags of opportunity. Along the way, some of my roles have been as a researcher, consultant, producer, host, facilitator and mentor. As well as being at the sharp end making in-the-moment decisions, advisory and strategy work has also beckoned. How lucky have I been to have made an impact in a sector in which I am now known internationally.

Whilst event professionals are not recognised as professionals at present, I believe we are heading that way. An event planner in the future will be someone that is regarded in the same way as somebody of a professional standing in terms of being a lawyer, or an accountant, or surveyor, or similar. And one of the ways we can demonstrate our professionalism is by understanding the theories, understanding the practice, and clearly linking, where we can, academia and industry together because then we all go forward and society benefits.

I am delighted and honoured to be able to write a few words to accompany this textbook. I wish you well, and I encourage you to read this textbook and fully absorb it, and enjoy your onward path into the world of events.

1.9 Summary

This chapter has discussed the evolution of events as part of human culture, from their historical foundations to their present-day status as part of a prominent global industry which is a major revenue earner for entire national economies. Such rapid and substantial contemporary development has nevertheless included the revival of many traditional events in a modern-day context, and the introduction of many new events, requiring the necessity for knowledgeable, qualified and professional event managers to deliver them.

All of the chapters in this book take the approach of presenting basic definitions and descriptions of the key management practices presently employed in the events industry, while linking these to the most important theoretical and management frameworks used to inform their successful practice. As event academics and practitioners, the authors have taken care to reflect present industry thinking and practice, while simultaneously attempting to challenge that which might be considered to be outdated or inconsistent. In such cases, an attempt has been made to propose new or adapted models and theories in order to stimulate debate and new practice in this fast-moving, international industry. To supplement this approach, many industry leaders and practitioners have been chosen to share their experiences in the 'Industry voice' sections.

Further reading

Bladen, C. and Kennell, J. (2014) Educating the 21st Century Event Management Graduate: Pedagogy, Practice, Professionalism and Professionalization, *International Journal of Events Management*, 18 (1): DOI:10.3727/152599514X13883555341724. For a broader coverage of the points summarised above.

Getz, D. (2008) Event Tourism: Definition, Evolution, and Research, *Tourism Management, 29* (3): 403–428. This is a very useful article for gaining an overview of the study of events and also includes references to many important sources.

Maslow, A. H. (1943) A Theory of Human Motivation, *Psychological Review, 50* (4): 370–396. Available at: http://psychclassics.yorku.ca/Maslow/motivation.htm. This article is the original source of Maslow's 'hierarchy of needs' model, a recurring feature of management literature.

References

Barron, P. and Leask, A. (2012) Events Management Education. In S. J. Page and J. Connell (eds) *The Routledge Handbook of Events*: 473–488, Abingdon: Routledge.

Bladen, C., Kennel, J., Abson, E. and Wilde, N. (2012) *Events Management: An Introduction*, New York: Routledge.

Electric Medway (2021a) About. Available at: https://electricmedway.co.uk/about/ [Accessed 21 August 2021].

Electric Medway (2021b) Launch Event by Electric Medway. Available at: https://youtu.be/RyVgOxsw37I [Accessed 21 August 2021].

Events Are GREAT Britain Report (2014) Available at: www.businessvisitsandeventspartnership.com/ [Accessed 12 April 2016].

Getz, D. (2005) *Event Management and Event Tourism*, New York: Cognizant Communications.

Getz, D. (2007) *Event Studies*, Oxon: Elsevier.

Getz, D. (2019) *Event Studies* (4th edn), Oxford: Routledge.

Goldblatt, J. (2010) *Special Events: A New Generation and the Next Frontier*, Chichester: John Wiley & Sons.

Goldblatt, J. (2014) *Special Events: Creating and Sustaining a New World for Celebration*, Chichester: John Wiley & Sons.

IFEA (2009) The Power of Celebration, Available at: http://www.ifea.com/joomla1_5/index.php?option=com_contentandview=articleandid=180andItemid=306 [Accessed 10 May 2009].

Thompson, H. S. (1970) The Kentucky Derby is Decadent and Depraved. *Scanlan's Monthly*, June. Available at: http://english138.web.unc.edu/files/2011/08/The-Kentucky-Derbyis-Decadent-and-Depraved.pdf [Accessed 31 July 2022].

Wilensky, H. (1964) The Professionalization of Everyone? *American Journal of Sociology*, 69: 142–146.

Chapter 2

Event project management

Feasibility, planning, delivery and evaluation

Contents

DOI: 10.4324/9781003102878-2

2.1 Aims

By the end of this chapter, students will be able to:

- understand the importance of event project management to the international events industry
- explain the organisational issues that must be taken into consideration when managing event projects
- relate event project management to conventional event planning theories and practices
- explain the processes related to effective event project management throughout the event cycle.

2.2 Introduction

Following our Chapter 1 discussion of the common event types that specialists are responsible for organising, we come to more of the considerations necessary when planning, delivering and evaluating such projects. As projects, events generally have fixed budgets, precise timelines and limited resources, including employees, suppliers, venues and volunteers. Organisers of such events are therefore responsible for the management and delivery of projects. Project management has developed processes and techniques to help plan, organise, lead and control events and can be used to make event projects more successful. This chapter discusses these techniques outside the simple application of limited, functional management theories and argues that, when applied correctly, event project management can produce better and faster results to plan and deliver events.

2.3 Events as projects

As can be seen in Figure 2.1, most events exhibit the characteristics of projects. This tendency generally increases with the size and scale of the event. Each of the characteristics of events is expanded in the following subsections.

2.3.1 Leadership

Events are often the ultimate responsibility of one lead events manager who coordinates specialist functions. The centralised and hierarchical nature of the leadership role can be dependent upon the scale of the event. A mega-event, such as the Olympic Games, has a national planning committee ultimately accountable to its international parent, while corporate events are often under the direct leadership of a single event manager. There will be more discussion of this unusual leadership role later in this chapter.

2.3.2 Budget

Events almost always have specific budgets allocated to them. As discussed in our chapter about events finance, the accurate calculation of such budgets will often include difficult predictions of fixed and projected variable costs in relation to forecasted attendee numbers. Such calculations cannot be considered reliable if made in isolation from other important project

Figure 2.1 The characteristics of events as projects

factors such as schedules, timelines and project life cycle stages. For example, cuts in government funding will inevitably curtail the provision and/or scale of public sector events.

2.3.3 Life cycle

Each event has a defined beginning and end within its life cycle. There are a variety of life cycles proposed in the field of project management to aid managers in distinguishing key phases throughout a project's life. However, such cycles for use by industries such as engineering or software development tend to accommodate the tendency in such industries for phases to be completed, leading to the definite beginning of the next. Event project managers do not often have this luxury, as they are required to handle multiple tasks, contractors and other (often complex and interrelated) factors simultaneously. This is particularly the case with large exhibitions, which can often take two years to plan and execute for delivery over a single week. In practice, this means that major exhibition organisers are likely to find themselves managing both this year's and next year's events at the same time. An international organisation such as Gartner, which operates across a number of continents at any one time, often has to have team members who are geographically spread, working on a variety of different projects at any given time. This requires effective communications, which can also make project management software packages such as Microsoft Project, Microsoft Teams and use of international databases imperative, so that team members can alter event details and immediate project updates can be sent to their colleagues using the company's international intranet.

2.3.4 Tasks

Events often require tasks to be performed that will not be repeated, even in the case of recurring annual events. The complexity of certain larger events requires that often the seemingly simplest of tasks or functions, such as catering, volunteer recruitment or theming, can be approached in a distinct manner in order to reinforce the uniqueness of a particular event from year to year. This obviously becomes even more complicated when an event changes location or venue, even if the concept of an annual event remains consistent. When the design and production details discussed in Chapter 3 are considered, they make the tasks involved even more complex and variable for different events. Successive Summer and Winter Olympics organising committees have experienced challenges as they try to learn from past events. Although the basic format of such mega-events remains constant, many of the problems and complexities differ due to changes in the city where the event is being held and factors such as culture, government legislation and even the basis on which initial bids by individual cities are made.

2.3.5 Cross-functionality

Event organisations are likely to be required to work cross-functionally without formal authority. This principle mainly depends on the type of event project being managed and the corresponding organisational structure required for optimal effectiveness and efficiency of execution. In other words, as most industries have clearly needed to adopt project management techniques in order to improve their performances, event managers have always, in a sense, been project managers because of an ongoing need for them to have versatile skills in a number of key business areas in order to be successful. Indeed, as this book suggests throughout, event project managers do not have the luxury of simply being good financial managers; they must also be effective marketers and human resource managers, as well as almost anything else that is required.

2.3.6 Teams

Events require working teams to be brought together only for the duration of a particular project. Most event organisations tend to vary their approach towards formality of event leadership and the corresponding organisational structure; it is not uncommon for the teams being employed on particular events to vary according to different factors. Goldblatt (2005) applied Toffler's (1990) earlier discussion of the 'pulsating organisation' to events, particularly in relation to the fluctuating numbers of volunteers required throughout the events cycle. Events such as trade exhibitions have often staggered delegate registration, giving priority to trade deals on the first day, the general public on the second day and students towards the end of the third day. Obviously, this is done for trade considerations, but it can result in some exhibitors leaving early and there being a need for fewer volunteers and other workers. These workers are required in larger numbers for the event set-up and breakdown, but not during the event. Thus, this organisation 'pulsation' takes place in accordance with the event cycle.

2.3.7 The event project life cycle

Events have a distinct timeline and life cycle. In Figure 2.2, Silvers demonstrates the link between an event's stages from initiation to closure and the levels of activity associated with these stages throughout an event's life, from start to finish. This classification has proven generally useful to event project managers to understand levels of activity required at the progressive stages of an event's conception, research, planning, delivery and evaluation, as discussed in Chapter 1.

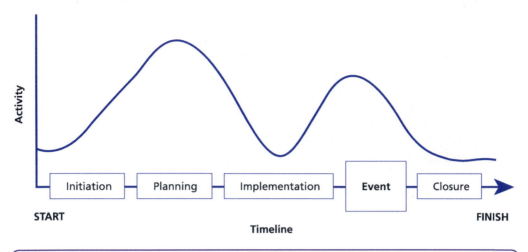

Figure 2.2 The event project life cycle
Source: Silvers (2007: 159)

2.4 Project management perspectives

When considering how to apply project management to events, a project leader should consider their overall perspective. As discussed by Kolltveit *et al.* (2007), there are six major perspectives to project management (see also Figure 2.3), all of which can be applied directly to the management of the event project.

● The *task perspective* focuses on the delivery of the event as specified, on time and within the set budget. Certainly, it is important to clients that such projects as most corporate events or weddings should meet the criteria specified beforehand since they represent the most tangible and measurable success factors for the event. Any event project team will need to focus on the scope of the event concept and operations, as well as clear targets, measurable results for evaluation, high levels of ongoing project supervision and tangible event legacy criteria. This has clearly been the approach thus far with the types of modern mega-events described in Chapter 10. These events, such as the Olympic Games, focus on the tangible measures necessitated by the adoption of the task perspective to events.
● The *leadership perspective* to event projects depends upon theories of leadership styles, communication styles and processes, decision-making, management of team characteristics and organisation, clear allocations of team members' functions and responsibilities, interim milestone delivery dates, reviews and feedback.
● The *stakeholder perspective* to event projects is heavily used in the events industry and focuses on identification of key stakeholder groups and the management of their relations to ensure event success.
● The *transaction-cost perspective* to event projects views the production of an event as a commercial transaction and mainly focuses on governance of the project and its cost structure with particular reliance upon contracts and innovation.
● The *systems perspective* to event projects views the event as an overall holistic system, rather than made up of individual, functional components such as marketing, finance, design and so on.

24

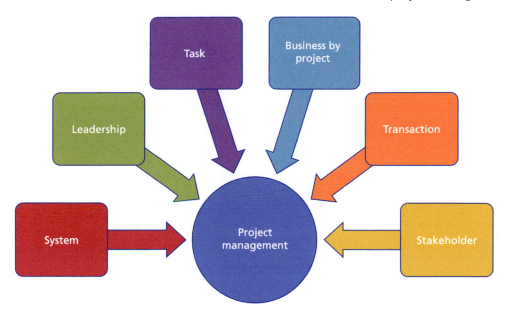

Figure 2.3 Perspectives on project management
Source: Adapted from Kolltveit *et al.* (2007: 4)

- The *business-by-project perspective* to event projects views events as individual investments which yield returns or benefits in their own right. This perspective relies upon
  investment methods and portfolio management, among others. While this approach is
  probably more common with the development of technological innovations through
  business start-ups, most large events management companies do, to some extent,
  maintain proprietary interests over a series of different event product concepts at any
  one time.

Kolltveit *et al.* (2007) found that the writers in the general project management field centre
on the 'leadership' and 'task' perspectives. Certainly, the main perspectives adopted by
events management writers to date tend to be based mainly on project tasks and stakeholder perspectives. It is argued that more investigation should be made into the relevance
of the other perspectives to the field, particularly those related to event leadership, due to
the specific nature of the event planner's role as project manager of the complex and highly
variable events.

2.4.1 The emerging importance of projects

The origins of project management can be traced back to its use during the large-scale government projects of the nineteenth century. It developed further through the building projects initiated as a result of the Second World War, moving project management on to the same methods
used in events management today. The field developed its own Project Management Body of
Knowledge (PMBOK) and its own professional certifications, such as the Project Management
Professional (PMP) Certification (www.pmcertification.net).

2.4.2 The core competencies of an event project manager

By applying the information provided by the PMP certification (see LaBrosse 2007: 99–100), we can see that an effective event project manager requires a variety of diverse yet interrelated core competencies that should be applied throughout the event project stages of initiation, planning, implementation, delivery and closure.

Event managers need to be able to select suitable projects, and in the event of multiple products they must be able to prioritise between them in relation to the requirements of their organisation. Such prioritisation will likely be related to strategic factors and overall feasibility. Initiation of the project will require the event manager to be able to assemble the initial project team and stakeholders, which may include provisional agreements from key personalities associated with such an event, such as top entertainers, leading sponsors, specialised designers and producers, as well as possible donors and benefactors in the case of voluntary and fundraising events. An event manager's ability to initiate an event project is also dependent upon their skill to develop an effective project contract so that further planning may proceed.

The event project manager will need to be a competent project planner of the event's key delivery milestones, processes and reviews in order to ensure that the project is kept on track through effective ongoing performance measurement. There is also a need to highlight possible areas of conflict between different functions of the event team. Additionally, this person must be a project leader throughout the event, careful to ensure that they capitalise on the skills of others who are involved in the project and knowing when specific tasks should be contracted out to other event specialists.

The event project manager will need to be competent to manage the event's scope, schedule, cost, procurement and resources. The risks to the satisfactory and successful delivery of the event itself (as opposed to 'risk management' of the health, safety and welfare of those associated with it, as covered in Chapter 8) will need to be accurately assessed and managed in the form of insurance and contingencies. As the planning and delivery of the event progresses, required changes will need to be identified and managed, aided by associated performance tracking and reporting. The appropriate media will facilitate communication throughout the event. In particular, stakeholders may need to be kept up to date with developments and teams will be involved in meetings to foster a constructive atmosphere of teamwork, consultation and feedback. Communication skills will also include the ability to negotiate with all parties associated with the event, both inside and outside the project organisation. The event project manager will eventually have to evaluate the overall accomplishment of the event's objectives and legacy, as well as document these findings.

2.5 Event project definition, organisation and framework

Following the foregoing discussion of events as projects and the various approaches an event manager can take towards them, it will be necessary to consider the most effective type of organisational structure for the event.

2.5.1 Functional and project-led organisations

Event organisations are often temporary and differ slightly depending on the project concerned. They will have a structure with predefined reporting relationships, functional 'departments' and systems to carry out the project. *Functional organisations* group their people into departments performing similar tasks, as is shown in Figure 2.4.

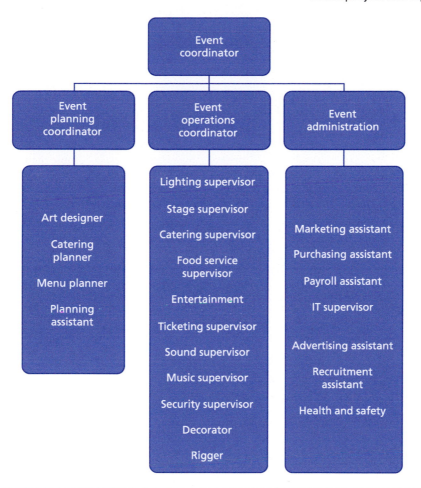

Figure 2.4 Functional event organisation

Project-led organisations group people into temporary teams for the duration of a project. The events industry clearly comprises both types of organisation. An international event venue, such as ExCel in London, will have a functional infrastructure of departments responsible for such activities as financial management, operational management, human resource management and so on. Event organisations, such as Gartner, a project-led organisation, will use different people on different events as the concept and brief dictate. An example of a project-led organisational structure is shown in Figure 2.5.

Matrix organisations combine functional and project-led structures in order to perform both focuses at the same time, as illustrated in Figure 2.6.

This structure enables both a project-led and a functional approach to events and is therefore particularly suitable for this industry. However, in order for the matrix to be project-led, it is important that key authority and responsibilities for important event project elements, such as budgetary and other resource control, reside with the project manager at the event level, rather than with the functional manager of the department under which the event is being delivered. Failure to adopt this approach will tend to weaken the matrix and relegate the event project manager to the more minor role of administrator.

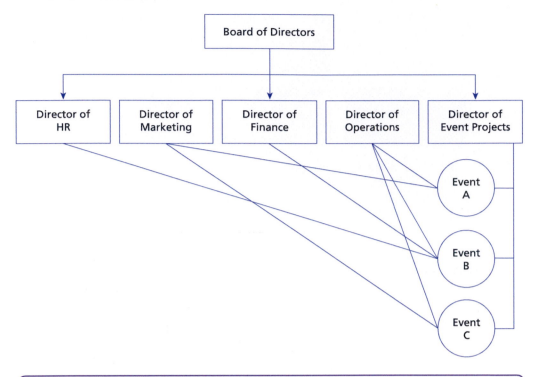

Figure 2.5 Project-led event organisation

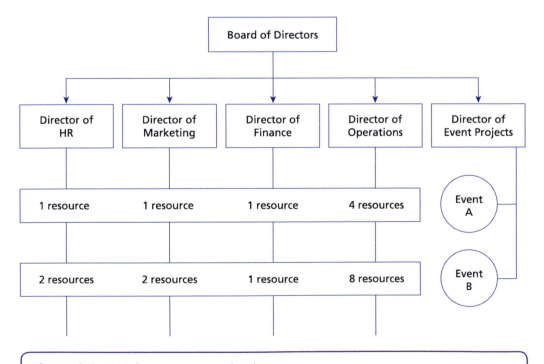

Figure 2.6 Matrix event organisation

It may be tempting to adopt the matrix structure without reservation, considering its appeal in combining the best of both functional and project-led structures. In many cases, this structure does profit the event in question, but there are a number of problems often associated with this structure. In particular, the decision-making processes of an event, especially during the delivery stage, must often be adaptable in response to crises or changes in the event's micro or macro environments. The matrix approach often slows down these processes since the project group must spend too much time in consultation across areas of responsibility before reaching a consensus. This can lead to serious delays and unnecessary project failures.

> ## Study activity
>
> 1 List the strengths and weaknesses of each of the above event organisation structures.
> 2 Discuss the most suitable organisation type for each of the following:
>
> - A venue specialising in corporate events.
> - An event company involved in creating and delivering one-off corporate events for a variety of leading brand clients.
> - The planning committee of the Olympic Games or another mega-event.

2.5.2 Project leadership

Whether an event organisation uses a functional, project-led or matrix structure for its events, its choice will, for the most part, dictate the type of leadership which is most practical for that particular structure. The leadership of the organisation, along with its structure, will in turn heavily influence its project culture, which will have its own influences on the delivery of the event. According to Pinto (2010: 130), project leadership 'involves inspiring, motivating, influencing, and changing behaviours of others in pursuit of a common goal'. Event project leadership therefore differs from management and administration tasks and responsibilities that are mostly functional, and focuses on the relationships between different individuals who are involved in the event.

Kurt Lewin, one of the pioneers of analysing organisations, carried out research into leadership styles. In their 1939 paper, Lewin *et al.* identified three main, prevailing leadership styles which shaped:

- authoritarian
- democratic
- laissez-faire work environments.

Authoritarian work environments are led by an autocratic leader who makes decisions on behalf of the team and divides work tasks and processes accordingly, providing critique of the team's performance while often not engaging closely with either the team or their activities. Democratic work environments have leaders who consult team members to arrive at a consensus regarding important decisions, offering guidance as required, as well as praise and constructive criticism throughout. Laissez-faire work environments have little tangible leadership input and the leader allows all major decisions to be made and executed by the team members, who demonstrate 'free-reign' and receive little input or feedback from their leader.

Turner *et al.* (2009) found that project success was increasingly linked to leadership competencies rather than tools and techniques, as had previously been thought. This finding built on the work of Dulewicz and Higgs (2005), which isolated three main project leadership styles: goal-orientated leadership, involving leadership and engaging leadership. Ironically, goal-orientated leadership, which involves the 'management by objectives' approach to events towards clearly defined results espoused by leading authors in the field (e.g. Bowdin *et al.* 2011; Goldblatt 2005; Shone and Parry 2010), appears more useful in environments that remain mainly stable in nature. However, many event practitioners might suggest that an event

Study activity

1   Which of Lewin's work environments would be best for:

- encouraging motivation and participation by event team members?
- encouraging innovation?

2   What do you think are the advantages and disadvantages of each?
3   Which type of leadership would you prefer to be following? Why?
4   Complete Table 2.1, adding 'High' or 'Low' to each cell.

Table 2.1 Leadership styles

	Leadership style		
	Autocratic	Democratic	Laissez-faire
Time required for decision-making			
Scope for innovation			
Promotion of participation			
Team member motivation			
Ability of team members to voice disagreement			
Scope for leader to make mistakes			
Direct/formal communication			
Open team discussion			
Quality of decision-making			
Clarity of mission			

project can be quite an unstable context for management, perhaps due to the intangibility of the perceived end result and the fluidity of the context in which it is being delivered. Involving leadership may therefore be more suitable for dealing with the transitory features common to events project organisation. Industry managers often find definitions, plans, resources and many other important project variables in a state of flux. The engaging leadership approach, however, appears to be impractical for anything other than the smallest or most specialised of event teams, due to the transformative nature of the leadership role and the necessary level of corresponding employee commitment. The particular attributes and competencies of such leaders are discussed later in this chapter.

2.5.3 Project organisation

Forming teams is an essential activity of any event project manager and is vital to the success of any event's production. The general considerations required in the management of event teams are mainly discussed in Chapter 5 of this book. However, simply selecting team members and allocating them to functional groups is not the most efficient or effective way of staffing an event, as this does not suit the common structure of the event organisation. It may also stifle the creativity of design described in Chapter 3. Therefore, team members and their formal and informal interrelationships should ideally reflect accommodation of the cross-functional activities associated with the events industry. For example, some of the tasks of the event's security detail will often also be involved with safety and customer service provision, so the team should be constructed to enable these important and interrelated capacities.

Teams and teamwork are usually more effective than individuals in events projects because:

- they allow more to be achieved as they can accomplish a much wider range of tasks and workloads
- team members usually have a wider range of skills, specialisations and thought processes that can be drawn upon in the solution of event problems
- team often make better decisions
- they often provide a better environment for motivation and can better support each other
- they are more open to risk-taking as risk is spread across more people associated with an event.

On further consideration of event project teams, according to Maylor (2010: 248–249), effective project teams require:

- clear goals
- a results-driven structure
- competent team members
- unified commitment
- a collaborative climate
- standards of excellence
- external support and recognition
- effective leadership.

For further discussion of important issues related to team management in events that include team culture, roles, motivation and evaluation, please see Chapter 5 on events human resource management.

2.6 Project parameters

2.6.1 Project scope

Project scope, though rarely called that, is probably the largest current area in events management literature. Most process diagrams, including the one shown in Figure 2.7, tend to relate to 'event planning'.

Figure 2.7 incorporates the main scope aspects, which according to Pinto (2010: 157) include concept development, statement of scope, work authorisation, scope reporting, control systems and project closeout.

The problem statement essentially denotes the *raison d'être* of the event, that is, the reason why it is taking place and what it intends to achieve. This can vary even when the same annual event is held in consecutive years at the same venue. It is vital to gather accurate information, from basic general observations to extensive environmental and other analyses. These activities can take months, or even years in the case of mega-events, and can form the largest part of the overall feasibility study for the event.

2.6.2 Project requirements and constraints

Constraints to the event's staging, financing and other practical options need to be considered as do contingencies and alternatives. Alternative design, themes, venues and entertainment options are often considered at this point in the event concept's development.

Figure 2.7 Event planning process
Source: Shone and Parry (2010)

2.7 Stakeholder requirements and needs

Stakeholder analysis is currently an important topic in events literature, with a much wider definition of the number of parties affected by an event's activities preferred to the narrower, profit-orientated definition used by other business-related fields. In other words, the wide-encompassing influences and impacts of events in communities and nations make it necessary to consider the needs of all parties affected by them in stakeholder analysis, whether they actively participate or not. This project stage will therefore include the analysis, monitoring and evaluation of the needs and requirements of investors, employees and attendees who seek to benefit from the event's delivery, as well as those of local area residents who may even try to avoid the event and its impacts completely, yet are greatly affected by them. This is discussed in depth in Chapter 14.

2.8 The project objective statement

Event objectives form the key direction for the following stages of the project's planning, delivery and evaluation. These objectives provide specifics for concept screening and feasibility analysis and form the overall direction of activities for the project team and associated event contractors to arrive at the accomplishment of the event's outcomes. These must be specific and measureable where possible in order to be effective indicators by which the event can be conceived, kept on track, effectively delivered and evaluated. To aid this, Doran's (1981) popular SMART acronym is often used to describe effective event project objectives:

● Specific
● Measureable
● Assignable
● Realistic
● Time-related

This acronym, though not at all scientific, is a useful guide to the formation of useful objectives. As with any business system, the project objectives will only be as effective as the consideration of the team that sets them, but making them as clear and communicable as possible will help to ensure their effective decoding by important stakeholders, contractors and others associated with the effective outcome of the event.

There is a great deal of discussion about the suitability of the application of such a 'management by objectives' approach to events management projects. Certainly, the prospect of a project team setting, achieving and evaluating the same objectives may potentially appear circular and self-fulfilling. However, the sheer scope of certain events and their potential for instability demands the clear formulation and communication of an effective project objective statement, although this may be modified as the project progresses.

Study activity

Set effective objectives for an event of your choice. Make sure they are specific and measureable. Can their achievement be effectively evaluated by a third party? Check them with someone else. What improvements can be made?

2.9 Project planning

2.9.1 Work breakdown structures

The process of an event project involves a variety of interrelated tasks and functions that must be broken down into smaller, more clearly distinguishable and easier-to-manage subsections. This work breakdown structure is essentially the basis for the Event Management Body of Knowledge (EMBOK) model and once again attempts to 'departmentalise' event activities into the previously criticised functional structure. On the other hand, it is reasonable to suggest that the successful future of the events management industry depends upon employees who can understand the working dynamics of the smaller elements of event work breakdown.

Work breakdown is important in event projects in order that a clear link can be observed between the event objectives and the tasks required to achieve them. Tasks might be practically divided into functional responsibilities, and event progress can be made more tangible for those participating in the event's delivery as well as for its stakeholders. It also enables more effective evaluation and cost allocation.

2.9.2 Project schedules

Time is crucial to the management and delivery of event projects, not least since event dates are often fixed because of venue and other resource availability as well as the need for upfront procurement payments and deposits. The flexibility of these factors also makes delays more likely than they might be in other project-related industries.

2.9.3 Resource breakdown structures

The main event project resources can be broken down into:

- *People* – including the expertise and skills of event specialists, such as designers, specialist entertainers, decorators, those associated with specialist staging activities and front-line personnel engaged in customer service delivery and other interactions.
- *Facilities* – including the venue, site and associated amenities, which can also include location and even destination attributes that contribute greatly to the success of any event.
- *Equipment* – including all plants and machinery, from transportation vehicles through to cooking equipment, lighting rigs, sound systems, scaffolds, portable dance floors, toilets and even personnel uniforms.
- *Finance* – as discussed in section 2.14 and Chapter 6.
- *Materials* – involving anything which can be used to make something else, such as timber, decorations, foodstuffs and paints.

2.10 Project optimisation

2.10.1 Critical path analysis methodology

Critical path analysis requires the analysis of all project tasks. Task dependency – that is, the relationship between the completion of one task before another can be commenced – also needs to be carefully considered. The construction of the critical path analysis of an activity network usually begins with breaking down the activities necessary for the planning of an event and

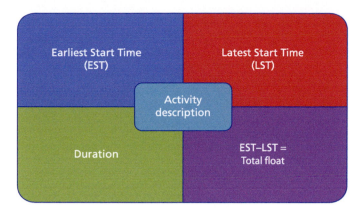

Figure 2.8 Activity notation

estimating as accurately as possible the earliest and latest start times and duration of each. This can then be represented as shown in Figure 2.8.

By noting each event activity using this method, they can then be represented as an activity network, displaying the relationships and dependencies of tasks to each other. The values in the bottom left of the boxes can be calculated in order to determine how long the project will take. The critical path is the longest path through the dependent activities. Please refer to the companion website for a worked example.

Critical paths often incorporate capacity planning, also known as capacity constraint buffers (CCB); a reserve allocated to project tasks that use the same resources. For example, project managers of specialist corporate events that use an event producer as a central agent for all event concept development, design and logistical arrangements will need to protect them as a resource at each stage of the project process. This becomes even more necessary if the producer is working on a number of different event projects simultaneously. A CCB must be applied to protect the producer's time as they transition from one part of a single project to another or from one project to the next.

2.11 Project evaluation and review techniques

An event project requires ongoing evaluation and review to avoid delays and to manage ongoing changes. Such delays or changes might lead to undesirable increases in costs in other types of project, but for event projects they might be lethal to effective delivery.

2.11.1 Evaluation criteria

It is important that the event project team have methods in place to ensure the ongoing evaluation of project scope in terms of its continued adherence to the parameters set by the event objectives. These controls will concern each of the financial, marketing, design and operational areas associated with the event. They will need to be supported by relevant documentation of such aspects as expenditure and communication to ensure that the initial event plan is being adhered to and not changed without authorisation.

These concerns will also extend to the ongoing monitoring of the event macro and micro environments. For example, international events rely heavily on attendance by visitors who arrive by air. Any major changes in airline pricing, perhaps as a result of government taxation or direct market factors, may greatly affect potential ticket purchases before the event and may require some corresponding strategic changes to be made.

2.11.2 Review techniques

The event project will require continual evaluation throughout its life cycle. In particular, many event projects are heavily reliant on stakeholder involvement and their promised legacy, as well as being commonly subjected to ongoing, critical media scrutiny. These factors, in addition to the usual financial requirements associated with non-event projects, such as return on investment and protection of profits, require that regular systems are in place to evaluate event achievement of its key deliverables. The basic process of event project evaluation involves four main reflective stages, as shown in Figure 2.9.

Key event areas which will require evaluation will likely include activity tasks, project milestones and budgetary indicators. Milestones, while being clear enough for all team members to readily understand, present problems if the project suffers serious delays. In such cases, the shortfalls are often revealed too late to be remedied effectively. One common way of evaluating and tracking project baselines is with the use of Gantt charts as shown in Figure 2.10.

The evaluation of any event project depends upon the clear definition and use of critical success factors. Pinto (2010) classifies these factors into the following areas:

- Project mission
- Top management support
- Project plans and schedules
- Client consultation
- Personnel

- Technical tasks
- Client acceptance
- Monitoring and feedback
- Communication
- Troubleshooting

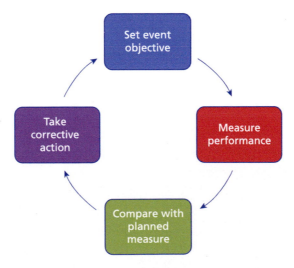

Figure 2.9 The event project evaluation cycle

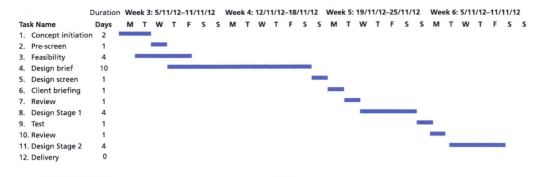

Figure 2.10 Event project tracking Gantt chart

2.12 Project crashing

Project crashing in events refers to speeding up the delivery process. This becomes necessary when costs can be saved, and when competitor offerings seem likely to steal innovation or successfully imitate other aspects of competitive advantage. Finishing event production early can significantly cut development costs, which may be distinctly advantageous, particularly if this development process has fallen far behind schedule.

The actual process of project crashing in events will involve increasing the productivity of the existing events team, increasing the resources allocated to the event, which may mean more people, plants and/or equipment, or altering the working methods. One way that crashing can be accomplished is by using technology more efficiently for such activities as project meetings, information sharing, ongoing team communication and operational concerns, such as ticketing, sales and reporting. As the project team becomes more liable for financial penalties due to delivery delays, the more likely it is that project crashing options will become attractive. Crashing can also be achieved by simply contracting out event-related tasks to third party agencies instead of handling them in-house, thus freeing up resources for reallocation elsewhere. Of course, outsourcing attracts its own set of problems and considerations.

> **Study activity**
>
> You have decided to crash an event project in order to save costs. Discuss some of the problems associated with contracting out your events management functions to third parties.

2.13 Project risk management

2.13.1 Definition of project risk management

Pinto (2010: 221) defines risk management as: 'the art and science of identifying, analysing, and responding to risk factors throughout the life of a project and in the best interests of its objectives'. In this section we intend to discuss risk management in the context of event projects from the perspective of loss in terms of the successful completion of an event. While we recognise that risks associated with the health, safety and welfare of event attendees and employees is an important area of management for event project leaders, we will discuss this in Chapter 8. Entrepreneurial risk management, which involves consideration of both monetary loss and gain, will be discussed in Chapter 6.

Anyone who has worked on even the simplest event project will recognise the complications caused by the unpredicted intervention of problems relating to resources, timings and changes, particularly in the context of the uncontrollable event macro environment. The ultimate success of such event projects invariably rests on the project team's ability to solve or lessen the impact of these problems. However, it cannot be argued that a successful project simply faces fewer problems than an unsuccessful one. It is more likely that the successful project manager can more accurately predict outstanding potential hazards that may come along throughout the duration of the project's schedule and has implemented satisfactory contingency measures well in advance. Thus, the art or science of successful event project risk management has to be in the manager's ability to predict the future as accurately as possible.

In order to predict such intervening variables before they cause problems, event organisers will need to ask themselves:

- How might these problems present themselves?
- What will be the symptoms or signs that such problems are occurring?
- What are the likely consequences of doing nothing?
- If something needs to be done, what should it be?

These questions are addressed as part of an internal and external analysis of the event organisation's environment, as discussed in Chapter 1.

2.13.2 Classification of project risk management

Risks need to be assessed in terms of their potential impact on the success of the project and where the source of their control lies. Wysocki (2007) classifies risk in the following four areas:

- Technical
- Project
- Organisational
- External

Sometimes projects fail because suitable technical resources, such as people, expertise or equipment, are unavailable. For example, in production-driven events (as discussed in Chapter 3), there is often an inevitable dependence on the creativity of the design team. Staff changes, departure from companies, disagreements and even illness or death can cause key team members to leave important projects, resulting in serious gaps. When this happens, it is not simply a case of replacing one person or role with another. For example, two events industry design directors may be considered of equal calibre, but they may have significant creative differences in the way they approach a project.

Charity events often rely on a steady stream of willing volunteers to maintain effective delivery levels. Failure to attract a suitable profile of volunteer can greatly impact on the success of event projects.

2.13.3 Use of buffers

Though work tends to fill the time available, event project managers can use time and cost buffers in order to offset the impact of several of these problems. As their name suggests, cost buffers include extra budget, which is allocated in emergencies, while time buffers are extra hours that can be allocated before the project delivery deadline to offset delays in the schedule. Again, though the application of these buffers seems fairly obvious in the context of traditional projects, the constraints of events as projects dictate unusual difficulties in a simple application of these principles. For example, the project managers for the Glastonbury Festival decided not to hold the world-class, internationally renowned music festival in 2012 due to reported resource shortages, which are claimed to have been caused by the London 2012 Olympic Games. According to one article, the key resources that were thought to be in short supply were police officers and portable toilets (Nicholl 2010).

2.14 Project cost breakdown structures

2.14.1 Total costs

Costing of event projects will likely emphasise price, cost or profit, according to which is the most relevant to the project in question. It can generally be approached from a top-down or add-on perspective, depending on whether a fixed budget is provided. Costs will generally be forecast for events using fixed and variable costs for the resource groups already listed earlier in this chapter, which will be subtracted from the forecast revenues eventually gained from ticket sales made at target prices. Clearly, there are complications to this approach, which relate to returns on investment, the cash flow considerations associated with events and other event-specific financial issues, which are covered in more depth in Chapter 6. However, it should be noted that the conventional project management methods regarding cost management tend not to be directly applicable to events as projects because events rarely present opportunities for guaranteed financial returns. Cost reductions to event projects can rarely be achieved by simple labour reductions, as is possible in other project-based industries, because of the labour-intensive nature of event projects. Also, many events are produced for the not-for-profit and public sectors.

2.14.2 Cost monitoring

For cost monitoring to be successful, the event project manager must allocate costs correctly to each of the project tasks. These should be reported at regular intervals by the individuals in charge of the relevant tasks' completion. In particular, it is essential with events that contractors are paid correctly, that ongoing expenses are carefully monitored and centrally authorised, and that costs are correctly allocated to the relevant event-department budgets.

2.15 Project implementation

Project implementation concerns the delivery of the event from its live opening to its close. This will involve the practical completion of all the processes related to the tasks with all their associated considerations covered so far in this chapter. The main articulation of this phase of an event will be incorporated into the events programme, which will include a statement beforehand of all the activities intended to be carried out, with the clear assignment of responsibilities for each. Depending on the type of event being staged, the project manager may decide to use a responsibility chart for each of the event programme elements, with an associated time schedule for their completion, as well as other relevant programme details, such as locations and other resource information. Each part of the event's delivery will require ongoing monitoring and reporting systems that should be as simple and as user-friendly as possible. These will enable each party to carry out the work successfully and to take effective remedial action if required. The major evaluative criteria the event manager is most likely to be concerned with include the completion of event delivery tasks, timings and associated cost controls. The more forthcoming and useful this review, the more likely it is that the project manager can remedy shortfalls in these important areas. Likely remedies will include the application of predetermined, contingent strategies that will often need to be applied in coordination with the most important event stakeholders. As complicated as these processes may sound, their successful implementation will depend directly on the soundness of the initial event project plan. They might well concern unforeseen circumstances stemming from the event's macro environment, such as adverse weather conditions or terrorist attacks, which may well require the overall strategic direction of the event to be significantly altered or even abandoned altogether.

2.16 Project shut-down

Event project shut-down can prove much quicker to implement than its initiation. An events-focused adaptation of Turner's earlier (1999) framework for finishing the work can be useful here and includes the following elements that can be applied to event completion:

● Produce checklists of outstanding work.
● Hold frequent meetings of event teams to ensure that closedown problems are identified and solved.
● Release event personnel from certain teams as they are no longer required, either onto other parts of the event closedown or from the project completely.
● Create a specific event closedown 'task-force' to complete outstanding work.
● Close down contractors and suppliers that are no longer required in order to avoid unnecessary cost.
● Support the event project manager with a deputy with finishing skills.

Considering this importance of stakeholder management, event objectives and planned legacies, it is also important for the evaluations of the event to be documented, including its problems, achievements and benefits. Some large event project management organisations, such as Gartner, also use this stage of an event to elicit attendee feedback through formal research processes, such as interviews and focus groups. Overall event evaluation will be a requirement for events that have involved the investment of public funds and those attracting a high degree of media coverage. Additionally, it will be useful in particular for events that will be repeated. Therefore, the project manager should ensure that the relevant information is planned for well before the event is delivered.

Disbanding event teams can be problematic if not planned well in advance. Many event personnel experience concerns about future employment, so there can be a tapering of team morale. It is therefore useful to plan for the schedule closedown as early as possible and some event organisations hold debriefing meetings and end-of-event parties, which may include recognition and rewards for performance achievement.

2.17 The required competencies of an event project leader

Following this in-depth analysis of the tasks of an event project leader, it is logical to present a brief consideration of some of the competencies needed for leading an event project effectively. Several studies (e.g. Dulewicz and Higgs 2005) suggest that an effective project leader should possess the intellectual, emotional and managerial skills outlined in Table 2.2.

Table 2.2 Event project leader competencies

Intellectual	Emotional	Managerial
Critical analysis and judgement	Self-awareness	Engaging communication
Vision and imagination	Emotional resilience	Managing resources
Strategic perspective	Motivation	Empowering
	Sensitivity	Developing
	Influence	Achieving
	Intuitiveness	
	Conscientiousness	

CASE STUDY 2.1

The 2017 Ealing Free Film Festival

One of the unique challenges associated with providing professional events management case studies is the competitive nature of this fast-growing industry and the resulting confidentiality that often surrounds its best examples of outstanding practice. However, the following is a real-world, industry case of event project management in action.

Project background

The first Ealing Free Film Festival was developed from an initial idea to hold a movie viewing for attendees on a local college campus. This was quickly developed by experienced project managers into a concept which utilised the Spacehive crowdfunding platform. The result was a successful two-day Free Film Festival on 11 and 12 August 2017 on Ealing Green. This involved crowdfunding from voluntary donations, using social media, web, direct marketing and word-of-mouth appeals, which raised the necessary budget in a three-month period.

The two-day festival screened the classic Ealing comedy *The Ladykillers* (1955) and the iconic musical *Dreamgirls* (2006) and involved project planning, which included the application for a licence from the London Borough of Ealing.

The project plan aimed to celebrate Ealing's Film Heritage by bringing film into the community and gathering local people together at free screenings.

The event's publicity promised:

> Free films are a great way to engage the local community and we aim to build connections and nurture partnerships with local businesses and individuals.
>
> This project will promote our ethnically diverse community and celebrate the area as a creative hub of artistic initiatives. The local community will benefit through the cohesion that film brings, allowing people of different backgrounds to share moments together through film.
>
> (Spacehive 2017)

The project steps involved included:

- Raising funding.
- Acquiring all the necessary film licences, permissions and permits.
- Collaborating with local businesses to promote and sponsor the project.
- Printing programmes and posters.
- Executing a sophisticated social media campaign to network with local businesses, residents and other stakeholder groups. This eventually was found to be the primary way to publicise interest and attendance from the audience not directly associated with the organising committee.
- Hire equipment, including screen, other audio-visual equipment, transportation, seating, etc.
- Organise staffing by volunteer workers.
- Liaison with Ealing Council.

The result was attendance by around 120 attendees each night, which brought a welcome buzz to the local Ealing area.

Project management

The Project Leader, as the key contact, liaised throughout the project with the central marketing team, including on marketing and social media. They had regular meetings as well as daily phone calls and emails.

- Planning:

  o duration – it was decided that the event would run for two days over a weekend

- client and stakeholder contact
- finance
- design
- selection of key speakers
- marketing
- social media
- risk and health and safety
- suppliers
- human resource management – choosing and training staff
- critical path development.

- Implementation.
- Evaluation.

Project management approach

The project was approached holistically. A project plan was formed, which outlined the date and specific details running up to the event, and focused on specific aspects, such as the site, obligations, design, guests, budget, suppliers and client (both invited guests and attendees) profile and information, and social media strategy.

Series project management

The project had a management plan. The main project management areas for the entire project could be listed as:

- Client contact and administration.
- Staff:

  - roles and responsibility of existing staff
  - deployment of internal marketing and design staff to support project
  - recruitment and training of staff to work at the event.

- Finance:

  - maintenance of overall budget to ensure no overspend
  - payment term negotiations for suppliers/vendors
  - analysis of resources.

- Suppliers:

  - supplier selection – audiovisual (AV) contracts, speaker and contracts.

- Marketing and design of entire project:

  ○ This was fundamental to the success of the event. It allowed suppliers to present their products in a manner that was approachable, friendly and fun in order to ensure an important return on their investment.

- Evaluation and feedback to client(s).
- Logistical concerns: health and safety, special needs, security, parking.

Industry voice

Lizzy Eaton, Oddity Events & Marketing

Events as projects

With a degree in event management under my belt I began my career in 2010, with what started with a fairly detached relationship with my work. I would get up, go to the office, do what I was paid to do, and go home without thinking about work at all till I was at my desk the following day.

As the years went by and I gained experience, skills and responsibility, my role as an event professional became part of my make-up. It takes a certain type of person to put themselves under this immense pressure when managing projects; the desire to please with a focus on structure, strict deadlines and achieving the seemingly impossible. This drives us to be perfectionists – never settling for anything less than excellence.

In the summer of 2018, after almost a decade of working my way around various event-project roles in organisations, I took the leap to start my own agency, Oddity Events & Marketing. We help corporate communications, advocacy and public affairs teams deliver event projects with personality to influential audiences (e.g. MPs, policy-makers, journalists and academics). As a fledgling agency we are constantly evolving and learning the best approach to deliver project results for our clients, never more so than in 2020. It was a rocky year for the events industry, but 2020 gave event professionals like me the opportunity to reflect on what drives us, our place in the workforce and the importance of our work on projects within the organisations we represent.

Despite the pandemic, event professionals rose to the challenge and proved their worth, reinforcing the value of the skills and resilience they bring to the table, as well as bringing a new perspective on what best practice looks like moving forward. As I take my business into 2021 there are three key things I will prioritise when planning an event project and advising my clients. These are purpose, consistency and community.

Purpose

When planning event projects, it's very easy for ideas to snowball as time goes on, so the purpose can sometimes get a little lost along the way. There is access to global information at all times, and as a society we are more stretched for time than ever. When event project managers invite people to events they should be mindful of the commitment each individual has made to engage, and ensure sure they leave with new knowledge that has made their attendance worthwhile. To achieve this, there needs to be a clear focus on why the event is being held with as little background noise as possible.

At Oddity, when a client comes to us with a brief we challenge them to establish some robust strategic objectives – the 'why' – so as the ideas for content and creative elements develop we can refer back and be accountable to the objectives. During the project planning process – particularly when they ask us to 'be creative' – we compare our ideas to 'the why' and ask ourselves if each idea we come up with will help us reach our goals. If the answer is no, then the idea needs to be parked and some budget saved. If it's yes, go for it. This helps to keep the project team focused and working toward the same target, and the event design and content is cohesive throughout. As a result, the attendee can absorb the key messages and information easily at the event as this has been at the forefront of the project planners' minds from conception to delivery.

Consistency

During the Covid-19 pandemic organisations have had to adapt their communications and marketing tactics in order to effectively reach their key audiences, but with a quality that is consistent with past activity. My interpretation of the event projects we deliver at Oddity is that they are a physical embodiment of a brand, an organisation, a campaign, a message. By default, it's up to my team to showcase the values and key messages of the organisations we represent, in the most literal and carefully curated sense.

Designing the attendee experience at corporate or B2B events is not just about reducing stress and making it smooth for all on the day; it's about influencing how the attendees feel when they physically interact with a brand or organisation, and how that interaction affects their opinion of that brand or organisation as a result. As a starting point, corporate event managers should try to align their event-project strategy with the brand values, policies and priorities of their organisation, in order to put them on display and reinforce a positive reputation. For example, if an organisation prides itself on being an inclusive employer, the event should be a showcase of inclusivity, with balanced speaker line-ups, accessibility for the disabled integrated within the experience design, and accommodating those who wish to pray with safe, private spaces. Or, if your organisation has a new sustainability policy, make your event as sustainable as possible, to highlight these new priorities.

Community

Every event-project has a life cycle, which rarely begins or ends with the event itself. When we invite people to events, we are inviting them to build a community with us, where common interests and values are shared among peers. With this in mind, events are the perfect vehicle to encourage advocacy and to directly influence the behaviour and actions of attendees. An engaged event community will take your message away and pass it on, extending the impact of your event further than the standard life cycle. This should be harnessed before, during and after the event day itself with thoughtful content and implementable calls-to-action to maximise your event's legacy.

This goes back to having a clear vision of the 'why'. When we understand the 'why' of our event, we can make the tone and messaging more authentic and compelling, so the community you build will be more willing to advocate on your behalf.

As mentioned above, these pillars represent what's important to me and my clients today in 2021, but as we've seen, a lot can change in a short space of time. It's important for event-project professionals to keep ears to the ground and respond accordingly with trends and expectations of our audiences. As their needs and demands evolve, it's critical that we don't become too rigid in our practices and we evolve and flex to ensure our event projects deliver excellence every time.

2.18 Summary

This chapter has attempted to demonstrate that events are projects, yet they are managed quite differently from those in other industries. The importance of proper applications of project management to the international events industry should now be apparent. Proper application depends on an initial understanding of the difference between the organisational structures and processes of event organisation, when compared to other types of business. While it is clearly possible to relate project management to many of the conventional event planning theories and practices discussed elsewhere, the particular processes related to effective event project management throughout the event cycle should be noted.

Further reading

Doran, G. T. (1981) There's a SMART Way to Write Management Goals and Objectives, *Management Review*, November: 35–36. This is the often-quoted, foundational paper for the understanding of SMART objectives, which is definitely required reading for any student of events management.

Kolltveit, B. J., Karlsen, J. T. and Gronhaug, K. (2007) Perspectives on Project Management, *International Journal of Project Management*, 25: 3–9. This paper provides a fuller discussion of our basic summary of *project management* perspectives, which provides useful models for understanding how to apply project management to events.

Pinto, J. K. (2010) Project Management, Trenton, NJ: Pearson. This book is a thorough overview of project management and includes many models and supporting examples from a variety of industries.

Silvers, J. R. (2007) *Risk Management for Meetings and Events*, London: Elsevier. This book is particularly useful for those wanting to understand more about project management and the risks associated with projects in particular.

References

Bowdin, G., Allen, J., O'Toole, W., Harris, R. and McDonnell, I. (2011) *Events Management* (4th edn), Oxford: Butterworth-Heinemann.

Dulewicz, V. and Higgs, M. (2005) Assessing Leadership Styles and Organisational Context, *Journal of Managerial Psychology*, 20 (1): 105–123.

Goldblatt, J. (2005) *Special Events: Event Leadership for a New World* (4th edn), Chichester: John Wiley & Sons.

LaBrosse, M. (2007) The Evolution of Project Management, *Employment Relations Today*, Spring: 97–104.

Lewin, K., Lippitt, R. and White, R. K. (1939) Patterns of Aggressive Behavior in Experimentally Created Social Climates, *Journal of Social Psychology*, 10: 271–301.

Maylor, H. (2010) *Project Management* (4th edn), Harlow: Pearson.

Nicholl, K. (2010) Glastonbury Loses Battle of Portaloo: 2012 Festival Off Because Olympics Needs All the Police and Portable Toilets. *Daily Mail*, 16 October, www.dailymail.co.uk/news/article-1321160/Glastonbury-2012-cancelled-London-Olympics-need-police-Portaloos.html [Accessed 12 November 2010].

Spacehive (2017) Ealing Free Film Festival, https://www.spacehive.com/ealing-free-film-festival [Accessed 6 October 2022].

Shone, A. and Parry, B. (2010) *Successful Event Management* (3rd edn), Andover: Cengage Learning.

Toffler, A. (1990) *Powershift: Knowledge, Wealth, and Power at the Edge of the 21st Century*, New York: Bantam Books.

Turner, J. R. (1999) *The Handbook of Project-Based Management* (2nd edn), Maidenhead: McGraw-Hill.

Turner, R. T., Müller, R. and Dulewicz, V. (2009) Comparing the Leadership Styles of Functional and Project Managers, *International Journal of Managing Projects in Business*, 2 (2): 198–216.

Wysocki, R. K. (2007) *Effective Project Management* (4th edn), Indianapolis, IN: John Wiley & Sons.

Chapter 3

Event design and production

Contents

DOI: 10.4324/9781003102878-3

3.1 Aims

By the end of this chapter, students will be able to:

- explain the relationship between the event production steps of concept, design and staging
- develop an understanding of events design as the production of experiences rather than the management of staging elements
- describe the common elements of the event attendee experience.

3.2 Introduction

Event design and production are among the greatest challenges facing the events specialist. As clients continue to demand ever more memorable and remarkable events for their participants, it is left to the event designer to fulfil the brief and the event producer to deliver desired outcomes. However, event design and production are difficult processes, which are also embodied in the wider activities associated with planning events.

Event design and production are distinct sets of activities from each other and are different skills from what are widely regarded as the functions of management. They therefore do not rely on the more specific management processes discussed in Chapter 2; instead they are generally creative and artistic, as well as being strongly grounded in traditional design principles.

'Event design' simply refers to the mental creation of an event before it takes place, first in the mind of the designer and then as it is communicated to those responsible for its production. 'Event production' therefore refers to the subsequent action of manufacturing or engineering an event's delivery, based on its initial design.

However, when approaching this topic with a view to successful industry practice, it is worth noting that the literature about event design and production is sparse, and also there are wide differences among industry practitioners about how to approach both areas. This chapter attempts to unravel some of this controversy and confusion about this important topic. Literature about processes and procedures in the industry has led to what many view as a 'managementisation' of what should be the production of authentic event attendee experiences. This emphasis has also led to confusion between both event design *and* production. Practitioners and academics have generally focused on staging and logistics when discussing both of these elements. What is really required from *design* is the clear establishment of an initial event concept, with corresponding design development following. Event *production* then involves putting this design into practice, using practical staging elements.

3.3 Recent developments

In addition to the challenges presented by the Covid-19 pandemic, recent developments in event design and production have been influenced by this need to produce authentic event attendee experiences. There is a demand to design an event to run as closely as possible to its theme. One of the ways this is evolving is a move away from the traditional event venues of conference halls or large hotels and selecting instead unique venues to capture the event theme, such as art galleries or venues with a history relevant to the theme. An example of this was the opening night event of New York Fashion Week in September 2014, where the event was held at the Irving Plaza because of its history as a rock venue. Another example was the 'What You

Will, Celebrating 400 Years of Shakespeare' event discussed in our second edition, which was held in the same room and at the same venue as the very first performance of Shakespeare's *Twelfth Night* – the Middle Temple Hall in London. This created an authentic experience both for the live audience and the online one on YouTube. Even more sophisticated digitisation of authentic online attendee experience has been required in order to adapt to various governmental and other public health requirements of the recent global pandemic. These will be discussed later in this chapter.

Advanced technology, using an iPad to order food preferences, or to vote in mini-questionnaires, for example, can be appropriate since they enable attendees to make prompt decisions about their own experiences, giving them choices, and providing them with instant gratification as their input becomes reality.

AV effects and lighting can create the atmosphere and visual effects necessary to complement event themes.

Live entertainers can be streamed in as holograms, both to create a unique space for an attendee's authentic experience and to heighten that experience by providing sensory stimulation. It is far less expensive to use holograms than to pay for live acts to travel, and therefore more entertainers can be employed at an event, which further adds to the attendees' experience.

3.4 Events as designed experiences

3.4.1 Events as part of the growing experience economy

In Chapter 1, the diverse scope of events was discussed, and it was established that it is often difficult to categorise, or even define, what they are. However, one common thread shared by all events is that they are experiences for those who attend them. Certainly, masses of attendees flock to the annual Glastonbury Music Festival, not because they cannot see its extensive, televised coverage, but because attending offers a particular experience that cannot be gained elsewhere. In fact, many music performers have overcome the impact to their earnings from revenues lost through illegal music downloading by switching their emphasis from generating profits through music sales to performing at live events. This change has led many previously retired acts to come back and play at large music event venues, such as the O2 in London.

In general, events, whether formally managed or not, can be considered as an industry that forms part of what Pine and Gilmore (1999) described as an emerging 'experience economy'. In a social, cultural and technical transition, our society, which used to be very much based on the consumption of products, now consumes a much higher proportion of services. The third phase of this consumption evolution has resulted not only in customers demanding services but also in having those services delivered as part of an overall, packaged experience.

Thus, the focus for event companies has changed over time. Industry successes, which are changing the face of the modern events industry, such as Top Gear Live, have moved from the traditional approach of car shows, which were largely presentations of manufacturers' vehicles. Potential customers and enthusiasts could try these cars and obtain information about them since they were consistent, durable products. These products, in turn, were being exhibited by company employees who, as service providers, customised their service offering, depending on the requirements and expectations of their customers. However, Top Gear Live turned this product and service relationship into an experience through the designed and produced event. This redefined the car event and produced a prosperous franchise for the organisers, who now hold five such events worldwide.

There has also been recent growth in the popularity of music and cultural festivals, increased media coverage of sporting and mega-events and an increasing reliance on the strategic value of faith, voluntary and corporate events to promote brand relationships. Clearly, the modern, international events industry represents a crucial facet of this new social architecture. These indications seem to support Jensen's (1999) observations that, as consumers of such experiences, we seem to be living in an ever developing 'dream society', where consumer perceptions of value, recognition of rarity and willingness to justify premium expenditure focus on the ability of successful business organisations to produce unique customer experiences. With such profound social and industrial changes, one could argue that the traditional management practices of the twentieth century might require reconsideration.

3.4.2 The event production process

Event planning is often presented as a rather simple process, comprising stages that build on each other towards the achievement of present objectives. Watt (1998), Shone and Parry (2010) and Bowdin *et al.* (2011) have all suggested this approach. However, event design is more of a creative set of activities that can often appear chaotic in its development due to its need to be revised. These activities are embodied in the 'spirit' of the event planning process. However, because *doing* event design and *learning* event design often involve very different outcomes, the specific explanation of what event design involves has proved more difficult to express. Anybody who has worked closely with expert event designers will often be impressed by how different their thinking processes and their verbalisation are, compared with those involved in more structured businesses, such as accountancy or law. It often seems that the 'out-of-the-box thinking' associated with design is difficult to put into ordinary speech.

Edward De Bono (1976) highlighted that thinking encompassed not only the logical and analytical 'types' of thinking we seem to spend so much of our studies and work lives practicing and perfecting, but also the importance of 'lateral' thinking, particularly in creative or artistic work, and that these three 'types' of thinking interact, as shown in Figure 3.1.

Lateral thinking involves the movement value of ideas. It is often concerned with taking an initial idea as a starting point and moving to the creation of new ideas. De Bono (2006) proposed four types of thinking tool to facilitate this process:

- *Idea-generating tools* that are designed to break current thinking patterns – routine patterns, the status quo.
- *Focus tools* that are designed to broaden where to search for new ideas.
- *Harvest tools* that are designed to ensure more value is received from idea-generating output.
- *Treatment tools* that are designed to consider real-world constraints, resources and support.

The realisation that artistic endeavour requires creative thinking processes is not new, particularly to those associated with the arts and the creative industries. However, the nature of the outcomes associated with events often requires much more final measurement of tangible success. Much of traditional business school education, particularly in the Western world, is concerned with the development of critical reasoning skills, relating to the evaluation of true statements and the questioning of errors – skills that mainly require analytical and logical thinking processes. While critical reasoning is obviously an important skill for events management specialists to develop and use in their work, it is much less useful for the event designer, whose 'craft' concerns the accomplishment of business outcomes through creative problem-solving.

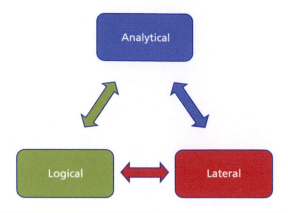

Figure 3.1 Three types of thinking
Source: Adapted from De Bono (1976)

3.4.3 The need for event designers to develop reflective practice

If the path to effective experience design in events cannot be satisfactorily pursued through the channels of traditional analytical, logical and therefore critical thought processes provided by mainstream business management practice and education, then the methods employed should perhaps attempt to incorporate more creative processes, possibly providing more opportunity to utilise right-brain functions. Certainly, the tasks associated with the more straightforward and organisational activities commonly associated with event planning may need to be rethought because of the creative requirements of reflective design.

Donald Schön (1987) proposed that in order to develop 'education for artistry' there would be a necessity for the formation of a 'reflective practicum', which represents a departure from the delivery and use of school knowledge and a move towards the use of reflection in action. For event designers to develop creative design practice which applies the tools of experience design literally 'outside the box' of conventional management activities, there is a need to articulate the difference between the two spheres of design knowledge, as compared in Table 3.1.

3.4.4 Content-based versus production-driven events

Berridge (2007) distinguished traditional management processes from the importance of recognising a particular design 'component' required throughout the event cycle to ensure the success of production-driven, creative events. This view has more recently gained popularity among events academics and practitioners alike.

Building upon the model of creative and reflective practice for event design, it is logical also to question the dominance of the linear event planning process models in which design seems to figure only as an implied part. For more detailed discussion on this topic, Berridge (2007) highlights at some length the fundamental distinction between management and design of event experiences.

Table 3.1 Comparison of 'school knowledge' versus 'reflection in action' as applied to event design

Event design according to 'school knowledge'	Event design according to 'reflection in action'
Designer relies upon critical reasoning – that is, the designer completes a preset schedule of logical steps.	Designer 'knows' in action – that is, various approaches are creatively synthesised using familiar pre-existing models from familiar past representations (e.g. culture) and other design settings in new combinations according to the design concept until an intuitive goal is reached.
The design process can be 'managed' or controlled according to predictability and bureaucracy. This allows the project to be constantly evaluated according to goals, timelines and tangible, measureable standards.	The design process becomes difficult for external parties and stakeholders to evaluate clearly. Measures of 'quality' are mainly perceived and realised from the reflective point of view of the designer.
The designer uses formal, commonly agreed categories of knowledge to inform the design process. This usually relies on a common body of knowledge and clearly 'right answers' which can be clearly articulated.	There is more of a view that design is somewhat about knowing more than we can say. Sensory design in particular often cannot be satisfactorily verbalised and also is not simply an intellectual activity.
The designer may view the design environment and its experience as separate from everyday life.	A designer may help the event attendee to coordinate everyday knowledge in action with other forms of privileged or received knowledge.
The designer's theory and experience are considered valuable, with higher levels of theory being brought to design having higher status. Design knowledge is also 'molecular' and not interconnected and there is a view of a more 'set' way and rigid answer to the set design task. Often there are single or set methods towards the required outcome.	The reflective designer uses on-the-spot experimentation, thinking about what they are doing as they are doing it. The designer allows themselves to be surprised and puzzled, responding to the puzzle as it progresses and unfolds, resetting the problem as appropriate. Separate methods are used, depending on the nature of the problem, including the invention of new ways to achieve outcomes in different projects. Overall, the practice is less of a method, but more of an art.
'Junk' categories are created for people who do not receive the design and event concept as expected.	The designer attempts to meet the attendee at their level of understanding.

Of course, linear models, such as those proposed by Shone and Parry (2010), should not be completely discarded, particularly in favour of a seemingly random replacement. It is simply hoped that there might be a proposition made that may assist the theoretical operationalisation of the design 'function' or component of the overall event planning process. Thus, the creative component of event design is carried out on the basis of a rationale for each event, which is based on traditional planning tools. The place of design in events is illustrated in Figure 3.2.

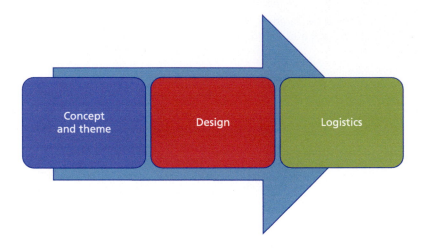

Figure 3.2 The three-stage event design model

CASE STUDY 3.1

Designing event experiences in a pandemic

Dr Carol Callinan

This discussion attempts to elucidate some of the challenges of the recent global pandemic and the strategies developed by event designers to meet new and ever-changing regulatory requirements and public health demands at the same time as attempting to deliver meaningful and satisfying event attendee experiences.

Events management has retained its user-centric orientation and focus on expectations and commitments of event owners and designers. Significant changes to the nature of events are evident resulting from the need for access via online virtual platforms. The use of online resources, whilst challenging, is equally liberating as this medium offers affordances and access to fresh audiences. Post-pandemic, events planning is continuing this trend, health concerns remain fundamental to design and are applied strategically to support the efficacy and success of the event. Many companies are planning to return to pre-pandemic organisation or structure in 2022, thus at the time of writing online events continue to replace and replicate traditional experiences. An appreciation of user-directed requirements for the online experience has interestingly extended the possibility for increased frequency in events. Digital dexterity concepts are now considered fundamental and present a strategic direction to successful evaluations.

Two areas which have observed significant diversification are the fashion and wedding industries. Event designers have needed to expand and significantly develop reach following the cancellation of many traditional events. Renegotiating the typical experience, fashion designers experimented with online streaming of events and an increased application of video-based media. Key fashion events have been rebranded, offering a broader remit and diversity in terms of engagement with designers and the physical location of the event itself. Significant shifts in weddings have included increased engagement with vendor teams, planners and designers. Traditional ceremonies have been replaced with increased outdoor events, a greater emphasis on the guest experience and extended or multiple day events.

Study activity

Watch the video clip at www.youtube.com/watch?v=q5r3FAxLOqE and answer the following questions:

1 Discuss the staging elements of the event. Write notes about the symbols used and the meanings they convey.
2 How have the designers linked the event concept to design and staging in this clip? How has New York been represented here as a destination in relation to the event?

3.5 Concept and theme

3.5.1 Event concept

The concept of an event and its theme, although different steps in the design process, are cohesive aspects, with the theme essentially becoming the main 'vehicle' through which the outcomes of the event are to be achieved. Goldblatt (2005) provided a useful framework, named the '5Ws', which has become the bedrock of most events, whether content-based or production-driven in nature. The 5Ws are explained by Goldblatt as the essential questions that should be asked and answered as the basis for any event before further decisions are made. These questions can be found in Figure 3.3.

While the questions have their own context in the overall planning of the event and form the basis of the widely accepted event planning frameworks, such as the one proposed by Shone and Parry (2010), they pose particular problems for the event designer in terms of the overall event outcomes to be accomplished by its design.

The focus on event attendees' experiences, as opposed to the simple management of an event's process, is a major departure from the more traditional practice of gathering together various logistical elements, such as catering, entertainment, sound, light and service, in the hope that somehow, with the right timings and programme, all those who attend will experience something special. Instead, the focus is on the psychology of event attendees and what will be achieved in their own experience. While in the planning context, discussed in Chapters 1 and 2, these five questions and their answers lead the quest for the establishment of event feasibility and present the event designer with more complex, creative problems to solve. In design terms, the reason why the event should be held becomes a question about what is to be achieved in the experience of its attendees. The event stakeholders often become agents in the creative process of design and may require accommodation by the event designer. This could also prove troublesome, making the design process more complex because of having to consider the additional opinions of the interested, yet not necessarily expert, parties. The venue and the date and time of the event, though often dictated to the designer, become crucial features of design, which either greatly complement or sometimes greatly hinder the cohesion with the theme and other important aspects of the event's delivery. The event product, or 'the

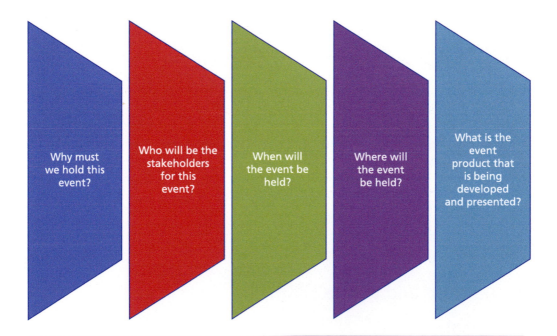

Figure 3.3 The '5Ws' of the event concept
Source: Adapted from Goldblatt (2005: 44)

event take-home', relates to the psychological, physical or even spiritual experience attendees should remember, perhaps reflecting on or acting upon them afterwards.

With respect to the event product, the design outcomes can be divided into cognitive, affective, decisional and psychomotor domains. Cognitive outcomes relate to the use of attendees' minds and may involve learning, which could include the delivery and assimilation of new knowledge. For example, an exhibition might seek to inform the public about the life and achievements of a particular historical figure. This would involve the conveyance of various types of information suitable for absorption by attendees, which could be retained in their memories.

Affective outcomes involve appealing to the emotions of attendees and can include their registration of new awareness, or surprise, excitement or even fear. Certainly, new awareness and appreciation of social issues, such as environmental sustainability, can be successfully achieved in event attendees by using suitable emotional stimuli, such as personal appeals or visual materials.

Decisional outcomes involve attendees making choices, such as those concerned with new purchases, voting or supporting causes.

Psychomotor outcomes involve physical activities, such as running marathons, playing sports or making political protests.

Once the answers demanded by the 5Ws have been ascertained, the relevant particulars from the outcome domains can then be decided on and articulated, and the designer can set specific design objectives. When these have been outlined, this concept can be linked to an appropriate theme.

3.5.2 Theme

Defining this important term from the existing literature has proved problematic. Authors such as Goldblatt (2005) and Monroe (2005) tend to apply the term in relation to a more traditional concept of the 'themed event', perhaps denoting a national flavour to food, entertainment, décor and other staging aspects. Getz (2007: 223) has provided the clearest definition so far, stating: 'A "theme" is a unifying idea or concept which gives meaning to the event, or is the object of celebration or commemoration'. Therefore, the theme, often established with the participation of stakeholders, is assigned with a view to being a dictating influence over all aspects of subsequent event design. This is contrary to the more traditional view presented by Bowdin *et al.* (2011), which places theming at the centre of logistics, without the key mediation of the distinct role of design in the production of event attendee experiences.

A more helpful analogy might be the use of genre in film and theatre production, which has been used to convey ideas and meanings more efficiently between directors, writers, costumers and all other parties responsible for every aspect of design. Part of the necessity of the use of genre was the difficulty associated with conveying ideas verbally. Words often convey linear thoughts and prove problematic in communicating creative ideas. As a result, directors developed forms of communication based upon visual media, such as storyboards. They also learned to talk to others responsible for important aspects of the creative process in terms of 'horror', 'romance', 'action' and other genre-based terms and concepts. This filtered into the marketing communication messages of studio advertising so that potential viewers of movie products might obtain clear ideas beforehand about particular offerings. Architectural firms have followed the same practice when communicating complicated building-design concepts to clients and other stakeholders through such devices as concept boards and scale models.

Similarly, in the case of event design, often the parties involved are unable to convey design ideas and instructions clearly without 'leakage' of meaning, potential loss of detail, as well as serious risk of potentially expensive design errors and client misunderstandings. Therefore, in addition to the theme being a central idea by which all the other elements of design can be determined, it also serves as an effective communication medium.

However, theming has thus far been approached at a level of complexity little more sophisticated than that offered by the existing tourism and hospitality management literature. For example, Getz (2007) briefly combined the topic with programme design. Malouf (1999) provided theming advice ranging from table plans to options for napkin folds. Goldblatt (2005) wrote a section about themed events, which offers suggestions about suitable design elements for events ranging from 'Hooray for Hollywood' through to 'Dickens of a Christmas'. Monroe provided a more extensive glossary of event themes including 'MASH', 'Dinosaur Dance' and 'Roman Empire'. It was Berridge (2007) who attempted to incorporate the components of theme into a clearer conceptual framework, which appears wholly inseparable from the design process itself and its planned outcomes.

Just as the big studio system of the twentieth century was often accused of effectively 'recycling' standardised and mass-produced art forms for general public consumption, the events industry may have also developed its own standardised forms. This has led to concern about inauthentic, artificially produced events.

As an important part of this ongoing debate, Brown and James (2004) notably discuss the potential risk of what they term 'ritual sacrifice' in the events industry. They argue that in its haste to become recognised as a mature field and profession, the industry is unconsciously deviating from its roots; the age-old foundations of events which were discussed in Chapter 1. These events were 'grassroots', cultural experiences that developed over centuries as authentic expressions of social community gatherings. However, Brown and James argue that these natural and often spontaneous expressions of social existence have been replaced by inauthentic, artificial, 'packaged' consumer experiences for generating profit.

CASE STUDY 3.2

Event luxury service design reconsidered

A timely reconsideration of the implications of the design and delivery of luxury event attendees' experience highlighted the place and important of semiotics. 'Semiotics' refers to signs or indications, and is important because it can potentially lead to greater levels of perceived customer authenticity in the service encounter. Semiotics is the study of sign processes, related to the production of meaning, mainly using non-language means, particularly through the senses, which are visual, auditory, tactile, olifactory, or gustatory. Such signs are used by event designers to engineer the stimulation of the senses of events attendees, in order that attendees may infer meanings, which they in turn use to form their event experiences.

A simple example of the practical application of semiotics to the design of the luxury event experience is the way the most popular music from different generations is used by DJs at luxury wedding events to elicit emotional engagement, through the stimulation of memories of particular times in their lives. Such theory helps to explain how attendees at an event are in themselves a community who agree on their collective meaning of communication codes regarding their understanding of objects encountered in events, whether they be dress, behaviours, symbols, colours, language or other aspects of design, which enable the content of the designed experience to be interpreted.

Therefore, event designers require an understanding of how event attendees process cognitive and emotional cues. Pictorial semiotics is also relevant as much of our roles as interpreters are based on the heritage of art and its pictorial representation throughout history. In the present day, it could be argued that films and other faster forms of media have a greater influence on interpretant-development than classic artworks. However, it should also be respected that traditional cues may be being disrupted by the role and pace of technological change, which is likely causing interpreters to develop and adapt new representations at a faster rate. Other important drivers of such change include culture and globalisation.

Source: Adapted from Bladen (2021)

Study tasks:

1 Considering the general overview of the information above, write down a list of key signs or signifiers you would expect to design for a luxury wedding.
2 For an event of your choice, study the main signs and symbols used to convey meaning to the event attendees in relation to the event concept. You may find the use of a YouTube video of the event useful here.

As is discussed more fully in Chapter 13, some produced events do still provide an escape for attendees from their usual routines. Chapter 12 highlights the essential part that event production plays in disengaging attendees from their normal thought processes, thereby enabling them to enter into a new set of relationships and experiences that are often related to unfamiliar branding concepts.

Pine and Gilmore (1999: 36) counter Brown and James's criticism by stating: 'There's no such thing as an artificial experience. Every experience created within the individual is real, whether the stimuli be natural or simulated'. Thus, while some in the marketing community continue to discuss more effective ways to deliver standardised products in customised service environments, the events industry's focus on the production of attendee experiences requires more consideration of an artificially produced 'experiencescape' in which the event attendee can engage in his or her personalised experiences at three operational levels of design, as shown in Figure 3.4.

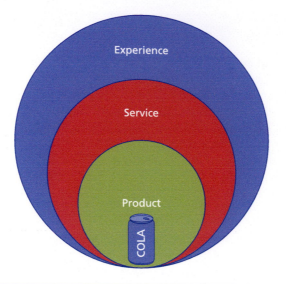

Figure 3.4 Three levels of the 'experiencescape'

Figure 3.4 demonstrates that the event attendee is often consuming standardised, tangible products, such as a branded soft drink, which is delivered through the medium of customised service provided by event employees, such as waiting or sales counter staff, within a personalised experiencescape that incorporates ambience, fragrances, light, space and other design aspects. It should be remembered that such attendees will always form their own personalised experience, which will often be as a result of stimuli artificially produced by the activities of the event organisation. These experiences will be positive or negative with respect to the achievement of the intended event outcomes. It is therefore the responsibility of the event designer to ensure that the experience which is personalised by each attendee mirrors these event objectives as closely as possible.

3.5.3 Inadequacy of the service design research

Since the popularity of service management literature began in the 1980s, several useful models for the design, delivery, measurement and recovery of customer service have been proposed. Foremost among these has been Zeithaml *et al.*'s (2006) model of service gaps and their associated measurement using the SERVQUAL questionnaire tool. Obviously, the events industry remains in many respects a service industry, and while the measurement of gaps in customer satisfaction related to service delivery remains relevant, from an event designer's viewpoint its use as an instrument of customer experience measurement appears limited. Such scientific methods are as inadequate in their capacity to evaluate the successful design and delivery of event experiences as they are in their measurement of people's opinions about art exhibits, or their views about theatrical productions. Major event organisations, such as Gartner, have attempted to address these issues by using flexible, one-to-one interviews with key event attendees after major productions. Event evaluation is discussed in greater detail in Chapter 14, but it seems that much more research is required into new ways to investigate the creative impacts of 'wow' factors on event attendees' perceptions of events and memory formation, in particular.

3.5.4 Experience blueprinting

It is therefore proposed that designers of the event experience clearly articulate, at least for their own reference, a 'blueprint' of intended attendee experiences throughout the event. This approach is an adaptation of Zeithaml *et al.*'s (2006) initial application of blueprinting to service design, which attempts to articulate service delivery actions, such as employee scripts, interactions and their associated performance standards. It is suggested here that the experience blueprint for an event includes similar details, though it should be supplemented by clear reference to the 'activities' of the various sensory stimuli involved in the design, such as programme, staging and timing elements, as well as their intended outcomes, such as attendees' memory formations, emotional flow, engagement and so on.

Such blueprinting of planned experiences should be carried out for the whole of the event cycle, which cannot be limited simply to the timelines required for operational delivery, but need to be centred on the experiences the attendee has at each stage. Just as marketers often find it essential to view a simple purchase as a multi-staged cognitive and emotional process, so event designers need to predict and design for the multi-phased nature of experience before, at and after events. Clawson's (1963) multi-phased nature of experience model helps to isolate some relevant, key stages of the attendee's experience, as shown in Figure 3.5.

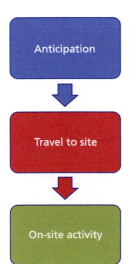

Figure 3.5 Five key stages of the multi-phased nature of experience
Source: Adapted from Clawson (1963)

It is also practical to suggest that some of the marketing and sponsorship issues discussed in later chapters should be carefully considered here to ensure cohesion of the event's design in relation to its overall branding and competitive positioning, as well as the service delivery aspects common to ticket sales and pre-event advertising and social media. These will also be important aspects of Clawson's 'anticipation' stage of attendee experience.

3.5.5 Attendee absorption and immersion

Any proposed blueprint, though subject to change as the event delivery progresses, should clearly provide an understanding of the levels of immersion and/or absorption, as well as the participation requirements and activities of attendees. Once again, such considerations should mirror the event concept requirements and will be informed by, and in turn inform, its chosen theme, thus influencing the event's design. Pine and Gilmore's (1999) 'experience realm' model helps us to understand these basic combinations of immersion and absorption, with participation levels at various stages of the event experience, as shown in Figure 3.6.

'Participation' can be active or passive, depending on whether event attendees directly influence the experience being produced. Classical music concert events generally involve little audience participation until the final applause, whereas the annual London Marathon depends upon the active participation throughout of its attendees, that is, the runners. 'Absorption' involves 'occupying a person's attention by bringing the experience into the mind', and 'immersion' is 'becoming physically (or virtually) a part of the experience itself' (Pine and Gilmore 1999: 31). The combination of these elements produces the four 'experience realms' of entertainment, educational, aesthetic and escapist events.

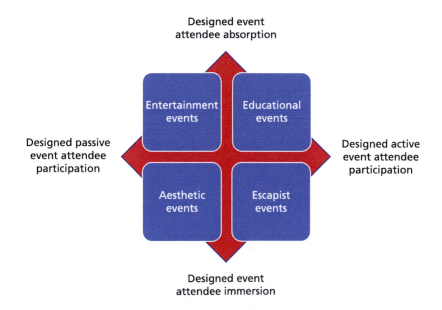

Figure 3.6 The event experience realm
Source: Adapted from Pine and Gilmore (1999: 30)

This model is not intended to depict a static rationale for an event, but refers to different levels of participation combined with absorption or immersion at different points of the event, depending on the prescribed outcomes of each stage. The level of participation by attendees at events needs to be carefully designed beforehand to ensure their appropriate level of engagement. Additionally, failure to implement the correct level of immersion can lead to serious shortfalls in attendee engagement and a lack of satisfaction. It might also be worth noting that attendees sometimes attempt 'unauthorised' immersion of themselves in experiences, which are mainly intended for absorption, such as football matches, the outcomes of which have suffered as a result of pitch invasions. In such cases, designers with planners, and even contract agents such as law enforcement officers, should ensure that steps are taken to minimise such disruptions.

3.6 Understanding event experiences

This view of the event designer's role therefore moves away from the traditional approach of simply planning events by using logistics. It focuses more on clearly defining the required experiences that attendees should have in relation to the planned outcomes and objectives set for the event, as well as the levels of required participation and immersion or absorption at its different stages.

3.6.1 The role of sensory experience

The basis of event attendee experience formation is sensory stimulation. Authors such as Goldblatt (2005), Monroe (2005) and Getz (2007) acknowledge the necessity of appealing to attendees' senses of sight, hearing, taste, touch, speech and emotions within the experience environment of the event. However, they tend to revert to lists of sensory categories and associated logistical options, without much explanation of their use or how they stimulate attendees to form experiences. The EMBOK model (www.embok.org) attempts to list design on behalf of the events industry as comprising:

- content design
- theme design
- programme design
- environment design
- production design
- entertainment design
- catering design.

Silvers also attempts to develop each of these categories, with a selection of logistical options under the heading of 'Management'. Not referring to EMBOK specifically, but more to the historical tendency of such lists, Berridge (2007: 34) observes:

> Oddly these are not always aligned with detailed examples of their use. Or any further explorations of the types of experiences that might be subsequently created. This is a common characteristic of academic study of events in general, to produce checklists of what could be included without necessarily any accompanying explanation of how they should be used or what they will produce.

3.6.2 Basic event attendee psychology

Bearing in mind that sensory stimulation provokes a psychological formation of experience in event attendees, general reference to some basic theories of psychology is appropriate here. Though it is not within the scope of this text to explain or critique these approaches, their importance and application to the design of event attendee experiences is crucial to the understanding of event design by the event designer.

3.6.2.1 Behaviourism

Behaviourism, one of the earliest schools of popular psychology, proposes that individuals learn through conditioning as a result of stimuli in their environment, as shown in Figure 3.7.

This school of learning is based on the two main theories: classical conditioning and operant conditioning. Classical conditioning was developed through experimentation on dogs by Ivan Pavlov (1927) and involved associative learning. Briefly, Pavlov demonstrated that individuals' naturally occurring stimuli – such as smelling food, which leads to the response of increased hunger – could be modified through conditioning to become a conditioned response associated with a modified stimulus. For example, when attendees arrive at a dinner event it would be usual for them to expect to eat at some later point. Seeing or smelling attractive food can stimulate hunger and appetite, but the event designer can use various sensory cues in the environment that are not directly related to food in order to condition the attendees to anticipate certain levels of luxury or extravagance in the pleasurable experiences awaiting them. Canapés, fine champagne and the dress code, as well as the formality and attentiveness of the food service staff, can all cause a conditioned response, as can table linen, cutlery choice and accompanying music.

B. F. Skinner's (1957) theory of operant conditioning as a development of Pavlov's classical theory demonstrated that individuals can learn as a result of punishment and reward from external stimuli, as is shown in Table 3.2.

This approach focuses on a person's response to stimuli and can be used with the correct corresponding reinforcement to modify behaviour. For example, attendees at an event often need to pass through processes which they do not consider satisfying or central to their overall event experience. These processes can include long queuing periods, or compliance with security or

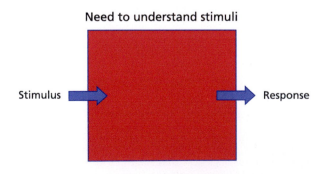

Figure 3.7 The stimulus – response mechanism

Table 3.2 Basic summary of stimulus – response via operant conditioning

	Outcome of conditioning	
	Increase behaviour	Decrease behaviour
Positive stimulus	Positive reinforcement (add stimulus)	Response cost (remove stimulus)
Negative stimulus	Negative reinforcement (remove stimulus)	Punishment (add stimulus)

other necessary crowd management procedures. Correct design can stimulate an appropriate response to verbal, visual or other cues which can instruct attendees in their required behaviours. Formally dressed security personnel can reinforce the need for adequate compliance with bag checks at events where there are valuable artefacts, camera use at art exhibitions or even physical examinations for weapons at football matches. Queuing configuration design can play a large part in the ambience of an event, reinforcing attendees' satisfaction levels and first impressions.

3.6.2.2 Psychoanalysis

The work of Freud, Jung and other popular psychoanalysts can also provide useful understanding to the event designer, who will often access previous experiences and associations from an event attendee's background and particularly their childhood. Many design strategies used in order to stimulate event attendee immersion encourage the use of basic and familiar instincts, often delivered in unfamiliar contexts. For example, businesses often use paintball competitions for team-building events, which could be little more than the re-enactment of school playtime. Dressing up in costume is common in events as diverse as carnivals, graduation ceremonies and Halloween. The gamut of childhood emotions, including fear, euphoria and competitiveness, can be variously called upon in event contexts by the appropriate design of sensory stimulation. As human beings, many of these instincts are experienced at an almost primal level and they can be enhanced by the tastes and textures of foods, food service, familiar music, colours and even smells. These can be used to stimulate attendees' memories, which in turn stimulate the required sensory outcomes. The deeper meaning of cultural symbols, rituals and contexts are discussed later in this chapter.

3.6.2.3 Cognitivism

Cognitivist psychologists such as Rogers or Schön extended the humanist agenda which resulted from the practical applications of the theories of the two foregoing psychological schools to propose that humans are sentient beings capable of forming their individual meanings from the world around them. The relevance of reflective processes to the design of event experiences has already been discussed in some detail with respect to the role of designer, but similar application could be made to the process by which event attendees make meaning of their experiences for themselves. Certainly, this approach will rely in part on those that have previously been mentioned, but attendees' past experiences will influence how they process a particular event's stimuli.

3.6.3 Sensory perception

An event designer should recognise the application of these schools in association with the role of perception. Perception refers to the interpretation of the information we receive through our five senses. Attendees at events constantly receive stimulation through visual, auditory, olfactory, tactile and gustatory cues in various amounts and combinations, depending on the particular event in question. It is the perception of our environment that distinguishes us from other mammals. Gestalt psychology, which is concerned with 'the whole', suggests we organise stimuli into groups according to four main types: similarity, proximity, continuity and closure. This means that event attendees group items based upon how similar they are, how close they are to each other, and according to continuous patterns, and they form their own interpretations of familiar objects in order to create their own experiences. Perceptual constancy allows event attendees to maintain their view of an object even though it changes in terms of size, shape and brightness.

Visual perception allows us to interpret size, texture, overlap, shading, height, clarity and depth. Visual perception is therefore an important consideration when designing events.

For example, attendees associate groups of dishes on a wedding buffet table in terms of food groups such as fish dishes, salads or vegetarian options, or visual indication of likely flavours, such as cultural specialities or desserts. They will expect to see a progression of courses at a typical wedding in the West; from hors d'oeuvres, to fish courses, main courses and desserts. Colours will provide indications of the variety of ingredients, possible freshness and potentially important differences between flavours of diverse items, such as cheeses. Cleanliness of the surroundings will be visually perceived. Grandeur of the setting can be communicated by the visual perception of the silver plate on the guest cutlery and the texture and brightness of the table linen. Though psychologists and philosophers understand more about visual perception than they do about any other type of perception, it is still crucial for the event designer to consider carefully its interaction with the other senses.

Auditory perception is the ability to identify, interpret and attach meaning to sound. Sounds are what we hear (McLachlan 1989), and are internal sensations which we experience directly as a result of public occurrences in the outside world of the event. For example, loud music at a music event can provide feelings of euphoria in one attendee and a physical headache in another. In 2009, a student suffered sudden arrhythmic death syndrome (SADS) after attending a club event, and heart specialists thought the cause could have been linked to the loud bass music. Though much discussion surrounds the nature of sounds in relation to the objects that produce them and the act of hearing, it is sufficient for our purposes here to state that objects produce distinct sounds and event attendees use the distinction between these sounds to make sense of their environment and the occurrences within them. With this in mind, the effects of music on human experience have been recognised since time immemorial. The effectiveness of themes can be reinforced or compromised by the suitability of the accompanying music and sound system logistics. Obviously, some events, such as music festivals, revolve completely around music. This has more recently led to discussions regarding the suitability of some popular music artistes' participation in such long-standing events, such as Glastonbury Festival in the UK. Music was a key design feature of the opening ceremony of the 2012 London Olympic Games, as the range of music was almost exclusively British, including classical works by British composers, performances by UK choirs and UK music from the 1960s onwards.

Musical motifs were used to bind the event together; a whistling theme for the ceremony and a bells theme for the entire opening day of the Olympics.

The other main senses involved in event design, though less well-documented, nevertheless remain crucial to the success of the event. *Olfactory design* involves appealing to the event attendees' sense of smell and has probably been the fastest developing area of experience design, thanks in part to its use by fast-food, retail, hospitality and leisure companies. *Gustatory design* relates to the sense of taste. While it is naturally closely allied with the olfactory sense, it has been used at events in catering for millennia. *Tactile design* involves the stimulation of the attendees' sense of touch to achieve outcomes in the psychomotor realm.

3.6.4 Memory

As attendees return home, the main residual effects of the event's concept and outcomes remain in their memories. Sometimes, whole societies can share a powerful collective memory of a particular event. It is therefore crucial that the most important moments in an event are signposted for its attendees and distinguished from the often huge quantity of other, peripheral information and stimuli being provided. Attendees can form and retain lasting memories of the event. It is vital in this process that various subsections of the experience are carefully designed and programmed. The psychological aspects of such subsections include a sense of time, excitement and mood, ambience and emotional flow. These are discussed at length by Graham Berridge (2007) and are often carefully combined to produce 'wow' factors, which can be defined as sensory crescendos where attendee consciousness reaches its peak. Such wow factors are designed moments when the *raison d'être* of the event is signified to all participants. For example, the captain of the European Football Championship's winning team raises the trophy in triumph as the high point and culmination of the whole tournament. Similarly, the torch-lighting ceremony of the Olympic Games often attracts the largest international media viewership. Film and other entertainment award ceremony presentations will schedule a specific moment to recognise a famous director for their lifetime achievement and contribution to the art form. Sometimes, though, wow factors are unplanned, such as the famous moment during the 1985 Live Aid event when Bono, lead singer of rock band U2, rescued a spectator from being crushed against security railings, creating an iconic, collective, cultural memory of a key event high point.

> ### Study activity
>
> Choose an event you attended. Try to recall its main memorable incidents and especially its wow factors. How were these delivered?

3.7 Event staging and logistics

Having decided the event concept and the specific design characteristics, it becomes more straightforward for the event designer to draw together a cohesive system of logistics in order to deliver the experience to event participants. Hopefully, the foregoing discussion has further clarified the importance of keeping to this order of design elements. Only when the event's outcomes are clear can it be determined on a sensory level which design elements will deliver them and which are the tools necessary for achieving this. Finally, the specific staging elements – such as timings, programming, service, audience participants, queuing arrangements, entertainment, sets and decorations, plants and flowers, seating design, table settings, catering and food service, lighting and rigging, colours and themes, sound and use of technology – can be definitively set, planned and delivered.

Industry voice

Kelly Strong, Event Designer

My career in the events industry has now spanned over 20 years, with the core of my career working in the events department at the Appointment Group, managing their MTV account. Now a self-employed event specialist and university lecturer in Event Management, when I was asked if I would like to offer my industry voice around 'design' to the third edition of this book, my initial thoughts were around the importance of understanding design and how design must consider the use of space and reflect on the flow of movement. The following case is an event that particularly comes to mind regarding the design experience it set out to achieve and the experience it actually delivered.

Firstly, I want to share some of the basics when it comes to design which will put this case into some additional context. Space should be your starting block and the foundation of your design. Thoughtful space planning should guide attendees on a smooth journey around the event. You need to consider where the attendees will enter and exit the space. If it is an indoor venue you need to consider where the bar is, where the cloakrooms are, the toilets are, where the stage is etc. If it is an outdoor space for a festival, for example, you need to consider where the stage or stages will be, where the catering will be, the toilet blocks, the self-camping site, the glamping site etc. Consider practical factors like not creating a bottleneck as people try to visit and return from the loos or not seating people near doors. Once you have a clear view of the space you are working with – either the set layout of an indoor venue or you are planning the layout of an outdoor space – you should think about the route you want your attendees to take. Think about how to break up the space ensuring you are achieving the right balance of furnished and empty space. You do not want certain areas being cramped and crowded, likewise you do not want areas feeling vacuous.

Secondly, when people think of design within events, it is normal to assume it just covers what the attendee will see. In reality, however, design stretches far beyond that. Large factors of design are of course those visual elements, but design also impacts other touchpoints. Think behind the scenes, the zoning of areas, the flow of the attendees and the location of activations. Everything that is experienced from start to finish at an event has been meticulously designed with a purpose in mind; to deliver a fantastic experience.

This particular event was a 'London Winter Festival Weekend'. Now, when most people think of festivals, they picture muddy wellies, open-air stages and the great outdoors. Over the last few years several traditionally outdoor events have developed an indoor version. Snowboarding, motorbike trials, motocross racing, surfing, monster truck racing as well as several extreme sports have all bore witness to indoor versions, many with huge attendances. The impetus for this event was to bring a traditional summer festival out of season and create an ultimate winter festival weekend destination for groups of festival goers from all over the UK. Traditionally festivals are outdoor events, and this was to host an indoor event attempting to recreate an authentic outdoor environment. If successful an indoor festival would offer event organisers a full year-round calendar in which to plan a festival, which would be a distinct advantage given the competition that takes place during the spring and summer months, and enable this event to stand out from the pack during a more traditionally quiet time of the year.

Considering other benefits, the most obvious advantage was that the festival would not be dictated by the elements, which is a huge benefit in the UK. The weather can be unpredictable and there is always a risk that a festival can become a washout or even be called off due to heavy rain or gale force winds for safety reasons. Additionally, a festival needs a host of elements to make it a success; staff, security, bars, food, stages, tents, ticketing etc., the list is never-ending! With an indoor venue a lot of these would already be on-site and available for use. The infrastructure production and cost requirements for an outdoor festival are huge.

Depending on the size, some outdoor festivals can require cost outlays of up to £600,000, if not more, and that is before a single ticket has been sold or an act booked. It is these costs that lead to the rising ticket prices for outdoor festivals. With an indoor venue and smaller overheads, it would be possible to price tickets more competitively, leading to a higher chance of success. Finally, according to The European Festival Market Report (2014), a study of festival goers found that they missed certain home comforts, such as clean toilets, a bed and phone reception. With an indoor festival attendee would not only have Wi-Fi but would more than likely stay at home or in a hotel for the duration of the event, meaning they have access to clean and comfortable facilities throughout. With all this in mind, the concept was to bring together 20,000 passionate, hard-to-reach festival goers who would be attracted to the event by a range of amenities and a vast amount of entertainment in an innovative environment. The concept was simply to create a festival destination based around several cultural indicators. With a well-known energy drink as the main sponsor, the event had an obvious 'living life on the edge connection'. Was I feeling optimistic about this concept? Of course! But it was very different to anything I had worked on before, and aside from the fact there are many other amazing destinations that could host a festival at this time of year, could an indoor festival really create the right ambience?

The idea was to have a central core stage of activity from which various zones were then linked. Like many events of this kind there was both an implicit and explicit indication of what the event would look like; in this case one vast, inter-linked festival albeit with different zones offering artists across various stages from main stage performances to rowdy roof-lifting stage sets, heavier blues rock stage sets to intimate songwriter sessions. Other zones would include a stage for the younger folk offering an array of opportunities to explore through music, craft, adventure and games, a food and drink zone, exhibition zone with craft stalls and vintage clothing, The Literary zone would bring great interviews, spoken word and poetry performances. The idea was to create a multi-phasic experience with the different thematic zones, but still be part of one single continuous experience of immersion within the festival zones. The choice of themes within the zones would conjure up an image of intensity, of closeness between guests, of constant interactions and of mutual and comple-mentary enjoyment and entertainment.

The main reason an attendee will attend a live event is for the experience. We needed to cater for each of their senses and deliver an experience which would genuinely amaze and add value. When we set about creating the envi-ronment, a lot of thought went into areas such as lighting, flooring, stages, wall textures and acoustics which would all help to create an experience people would want to talk about. My experience in the industry had taught me that a fundamental part of event design is how the attendee experiences the space. My concern with such a large amount of attendees in one area was that we needed to put a lot of thought into how they would flow around the venue and experience all the zones, how they would know how to navigate the zones and overall space, and more importantly would they be able to find important facilities like the toilets and smoking areas which needed to not be too far away at any given time. We knew the main area needed to work in harmony with the other zones to deliver an overwhelmingly positive experience.

The actual experience of the festival was however very different to what we set out to achieve. Although the zones were credible and enjoyable in their own right, the overall impact of the event was just lost in the large hall of the venue at London's ExCel. Rather than captivating the attendees as a series of interlinked festival zones, each zone appeared to stand alone in isolation from each other. The compactness of space and the forced flow of guests were lost either due to the distance or the space between each zoned area. We very soon realised that rather than the attendee be lost in this artificial festival world and carried along by the wave of revelers, they appeared to be struggling to maintain momentum. Exiting from one zone to another was not a seamless transition, rather it was a profound jolt to the senses and the attendee was reminded that they were actually in a purpose-built event venue and not in a rural outdoor setting. Thus, space and flow interrupted rather than intensified the immersion of the guests.

3.8 Summary

This chapter attempts to provide a clear, introductory overview to a topic which is crucial to the success of designed and production-driven events, yet about which remains much misunderstanding and confusion. The relationship between the event production steps of concept, design and staging has been highlighted, with a focus on events as the production of experiences rather than the simplistic, yet common, management of staging elements. This has been discussed from the perspective of the event attendee's experience, with a focus on the psychological outcomes of design and production.

Further reading

Berridge, G. (2007) *Event Design for Experience*, Oxford: Butterworth-Heinemann. This well-written book provides a thorough, literature-based review of some of the concepts discussed in this chapter from the multidisciplinary perspective of experience design.

Brown, S. and James, J. (2004) Event Design and Management: A Ritual Sacrifice? In I. Yeoman, M. Robertson *et al.* (eds) *Festival and Events Management,* Oxford: Butterworth-Heinemann. This seminal chapter provides an interesting and critical discussion of some of the issues associated with event design and production regarding cultural authenticity and the wider implications of escapist events.

Jensen, R. (1999) *The Dream Society: How the Coming Shift from Information to Imagination Will Transform Your Business*, New York: McGraw-Hill. Though not directly related to the events industry, Jensen's thoughtful and well-written book discusses the movement in society away from tangible products and services to the demand by consumers for the designed experience and the importance of story-telling and other methods applied by the modern-day marketers of such offerings.

Pine, B. J. and Gilmore, J. H. (1999) *The Experience Economy*, Boston, MA: Harvard Business Review. A foundational text for anybody interested in the models of experience design, which also uses many examples from a variety of consumer industries.

Weblinks

11 Ways the Pandemic Has Changed Wedding Traditions Forever: www.brides.com/ways-covid-19-pandemic-changed-weddings-5118315

Fashion Month's Realignment: A New Pace: www.voguebusiness.com/fashion/fashion-months-realignment-a-new-pace-eckhaus-latta

IOC Issues Glowing Review of Beijing Games, *New York Times*: www.nytimes.com/2008/11/27/sports/olympics/27olympics.html?_r=0

London 2012: The Opening Ceremony: www.olympic.org/news/london-2012-the-opening-ceremony/204829

London's RHS Chelsea Flower Show Fit for Royal Visit: http://news.bbc.co.uk/1/mobile/england/london/8699866.stm

What You Will: Celebrating 400 Years of Shakespeare in the English Language: www.eventbrite.co.uk/e/what-you-will-celebrating-400-years-of-shakespeare-in-the-english-language-tickets-8478155391

References

Bladen, C. (2021) The service semiotics of luxury events: An exploration for future research and events management industry practice, *Research in Hospitality Management*, 11 (1), 53–57, DOI: 10.1080/22243534.2020.1867374.

Bowdin, G., Allen, J., O'Toole, W., Harris, R. and McDonnell, I. (2011) *Events Management* (3rd edn), Oxford: Butterworth-Heinemann.

Clawson, M. (1963) *Land and Water for Recreation: Opportunities, Problems and Policies*, Chicago, IL: Rand McNally.

De Bono, E. (1976) *Teaching Thinking*, London: Penguin Books.

De Bono, E. (2006) *Thinking Systems Lateral Thinking: The Power of Provocation Manual*, Clive: De Bono Thinking Systems.

Getz, D. (2007) *Events Studies*, Oxford: Butterworth-Heinemann.

Goldblatt, J. (2005) *Special Events: Event Leadership for a New World* (4th edn), Chichester: John Wiley & Sons.

Maclachlan, D. L. C. (1989) *Philosophy of Perception*, Englewood Cliffs, NJ: Prentice Hall.

Malouf, L. (1999) *Behind the Scenes at Special Events: Flowers, Props and Design*, New York: John Wiley & Sons.

Monroe, J. C. (2005) *Art of the Event: Complete Guide to Designing and Decorating Special Events*, New York: John Wiley & Sons.

Pavlov, I. P. (1927) *Conditioned Reflexes: An Investigation of the Physiological Activity of the Cerebral Cortex*, translated and edited by G. V. Anrep, London: Oxford University Press.

Schön, D. (1987) Educating the Reflective Practitioner, presentation to the meeting of the American Educational Research Association, Washington, DC, 20–24 April.

Shone, A. and Parry, B. (2010) *Successful Event Management* (5th edn), Andover: Cengage Learning.

Skinner, B. F. (1957) *Verbal Learning*, New York: Appleton-Century-Crofts.

Watt, D. C. (1998) *Event Management in Leisure and Tourism*, Harlow: Longman.

Zeithaml, V., Bitner, M. and Gremler, D. (2006) *Services Marketing*, Maidenhead: McGraw-Hill.

Event operations

Contents

DOI: 10.4324/9781003102878-4

4.1 Aims

By the end of this chapter, students will be able to:

- explain the key elements of event operations
- evaluate the need for event operations within the wider framework of event planning
- understand how to manage the flow of resources around an event – the products and services that are present in the event supply chain
- understand how decisions are made regarding the utilisation of resources in the event operations process
- recognise the importance of quality in event management and how it results in competitive advantage
- understand how knowledge of stakeholders (including customers) can create a competitive advantage due to the quality of service provision
- recognise the importance of contracts and to understand the basic contractual requirements for events
- analyse individual event requirements from a logistical perspective.

4.2 Introduction

Operational planning takes place after the strategic plans have been put in place – the event manager has developed a concept, tested it for feasibility (using situational analysis and market segmentation), chosen a venue, considered the event design and drawn up a strategic project plan. The next stage is to develop and implement the operational plan.

Whilst much that is written about the management of events focuses on the outputs of the event (the experience itself), operational management ensures that you also consider all the resources that are needed in order to create and deliver that experience. It is therefore of vital importance to the success of an event. After all, without operational planning, there simply would be no event!

> ### Study activity
>
> Consider the ingredients for the full breakfast you had this morning. Unless you live on a farm and have the animals to produce the products yourself, then those ingredients have passed through several different processes and people or organisations before they landed on your plate. What would those steps be?

When you describe the different processing steps that are needed in the study activity, from the farmer who produces the meat, to the company that makes the plastic to wrap the food in, to the transportation of your food from farmer to shop etc., you are describing all the different operational processes that resulted in your meal. In an events context, operational planning is therefore the consideration of all the things that you will need to run an event,

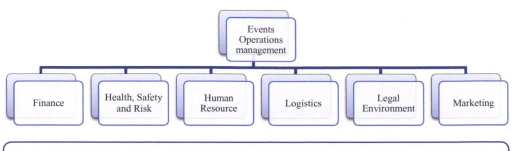

Figure 4.1 The key areas of managing event operations

and the putting together of a plan of how to get all of those resources to be where you need them to be, at the right time.

Operational management in events is therefore the activity of managing the resources that create and deliver the organisation's goods and services (Tum *et al.* 2006). It is the detailing of the skills and resources needed to deliver an event (Bowdin *et al.* 2011) and must therefore consider all areas central to event delivery. The event manager must consider all elements of the event and decide what resources, skills and equipment will be needed to deliver them – this, in a nutshell, is event operations.

Study activity

Draw a model that demonstrates the event planning process as described in the book so far. It should include the order of the processes and indicate how one element feeds into another. Include the following areas:

- The planning process:

  - event concept development including 5Ws and SMART event objective setting
  - event design
  - event feasibility testing including SWOT/PEST analysis
  - event project planning.

- The operations process:

  - financial planning
  - health, safety and risk
  - human resource management
  - logistical operations
  - the legal environment
  - marketing.

As every event is different and individually complex, there is no set formula for which operations will need to be planned. However, we can generalise, to some extent. Typical areas for planning include decisions around a staffing strategy; plans that cover the organisational approach to marketing and sponsorship; operational planning to evaluate health, safety and risk factors; and financial control systems. All these issues are key event operations requirements and are therefore explored in detail in the chapters that follow this one. Figure 4.1 shows the key areas of operational management.

As Tum *et al.* (2006) so clearly point out in their excellent – if now dated – book on the management of event operations, event operations are concerned with the day-to-day management of an event, which includes the implementation, control and administration of the planning process. As event operations is, effectively, everything that an event organisation does, it is difficult to describe within the confines of one chapter. Instead, this chapter will focus on the process of operational planning, which includes the introduction of various operational models and strategic operational planning, the tensions between quality outputs and cost-effective events, supply chain management and event logistics – including the logistical planning both for customers and on-site at venues/event sites.

4.3 Why do operations matter in events?

Event operations managers are the people who are responsible for planning and delivering the creative design of an event experience. Without operational planning, the event concept would remain just that – an idea that is floating around on paper. Those responsible for operational planning take the idea and make it reality; they are responsible for producing the right event experience, at the right time, for the right quality and at the right cost. It's a big job and it matters because it is the operations that make events happen.

Sound operational planning ensures that the event meets all the stakeholders' expectations and – if the operations of an event are run well – adds value to the event itself. Effective event operations can even help to ensure that the organisation is profitable, because the operational decisions determine how much money is spent on all the different areas of an event, and it is through our operational plans that we can reduce overhead costs (e.g. by negotiating a better

Study activity

Consider this quote from O'Toole (2011: 253): 'The operations of the event are the attendee's main experience. The site, the logistics and the programme are the areas of concern'.

The implication is that it is the output of event operations (how clean the toilet was, how good the food is, whether the venue looked right) that will make up the attendee's main experience. Others might argue that it is the designed event experience – the emotional responses to all the aesthetics and theming and the associated memoires – that make up the attendee's experience. What do you think? Is it operations **versus** experience, or operations **and** experience?

price with a supplier, or using less of one resource than we have budgeted for). So event operations matter because they create the physical event experience, and they deliver value to the different stakeholders.

4.4 Event operations transform resources into experiences

How does operations add value to the event experience? It transforms inputs into outputs that satisfy the various stakeholders' wants and needs. This idea is described by Slack and Lewis (2017) as the input-process-output model of operations (here, we describe it as the IPO model). This model suggests that operations transforms inputs – the resources that are needed to run an event – into outputs – the event experience itself. In order to help you to understand the IPO model, it is often easier to ask you to think of your own experience as a student. The operational process of a university student would look something like that shown in Table 4.1.

Table 4.1 The operational process of a university student

Input	Process	Output
Student	Independent study	A good degree
Lecturers	Engaging with seminars	Graduate job
Library	Attending lectures	Pride
University buildings	Submitting assignments	Confidence
Books and reading material	Doing the reading	Transferable skills
Computer	Submitting assignments	Employability skills
Internet access	Feedback from lecturers	

All events can be analysed using the IPO model (see Figure 4.2).

Figure 4.2 The IPO model

Essentially what the IPO model shows us is that operations managers are responsible for two things:

- Managing the resources that are needed to run the event (e.g. the physical resources such as the venue, the machines, the computers and the people and their knowledge, skills and expertise).
- Planning, implementing and controlling the processes – organising the resources to create the best possible event experience, at the right time, for the right cost.

Study activity

Apply the IPO model to an event of your choice.

- For the inputs, you need to think about all the resources you will need to run your event (think physical resources – staging, lighting, staff, trucks AND intangible resources – knowledge/health and safety awareness etc.).
- For the process, you will need to think about all the operational process that you will need to undertake in order to transform your list of inputs into an event. For example, financial management, project planning, training of staff etc.
- For the outputs, you will need to think about the outcomes of your operational process. For example, a safe event; well trained staff; an event experience that meets the customers' expectations.

4.5 Event operations strategy

Before we start to think about planning and designing the operations of an event, we should consider operational strategy. This means thinking about the strategic direction of the organisation, as Slack, Brandon-Jones and Johnston (2019: 74) suggest:

- *Strategy* – 'is the total pattern of the decisions and actions that influence the long-term direction of the business'.
- *Operations strategy* – 'the pattern of decisions and actions that shape the long-term vision, objectives and capabilities of the operation and its contribution to the overall strategy of the business'.

In other words, operations strategy is the tactics used in order to deliver the long-term objectives of an event organisation – it answers the question 'How do we get there?' posed by the strategic plan. The outputs of our event operations must meet the objectives of that event. Operations strategy links the decisions associated with operations to the marketplace, the environment in which the organisation operates and the overall objectives of the organisation. It can be viewed as the specific decisions and actions which set out how the event experience will be delivered. Successful operations managers must therefore plan, execute and control operations within the framework of the corporate plan.

Without a strong operations strategy, event organisations will find it difficult to keep up with the changing markets and struggle to compete. Slack and Lewis (2017: 10) describe four perspectives on operations strategy:

- **Top-down perspective** – this reflects what the entire organisation wants to do. In events, that would mean that the event operations must reflect the directions from the top of the organisation.
- **Market requirement perspective** – this is when what the market wants is translated into operational decisions. From an events perspective, this means that if the consumer market wants a cheaper event, the operations will need to be run in a more cost-effective way, so that ticket prices can be slashed.
- **Bottom-up perspective** – this is when the day-to-day experiences of an organisation suggest what operations should do. For events, this would mean that if, for example, the operations were focused on a high-quality event, the strategic position of the organisation would eventually be to offer high-quality events.
- **Operations resource perspective** – this basically means that the organisation does what the operations resources can do; it exploits the capabilities of its operations.

No matter which perspective an event organisation takes in terms of their operational strategy, what it really comes down to is the ability of event operations to provide a competitive advantage for the organisation. That's because event operations strategy helps to improve products, services and processes. If event operations are organised effectively, then the event organisation becomes more effective in the competitive environment.

4.6 Managing quality in event operations

We have established that event operations involves the control of the process that transforms the resources needed to create an event into the final event experience. Event organisations must therefore strive to maximise the quality of this process in order to meet the various stakeholders' needs, demands and wants. Events have a wide range of stakeholders and, as O'Toole (2011) suggests, they often have different objectives which compete – what one stakeholder wants might be very different to another. Identifying existing and potential stakeholders and mapping their expectations is therefore an important part of the planning process – and it also helps with the planning of the event operations, because you can add value to your event by understanding what your stakeholders want, and trying to give it to them. And, as stakeholder theory suggests, a company is only successful when it delivers value to its stakeholders (see Freeman 1984 for discussions on this). If we use the right resources for our event, it is possible to satisfy the diverse needs of our various event stakeholders, whilst also keeping within the strategic objectives of the event and making a profit (Tum et al., 2006). The way in which we do this is through the delivery of a quality product. But what exactly is quality?

In a service encounter, such as the delivery of an event, quality is normally defined as the extent to which the event has met the expectations of the customer. However, as Getz (2012) points out, quality means different things to different people. In events, quality is particularly difficult to define because of the wide range of stakeholders that we need to satisfy – for us, quality refers not just to meeting the customers' needs, but also to thinking about what our sponsors want, or what the client has demanded or the supply chain need. So when event organisers ask their stakeholders what they want from an event, they get a wide range of responses!

Think for a moment about what quality in events mean to you. Does it mean an event that has the best line up? Or an event that exceeded expectations? Or an event that was better than all the other ones? Each of you will be thinking about different things, because perceptions of quality differ vastly. However, the basic requirement for every event is that the event must meet the customers' expectations (which can be identified in earlier stages of event planning, through detailed marketing analysis). There are several metrics that we can use to consider what customers might mean by a quality event:

1 A service that is free from error (Slack *et al.* 2019).
2 An event that conforms to the original specification (Tum *et al.* 2006) – e.g. if a conference designed to create new business opportunities doesn't involve any networking opportunities, then it has not served its purpose.
3 The product meets the customers' needs or expectations.
4 The event meets the standards set by the marketing material (e.g. promise 200 stands at your exhibition, deliver 200 stands at an exhibition).
5 Slack also suggests that organisations can adopt a value approach – for events, this means that the attendees may accept a lower quality event if they are paying less to attend it.

4.6.1 Quality service provision

There are several quality initiatives that we can use to set standards in our event operations, which will help us to manage the quality of our processes. Some of the key ones are briefly outlined below – there is plenty of literature on all of these, so readers are encouraged to read more widely around them all.

4.6.1.1 Total Quality Management (TQM)

This is a holistic approach that sets standards for organisations, and provides measure to see if the organisations meet those standards. TQM seeks to create an event company that continually improves the quality of its services (Bowdin *et al.* 2011). It requires a culture of quality throughout the event operations and extending out into the supply chain – everyone involved in the process of delivering the event experience, from the caterers providing the food, to the staff greeting the guests or the audio visual company providing the lighting, must be focused on doing their very best for the organisation. For events operations, this is the challenge of TQM – the industry works with a network of outsourced suppliers, and ensuring that they buy in to this vision of a quality service provision can be difficult.

The challenge for applying TQM to event operations is that organisations need to go beyond just satisfying the basic customer needs – in order to gain a competitive advantage through the quality of the service, organisations need to exceed performance measures. To explain this, consider the following situation:

> You are an event operations manager, and you have arranged a coach to take your guests from the hotel where they are all staying to the conference venue. Which of the following scenarios offers the best quality service provision:
>
> 1 The coach turns up on time, the guests found the coach waiting outside the hotel for them, boarded it and arrived at the conference venue in plenty of time for the event to start.
> 2 The coach arrives at the hotel early. A member of staff waits in the lobby for the guests, greets them and takes them to the coach. It's raining so the guests are all offered an

umbrella for the short walk. When they board the coach, the driver politely greets each of them. They notice that the coach is sparkling clean, and on each of the seats is a bottle of water and a welcome note from the event organisers. There is classical music playing and the coach smells lovely. When everyone is safely onboard, the driver takes the shortest route possible, ensures everyone disembarks carefully, and a member of staff takes them into the conference venue.

Of course, it's the second example that offers Total Quality Management – you can see the difference quite clearly!

4.6.1.2 Just in time management (JIT)

'Just in time' is probably the most common management tool in the events industry. It short, it places an emphasis on customer service, and focuses on costs and timings. The basic principle is that everything that is outsourced should arrive at the venue *just in time* – this means that resources don't arrive early or late! If they arrive early, there is usually a cost associated with the storage of them, or security to look after them, or payment of additional staffing resources from the supplier. If they arrive late, they jeopardise the entire event experience. So good operations managers try to ensure that all their resources arrive *just in time*! There is clearly some risk associated with this initiative, and event operations managers must therefore have a high level of trust in their suppliers, because they can easily be let down here.

4.6.1.3 SERVQUAL

SERVQUAL is a very well-established approach to service quality which relates to understanding the customers' expectations and ensuring you meet them. SERVQUAL suggest that it is often the smallest things that decide whether people had a good time – the quality of the food, the length of queue for a drink, the state of the toilets. SERVQUAL therefore focuses on issues such as reliability (did it run on time, was it what customers expected); assurance (was it safe?); and customer service (were the staff friendly, did customers receive the right attention?). As Tum *et al.* (2006) suggest, it is generally quite easy to add value to the event through better quality service provision – think about cleanliness, consistency, reliability and friendly and helpful frontline staff.

Study activity

Think of the most recent event you attended. How would you describe the experience? Did you think it was of 'good quality', and if so, why was that?

- List the good quality aspects of the event.
- List the poor-quality aspects of the event.
- Create some recommendations on how that event could have improved its service provision.

> ### Quality versus Cost
>
> There is a good maxim that sums this up:
>
> There are three kinds of service, but you can't have all three:
> Good – Cheap – Fast
> Good and cheap won't be fast
> Fast and good won't be cheap
> Cheap and fast won't be good

One of the challenges of offering an excellent quality of event operations is that quality does not come cheap. There is a constant tension in the events industry between quality maximisation and cost minimisation. The events industry often works to very strict, tight budgets and a driving force for operational decisions is often cost (can we get it cheaper?!). The industry also has risks associated with rising or unexpected costs – e.g. more guests register than was planned; certain food or drink prices suddenly rise; suppliers suddenly face increasing demand and hike their prices up accordingly. The industry therefore always walks a very tight line between trying to minimise the costs and always providing the best product they can.

The best event experience, at the cheapest cost, is very difficult to do – but the answer lies in solid operational planning. If event managers think carefully about the event they want to deliver, and the resources they need in order to do so, then you can become much more efficient in the way you deploy the available resources in order to offer not just an event within budget, but also an event that is of high quality and offers value to stakeholders. In other words, quality service provision enables the efficient use of resources.

> ### CASE STUDY 4.1
>
> # The Fyre Festival
>
> **Location:** Great Exuma, Bahamas
>
> One of the most notorious event scandals of recent years – the Fyre Festival – can be viewed as an example of how not to run your event operations. The festival was promoted as a luxury music festival by its founders Billy McFarland and Ja Rule – the event was due to take place over two weekends in April and May 2017, in the Bahamas. Promotional videos of supermodels were released, promising 'the best in food, art, music and adventure' on a private island they suggested was once owned by Pablo Escobar. Many social media influencers, including Kendall Jenner, were paid to advertise the event through their media channels and day tickets were priced from $4,500 to $41,500, with VIP packages (including flights and luxury accommodation) for $12,000.

Reports suggest that McFarland was surprised by how much professional event organisations would charge to run his event for him, and shocked to be told that an event like the one he had planned would cost at least $50 million to stage, in the timeframe that he had promised in his advertisements. Most consultants told him he would need at least another year to plan his event. At this stage, the organisers decided to press ahead, doing things themselves, despite having no prior event experience.

By the date of the inaugural weekend, 5,000 tickets had been sold and a plane had been hired to take festival goers from Miami to the event. Behind the scenes, however, there was an unfolding litany of disasters, including major issues with financing, last minute changing of the catering company and many of the booked acts pulling out, as they became aware of the lack of planning for the event.

In order to raise funds for the event, ticket holders were advised that the event would be cashless and encouraged to put thousands of dollars onto a digital Fyre Band (an RFID wristband) in advance of the event. This was despite the organisers being warned that it was likely that the internet connectivity and any Wi-Fi would be so poor that the bands would be useless. About $2 million was taken from festival goers on these bracelets, and according to a lawsuit, 40% of this money was used by McFarland to pay off a short-term loan.

When ticketholders arrived on the island, the festival site was not ready. There were issues with security, food (the pictures of the cheese sandwiches guests were given as their 'luxury' food, for which they had paid hundreds of dollars, quickly went viral), accommodation (as did the images of the mattress dumped on sand, and poor-quality tents, of the kind used for disaster relief) and artist liaison. People waited for hours to be registered, and despite their being around 500 ticket holders arriving on that first day, there were not enough tents and beds for all the guests. A myriad of other problems were reported, including mishandling of guest baggage, no lighting around the site, a lack of medical personnel and theft of personal belongings. In the early morning, it was announced that the festival would be postponed (it was of course eventually cancelled) and guests were reportedly stranded, with no flights back to Miami available.

In the end, McFarland pleaded guilty to fraud and was sentence to six years in prison and ordered to forfeit $26 million. The organisers are still the subject of several lawsuits and class actions suits related to defrauding ticket buyers.

Study questions:

● Watch one of the documentaries on the Fyre Festival, or do some further reading. Then try to list all the operational processes that went wrong. Can you identify the root causes for these issues?

For further information on the festival, two documentaries were released in 2019: Hulu's *Fyre Fraud* and Netflix's *Fyre: The Greatest Party that Never Happened*. Watch the promotional video: https://youtu.be/mz5kY3RsmKo.

Sources: Wikipedia (n.d.), Baggs (2019)

Image 4.1 Rokers Point Settlement, Exuma, The Bahamas

4.7 Supply chain management

Events operations can either be performed in-house or by the purchasing of services and products from other organisations. In reality, very few organisations have the resources to supply all the inputs needed to run an event. Event operations do not, therefore, exist in isolation; instead every event experience is part of a larger and interconnected supply network. Events are supplied by the products and services that are needed to create an event experience and, as events are diverse, the range of suppliers is diverse. In an event, there can be many different supply chains, through which a variety of resources flow. This results in a large set of organisations who must come together in order to supply the resources needed to run an event. This is the supply network and it includes not just the supplier, but also the suppliers' supplier and the suppliers' suppliers' supplier and so on.

This use of a range of outsourced, external, organisations to supply the resources for an event is a traditional market supplier relationship. Think here about how event organisations must hire a venue, and an outside caterer, and an organisation to run the audio-visual aspects of an event. This use of external suppliers has a number of benefits for an event organisation, including:

- Maintains competition between alternative suppliers.
- Ensures you get specialist support and innovative products or services.
- Ensures that you get the best price.
- Is inherently flexible – changing suppliers is often easy and fast.
- Helps event managers to concentrate on their own core activities – that of delivering the experience.

Event operations

But external suppliers also bring with them some potential issues:

- There are uncertainties – once you have placed that order, you lose control over how it is fulfilled.
- Choosing who to buy from takes time and effort.
- An overreliance on suppliers can 'hollow out' the company.
- Short-term relationships that are price orientated can create issues in support and reliability.

(Adapted from Slack *et al.* 2011)

Study activity

Event supply chains have one particularly challenging feature – all the suppliers must be managed and coordinated into one event which is delivered at the moment it is consumed. Considering what you have just read about external suppliers, can you list some of the problems that might be caused by relying on other organisations to resource your event?

Types of relationships in the supply chain

- **Business-to-consumer relationships (B2C)** – relationships that are the final link in the supply chain, involving the ultimate consumer (i.e. the event organisation and the audience member OR the client)
- **Business-to-business relationships (B2B)** – when one company purchases goods or services from another company (i.e. when the event organisation uses an outside catering company).

(Slack *et al.* 2011)

It is also important to recognise some suppliers are more significant than others – there are primary and secondary suppliers:

- *Primary* suppliers – fundamental to the implementation and delivery of a safe and successful event. Can sometimes be referred to as 'critical suppliers'.
- *Secondary* suppliers – influence the quality levels of the event.

Study activity

List all the suppliers you think would be involved in delivering Glastonbury Festival. Can you categorise them as primary or secondary suppliers?

4.7.1 Supplier selection

Because event operations do not exist in isolation, organisers are heavily reliant on their supply chain. Event managers are responsible for providing events at the right cost, the right time, to the right specification and quality and for the right duration. They are trying to achieve a wide range of objectives, as set by stakeholders. In order to do this, the event manager must purchase all the resources that make up the event. This makes selecting the right supplier of the utmost importance.

Slack *et al.* (cited in Tum *et al.* 2006) suggest that the people responsible for selecting the suppliers provide a vital link between the operation itself and suppliers, because they must understand the requirements of all the processes within the operation and also the capabilities of the suppliers who could potentially provide products and services for the operation. Purchasing can also have a significant impact on any operations costs, and therefore profits. In order to ensure that operations remain profitable, Slack *et al.* describe the five rights of purchasing:

- At the right price
- Delivered at the right time
- Goods and services are of the right quality
- In the right quantity
- From the right source

The event supply chain can be unwieldy and complex, but it is a necessary element of the operational process. Finding the right supplier can be difficult and time consuming – good supply chains are based on relationships. How those relationships are managed is vitally important to the success of the event – the key to a successful supply chain is building a good relationship that can be maintained and deepened over time. Atrek, Marcone, Gregori, Temperini and Moscatelli (2014: 376) established eight elements which contribute to relationship quality between company and supplier:

1 Quality of the products
2 Quality certification for the standard requirement
3 Flexible and timely services
4 Availability of the salesperson
5 Speed response time to request of the company
6 Willingness to review economic conditions with the view to develop future relationships
7 Terms of delivery
8 Wide range of materials in stock

4.7.2 Supplier procurement

Suppliers for events are often selected via a tendering process which involves a request for proposals (RFP) to several competing organisations. This typically includes a description of the event concept, details of the event plan as they currently stand and an outline of any particular business problems. It will also include a full outline of the requirements of the supplier. These RFPs are sent to a variety of organisations offering the services required, with a deadline for submissions. The potential suppliers will review the request and decide if they wish to bid for the contract. If they decide to go ahead, they submit a proposal, which will include specific suggestions on how to meet the needs and wants of the event organiser and, depending on the type

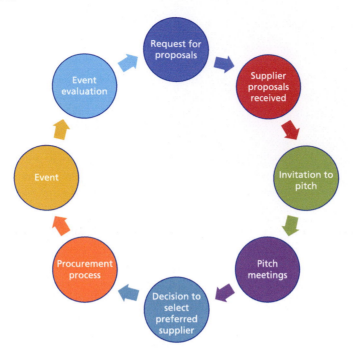

Figure 4.3 Supplier tendering process

of work, may also include creative solutions to business problems outlined in the proposal. A small selection of these organisations will then be invited to pitch their proposal at a meeting, and from this the event manager will pick their preferred supplier.

Once the preferred supplier has been identified, it is often necessary to go through procurement. This is the process of making a buying decision (i.e. selecting a supplier) that promotes fair and open competition and also protects the events organisation from fraud. It commonly involves all the processes from preparation of contracts through to the invoicing and receipt of payment, and often concentrates on researching the supplier, value analysis, detailed contract specifications and the agreement of financial processes.

The selection of suppliers via a tendering process is outlined in Figure 4.3.

4.8 Event supplier contracts

'The contract is the documentation of the relationship between the event and the various stakeholders' (Bowdin *et al.* 2011: 330); it is an agreement that sets out the responsibilities between two or more parties and it is legally binding. Typically, contracts are written; oral contracts are becoming less common in the industry, as all stakeholders understand the need to have formal contractual obligations in order to guard against future problems.

Events involve dealing with many suppliers, and each of these relationships should be legally supported through the provision of a contract. Suppliers include audio-visual, security, catering, staging, florists, marquee and furniture, staffing agencies, technology providers and marketing and PR agencies.

These contracts need to be carefully worded to ensure that there is protection for either party if the event is cancelled, and also to ensure there is provision and protection in the case of non-supply by a supplier.

4.8.1 Contract law

Contract preparation and execution are vital parts of the events management role, so it is important that event managers understand the key terms used within them. Goldblatt (2013: 181–182) defines the key terms of an events contract as:

- *Parties* – names of parties must be clearly defined.
- *Offer* – 'the offer is the service or product tendered by one party to another', including consulting services, products, entertainment, sponsorship deals and so on.
- *Consideration* – the consideration clause defines what one party will provide the other upon acceptance of an offer. This is usually money or rights.
- *Acceptance* – 'when both parties accept an offer, they execute (sign) the agreement confirming that they understand and agree to comply with the terms and conditions of the agreement'.

Matthews (2008) offers a comprehensive breakdown of the requirements of contract provision. He suggests that a contract is made up of two main parts: terms and conditions, and the clauses. *Terms and conditions* are considered essential to the contract and include contact information (including legal names, full addresses and so on); event details (including venue, specifics of product/services, additional requirements, details of general liability and additional insurance, and compliance with regulations and standards); financial information (including details of cancellation and compensation, plus taxes and deposits); rider information.

Clauses comprise the fixed part of the contract. They define and expand upon the terms and conditions, and might include:

- *Cancellation* – usually this is expressed as a percentage of the total value of the contract, which is payable upon cancellation by either party. Cancellation policies usually operate on a sliding scale, with 100% of the contract value within 14 days of the event date.
- *Force Majeure* (act of God) – this clause removes liability from the contracted party should they be prevented from delivering their obligations due to an act of God. Acts of God are defined as unavoidable circumstances that are outside of the party's control – in event contracts, they tend to relate to the weather, natural disasters, transportation issues and terrorism.
- *Billing* – including payment terms and schedules.
- *Insurance* – including details of insurance held by the contracted parties.
- *Indemnification* – protection of the contract signatory against losses incurred by an event. Liability clauses are also included and are important for events, as many suppliers will not expose themselves to liability and will attempt to remove this clause. Event managers are advised to seek legal advice on this clause, as it relates closely to insurance and can invalidate policies and contracts.

(List adapted from Goldblatt 2013)

Whilst these lists and generalisations are useful as a background to event contracts, some contracts are vital to the successful delivery of an event and require special consideration. These are listed in Figure 4.4 and explored in more detail in the following sections.

Venue
Sponsorship/exhibition
Audiovisual (including lighting and sound)
Entertainment/artist
Catering (including food and beverage suppliers)
Event structures (marquees/staging, set building, fencing, etc.)
Security and staffing
Event production
Decor, design and theming (including florists, furniture suppliers, etc.)
Hospitality provision
Technology providers
Marketing/PR agencies

Figure 4.4 Event contracts may be required for a number of suppliers and providers

4.8.2 Venue contracts

The venue contract is one of the most complex contracts. It contains many specific clauses and, when dealing with these agreements, a number of issues must be taken into consideration. Again, these are usually legally binding. They can be summarised as:

1 Cancellation clauses, including details of refunds available and costs payable in the event of a cancellation by either party.
2 Payment terms, including deposit details and payment schedules.
3 Full details of costs and estimated event spend at the venue (including projected food and beverage costs, room hire charges, furniture and linen hire, tips and service charges, taxes, set-up charges and so on).
4 Attrition clause, which sets out the food and beverage minimum spend. If your customers do not attend, the event organiser will be required to pay this fixed fee. If the venue is a

Cancellation Terms

Unless otherwise agreed in writing by the University, these conditions apply and are additional to any specific agreement concluded for the hiring of University Premises and/or Facilities.

1. Definitions

"Hirer" means the company, entity, institution or person hiring the Premises and/or Facilities from the University. "Premises" means all premises which are being hired by the Hirer (including car parks and grounds).

"University" means University of Greenwich.

"Facilities" means all services, equipment and apparatus belonging to or provided by or on behalf of the University to the Hirer.

2. Booking, Deposit and Confirmation

2.1 The submission of a Hiring Agreement does not constitute a hiring. The University reserves the right to decline an application at its sole discretion.

2.2 This Agreement shall not be effective until the potential hirer has submitted a signed Hiring Agreement and paid a non-refundable deposit for the Hire of Premises and/or Facilities to the University and the University has accepted such Hiring Agreement.

2.3 The Hiring Agreement sets out the amount of non-refundable deposit(s) and the date(s) by which such deposit(s) shall be paid by the Hirer. The Hirer acknowledges that if the University does not receive the non-refundable deposit (s) by or before the relevant date(s), the Premises may be hired to a third party or become non-available. The non-refundable deposit(s) will be based on minimum number of guests or attendees.

The Hirer agrees that the initial pre-paid deposit(s) are non-refundable and non-transferable in the event of the booking being cancelled for whatever reason.

2.4 All catering will be undertaken by the University unless agreed prior in writing by the parties. Final confirmation of the number of guests or attendees for catering purposes must be received by the University one week before the start of the period of hire.

3. Charges, Deposits and Payment

3.1 The charges for the Facilities and the Premises will be communicated to the Hirer prior to or at the time of booking and will be set out in the University Hiring Agreement.

3.2 The Hirer agrees that these charges may be increased by the University between the time of booking and the period of hire in the event of any increase in the costs to the University of providing the Facilities and/or Premises for reasons beyond the University's control.

3.3 The University shall issue (after the period of hire) a final invoice for the charges for the hire of the Premises and/or Facilities plus any applicable VAT, less any deposit(s) already pre-paid by the Hirer. The Hirer shall pay the outstanding amount within 30 days from the date of the invoice.

4. Cancellation and Charges

4.1 All cancellations must be submitted in writing to the University. Failure to confirm cancellation in writing may result in the Hirer being liable to pay the full amount of the estimated charges for the hire.

4.2 Unless minimum numbers are guaranteed by the hirer and stated on the hiring agreement the following shall apply; if the hire is cancelled or the number of guests or attendees is reduced:

a) 365 days or more before the date of hire, there is no charge other than the initial non-refundable deposit (if applicable)

b) between 364 and 180 days before the date of hire, there will be a 20% charge of the estimated total amount.

c) between 179 and 90 days before the date of hire, there will be a 40% charge on the estimated total amount.

d) between 89 and 15 days before the date of hire, there will be a 60% charge on the estimated total amount.

e) 14 days or less before the date of hire, there will be a 100% charge on the estimated total amount.

Notwithstanding the above, the University may, at its sole discretion and in any case after the period of hire, refund part of the initial pre-paid deposit(s) if the same Premises are hired to a third party.

4.3 In addition to the amounts set out in clause 4.2 above, the Hirer shall reimburse the University in full for any expenses already incurred or committed by the University (with the Hirers consent) for or on behalf of the Hirer including but not limited to musicians, florists, equipment hire, catering and accommodation.

4.4 Neither the University nor any body responsible for the management of the University shall be held liable or required to pay compensation to the Hirer or any third party for any loss or damage sustained as a result of or in any way arising out of the cancellation of the hiring.

4.5 The hire charges relate to the times of the booking. The Hirer will be responsible for ensuring that the Premises are vacated by the finishing time agreed at the time of the hiring. In addition to the rights and remedies that the University may have against the Hirer, if an event continues beyond thes times the Hirer will incur additional hire charges.

4.6 In any case, the University reserves the right to enter the Premises and terminate any event which extends beyond the contracted times of hire without any liability to the Hirer.

5. Liability

5.1 Where the Hirer is an unincorporated association, the person or any member, servant or agent thereof signing the Hiring Agreement or such other document requesting the use of the Premises and/or Facilities undertakes personal liability for all charges in respect of the hiring and for the compliance with the terms of the Agreement. The liability of the unincorporated association and such person or any member, servant or agent thereof shall be joint and several.

5.2 The Hirer shall indemnify and keep indemnified the University against all actions, claims, demands, costs and expenses of any nature which may be brought against or suffered by the University as a result of or in connection with the use of the University Premises and/or Facilities by the Hirer, its guests or any other attendees. For the avoidance of doubt, the Hirer shall be responsible for any damage, other than fair wear and tear, to University property (or that belonging to any individual or organisation).

Figure 4.5 A sample venue contract

Note: This is an example of part of the terms and conditions section of a booking contract.

Booking Contract   **Ref: 203**

5.3 The University accepts no liability for any interruption or curtailment of the hiring as a result of the actions of any third party (including any guests or attendees of the event organised by the Hirer), howsoever caused.

5.4 In no circumstances will the University be liable or accept any responsibility for loss of or damage to any personal property, car or other vehicle (or the contents thereof) which may be brought or left within the premises.
All persons using the University's Premises or Facilities must take their own precautions to protect their property.

5.5 The University reserves the right to let other parts of its Premises and/or Facilities to other persons or organisations simultaneously with the hiring and accepts no liability for the actions, omissions or conduct of such other persons or organisations.

5.6 The University's maximum aggregate liability in contract, tort or otherwise (including any liability for any neglect, act or omission) howsoever arising out of or in connection with this Agreement in respect of any one or more incidents or occurrences shall be limited to a sum equal to the charges paid by the Hirer to the University under this Agreement.

5.7 The University shall not be liable for any indirect, special, incidental, or consequential loss or damage nor for any loss of business or profit.

5.8 The limitations set out in clause 5 shall apply to the extent permitted by law. Nothing in this Agreement shall exclude or restrict either party's liability for death or personal injury resulting from the negligence of that party or to any extent not permitted by law.

5.9 The University will require the Hirer to take out such insurance policies as the University may reasonably deem appropriate in respect of the hire.

6. Health and Safety and Conduct

6.1 The Hirer shall comply and must ensure that all guests and attendees and any person entering the Premises comply with any applicable health and safety laws and regulations (including the Health & Safety at Work Act 1974) and any of the University's health and safety guidance, policies, procedures or rules.

6.2 The University reserves the right to cancel the hire, upon notice to the Hirer (and without any liability thereof), if the University reasonably believes that any condition contained in this Agreement is or may be breached or that the safety of persons or property is or may be endangered as a direct or indirect result of the hiring.

6.3 The Hirer shall be solely responsible for keeping and maintaining proper order, for observing fire, safety and security regulations at all times and for providing efficient supervision on the occasion of the hire (including controlling and regulating the ingress and egress of all persons attending the event).

6.4 The Hirer must ensure that any University Premises are maintained in a clean and tidy state at all times during the hire. If any parts of the Premises are in disorder at commencement of the hire, this should be reported to a member of University staff immediately.

6.5 In the event of any damage, the University may make good the damage and the Hirer, by acceptance of the hiring, will thereby be deemed to have undertaken to pay the cost of such reparation.

6.6 The Hirer shall not install and use on the University's premises any electrical appliance, amplification equipment or lighting fittings without the priorwritten permission of the University. The Hirer is wholly responsible for the safety of such installation at all times whilst it remains on the University's Premises and for any injury caused to any person or property arising in connection with such installation and usage. Consent by the University to such installation and usage does not imply the safety or suitability for use of the said installation or acceptance by the University of liability for damage or injury arising in connection with the said appliance.

6.7 The Hirer must ensure that no child under the age of 14 years is admitted on the University's premises unless during the whole time such child is accompanied by an adult person, (minimum requirement of one adult per 10 children).

6.8 All persons under the age of 18 years (and over 14 years) must be under the control of at least one adult who should be clearly identifiable as such and who will be held responsible for any actions or liabilities incurred by such persons, (minimum requirement of one adult per 15 children).

6.9 University property shall not be moved except with prior written permission of an authorised officer of the University.

6.10 Smoking is not permitted in any part of the University except areas which are clearly designated.

6.11 No pets or other animals, except guide dogs, are permitted on University premises without prior written permission of the University.

6.12 The authorised representatives of the University shall have free access to the Premises at all times.

6.13 No part of the Premises may be sublet, or reassigned by the Hirer to any third party.

7. Overnight Accommodation

Where the hire includes use of the University premises as overnight accommodation the Hirer shall:
  (a) provide the University with a full list of persons who will be resident on the hired premises overnight not less than 7 days before the commencement of hire;
  (b) ensure the hired overnight accommodation is used only by persons specified on said nominal list unless agreed prior in writing by the University;
  (c) receive keys on the day of arrival no earlier than 16.00 and
  (d) vacate the room and return the key(s) by 09.00 on the day of departure.

8. Licensing Considerations

8.1 The Hirer must ensure that the maximum number of persons permitted to be present in any indoor facility under the licensing arrangements shall not be exceeded at any time.

8.2 No alcoholic liquor, food or other refreshments, other than those supplied by the University, shall be sold or consumed by the Hirer (or any of the guests or attendees) on the University premises without the prior written consent of the University. Alcoholic liquor shall only be consumed on the premises upon prior written approval of the University and subject to the obtaining of any specific licence that may be necessary.

Figure 4.5 (Continued)

hotel, and the contract includes room bookings, there will be an attrition clause regarding the minimum number of rooms that must be paid for, even if they are not occupied.

5 Provision of personnel and security, including overtime rates and numbers of staff required.
6 Access times and overrunning clauses, including date of event, start and end times, service times for food and beverages.
7 Venue damage, including indemnification, insurance, liability issues, licences and permits.

The venue contract should be viewed as an opportunity for the event organiser to negotiate rates and charges. Particular attention should be paid to the payment terms. Getting this right will ease cash flow and ensure financial stability throughout the event process. The venue is often the largest expense on an events budget, so ensuring that the payment schedule allows the event manager to generate some revenue before meeting most of the costs will help prevent cash flow issues.

Similarly, cancellation terms and penalties need close attention and are often open to negotiation. Contracts with venues also usually set out the minimum numbers required for the event – this figure represents the least number of guests the event organiser must pay for, no matter how many guests actually attend. It should *always* be negotiated, as it is usually possible to cut it by 10–20%. Event managers should also look closely at food and beverage prices, which are often highly negotiable and may contain hidden costs, such as the supply of linen, chairs and tables, which can be easily removed. Figure 4.5 shows a sample venue contract.

Organisers should note, too, that many venues will issue operational and safety guidelines, detailed in their terms and conditions and hiring policy. These must be in place during the organisation and running of an event in their space; failure to comply with these guidelines can result in the cancellation of your event. An example of this can be seen in the case study below.

CASE STUDY 4.2

Oktoberfest

Location: London, UK
Venue: Tobacco Docks, London

In 2015, Oktoberfest London opened for one night only and was cancelled the next day, before most of the weekend activities could take place. Oktoberfest London was set to be a version of the German beer festival, held in the UK. It was expected that around 24,000 people would attend – tickets ranged from £10 to £1000 for tickets for groups, inclusive of food and drinks. It was due to run from Thursday to Sunday inclusively, with a number of 'sessions' running each day.

The venue pulled the event after one day because of issues with staffing and other managerial and operational aspects on the opening night and due to concerns with their compliance with the 2003 Licensing Act. The venue released a statement that stated: 'We were not convinced the operational changes we required the organiser to make would be able to be put in place by Oktoberfest UK in time for this weekend's events to run safely and efficiently, and at that point agreed with them that these events should be cancelled' (Tobaccodocklondon. com/news). In addition, the venue's statement said: 'The decision [to cancel the event] was not based on guest numbers nor the nature of the event – both of these were well understood in advance – but on the management and operational systems and insufficient serving staff both in terms of numbers and experience that had been put in place by Oktoberfest UK'.

The company organising Oktoberfest UK went into administration, and are currently not trading. Ticket holders for the cancelled session needed to apply to the administrators for a ticket refund. Other event organisers have been more successful in bringing Oktoberfest to the UK – see Image 4.2.

Image 4.2 Oktoberfest in Munich, which event organisers tried to replicate in the UK – to varying degrees of success
Sources: McShane and Edmonds (2015), Livesey (2015)

4.8.3 Entertainment contracts

Entertainment contracts are agreements drawn up between the event organiser and those people supplying the entertainment. Typical entertainment options include after-dinner speakers, celebrities, bands, DJs, singers, cabaret acts, masters of ceremonies, comedians, magicians and musicians. Special considerations for this type of contract will include non-attendance, exclusivity (the prevention of headline acts performing at similar events around the same time), cancellation terms for either party and insurance clauses.

Particular attention should be paid to the non-attendance – or 'no-show' – clause in the contract, as artists pulling out of an event at the last minute – or simply not showing up – can be a major problem for event organisers. Having a clause that clearly states the implications of a last-minute cancellation will go some way to protecting the event organiser and will at least result in financial remuneration, if not artist replacement.

Another key element of the entertainment contract is the rider. This is usually attached to the contract (hence the name: it 'rides' the contract) and specifies particular demands that the event organiser needs to meet. These can include audio-visual and technological requirements and hospitality demands (specific food, drink, room layouts and so on). Silvers (2004) suggests that riders can run to a hundred pages or more and often contain sensitive material, such as how an entertainer achieves a specific effect. Rider requests should be carefully examined as they are often used by entertainment suppliers to increase their fees, making them extremely costly for event organisers. Event organisers should therefore enlist the help of talent buyers or agents – and should acquire legal advice from solicitors – before negotiating entertainment contracts.

4.8.4 Sponsor and exhibitor contracts

Contracts with sponsors and exhibitors are unique as they refer to a one-off relationship and the obligations that stem from that relationship. Sponsors and exhibitors are usually brought on board by a specialist sales representative and they will often draw up contracts directly. However, it is essential that the event manager directly responsible for event delivery reads these contracts carefully prior to signing to ensure that all the specifics are deliverable. Special considerations for sponsor and exhibitor contract agreements include:

- exclusivity (no other sponsors/exhibitors from the same sector can be involved)
- hospitality rights, including complimentary tickets
- branding on marketing collateral and on-site brand presence
- cancellation terms, including if the event is cancelled and if the sponsor/exhibitor wishes to terminate the relationship
- payment terms – payment is preferable upon signage of the contract
- length of contract – contracts can often cover a relationship lasting for a number of years (sponsorship of a repeat event over a three-year period, for example). These contracts need to be carefully considered in order to ensure that the event will be able to deliver all obligations each year.

4.9 Event logistics and capacity management

The term 'logistics' is used to describe the movement of products and resources. Events management draws heavily on management logistics theory in order to understand how to manage the flow of goods, resources and information effectively. However, much of this theory relates to supplying the product to the customer – event logistics, by necessity, must consider a logistical approach that brings the customer to the product (the product cannot go to the customer; the customer must come to the product).

At first glance, event logistics can seem incredibly daunting – there is so much to plan and organise that it can feel like an impossible task. To simplify the process, it is sensible to reduce the number of logistical considerations. It is useful to consider two broad areas of event logistics – the customer and the venue/site (see Figure 4.6). (In the past, event academics have talked of a third area – the product – but this is usually defined as the entire event, and is therefore confusing.)

Events can be seen as a large jigsaw puzzle, with all the elements needing to be slotted together to complete the picture – it is the role of logistics to ensure that these elements all fit and are brought together at the right moment.

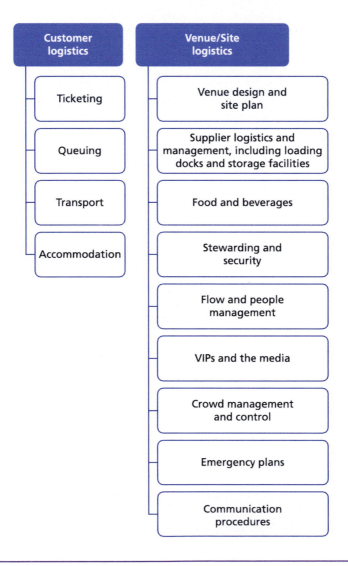

Figure 4.6 Event logistics

4.9.1 Venue/site logistics

Event venues or sites can vary enormously. Corporate events taking place in a five-star hotel have very different on-site logistical requirements from those of a festival taking place in a desert in the middle of Arizona. The event logistics manager must therefore think carefully about their specific venue and the logistical requirements of their choice. Some of the key considerations can be seen in Figure 4.7, and each will be discussed in more detail throughout this section. It is important to stress the individual nature of every event and the fact that these individual aspects will result in very different logistical requirements.

4.9.1.1 Venue design

Much of the information in this section is adapted from *The Event Safety Guide* (HSE 1999).

GENERAL PRINCIPLE OF VENUE/SITE DESIGN

The guiding principle for the design of venues or sites is to provide an arena where the audience can enjoy the entertainment in a safe and comfortable atmosphere. The venue must be suitable for the event's needs and for the needs and wants of the audience.

The choice of a venue is one of the hardest and most important aspects of an event – it is often easy to get enthusiastic about a fantastic venue and forget that the audience's enjoyment is key. Questions such as those in the list below should be paramount in any venue or site decisions:

- Will the audience like the venue?
- Do they have a clear sight of the stage?
- Can they find the location easily?
- Are the transport links adequate?
- What about the catering and general service?
- How large is the site, and how easy is it to navigate?
- What facilities are available?

SITE SUITABILITY ASSESSMENT

Once a potential site or venue has been identified, it is essential to visit it to assess suitability well before the event. In order to assess the suitability effectively, the event manager must have a proposed capacity in mind, have some ideas of the concept and theme, and have an idea of the programme – what you want to happen and when. This provisional plan will need to be flexible to work with the venue, but the more detail you have, the easier the site assessment will be.

Three crucial areas should be considered on the first visit to a new venue or site:

1 Available space for audiences and temporary structures – stages, marquees and so on.
2 Backstage facilities – how much room will the crew have? Do you want back or front projection? Is there room for performers? Crew equipment? Crew areas?
3 Parking/camping, rendezvous points and transport.

This visit allows the event manager to determine what facilities are available. Event managers should check such facilities as rooms and layouts, location and access, ground conditions,

Venue/ site design

Supplier logistics and management

Food and beverages

Stewarding and security

Flow and people management

VIPs

Crowd management and crowd control

Communication

Health and safety and emergency procedures

Figure 4.7 The key areas of venue logistics

traffic routes, first-aid provision, toilets, waste-disposal areas, power, water, gas and electrical supplies, fire exits, stages, barriers, exits and entrance areas, hospitality areas, sight lines and so on.

Once the visit is completed, it is usual to produce a pre-design appraisal of the site. The final design will depend on the nature of the entertainment, location, size and duration of the event. It will also need to take account of the geographical, topographical and environmental infrastructure. This appraisal of the site visit will typically cover:

- proposed occupant capacity
- artist profile
- audience profile
- duration and timing of event
- venue evaluation
- alcohol availability
- audience: seated or standing?
- audience movement between facilities/entertainment
- single stage/multiple-arena complex etc. (HSE 1999)

4.9.1.2 Site plans

Once the event design is in place, the event manager can begin to put together the site plan. Such plans are the primary means of ensuring communication is flowing and that the various managers (stage manager, lighting manager, production manager and so on) working on an event understand the key elements. Their main purpose is to indicate the proposed areas to be

Figure 4.8 Contents of a site plan

used by the event and the locations of various activities within the event site or venue. These plans are also key tools for communicating logistical requirements – they should, if produced correctly, alleviate the need for explanation and highlight key areas of concern.

Figure 4.8 provides a list of what should be included in a site plan. It should be noted that these plans need to be far more detailed than the venue or site maps that are given to the customer. The final site plan will often not be ready until the day of the event set-up, when ticketing and entertainment have been finalised.

Figure 4.9 shows a site plan for the University of Greenwich. The Greenwich campus is a World Heritage Site, with a stunning location on the banks of the Thames in London and classical buildings designed by Sir Christopher Wren. It is an ideal venue for academic conferences, celebratory meals, public lectures and fundraising events, and it has a wide range of rooms and facilities, making it important that event organisers, suppliers and attendees can all navigate the site easily. The site plan details the layout of the venue and allows event organisers to get

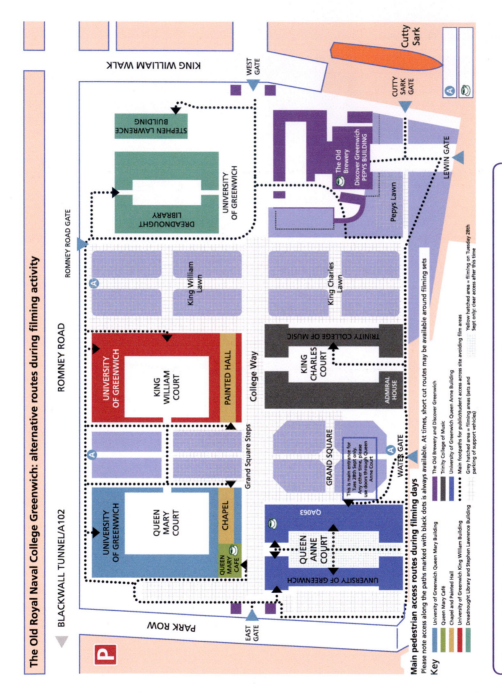

Figure 4.9 Example site plan: the University of Greenwich

a visual feel for the layout; it also directs suppliers to the right part of the campus and helps attendees arrive in the right place.

4.9.2 Supplier logistics and management

The main thrust of logistics is the flow of equipment, product and people around the venue and to the places where they need to be, when they need to be there.

Therefore, one of the key areas that needs to be considered is the coordination of all the event suppliers – how and when they will reach the site, and how they will move around the venue, must be planned carefully. It is the logistics manager's responsibility to do this. Ensuring that your suppliers know how to find the site and where and when they need to be available is essential, so each supplier will require a detailed briefing. This can be a very complex process. For example, a conference for a hundred delegates may require the coordination of a caterer; an audio-visual organisation; lighting and stage set production companies; room dressers to create a specific theme; furniture-hire companies; drinks suppliers; entertainment; and a cleaning company. Each of these organisations will have their own set of requirements and their own timelines for set-up. They will also require specific access (often through loading docks) and a large amount of storage space for equipment.

4.9.2.1 Food and beverage

The provision of food and beverages should be an important part of the logistics plan, with ample time built in to ensure that the catering is provided properly. Caterers at an event have very specific logistical requirements that will vary depending on the size of the event and the type of venue used. A large trade show may involve 20 different catering suppliers – each caterer must be on-site, set-up and equipped with the necessary facilities in good time before the show opens. They will usually need access to running water and waste disposal, refrigeration and gas supply/electrical power points, and will have lots of equipment and a large amount of perishable goods. Moreover, they will have strict times for how long they need to set up, and how long they need to be on-site before the event opens. All of these issues will need to be considered when drawing up the logistics plan.

4.9.2.2 Stewarding and security

One of the key security issues for the logistics manager is ensuring that the right people have access to specific areas during set up, at the event itself and during the shut-down process. This can be managed by giving suppliers or VIP guests laminated badges (for example, a creative event producer who works closely with the event manager, the audio-visual team and the entertainment will probably need an 'Access All Areas' badge). Colour-coded wristbands can also be used, acting in the same way as badges to control the movement of staff and suppliers. It is the responsibility of the logistics manager to issue these control methods (badges or wristbands), to ensure that every supplier and staff member has the correct access level.

4.9.2.3 Flow and people management

Events of any scale feature a large amount of movement in the venue or on-site. Suppliers will move around with their equipment, sponsors and exhibitors will move around with their resources, and customers will move around once the event starts. This movement of people around the event venue or site is known as the 'flow', and the people who move around are often referred to as 'event traffic'.

The flow of event traffic grows more complex as the event grows. A small networking dinner for 50 can be straightforward, with only the caterers and the venue staff to consider during set-up, and with the flow from the kitchens to the dining room being uncomplicated (in the right venue). However, a festival with a vast number of venues within a single site will have hundreds of suppliers (including caterers, audio-visual suppliers, lighting engineers, staging set producers, entertainment, VIP guests, security personnel, gate, fence and crush barrier builders, water and electrical engineers, first-aid operatives, toilet suppliers, vendors, media, waste removal and equipment transporters). All these suppliers need to be controlled and need to be able to flow around the site without inhibiting other suppliers during the set-up and shut-down processes.

Once the event has started, the need to move people around the site does not lessen – in fact, the flow of event traffic becomes even harder to manage as suppliers often still need to move equipment around but will now also have to contend with customers. An experienced logistics manager will consider where the customers will be at all times, and will ensure that the rest of the event traffic flows around them. So they may suggest that suppliers cannot move equipment during peak times – such as arrival, coffee breaks or lunch sessions – or they may ensure that the supplier traffic is flowing in a different direction to the customer flow.

The Burning Man Festival – held in the Nevada Desert each August – has encountered problems with event traffic moving around the same site as event customers. In 2003, a woman was killed when she fell under the wheels of an 'art car'. In the same year, a truck carrying 30,000 pounds of ice rolled over and injured a person (Associated Press 2003). These examples highlight the importance of considering the entire flow of event traffic prior to the event as part of the overall event plan.

4.9.2.4 Communication

Communication between staff is a key logistical concern. From an operational point of view, all staff members and suppliers need to be able to communicate quickly and effectively; finding the right solution to facilitate this is therefore essential. For small events, this can be as straightforward as mobile-phone usage. However, for larger events, this can be impractical, expensive and difficult to manage – particularly as the event manager may want to communicate the same message to more than one other person at a time. In such circumstances, the use of hand-held, two-way radio transmitters is useful. For complex events, several radio channels may well be in operation, with security operating on one, suppliers and contractors on another, and event staff on a third. The employment of runners who can physically take messages from one area to another is another common, and useful, communication technique.

It is recommended that a communications plan is devised prior to the event. Typically, this will include full contact details of all staff members and suppliers and pager, radio call IDs, phone extension and mobile phone numbers, as well as where each person will be stationed during set-up, event time and shut-down. Communication planning should also consider emergency situations, should be part of the overall project management plan, and should be included in the risk assessment (Bowdin *et al.* 2011).

4.9.2.5 Health and safety and emergency procedures

Event operations and the logistical planning for an event must include emergency procedures, which can range from evacuation procedures and the amount of first aid on-site through to

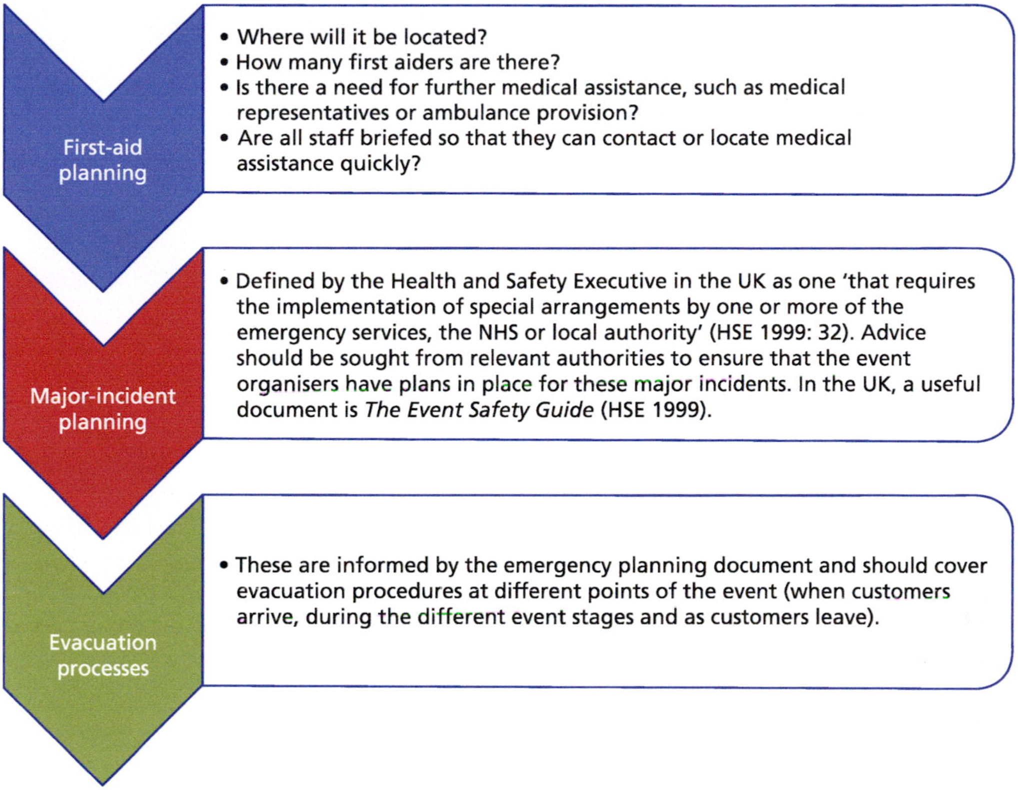

First-aid planning

- Where will it be located?
- How many first aiders are there?
- Is there a need for further medical assistance, such as medical representatives or ambulance provision?
- Are all staff briefed so that they can contact or locate medical assistance quickly?

Major-incident planning

- Defined by the Health and Safety Executive in the UK as one 'that requires the implementation of special arrangements by one or more of the emergency services, the NHS or local authority' (HSE 1999: 32). Advice should be sought from relevant authorities to ensure that the event organisers have plans in place for these major incidents. In the UK, a useful document is *The Event Safety Guide* (HSE 1999).

Evacuation processes

- These are informed by the emergency planning document and should cover evacuation procedures at different points of the event (when customers arrive, during the different event stages and as customers leave).

Figure 4.10 Key features of health, safety and emergency planning

major-incident or disaster planning. Each event will need its own specific procedures, but the basic requirements are outlined in Figure 4.10.

It should be noted that much of the health and safety and emergency procedural planning will take place during the production of the risk assessment documents. It is imperative that these issues are taken seriously, as events can be shut down very quickly if the relevant authorities perceive health and safety or emergency procedures are inadequate. More detail on risk assessment is provided in Chapter 8.

4.9.3 Customer logistics

An event's customers are usually perceived as those who pay for it, although, of course, many events (particularly culturally focused and local community events) are free. The customer is therefore better defined as someone who is attending an event.

Each event will need a different logistics plan that caters to the needs of its specific customer base. For instance, the transportation, ticketing and accommodation plans for the Burning Man Festival, which attracts customers from around the globe, will need to be vastly different from those for a community festival, such as a Holi Festival in India, whose customers all come from within a five-mile radius. The key areas for consideration in customer logistics are shown in Figure 4.11, and are discussed in detail in the following sections.

| Ticketing | Transport | Queuing | Accommodation |

Figure 4.11 The key areas of customer logistics

4.9.3.1 Crowd management and crowd control

Management of the customer base should be a priority for anyone concerned with operational planning of events – from a logistics point of view, the customer base is a crowd. Priority should be given to planning proper operating procedures, as the impacts of not managing a crowd correctly can be incredibly damaging and sometimes even tragic. See for example, the fire at the Colectiv club in Bucharest in October 2015, in which 41 people died – at the time of going to press, investigations are ongoing but allegations are that the venue was over-crowded and lacked the required number of emergency exits. At the German Love Parade in 2010, police attempted to stop people reaching the parade area, which led to a stampede and the death of 19 people (BBC 2010). Unfortunately, there are several similar examples, all of which highlight the importance of a thorough understanding of the issues relating to crowd management and control, and of the need for a robust strategy at every event, no matter how small or large.

It is important to distinguish between the techniques of crowd *management* and crowd *control*: the former is concerned with moving the crowd effectively, whereas the latter is a reactive process relating to the steps that are taken once a crowd (or part of a crowd) has started to behave unexpectedly, often in a disorderly or dangerous manner (Abbott and Geddie 2001).

It is essential that event managers have a basic understanding of a crowd's basic sociological behaviour. Much has been written on this (see, for example, numerous journal articles in the *Journal of Events Management*: Berlonghi 1995, Fruin 2002, Abbott and Abbott 2000, the HSE 2000 guide *Managing Crowds Safely*, as well as online resources, such as those provided by the International Centre for Crowd Management and Security Studies (www.iccmss.co.uk) and consultants (www.crowddynamics.com)).

The main aim for logistics managers is that they have practical measures in place for an effective crowd management plan. The basics for this plan should include the control of the entry, exit and movement of people around the site. In addition, Abbott and Abbott (2000) suggest that communication, signage, ushering and security, alcohol distribution and on-site legal counselling all need to be considered. Managers must also be able to identify crowd issues, and have carefully thought-through crowd control procedures in case the crowd loses control. For an in-depth analysis of crowd control plans and advice on how to formulate them, it is recommended that students read Abbott and Abbott (2000).

Crowd management is covered in more detail in Chapter 8.

4.9.3.2 Ticketing

The distribution, collection and security requirements relating to ticketing should be a key concern for the event manager. From a customer's perspective, the process of purchasing, receiving and using tickets is often the first impression they will have of the event, and it marks the start of a relationship between the customer and the organiser. It is therefore vital that this impression is a good one.

From a logistical perspective, whilst not all events have an entrance fee, ticketing should always be a consideration, as it enables the organiser to control customer numbers and monitor the flow of guests throughout the event.

A key issue to consider is how much of the ticket sale allocation will be pre-event. Ticketing is usually an essential part of the cash flow – event finance tends to be unbalanced, with most costs happening before the event takes place (see Chapter 6 for an in-depth look at event finance). Revenue generated by advance ticket sales therefore often covers expenses that need settling before the event date (Cherubini *et al.* 2007).

As well as helping the cash flow, selling tickets prior to the event allows the organiser to know exactly how many customers will be attending, which enables them to plan operationally in terms of food, beverages, staffing and so on.

Increasingly, events tickets are being issued electronically, with barcodes or QR codes that can be scanned by security staff equipped with hand-held scanners. This method increases the speed of entry and reduces the risk of fraudulent tickets. It also saves the organiser printing and mailing costs.

Another ticketing technique that often utilises QR coding technology is sending tickets to mobile phones – known as mobile ticketing. This process allows customers to order, pay for, obtain and validate tickets via their mobile phones. The most common method of mobile ticketing involves customers receiving their tickets in an SMS after texting a code to the organisers. The price of the ticket can either be added to their next mobile phone bill or debited from a previously set-up account. These mobile tickets are then visually inspected or scanned at the entrance to the event, thereby reducing production and distribution costs and increasing customer convenience.

With the increasing use of phones that support applications, it is expected that these tickets will become the main form of ticketing at future events. However, it should be noted that such tickets create a revenue issue for event organisers because mobile-phone operators often insist on a large percentage of the overall ticket price.

One logistical consideration related to tickets is the resale of tickets over and above face value. There is an increased concern among the industry that secondary ticketing sites (where tickets are re-sold) are unfair for consumers and are creating unfair ticketing prices. In 2015, 80 leading figures from the events industry wrote to the government to ask them to introduce controls for these websites. The government voted on the relevant clause in the Consumer Rights Bill and rejected the opportunity to make secondary ticketing sites more transparent.

4.9.3.3 Transport

It is a common misconception among event managers that the way in which customers travel to the event is outside of their control and therefore not their concern. In fact, the way that customers are transported to an event is an important part of the overall logistics planning process. Bowdin *et al.* (2011) describe transport to the site as the customers' first physical commitment to an event.

From a logistical point of view, it is essential to establish *when* customers will arrive at an event. Event managers use two words to describe the arrival of customers: *dump* refers to customers all arriving at around the same time (for a music gig or a conference, for example); and *trickle* refers to customers arriving at different periods throughout the event (as they do at an exhibition or trade show). It is essential that those responsible for the logistics plan understand when their customers will arrive so that plans to accommodate them can be drafted.

How customers will reach an event is a key question and one that is usually considered fully during the planning stages. Below are some of the questions that should be asked of the venue, from a logistics point of view:

- Does the venue have good transport links?
- How reliable are the transport links?
- Are there likely to be problems with the transport – strikes, engineering works and so on?
- Is the venue near to major transport hubs, such as train stations and airports?
- Will travel to the venue represent an additional cost for the customer?
- If so, will this additional cost make the overall event proposal less attractive to the target market?

When considering major and mega-events (such as the Commonwealth Games or Glastonbury), transportation logistics become particularly important. As Bowdin *et al.* (2011) point out, permission must be gained from local councils, highways agencies or police, and road closures often need to be arranged as part of the logistics planning. Ensuring that roads are clear, that there is enough signage to direct traffic, that one-way systems are in place and so on will enable suppliers and customers to arrive and depart quickly and with minimum disruption to the local area. It is especially important to consider the transportation logistics for events that take place in usually quiet, tranquil areas, as disrupting the local community can cause repercussions for the event organisers, including pressure not to return in the future.

4.9.3.4 Queuing

Once the ticketing method has been decided, and the guests have arrived on-site, the logistics manager must consider how the guests will present their tickets for inspection in order to gain entry to the event. This will involve some form of queuing – and as this is often the customer's first physical impression of an event, it is one of the key aspects for the logistics manager to consider.

There are many techniques for managing queues, as well as a vast array of literature covering all aspects of queuing, from waiting times to physical management, much of which is too detailed to discuss here. (See, for example, Oakes and North 2008, Shelby *et al.* 1989, Jenner 2010, and the excellent work carried out by the International Centre for Crowd Management and Security Studies (www.icmss.co.uk).)

This section will touch on the three major techniques for queue management. It should be noted that we are concentrating on entrance and ticketing queues but there are similar issues and techniques for queuing once inside the event. Gaining access to toilets, catering, showers, activity booths, exhibition stands and so on usually involves queuing and therefore demands some attention to ensure that it is managed effectively.

PHYSICAL QUEUING

The most common form of queue management is the physical queue. The logistics manager must ensure that queues are designed to make the wait as pleasant as possible. Queues should

Image 4.3 People queuing for Dismaland
Source: Helen Boast: Getty Images

be kept simple for customers, with waiting times kept to a minimum and protection from the weather in place (rain and hot sun are two important issues here). The right number of personnel should be on hand to deal with the queues and the waiting times should be signalled as often as possible to manage customer expectations.

There are several strategies that help to achieve a pleasant queue environment, including:

- *Queue capacity*: expanding the queue capacity allows more customers to join. This can be done by increasing the lane size or the length of the queue, or (more usually) by designing a line that zigzags. This shape allows for a larger number of customers to queue in a smaller area and ensures that customers cannot perceive the true length of a particularly long queue.
- *Queue entertainment*: TV screens, music or entertainers can be used to distract customers from the length of their wait.
- *Signage* that indicates the length of the queue is advisable.
- *Secondary queues*: VIP queues or fast-track queues for guests who have paid a premium are becoming ever more popular at events.

Once inside, customers will be faced with queues for the toilets, food, beverages and merchandise, all of which need to be given the same level of consideration as the entrance/ticket queue, as they often have the largest impact on a customer's event experience.

Virtual queuing

All queuing systems have problems – the main one being that the customer must arrive ahead of time and wait in line. A recent development in managing queues has sought to alleviate this through the use of virtual queues. This technique allows the customer to enter a virtual queue via their mobile phone or the internet, and await an alert that tells them when they are nearing the front of the line. They can then make their way to the event, greatly reducing their physical queuing time at the entrance. This technique seems to increase the patience of customers and ensures that there are fewer no-shows.

Exit strategies

Techniques that ensure the safe exit (egress) of customers from an event also include elements of queuing theory. For example, staggered leaving, as operated at most football grounds (one set of fans waits in the ground until the other set of fans have left the venue and the surrounding area), ensures the safety of the customers. Stadium music gigs often empty VIP rooms first, while those standing are usually the last to leave the arena. And festivals must consider exit strategies if they are to avoid chaos – thousands of vehicles all leaving a remote area at the same time can result in long queues and extremely frustrated customers. Fruin (1984) discusses time-based control techniques, such as metering (a strategy used to control the rate of arrivals and degree of crowding at a known pedestrian bottleneck) and processing rates (the capacity and the time taken to move through or towards certain areas at the event). These strategies, when implemented properly, will help to prevent critical crowd accumulation.

4.9.3.5 Accommodation

Many events must consider customer accommodation. These are usually events that span several days or continue late into the evening, making travel home difficult or unnecessary. Examples include corporate team-building weekends and cricket test matches. When dealing with accommodation, it is essential that the logistics manager considers the time taken to travel to the site and the efficiency of transportation links, as well as whether the available accommodation matches the needs and expectations of the customers.

4.9.4 Logistics planning folder

It is advisable to create a logistics planning folder (sometimes known as an event manual) that can be consulted when on-site. These are frequently now contained on netbooks or tablet computers, so that they can be updated easily and so that the information is available to a large number of users simultaneously. The contents of a planning folder are shown in Figure 4.12, with details of each section given below.

- Contact list, including full contact details of all contractors and suppliers, entertainment details and sponsors' and exhibitors' details. These should be up-to-date and include mobile phone numbers.
- Venue or site plan – several spare copies should be made.
- Project management plan. This could be presented as a critical path, a timeline or a Gantt chart. It is essentially a checklist of everything that has been done and everything that needs doing.

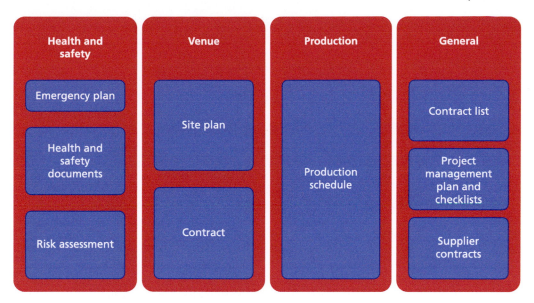

Figure 4.12 Contents of a planning folder

- Production schedule. This is a detailed schedule of all activities during the day(s) of the event.
- Contracts signed with audio-visual suppliers, entertainment suppliers, sponsors and venues will help to resolve any on-site disagreements quickly.

4.9.5 Event shut-down

The event manager's job does not end as soon as the customers have left. Rather, it continues right through the process of breaking down all the equipment and removing all signs of the event from the site or venue. This process is known variously as the event shut-down, the site phase-out or the event breakdown, and it is as important a part of the logistical planning as the set-up and staging of an event.

Smaller events may require hardly any shut-down. It may just be a case of ensuring that the venue is clear of debris and customers have not left behind any personal items. Conversely, events on a larger scale require a complex and thoughtfully put-together shut-down schedule that coordinates all suppliers and works to strict timelines. The shut-down for large events will include the breaking down and removal of all equipment; the final dealings with the entertainment, including payment; cleaning and removal of staging areas; and any outstanding financial transactions. Finally, all sponsors, exhibitors, staff and contractors must be thanked and left with positive thoughts of this event and encouragement about the next event.

Once all of this has been completed and the site is clear, the event manager's shut-down will continue for several weeks back in the office. Figure 4.13 shows the processes involved in the total shut-down of an event. The key point is that operational processes should be assessed and evaluated against original plans to examine their effectiveness. Lessons will always be learned from this process and it is essential that it takes place within a few weeks of the event, whilst memories are still clear.

Event operations

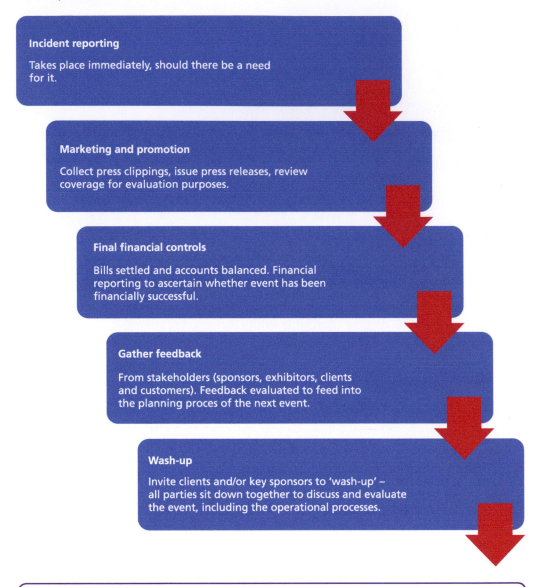

Incident reporting

Takes place immediately, should there be a need for it.

Marketing and promotion

Collect press clippings, issue press releases, review coverage for evaluation purposes.

Final financial controls

Bills settled and accounts balanced. Financial reporting to ascertain whether event has been financially successful.

Gather feedback

From stakeholders (sponsors, exhibitors, clients and customers). Feedback evaluated to feed into the planning proces of the next event.

Wash-up

Invite clients and/or key sponsors to 'wash-up' – all parties sit down together to discuss and evaluate the event, including the operational processes.

Figure 4.13 The event shut-down process

Industry voice

Olly Galvin, Operations Manager, Galvin Events Ltd.

 When planning operations management for music festivals I always take the event site as the starting point. Each site is unique in the requirements it places on the supply chain and event logistics, both of which must be accommodated by event operations planning in order to deliver a high-quality event to the audience. Specialist experience is required to ensure that the site's requirements are understood in the planning phase which is why I always make sure that I have visited the site with each key contractor to discuss their planning and requirements.

The site location can present a number of challenges. If it is close to residential properties there may well be conditions on the event license relating to audio levels at these properties. This will affect the whole site layout as it will influence the position and direction of stages, as well as meaning that we need to employ a sound control specialist to ensure that we do not exceed the audio levels stated on our license.

The location can also have a huge impact on our logistics. Narrow roads and weak bridges can make it impossible for key suppliers to bring infrastructure on-site on their normal lorries, slowing down the delivery of their element of the event. I have worked on a site where a weak access bridge to the site meant we had to install one kilometre of temporary trackway across the site just to bring the suppliers' lorries on-site. This added a significant amount onto the hire costs for the event, as well as increasing the time the construction of the event site took, adding extra days onto the crew wages bill, along with accommodation and catering costs.

The road network in the local area can cause huge traffic jams for the audience arriving in their own vehicles without proper management, so we will often need to add a traffic management company to our supply chain. For events with inadequate road networks there are a number of alternatives available to us in the operations planning phase, including emphasising public transport and providing a shuttle bus service to the site itself, encouraging transport sharing or staggering the audience's arrival times to avoid everyone arriving at the same time. This can also help with customer ticketing – staggered arrival times mean less time spent queuing to enter the event, and if we can predict when customers will arrive we can resource our ticket checking areas appropriately.

The site's location can bring immediate neighbours into the stakeholders group as well. Difficult neighbours can cause issues for the event – I've worked on festivals in the middle of farmland where the neighbouring farmer has demanded payment to stop him dumping slurry at the boundary of his land and our campsite!

The terrain will also influence our planning. Hills and woodland can interfere with Wi-Fi and radio signal so engaging a competent supplier who can overcome these issues is crucial. Poor radio communications can lead to failed information sharing between the management team, resulting in a low-quality or dangerous event, and Wi-Fi is so heavily relied on by events that without it our ticketing systems can fail and traders would be forced to cease trading.

The terrain will have a significant impact on the location of stages, and also on our staffing costs. If we locate stages in enclosed areas we need to allocate security staff to ensure that the area's capacity is not exceeded.

Bodies of water on the site can present opportunities as well as challenges. I have worked on sites where large lakes meant that we needed to hire lifeguards to patrol them, and I have built floating stages on other lakes as well as bridges over rivers to help with crowd flow.

If we have an event site with poor drainage we will need to take steps to prepare for a waterlogged site. Vehicle tracking needs to be bought in at the start of the event build to make sure that our suppliers can move around the site. Without this contingency we will see delays in the supply chain that will have a significant impact on our ability to deliver the event; stages may not be ready to open on time if the audio equipment can't be installed, and bars could run out of stock on the first day, severely impacting both the audience experience and the event's finances. Similarly, we will need to plan for waterlogging from an audience perspective, having aggregates on standby that we can deploy in the worst affected areas to keep the crowds moving around the site and ensuring that the car parks do not get blocked with stuck cars. The worst case scenario in these terms is a flooded site, forcing us to cancel the event for health and safety reasons. A site I was managing a few years ago flooded the day after the event (luckily the audience had already left!). Even at this stage the flooding had a huge impact on the event itself, as damaged equipment and a severely delayed supply chain removing infrastructure generated significant costs that we had not planned for.

We have seen how the event site can place demands on the operations of an event, and how these demands often result in additional infrastructure and staffing requirements. These additional requirements will often generate further costs themselves; every extra member of staff on-site needs to be provided with accommodation and food and will require sufficient welfare facilities while they are on-site. Good operational planning will be able to account for all of these factors to make sure that the event is delivered with the highest quality while remaining inside the budget allocated.

4.10 Summary

This chapter has highlighted the importance of events operations – it is the underpinning of all event planning and, without event operations, there would be no event. Event operations is described here as the transformation of all the resources (or inputs) that are needed to run an event into the event experience – event operations make events happen. The chapter has sought to highlight the central importance that operations have in strategic decisions, including that key tension between running events within a strict budget, whilst providing the best event experience possible.

Throughout the chapter, it has been made clear that every event is different and individually complex, so there is no set formula for operations. The importance of the supply chain or supply network that supports event operations was highlighted and then the chapter focused on the key operational aspects of event delivery itself – logistical planning and capacity management.

The planning of event operations to decide which resources, skills and equipment will be required is an essential part of the events management process and needs to be considered fully within the context of both the event planning process and health, safety and risk analysis.

Review questions

1. Why are operations management important to the success of an event organisation?
2. Can operations have a leading role in determining the strategic direction of an event?
3. Describe the tensions between cost minimisation and quality maximisation in the events industry. Why do they occur, and what can be done about the conflict of trying to offer the best event at the cheapest cost?
4. Discuss the use of the IPO model as applied to event operations.
5. Read Olly Galvin's industry voice – were you surprised by the number of things he suggests you need to consider when thinking about site management? What was the most interesting point that Olly made?

Further reading

Lai., I. K. W., Hitchcock, M., Ting Yang and Tun-Wei Lu (2018) Literature Review on Service Quality in Hospitality and Tourism (1984–2014): Future Direction and Trends. *International Journal of Contemporary Management*, 30(1): 114–159. Whilst focusing mainly on related leisure industries, this article is very useful for students studying events too – the discussion of future direction is particularly informative, and the literature on hospitality and tourism is certainly also relevant to the events industry.

O'Toole, W. (2011) *Events Feasibility and Development: From Strategy to Operations*, Oxford: Elsevier Butterworth-Heinemann. A comprehensive review of strategy and operational management specific to the events industry. Fairly practical in its nature, but very useful and, despite the age of the book, still highly recommended.

Tkacynski, A. and Stokes, R. (2010) Festperf: A Service Quality Measurement Scale for Festivals. *Event Management*, 14 (1): 69–82. An interesting study on a performance only measurement of quality in a festival setting.

Tum, J., Norton, P. and Wright, J. N. (2006) *Management of Event Operations*, Oxford: Elsevier. An incredibly detailed view of the management of event operations, useful for those who need to look in depth at a specific operational aspect. The book is particularly strong on operational techniques, such as forecasting and gap analysis. Tum *et al.* also provide a useful overview of the supply chain management of event operations. It should be noted, however, that the event operations management model proposed in this book is very complex and may well include too much under one 'umbrella' term.

Video links

Extraordinary Events Podcast – Who Are the Event Stakeholders? https://podcasts.google.com/feed/aHR0cHM6Ly9mZWVkcy5idXp6c3Byb3V0LmNvbS8xMjAyNDM1LnJzcw/episode/QnV6enNwcm91dC01MTMxMTg2?sa=X&ved=0CAwQzsICahcKEwjYyKCur8rrAhUAAAAAHQAAAAAQAQ

How to write an event planning checklist, International Institute of Event Management: https://youtu.be/Q_Ece-fPKuw

IOC Media: Venue & Event Operations. This video introduces you to venue and event operations on a mega scale: https://youtu.be/aUQJguPlLkg

People and Crowd Management Planning – Safety and Security for Meetings and Events (MPI): https://youtu.be/lE-GNcr1nxs

What Is Supply Chain Management? (Brigham Young University): https://youtu.be/AwemFfdD6VI

Weblinks

Crowd Dynamics: www.crowddynamics.com. Crowd Dynamics is an independent specialist consultancy in crowd movement, transport planning and movement strategies. We are uniquely positioned to support clients who need the safe and efficient movement of people on all transport modes in the built environment and within the public realm.

Extraordinary Events Initiative: www.extraordinaryeventsinitiative.com. The Extraordinary Events Initiative started as a movement to elevate event education for everyone, everywhere. This initiative is affiliated with the University of Nebraska Lincoln and provides objective, quality education that is unbiased from corporate/association promotions and is not a for-profit entity. Although we have many great industry partners, this initiative is self-funded through low-cost fees on some of the content. This resource is useful and available for everyone – no matter your skill level in events. @eventinitiative on Facebook and Instagram.

Managing crowds safely – Health and Safety Executive: www.hse.gov.uk/event-safety/crowd-management.htm

Picking the right venue for your event – Eventbrite: www.eventbrite.co.uk/blog/academy/event-management-checklist-venues-ds00/

Want to know more about the inputs and outputs of the operations model? www.open.edu/openlearn/money-business/leadership-management/understanding-operations-management/content-section-3.2

References

Abbott, J. L. and Abbott, S. M. (2000) The Importance of Proper Crowd Management and Crowd Control in the Special Events Industry, in J. Allen, R. Harris, L. K. Jago and A. J. Veal (eds) *Events beyond 2000: Setting the Agenda, Proceedings of the Conference on Evaluation, Research and Education, Sydney, July 2000*, Sydney: Australian Centre for Event Management, University of Technology.

Abbott, J. L. and Geddie, M. W. (2001) Event and Venue Management: Minimizing Liability through Effective Crowd Management Techniques, *Event Management*, 6: 259–270.

Associated Press (2003) Woman Killed at Festival. *New York Times*, 1 September. Available at: www.nytimes.com/2003/09/01/us/woman-killed-at-festival.html?ref=burningmanfestival [Accessed 9 June 2011].

Atrek, B., Marcone, M. R., Gregori, G. L., Temperini, V. and Moscatelli, L. (2014) Relationship Quality in Supply Chain Management: A Dyad Perspective/Tedarik Zinciri Yönetiminde İliski Kalitesi: Çift Yönlü Perspektif. *Ege Akademik Bakis*, 14 (3): 371.

Baggs, M. (2019) Fyre Festival: Inside the World's Biggest Festival Flop. *BBC News*, 18 January. Available at: www.bbc.co.uk/news/newsbeat-46904445 [Accessed 31 July 2022].

BBC (2010) Stampede at German Love Parade Festival Kills 19. Available at: www.bbc.co.uk/news/world-europe-10751899 [Accessed 30 December 2010].

Berlonghi, A. (1995) Understanding and Planning for Different Spectator Crowds, *Safety Science*, 18: 239–247.

Bowdin, G., Allen, J., O'Toole, W., Harris, R. and McDonnell, I. (2011) *Events Management* (3rd edn), Oxford: Butterworth-Heinemann.

Cherubini, S., Iasevoli, G. and Lauretta, G. (2007) Events Ticketing Management: The Case of the Olympic Winter Games Torino 2006 and the FIFA World Cup Germany 2006, presentation at Marketing, Trends in Europe Conference, Paris, 26–27 January.

Freeman, R. (1984/2000) *Strategic Management: A Stakeholder Approach*. Boston, MA: Pitman.

Fruin, J. (1984) Crowd Dynamics and Auditorium Management, *Auditorium News*. Available at: www.crowdmodelling.com/Fruin2.html [Accessed 4 November 2011].

Fruin, J. (2002) The Causes and Preventions of Crowd Disasters. Available at: www.crowdsafe.com/FruinCauses.pdf [Accessed 24 February 2011].

Getz, D. (2012) *Event Studies* (2nd edn), Oxford: Butterworth-Heinemann.

Goldblatt, J. (2013) *Special Events: Creating and Sustaining a New World for Celebration* (7th edn), New York: Wiley Global Education.

Health and Safety Executive (HSE) (1999) *The Event Safety Guide*, Norwich: HSE Books.

Health and Safety Executive (HSE) (2000) *Managing Crowds Safely*, Norwich: HSE Books.

Jenner, T. (2010) Whose Queue Is it Anyway: A Study of Responsibilities for Post-Event Queuing, *Journal of Crowd Safety and Security Management*, 2 (1): 15–23.

Livesey, J. (2015) Oktoberfest London Cancelled. *Mirror*, 9 October. Available at: www.mirror.co.uk/news/uk-news/oktoberfest-london-cancelled-organisers-call-6603965 [Accessed 2 August 2022].

Matthews, D. (2008) *Special Event Production: The Process*, Oxford: Butterworth-Heinemann.

McShane, A. and Edmonds, L. (2015) Oktoberfest London Cancelled. *The Standard*, 9 October. Available at: www.standard.co.uk/news/london/london-oktoberfest-cancelled-half-an-hour-before-doors-were-due-to-open-because-of-operational-issues-a3086611.html [Accessed: 2 August 2022].

Oakes, S. and North, A. C. (2008) Using Music to Influence Cognitive and Affective Responses in Queues of Low and High Crowd Density, *Journal of Marketing Management*, 24 (5–6): 589–602.

Shelby, B., Vaske, J. J. and Heberlien, T. A. (1989) Comparative Analysis of Crowding in Multiple Locations: Results from Fifteen Years of Research, *Leisure Science*, 11: 269–291.

Silvers, J. (2004) *Professional Event Coordination*, Hoboken, NJ: John Wiley and Sons.

Slack, N. and Lewis, M. (2017) *Operations Strategy* (5th edn), Harlow: Pearson.

Slack, N., Brandon-Jones, A. and Johnston, B. (2011) *Essentials of Operations Management*, Harlow: Pearson.

Slack, N., Brandon-Jones, A. and Johnston, B. (2019) *Operations Management* (9th edn), Harlow: Pearson.

Tum, J., Norton, P. and Wright, J. N. (2006) *Management of Event Operations*, Oxford: Butterworth-Heinemann.

Wikipedia (2022) Fyre Festival. Available at: https://en.wikipedia.org/wiki/Fyre_Festival [Accessed 31 July 2022].

Chapter 5

Event human resource management

Contents

DOI: 10.4324/9781003102878-5

5.1 Aims

By the end of this chapter, students will be able to:

- explain the human resource challenges of managing events
- model the process of event recruitment and selection with respect to events organisations
- appreciate the complexities of leading event employees and volunteers
- establish suitable methods of event employee learning and development.

5.2 Introduction

Though human resource management (HRM) has been studied and practised for decades, effective staffing, training, management and motivation of event employees and volunteers differ from what is often observed in traditional, static business organisations. This is mainly because of the challenges posed by an event's vastness and the disjointed and 'pulsating' nature of the temporary events organisation. Therefore, modern events managers need to be more proactive and flexible than managers from other professions, which deal with more permanent, ongoing, day-to-day businesses. It is argued that traditional business models, research and industry practice are not sufficient with respect to the particular uniqueness of managing the event's human resource. These variations also extend to the leadership style in the new vibrant events organisation, with a view to recognising, developing and designing the role of staff and their interactions with event attendees.

5.3 The event human resource challenge

The event human resource behaves differently from that in other organisations, requiring different planning and management activities. This runs counter to traditional views of more monolithic, hierarchical organisations, whose staffing priorities are generally filled to accommodate their own missions, goals and cultures. Instead, event organisations are required to vary staffing in accordance with each event's size, use of volunteers and permanent staff, task scheduling, roles and expertise, in addition to the particular client's and/or venue's needs.

Building on Chapter 2, the main human resource particularities of events organisations arise because, unlike static organisations such as retailers or cinemas, event organisations tend to be project-led, rather than simply designed with a view to their ongoing function. This is because project-led event organisations respond to the requirements of each individual event they undertake, making traditional functional structures, and their associated processes, less helpful when assessing how to staff events and manage event workers effectively.

Events tend to be delivered by 'pulsating organisations' (Toffler 1990), which cause their processes and practices to be constantly revised, in line with the fluctuating event environment. Different operational demands, even on different days of the same event, mean skills and numbers of workers required vary. Along with cost-control considerations, these varying personnel requirements create an ongoing need to alter demand for labour, requiring a mix between sufficient numbers of permanent employees and flexible workers, which usually include those on zero hours contracts, and volunteers.

Study activity

1 What are zero hours contracts? How do they work?
2 What are the benefits and drawbacks of using such contacts in the events industry?
3 Discuss some of the ethical as well as business conditions under which zero hours contracts can be managed in order to maintain efficient costs, customer satisfaction and employee loyalty.

Terminology, as it applies to event staffing, has altered significantly in recent years, in line with its increasing complexity. Twenty years ago, a practitioner or student would have referred to the staffing of an event as a function of 'personnel management', rather than using the current term 'human resource management'. This change mainly resulted from the increased complexity facing HR professionals, due to ongoing economic and cultural changes. At the same time, the expectations of how employees perform in organisations has also developed, in line with expectations of what people hope to derive from work itself.

Study activity

1 What do employees expect from work beyond customary contractual pay and conditions?
2 Generate some ideas about ways in which workers could have their work satisfaction and productivity improved.
3 What are some of the main initiatives that could be implemented to promote work–life balance within events organisations? Research and discuss, using examples from work organisations.

5.3.1 Event personnel

While previously the events workforce was primarily treated as a resource, to be recruited in large enough numbers from local communities (Goldblatt 2010), societal and industry changes regarding the role and treatment of temporary staff have increased the complexities and considerations associated with modern event leadership. Also, the increased academic and industry focus on holistic event design and service management has made it necessary for HR managers to evolve their function as well. Therefore, rather than simply generating staff in significant enough numbers to provide presence and atmosphere, or carrying out basic, practical tasks, HR managers must recognise that events are comprised of people; the co-producers of event customer experiences.

Thus, Van Der Wagen (2007: 5) refers to events as 'a new context for human resource management'. She argues that people are not just an essential resource for an event, but also a key success factor. Building on this important point, events as gatherings of people are conceived, designed and delivered by people, for people. They decide the all-important '*raison d'être*' of the event which is crucial to an event's authenticity. As discussed in Chapter 2, if an event's designer needs to decide whether attendees should be immersed or absorbed in a particular experience, event staff will be essential to achieving this. Such an important role will often be key to an event's successful staging and the ultimate expression of its planned legacy.

This new strategic role of HRM for events demands greater concern for the philosophy of events and event organisations, not just attention to processes and staffing. This new view is important to event managers, considering the strategic nature of most events and the way they are managed by ad hoc organisational structures, which are often formed, revised and disbanded according to fluctuating needs.

As industry focus continues on the all-important, memorable wow factors of design-driven events (see Chapter 3), so the essential element of interaction between staff and customers also comes to the forefront of successful, quality experience-facilitation. This continues industry departure from the basic '4Ps' marketing mix of product, price, place and promotion, earlier found to be inadequate for service industry use (Booms and Bitner 1981; Bitner 1993).

Currently, successful events incorporate the additional components of people, process and physical evidence into their design and staging plans to emphasise the essential and complementary role that human resources plays in the design and production of event attendee experience within event experiencescapes. Also, the extent to which other, related event elements play their part, such as communication and the flow of activities, should not be underestimated, and are actioned by the event workforce. Even the staging elements, which comprise the remainder of the holistic experiencescape discussed in Chapter 3, are also delivered by people.

5.3.2 Understanding event professionalism

As events have continued to be mass-produced in increasing, record numbers, the industry need for workers with appropriate skills and attributes has also increased. However, though the numbers of skilled professionals required are not debated, there are conflicting opinions concerning the specific skills and attributes required.

5.3.3 Establishing the desirable attributes of event personnel

With the increasing demand for suitably skilled events personnel have come various attempts by the industry and academic institutions to define and categorise the desirable attributes of such workers in terms of competencies. As the learned capacity to do certain activities, the required competencies of event staff will vary in part according to the requirements of the particular event in question. Thus, the professionalisation of the event manager continues, as is illustrated in the following case study.

CASE STUDY 5.1

Do events management degrees adequately equip graduates for the events profession?

Bladen and Kennell (2014) explained at the time that there was discussion still about whether events management can in fact even be considered a profession, due, among other factors, to its lack of a coherent professional body and professional qualifications. For those in doubt, an event manager is an actual profession requiring specific expertise, skills and qualities, and there are now many professional bodies in this sector. There has been much debate over the event manager's profession being just a fun job, party animals who have embarked on a career that gives them a fun lifestyle while earning money. This could not be further from the truth and hence why we have event management degrees. Apart from requiring a variety of skills and qualities, being an event manager demands specific background, expertise and know-how. If you happen to work on an event that does not have a big team you will find yourself combining a number of professions and skills into one role. It is important to constantly gain new expertise and a degree can offer that.

To serve the recruitment needs of the ever growing, international events sector, there has been much recent discussion about whether degrees in events management are the most effective route towards the professionalisation of graduates within the field. The reason being that, there has been a tendency with some to suggest that the practical nature of the profession can only be learned by practical, hands-on work experience. Events management is a competitive area and its true experience can be just as important as the degree subject for getting a job in the sector. Events management degrees have really evolved, with some universities holding employer advisory group meetings, inviting leading event professionals to contribute to the content and assessment styles within the degree to assist in embedding those all-important employability skills. Additionally, it is worth noting that experience in any role involving customer service will raise your profile, especially in hospitality or tourism. Many events organisations look for casual staff to help out at their events, and this can be a good way to gain skills and build up contacts in the sector while obtaining your degree. University extracurricular activities can give you valuable experience, for example, organising the end of term ball or a fundraiser for a university society. In the run up to a large event, and during the event itself, staff may need to work long hours and be very adaptable, so any role where you can demonstrate an ability to work hard and think on your feet is useful.

Though this does still appear to be the continuation of an age-old debate between those who champion practical, on-the-job training, versus those in favour of the longer-term, career emphasis provided by professional degree education, it seems that both are required for new employees wishing to pursue a career in events management – from the point of first-job entry level into operations as well as far beyond this to a long-term career path and events leadership.

5.4 Finding the right people

Study activity

1 What general skills and attributes do effective professionals in the events sector require?
2 Choose a specific area of the events sector and carry out the following tasks:

 ● Write down the specific skills, tasks and competencies required of a manager working in the area.
 ● Discuss ways in which these could be developed.

3 Carry out a personal SWOT (strengths, weaknesses, opportunities and threats) analysis to establish your current suitability for the management position discussed in Q2. Produce an action plan for each of your strengths and weaknesses, along with specific methods by which they may be effectively developed. Write a set of personal development goals for the next year, with measurable timelines for their achievement.

5.4.1 Recruiting

For every event, there is the necessity to attract, screen and select adequately qualified workers either through a formal or informal process, which involves:

 ● determining the vacancies
 ● sourcing strategy
 ● preparing and publishing information
 ● processing and measuring applications
 ● notifying applicants.

(Tyson and York 2000: 106–107)

Invariably, due to the sheer scale of many events, it is common practice for event organisations to use recruitment intermediaries to assist with what can often be a resource-intensive and specialised activity.

Study activity

1 What do you consider to be the advantages and disadvantages of using an events recruitment company to staff events?
2 Find a specialist events recruiter.
3 Research this company's website.
4 What are their main target markets?
5 What other activities do they appear to be involved in other than recruitment?
6 What professional experience does the company appear to use in its business?

Whether the event organisers use recruitment agencies, or manage this process in-house, it is important that effective procedures and processes are formulated, possibly for each individual event if required, in order to ensure that the most suitable candidates are matched with the planned jobs. Ineffective recruitment may lead to significant shortfalls in performance, and in the events industry where, as the cliché states, 'you are only as good as your last event', failure is much more difficult to rectify than in many other industries.

Recruitment and selection methods should attract sufficient numbers of suitable applicants and should provide scope for fairness in relation to their chances of being selected. According to Pilbeam and Corbridge (2010: 137), recruitment and selection involves:

1 Attraction of suitable candidates.
2 Reduction of unsuitable candidates.
3 Selection of suitable candidates.
4 Transition of a successful candidate to an effective employee.

The typical constraints to these activities experienced by most organisations, such as a shortage of qualified candidates and issues relating to the organisation's macro environment, are even greater for event organisers. They also have to consider the temporal nature, geographical movement, complexity of stakeholder relationships and fluctuations in environmental factors, including media coverage, that are associated with the events industry.

5.4.2 Designing event jobs

Prior to beginning the process of recruitment, the event planner should complete an in-depth job analysis to assess the positions which need to be filled. This will include the collection of information about the tasks to complete before, during and following event delivery. Obviously, the more rigid and less changeable the event concept and plan are, the simpler this task will be. Any changes will require subsequent revision, perhaps adding cost buffers to timelines and budgets.

The end result of the job analysis will be a list of job descriptions, which group the various tasks coherently, and job specifications, which clarify the specific competencies of the candidates who will be recruited for these jobs.

5.4.3 Clarifying job designs and descriptions

A job description should include the following key information:

- Job/role title.
- The event-related tasks and activities that the job should achieve. These will be linked to the objectives of the role. Performance indicators can also be stipulated here.
- Levels of responsibility and any departmental affiliations within the event organisation, as well as the name of the person to whom the successful applicant would report.
- Pay scale.

5.4.4 Establishing applicant suitability

Once the parameters of the job are established, then what is required of the applicants becomes the focus, including:

- Formal qualifications, event-related certifications (such as first aid), criminal record checks, health and safety certifications and so on, as required by the event and its predicted target markets.
- Competencies, including skills, knowledge and prior experience.
- Any physical characteristics required for the role, such as heavy-lifting capabilities.

Each of these may be expressed in terms of 'essential' (minimum) and 'desirable' requirements to avoid misunderstandings during the selection phase, and to ensure that the event hires the best individuals for the various posts.

Many events are vast undertakings, requiring a diverse scope of abilities to achieve them. As Boxall and Purcell (2008: 176) observe: 'Thus, as we move up from low-complexity work (such as routine clerical work) to jobs where greater ambiguity is involved in decision-making, differences in skills and judgement become more pronounced and are more consequential for the organisation'.

This means that, as event tasks become more complex, there is a need to find people with a wide range of skills. An event producer, for example, may possess the highest levels of innovation and creativity, yet these talents matter little if they are unable to communicate effectively. Obviously, the ideal candidate will be both creative *and* an effective communicator.

However, it is important not to set required competencies, skills, attributes and qualifications too high. Physical or skill requirements should not discriminate against applicants with disabilities, unless these qualities are essential for the job. Many event organisations provide on-the-job training or certifications, and carry out criminal record checks according to legislative requirements, but these can be costly and prove impractical within tight timelines so that it is often impossible to hire applicants who do not already have them.

1 For events local to you, what are the legal requirements regulating employees? Consider the certifications you would be expected to possess in order to work in your country.
2 What are your country's main disability discrimination laws? Provide examples of steps an event manager might be able to take in order to make event jobs more accessible to the physically and mentally challenged applicants.

5.4.5 Communicating event vacancies through traditional and online media

Potential event employees are attracted by various methods, including basic advertising, word-of-mouth referral and formal recruitment sources, which include job centres, industry fairs, schools, colleges and universities. While job adverts and messages remain relatively consistent, the use of such social networks as Facebook, Twitter and LinkedIn has changed many of the ways in which recruitment takes place, presenting new challenges for both employers and applicants.

Applicants no longer maintain a passive role in the application process, but rather engage in two-way, adaptable messages, often in 'real-time'. For example, many Facebook groups have been formed specifically to publicise both paid and voluntary employment vacancies in the domestic and international events industry. Though often free, or supported by advertising, such online vehicles sometimes apply a commission for referral, which can lead to events organisations paying a variety of charges. These can range from an almost negligible 'click-through' fee to substantially larger commissions for the placement of high-level events executives. It should be noted that the legal framework governing such media is changing fast in order to bring it more in line with the laws governing offline practices, and this should be monitored closely to avoid litigation.

Study activity

Discuss, using examples from your own research, what the potential opportunities and possible pitfalls might be to the use of social media by event professionals. You might include in your discussions areas such as:

- Relationship-building between organisation and applicant.
- Legal considerations regarding contracts, descriptions.
- Management of recruitment messages and corporate image.
- Communication styles.
- Exclusion of certain social groups.

5.4.6 Screening

Following the receipt of applications via the sources discussed in the previous section, a process of screening should be applied to eliminate unsuitable applicants and reduce the numbers of less suitable candidates in favour of those who more closely match or even exceed the particulars of the planned job specification. It should be remembered that this part of the selection process involves subjectivity on the part of those responsible for selection.

There must be mutual trust and respect between employer and applicant, as a psychological contract is formed between both parties which is based on their expectations of one another as well as assumptions and inferences derived from their mutual interactions, in addition to any formal communication or legal contracts. Certainly, many premature breakdowns in the formal, contractual relationships between employers and employees can be traced back to this less formal, yet often more important, psychological understanding.

Study activity

What are your likely expectations of your employer? Which of these can be classified as comprising the 'psychological contract' between both parties? List these and discuss ways in which you think events organisations can improve their management of employee expectations from the very start of the employment relationship.

5.4.7 Selecting

Prior to any events organisation's recruitment of new employees, there is a challenging process whereby the events recruiter attempts to use selection processes to predict on-the-job performance. To this end, the events manager may employ a number of measurement tools to assess a candidate's suitability. However, this can be problematic as there is no real capacity for a trial period of employment in the events industry, as events are time-constrained and also vary considerably from each other.

Torrington *et al.* (2009: 171) highlight that selection methods can be determined on the basis of a combination of the following factors:

- selection criteria for the post to be filled
- acceptability of and appropriateness of the methods
- abilities of the staff involved in selection
- administrative ease
- time factors
- accuracy
- cost.

Because of the people-centred nature of events work, those involved in the selection process are likely to favour face-to-face contact with applicants – ideally in a one-to-one interview – in order to gain an accurate impression of their interpersonal skills. Such meetings allow the interviewer to make an assessment of the candidate's suitability and to present a realistic job preview. However, time, cost and other resource constraints usually make wholesale use of such methods unfeasible, particularly for larger events, and this has increased the popularity of the use of real-time, virtual face-to-face media such as Skype. Methods that are widely used in event selection processes include:

- application forms
- interviews – face-to-face, group, or via telephone/webcam
- aptitude tests
- group interviews and problem-solving exercises, business games, competitions and so on
- work sampling, including written work, business plans, portfolios and presentations
- references.

Several of these will usually be used in combination, depending on the type of event in question. References are especially important, with many event specialists relying on the recommendations of credible referees, such as university teaching staff and the applicant's previous employers.

5.5 The challenges in practice to the events industry

Certainly, the process discussed thus far is widely accepted and practised and it finds application in the international events industry. However, many events managers will no doubt take issue with many of the time, detail and documentation requirements implied here. This will mainly be due to the usual time and resource limitations commonly associated with events. It will also reflect the transitory and temporal nature of events, discussed earlier in this chapter. Indeed, there would appear to be little benefit in mapping out job descriptions and the qualities and qualifications of the people required to perform them if one event differs widely from the next. Most event roles maintain a large degree of consistency across different events, but the processes already described are indicative of useful concepts rather than the specifics, because of the rapid changes in events organisations and the specified outcomes of their event concepts.

5.6 Formulating and conducting event induction and acculturation

5.6.1 Induction

While traditional new-employee induction to most workplace organisations is intended to promote effective adjustment and integration of the new employee into the new workplace, in the events industry it involves much more. Though it was formerly assumed that induction was a first-day familiarisation tour, in the events industry it begins at interview and continues to the end of the worker's involvement with the event, or with longer engagements until the employer and employee have reached a mutual understanding of their relationship.

A distinction also needs to be drawn between the employee's induction to the event organisation and their induction to the current event. The weight given to these two elements depends on the kind of event, the stage at which the employee joins and the type and expected duration of their role. In events, the new-employee induction is crucial: it can safeguard lives and ensure the health and welfare of customers, colleagues and the employee themselves, primarily because of the intrinsic dangers associated with many event sites and venues. Please see Chapter 8 for more information.

Virtual induction is practised by several events companies, which post important familiarisation and training materials for specific events on websites and company intranets for use by new and existing employees. These sites provide crucial event information about company policies and procedures, employee duties, site plans and so on. This supplements the usual induction, which informs new employees of the procedural and legal guidelines they must follow and gives them an opportunity to ask questions. In many events, the concept will be explained in relation to the employee's role. Event organisers will often pair new workers with those who are more experienced in order to familiarise them with an event.

5.6.2 Organisational culture and events

During this induction phase, the employee will gain an impression about various cultural norms they will be expected to observe during their time working on events. Schein

---

Table 5.1 The factors comprising organisational culture

Beliefs and assumptions

- What does the organisation do?
- What business(es) is it in?
- What does it seek to achieve in the future?
- Who are its stakeholders?

Values

- What do its stakeholders want from the business?
- What are the standards of behaviour of the people associated with the organisation?
- How do the personal and professional values of the people align with those of the organisation?
- How does the organisation view 'progress'?

Norms

- How do the people associated with the organisation commonly:
  - behave?
  - interact?
  - communicate?
  - implement/react to change?

- How do these norms match corporate guidelines and expectations?
- What is the relationship between the groups in the organisation, the national cultural groups, the organisational culture and the corporate culture?

Signs

- Organisations often display outward indications of how they work, such as employee uniforms or visible price or service promises. How do such tangible signs relate to or contradict each other?

(2010: 7) writes about culture in organisations and observes: 'Cultural forces are powerful because they operate outside of our awareness. We need to understand them not only because of their power but also because they help to explain many of our puzzling and frustrating experiences in social and organisational life'.

The organisational culture of an events company gives each of its events a specific 'personality'. According to Schein, organisational culture is mainly made up of the factors developed in Table 5.1.

It is important to understand the organisation's culture because, whenever a new employee joins, they will very quickly reach their own conclusion about it, based on their assessment of these factors.

In addition to generic, organisational principles, the combined influences of other types of culture found in an organisation should also be considered, such as group culture. For example, members of an event banquet service staff team are likely to have their own set of assumptions, values, norms and signs that are additional to those of the parent organisation, or of the event they are working on. Group culture distinguishes its members to some extent from other groups and such distinctions can cause conflicts between them. When other cultures, such as national cultures or ethnic cultures, are combined with group cultures, the culture of the event itself and the corporate culture of the parent organisation, the HRM implications for the event manager can be challenging.

5.6.3 Team building

Event team building is also more complex than functional HRM suggests. Goldblatt (2010) highlights some of the complexity of leading and managing event teams, particularly from an outsourcing perspective.

Many event managers make the decision to outsource the skill sets required for particular events. Many new to the industry, such as events students, prefer instinctively to retain direct control over the more creative aspects of an event, such as design and production, often intending to outsource some of the more 'mundane' tasks, such as cleaning. However, in practice more experienced event managers understand that the distinctiveness of the event might depend upon the effective delivery of 'wow' factors and other creative staging aspects which require expertise that is rarely found within the skill set of the existing team. There are other factors in play which also contribute to this perspective, including legal and safety restrictions, and the required capital and talent investment. These factors may be outside the scope of many general events management organisations, particularly for irregular use for individual events.

The construction, management and leadership of event teams, particularly in the context of these discussions regarding group culture, can prove challenging for any event manager and is another contributory factor that makes management in this industry distinct from that of other areas of management practice. For a wider discussion of event leadership and organisation structure, refer to Chapter 2.

Some event organisations take a psychological approach to the construction of teams. Psychometric tests can be used to assess the personality traits of individuals as early as the selection stage of the HRM process. Whether event managers favour this option will mainly depend on their own experiences with regard to predicting future employee performance.

In a team-building context, the most effective approach will be taken depending on the planned purpose of the team in question. Event teams can provide basic event delivery, such as customer service or various staging provisions. Others might be responsible for relatively complex problem-solving activities. The psychological characteristics, skill sets, and competencies of employees performing these roles will vary according to their specific planned context.

The combination of the above characteristics of individuals within the team should also be considered. Pfeffer (1998) found teams to be much more effective than individuals at organisational problem-solving. In the context of creative design, the more diverse the team, the longer the decision-making process, but the more effective the final result. According to the Gorge Group study (1994; cited in Walton 1999), excellence in team problem-solving performance was based on the creation of synergy between members, the building of commitment towards a common goal, the fostering of independence, constructive debates and mutual concern and respect for each other.

It should also be stressed that teams in the events industry are increasingly virtual in nature, particularly in vast, international parent companies. This enables the principles above to be facilitated through the use of information technology media, as discussed earlier in this chapter. It is therefore possible for event specialists in the field to be supported by members of a virtual 'back office' of personnel, many of whom they may never meet in person.

5.7 Developing effective communication with event workers

Boxall and Purcell (2008) focus on the management of the 'employee voice' in organisational decision-making through the promotion of employee involvement strategies. This approach is collectively influenced in the events industry by the involvement of trade unions and professional associations, whose scope and power will vary widely depending on the country concerned.

Effective communication, according to the Gorge Group (1994), is based on the organisation:

- proactively building a shared understanding
- focusing on the needs of others and predicting their questions
- communicating most effectively outside meetings.

5.8 Event employee learning and development

The events organisation should facilitate various degrees and types of employee development in order to maximise performance. The specialised field of HRM views these activities as the facilitation and promotion of cultures and processes that allow employees to learn. Formal training programmes certainly have their part to play in increasing the effectiveness of event employees, particularly in mandatory, operational management areas, such as safety. However, the genuine differentiation of event offerings may hinge on the promotion of a learning organisation where people are encouraged to keep learning and improving and are supported with the resources to do so. For example, the official London 2012 Olympic Games volunteering programme, while a vehicle for the achievement of much of the social legacy portion of the bid, successfully encouraged volunteering by promising that volunteers would gain skills in return for their activities in the lead-up to and during the Games.

5.8.1 Reflective practice

Kolb's learning cycle can be applied to the events industry as shown in Figure 5.1. This adapted model is an ideal starting point for the development of the learning events organisation as it focuses on problem-solving.

Another key HR function is to conduct a formal, organisational programme of learning and training for events by:

1 identifying the development need
2 designing the development activity
3 carrying out the development activity
4 evaluating the success of the development activity.

These four areas constitute the 'people development strategy' of the organisation, within the wider context of the business strategy, in relation to the business environment.

The identification of the development need will take place via various formal and informal systems. As Bowdin *et al.* (2011) point out, this can be linked to the appraisal systems of the organisation, although this approach will not be practical for most events organisations, with temporary and short-term workers. Certainly on-site, employee observations, customer complaint logs and other management information systems are useful indications.

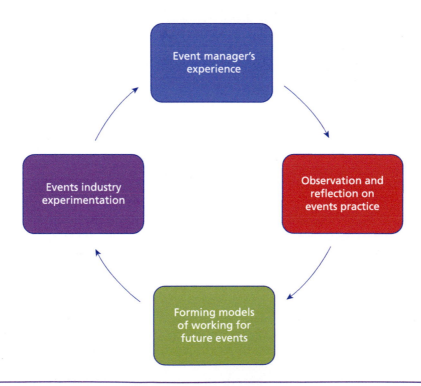

Figure 5.1 Kolb's learning cycle
Source: Adapted from Kolb (1984)

Designing and carrying out the development activity will involve the planned use of methods of learning and development, which may include items in the following list, also developed from Torrington *et al.* (2009):

- off-job methods, such as education and training courses
- on-job learning methods, such as coaching, mentoring, peer relationships, individual or group self-development
- e-learning methods.

Evaluation of the learning is likely to be continual and will rely on the accurate assessment of behavioural or attitudinal changes in line with the initial objectives set following the needs analysis. There are also employee-centred assessment methods, such as self-administered questionnaires, which are designed to measure the satisfaction derived from the learning process.

5.9 Motivating, maximising performance and retaining employees

Motivation of employees is too vast a topic for the scope of this chapter. In 'Maslow's hierarchy of needs' motivation model, reviewed briefly in Chapter 1 in relation to general event-attendees' motivation, it can be seen that employees' motivation results from unfulfilled human needs and suggests a human tendency to pursue the satisfaction of needs in a hierarchical order towards self-actualisation. Festinger's (1957) *Theory of Cognitive Dissonance* states that such dissatisfaction will result in psychological discomfort which the individual will seek to overcome.

However, in the context of Maslow's hierarchy, Herzberg's 'two-factor theory' demonstrates that event employees are likely to view aspects of work differently according to whether these are:

- motivators (e.g. challenging work, recognition, responsibility) that give positive satisfaction, arising from intrinsic conditions of the job itself, such as recognition, achievement, or personal growth
- hygiene factors (e.g. status, job security, salary and fringe benefits) that do not give positive satisfaction, although dissatisfaction results from their absence; these are extrinsic to the work itself, and include aspects such as company policies, supervisory practices, or wages/salary (Hackman and Oldham 1976).

To overcome the simplifications of Maslow's and Herzberg's theories, Vroom's 'valency expectancy theory' proposed that the degree of effort an employee would exert to satisfy a need depended directly on the expectation that their efforts would achieve their predicted goals. It is expressed as:

$$\text{Force (F)} = \text{Valency (V)} \times \text{Expectancy (E)}$$

In order to supplement these models' contributions to the wider understanding of employee motivation in an events context, more research has been conducted into the motivation of a particularly important group of event workers: volunteers.

5.9.1 Event volunteers and motivation

Many events survive because of the availability of a pool of willing and often repeat volunteers. However, as Bladen (2009) found, there are significant gaps in understanding as to the motivation of this crucial human resource. It is recognised that repeat volunteering will be based to some extent on the favourable evaluation by volunteers of their initial experiences. This is particularly crucial because, as Bowdin *et al.* (2011) state, event organisations that use large numbers of volunteers tend to recruit far more than were needed and then shed the unsuitable ones. This process, if practised by repeat event organisers, could jeopardise the sustainable future of such events. Additionally, researchers should examine such attitudinal factors as potential predictors of volunteers' future behaviours. Some volunteers are altruistic and desire to benefit others with little expectation of reward for so doing (Flashman and Quick 1985; Cuskelly *et al.* 2006). However, some repeat volunteers may be egoistic, doing so out of a self-interested desire to benefit themselves, while core – or 'career' – volunteers continue to volunteer because of the intrinsic rewards associated with the volunteering experience itself (Stebbins 1996).

> ### Study activity
>
> Have you ever volunteered for an event? What were your reasons for doing so? Were they mostly based upon altruism or egoism? Why?

5.10 Remunerating staff

Remuneration relates to the total benefit to a person for working on an event and is more inclusive a concept than simply 'pay' for a job done. The events industry provides tangible benefits in the form of money paid to workers, though most volunteers can expect little or no payment for their services, except perhaps reimbursement for certain 'out-of-pocket' expenses, such as travel to the venue. Event managers need to consider their chosen reward strategy for remunerating their employees carefully. Certainly, if the motivation of the staff depends on rewards, then the reward package must be sufficiently substantial to attract applicants and retain them once they become employees. The largest pressure for many events is that such a strategy is not only costly, because of the vast numbers of staff needed, but also self-defeating, because with such high labour costs many events would cease to be sustainable.

There is still much debate about the roles of and rewards granted to volunteers. There are substantial ethical concerns about the long-term sustainability of volunteering in the events industry. Many volunteers are students, who view their participation in events as work experience with a view to future employment. However, there is also the question of whether students should be expected to work for free as a standard part of their training while the event organisations profit from their efforts.

When setting payment levels, employers must consider the market rate for that type of employment. There are minimum-wage restrictions in the UK, the USA and Australia, as well as other considerations when setting pay levels. Other industry payment methods such as a bonus or commissions are less common. In many countries, it is routine to consult trade unions, although this is unusual in the UK events industry. There are also restrictions regarding the equal payment of workers, particularly based on gender. It is still reportedly legal and fairly frequent in the UK, the USA and Australia that female employees on average earn less than their male colleagues, often for the same work.

CASE STUDY 5.2

Events volunteer management

Since first addressing the topic of staffing events using volunteers in our first edition, there has been much more attention to the complexities associated with recruitment, training and management of a temporal and essentially external resource, compared to traditional notions of the day-to-day HRM functions of employees in static organisations.

Whilst this encouraging growth in developing methods to better manage an event volunteer workforce is encouraging, there remains a general need to reconsider the core view of why people volunteer for events, who they are, what they receive from the experience, and how they can be better prepared and utilised in relation to the delivery of satisfying event experiences.

As with much of events management in practice, there is a rather general categorisation of knowledge and terminology, resulting in an understanding that whilst the success of an event often depends directly on the large-scale access to a temporary and cost-effective human resource, and although a general application of generic human resource processes is applicable and often legally required by regulatory bodies, little else about events volunteering resembles the knowledge supplied in accordance with wider, generic industry human resource practices. This results in the opportunity for more academic and industry research and knowledge sharing in the field, by scholars and practitioners alike.

The motivations of volunteers to participate in events continue to be linked to their derived satisfactions, which can be found in the benefits they yield. Some are motivated by specific intentions to increase marketable work experiences, perhaps to 'break-into' future industry employment opportunities. Others use volunteering to gain personal satisfaction from helping others and to contribute to their own communities or interest groups. Some volunteers simply like to keep busy and perhaps even use temporary events work as an opportunity for an alternative form of tourism. The emotional component of these different motivations still lacks understanding and is worthy of future investigations.

What is certain is that technologies which promote the registration and bonding of volunteers are increasingly moving to the forefront of volunteer management. This may make the event itself less important than the communities that issue from the practice of volunteering processes.

This is an interesting area, and it will prove encouraging to see how future investigations continue to shape the way we hire, lead and further develop volunteering as a way of life, to the benefit of the events sector, our attendees and those who work in it.

Study tasks:

1 Reflect on your own experiences of volunteering. What did you gain from the experience? Would you say there were differences between the experience you initially signed up for and your final evaluation of it?
2 Think of an event that uses volunteers as part of its delivery. Consider how you could effectively research their experiences of volunteering. Which research methods would you apply? What are the complexities or challenges you could anticipate? How could you overcome these?
3 From the discussion above, list several areas of events volunteering that require more research. Take one of these and develop a research proposal.

Study activity

1 Using this case, and the industry voice section, discuss some of the challenges facing an organisation in managing event human resources.
2 Consider your up-to-date CV, or employment résumé. What changes could you make to the way you would present yourself to such a company to make yourself more employable?
3 Practice writing a cover letter to an organisation of your choice, introducing yourself as a potential applicant and describing your background as it benefits your potential employer.
4 Imagine you have been called for an interview. Write down some questions you are likely to be asked by the interviewer and your possible responses to them.

Industry voice

Dr Ingrid Kanuga

❝ Managing people in practice

I have been fortunate enough to be involved with a wide range of events, including mega-events, hallmark events, multi-national conferences, national award ceremonies, day-to-day conferences and banqueting and unique weddings. In this section I look back at my experiences and those which involved managing people in practice.

I started my career in events as part of the 'Disneyland Paris Millennium Celebration Crew' for the turn of the millennium in 1999/2000. Working at this mega-event I was exposed to the absolute importance of planning and managing every possible detail of such a unique event. Guests attending the celebrations were paying €1500 per person to access the park and could upgrade their packages with a five-course banquet dinner show and a New Year's breakfast in the morning. The event planning team took two years to plan every single detail, from the recruitment and training of the crew to risk management in case of security breaches or natural disasters. As it happens, the area was struck with a tornado just a few days before the actual event and the park had to be closed for the first time in its history. On the eve of 31 December 1999 every single part of the event went as smooth as planned. For me, the key to this success seemed to be its people, the method through which they had been recruited and the intense training they received. The crew I was part of were approached at Hotel Management Schools in the Netherlands. The thought behind this was that we were passionate about the industry, would know the basics of customer service and were able to speak multiple European languages. We received part of our theory in The Netherlands and were then transported to free housing at the edge of the resort. Here we received breakfast every day and we were given cards with credits to eat lunch and dinner in the various staff restaurants. Transportation to the training facilities and our place of work was part of the package. For two weeks we had intense training where we rehearsed every detail of the actual event as if we were actors in a show. In addition to our financial renumeration additional benefits included unlimited access to the park and four guest passes for our friends and family to visit before the actual event. After we completed our temporary job, each of us was given a certificate, a reference letter and various souvenirs.

I reflect on this event because I learned that when a company understands the importance of managing *people* as invaluable assets of their company, their actual guests or customers will receive high-quality and passionate service. In the events industry the detail and planning is immensely important but it is the people who deliver the vision and can make or break an event. Therefore HRM strategy needs to focus on developing a culture which values the human and social capital from the beginning to the end of the employee life cycle.

From employee to operational events manager

Investing in people and giving them a sense of *belonging* further helps an organisation with employee retention and succession planning through effective talent management. My experience in Disneyland Paris led to me actively seeking a career with the organisation. Towards the end of 2000 I joined Walt Disney World, in Florida. Again, I received extensive training before joining their operations and then extended this with their 'Disney Event Production' course at the Disney University. Applying the theory in practice daily allowed me to quickly progress my career into events management.

I joined the NEC-Group in Birmingham in the fall of 2002 as a junior events manager at their International Convention Centre. Although my job title was 'junior', the role was rather big! On a day-to-day basis I was involved with managing the conference and banqueting for around 300 delegates. This meant an operational team of around 20 staff. On the weekends I joined my more senior colleagues where we managed large events from medical conferences attended by up to 10,000 delegates to the BAFTA award ceremonies. During these events I would manage around 100 staff, most of them employed via recruitment agencies. As I became more experienced in managing people, I learned that besides being organised, it helps to know what motivates your staff and which other priorities they might have. Within a few months I managed to build a good relationship with the regular employees and understood their skills and strengths. I also knew their preferred hours of work because of other commitments, and I learned who was comfortable talking to clients and who preferred to just serve. Some staff were quick in setting up rooms and clearing, others were better at the actual customer service. Building a relationship of trust and mutual respect meant some small events could practically run themselves, allowing me time to plan for the following week. When *managing people in practice* it is important to utilise strengths. Every member will have a different skill set and although we can develop weaknesses they often enjoy using and strengthening their natural talents more. Understanding their commitments outside of work and using this knowledge when assigning shifts and events helped to ensure that absence was minimal.

It took me a little longer to learn how to manage the agency staff, or in today's events the staff on zero-hour contracts or gig employees. The employees varied from week to week and for many it was their first time working in our industry. As time progressed, I became better at planning initial event briefing sessions which also included handouts to the staff with details of the client, the layout of the venue and even steps of service. I would spend an hour before actual operation started briefing and training staff and where possible I would allocate permanent staff to groups of agency staff. In addition, I would always plan an extra 10% headcount, knowing that if a better opportunity came along the agency staff might not show up for their allocated shift.

In 2003 I was approached by the leadership team of the National Exhibition Centre to help with the account management of clients attending ITMA, the world largest textile exhibition. This hallmark event includes 1400 exhibitors from 140 countries. For six months I worked with international clients on planning their stands and catering needs for the event, before delivering it during the actual exhibition. This experience even further emphasised the need for effective communication between departments, clients, operational management and operational staff and it is most certainly one of the top skills of effective leaders.

My final role in operational events management was working for the Crown Plaza as their 'Guest Services Manager for Events and F&B'. This was a new property, and I was tasked with the recruitment and training of an entire events team, including supervisors and assistant managers. During the week, the team worked mostly with corporate clients having meetings at the hotel and making sure they were catered for with coffee breaks, refreshments in their meeting rooms and lunches. In the evening we would reset the rooms ready for the next day. Weekends were busy with weddings. These would start with the families arriving on the morning of the event, followed by their ceremony, sit-down meals and evening receptions which continued into the small hours of the night. Being responsible for the entire *employee life cycle* I learned that *managing people in practice* starts with sourcing and recruiting people who have the *right attitude* and fit within *the culture* of the team. A skills gap could be overcome with the right training and coaching. Developing a work ethic which included mutual respect, an understanding of commitments outside the workplace and motivational needs led to a team that could run the day-to-day events with little involvement of myself. This freed up my time to develop staff into new roles, meet our prospective wedding clients and work together with department heads to ensure all aspects of each event went smoothly: from initial sales conversations to checking-out of the hotel.

From operational manager to strategic HRM

My passion for *managing people* led to me completing my MA with a focus on HRM. After ten years in events, five of which were in operational management roles, I transitioned to a strategic, corporate HR role. Here I focused on learning and development for our 3000 employees and in particular our graduates. The lessons I learned from *managing people in practice* always influenced my HR decisions and still impact my work today.

5.11 Summary

This chapter has analysed the human resource challenges of managing events and it should be noted that there are significant differences between management of the human resources associated with events and the management of ordinary employees in other industries, due to the temporal project structure of the event organisation. Therefore, the process of event recruitment and selection also tends to differ significantly from that found in other businesses, and these differences are compounded as the scale and duration of the event being managed increase. Also, the complexities of managing event employees and volunteers relate closely to the pulsating nature of the organisation and therefore require constant review throughout the event cycle so that short-term changes can be made in response to the usual fluctuations in customer attendance and the various transitions through the stages of the event cycle. Through employee retention methods, employee learning and development can be facilitated in conjunction with the strategic requirements of the event and its organisers.

Further reading

Cuskelly, G., Hoye, R., *et al.* (2006) *Working with Volunteers in Sport: Theory and Practice*, London: Routledge. Focused on sporting events, this book gives a thorough introduction to volunteering in events, including useful references to the research in the field.

Schein, E. (2010) *Organizational Culture and Leadership*, San Francisco, CA: John Wiley & Sons. This book is a good overall introduction to this important topic.

Van der Wagen, L. (2007) *Human Resource Management for Events: Managing the Event Workforce*, Oxford: Elsevier. A thoughtful and practical overview of HR in events, this book has the added advantage of being thoroughly events-related.

Weblinks

A Voice for Radiotherapy: www.cancerresearchuk.org/support-us/campaign-for-us/our-campaigning-successes/a-voice-for-radiotherapy

Race for Life/Cowan Global: https://cowanglobal.wordpress.com/tag/race-for-life/

Volunteer – Support Our Events – Race for Life: http://raceforlife.cancerresearchuk.org/support-our-events/volunteer/index.html

References

Bitner, M. J. (1993) Managing the Evidence of Service, in E. E. Scheuing and W. F. Christopher (eds) *The Service Quality Handbook*: 358–370, New York: Amacom.

Bladen, C. (2009) Towards an Olympic Volunteering Legacy. Proceeds of the 2008 People, Place, Enterprise: The Olympic Legacy Conference, University of Greenwich.

Bladen, C. and Kennell, J. (2014) Educating the 21st Century Event Management Graduate: Pedagogy, Practice, Professionalism and Professionalization, *Event Management*, 18: 5–14.

Booms, B. and Bitner, J. (1981) Marketing Strategies and Organizational Structures for Service Firms, in J. Donnelly and W. George (eds) *Marketing of Services*, Chicago, IL: American Marketing Association.

Bowdin, G., Allen, J., O'Toole, W., Harris, R. and McDonnell, I. (2011) *Events Management* (4th edn), Oxford: Elsevier.

Boxall, P. and Purcell, J. (2008) *Strategy and Human Resource Management*, Basingstoke and New York: Palgrave Macmillan.

Cuskelly, G., Hoye, R. *et al.* (2006) *Working with Volunteers in Sport: Theory and Practice*, London: Routledge.

Festinger, L. (1957) *Theory of Cognitive Dissonance*. Available at: www.simplypsychology.org/cognitive-dissonance.html#leon [Accessed 7 July 2017].

Flashman, R. and Quick, S. (1985) Altruism Is Not Dead: A Specific Analysis of Volunteer Motivation. In L. Moore (ed.) *Motivating Volunteers*: 155–168, Vancouver: Vancouver Volunteer Centre.

Goldblatt, J. (2010) *Special Events*, John Wiley & Sons.

Gorge Group (1994) Getting Results in Network Organisations, presentation at the ASTD annual conference, Anaheim, USA.

Hackman, J. R. and Oldham, G. R. (1976) Motivation through Design of Work, *Organizational Behaviour and Human Performance*, 16: 250–279.

Kolb, D. A. (1984) *Experiential Learning Experience as a Source of Learning and Development*, Upper Saddle River, NJ: Prentice Hall.

Maslow, A. H. (1943) A Theory of Human Motivation, *Psychological Review*, *50* (4): 370–396.

Pfeffer, J. (1998) *The Human Equation*, Boston, MA: Harvard Business School Press.

Pilbeam, S. and Corbridge, M. (2010) *People Resourcing: HRM in Practice*, Upper Saddle River, NJ: Financial Times/Prentice Hall.

Stebbins, R. A. (1996) Volunteering: A Serious Leisure Perspective, *Nonprofit and Voluntary Sector Quarterly*, *25* (2): 211–224.

Toffler, A. (1990) *Powershift: Knowledge, Wealth, and Power at the Edge of the 21st Century*, New York: Bantam Books.

Torrington, D., Hall, L. and Taylor, S. (2009) *Human Resource Management* (7th edn), London: Pearson Education.

Tyson, S. and York, A. (2000) *Essentials of HRM* (4th edn), Oxford: Butterworth-Heinemann.

Van der Wagen, L. (2007) *Human Resource Management for Events: Managing the Event Workforce*, Oxford: Elsevier.

Walton, J. (1999) *Strategic Human Resource Development*, Harlow: Pearson Education.

Chapter 6

Event finance

Rob Wilson

Rob Wilson is Head of Department for Finance, Accounting and Business Systems in the Sheffield Business School at Sheffield Hallam University, UK. His subject specialisms are financial reporting, management accounting and economic decision-making in the sport and leisure industry, and his main research interests are in the financing of professional team sports and the economics of major events.

Contents

DOI: 10.4324/9781003102878-6

6.1 Aims

By the end of this chapter, students will be able to:

- appreciate why financial skills are an important part of the event manager's portfolio of skills
- articulate key financial terminology that is often applied to events
- understand the meaning of budgeting in operational, tactical and strategic events management contexts
- analyse budgeted against actual performance using recognised evaluation techniques
- understand sources of event funding and how to secure such funding
- monitor and evaluate an event's financial performance.

6.2 Introduction

This chapter examines the importance of event finance and places it in a context that should be easily understandable for any event manager to apply to their event, whether that event is a major undertaking like the Olympic Games or a local community fair or farmers' market. For all events, it is essential that the overall governance is underpinned by sound financial management so that the event runs successfully (from a financial viewpoint at least). Without needing to be a fully qualified accountant or having specific training in finance all event managers should be able to answer two fundamental questions. First, is the selling price higher than the cost? In other words, will the event bring in more money than it pays out? Or, is the event going to make a profit? If you are managing a small community not-for-profit event it is simple to modify this question to; is the event operating within the resources allocated to it? If the answer is 'no', then the event will struggle and could prove to be unsustainable.

The second question an events manager must answer is; can this event continue? In financial terms, this question relates to the event's ability to pay its creditors (people that it owes money to for goods and services). Many events will never take place due to an inability to meet these obligations because they have not considered cash flow and have run out of money to pay creditors before the event can generate revenue. Yet, being unable to meet these basic requirements is not uncommon and is the reason why you see businesses, organisations and events management companies going bankrupt. Event managers must ensure that they can pay their bills as they fall due and understand how to negotiate payment dates that fit in with income streams. Moreover, the sustainability of events is an increasingly important component of an event plan and you will need to demonstrate how you can generate the income to meet your expenses.

Before we start, we need to establish some ground rules; put simply, finance is not only about numbers, and you do not have to be a skilled mathematician to understand finance or manage money. Instead, you need to understand the guiding rules and principles that help to compile and structure a set of financial documents. As students or managers who work within the events industry, it is important that you appreciate the importance of financial management and responsibility and that you can communicate key financial information to both the internal and external stakeholders. The net result of these skills, coupled with those you have considered already, and will consider later, and elsewhere in this book, will enable you to set up, run and manage successful events.

A successful event cannot happen without sufficient financial support and, by definition, financial management. The most significant, and perhaps most routine, error in committing to an event is to do so without securing the necessary financing (or funding) at a very early stage. This will be a worry for any event manager from beginning to end and can ultimately mean the event is presented in a less than satisfactory way, which hinders success and event sustainability planning.

Many event managers shy away from managing money and financial performance because they are scared of the associated terminology. They will often focus on sexier components, such as marketing or volunteer training, rather than managing the basic functions of financial control. Financial viability, however, should be the key issue of any event planning process, and if the expenses far outweigh the income streams, then managers should not be afraid to cancel their event. In not doing so, they compromise the future of similar events, acquire a poor image for their organisations and reduce the ability for bidding groups to bring other events to the region.

Unfortunately, the events industry has lagged behind other business sectors from a financial management point of view. For the most part, event marketing, planning and strategy have dominated events management education which has led to a growing maturity in such areas. Financial management has often been overlooked, anecdotally because individuals claim to have a fear of numbers. There are still many event managers and graduates with events management degrees who struggle to understand even the basics of a budget or cash flow statement, let alone have the confidence to make informed judgements on the financial health of their event. However, every organisation – ranging from multimillion-pound operations through to small, local, voluntary sports events – needs to manage money and make routine financial decisions. Therefore, if organisations must do this, the chances are that successful managers will have to understand, communicate and use financial information too.

6.3 Financial terminology

Understanding the nature and application of finance is often a question of understanding the terminology that financial experts use. Demystifying this terminology is the first step in managing finance effectively since it will help you to understand what things mean and why they are important. Understand this and you will be able to apply it later in the chapter.

Essentially, there are two types of accounts: financial and management. Depending on the nature of a user's information needs (explored in more detail later in the chapter), the style of the accounts and financial documents may be quite different. From the section above, you should have noticed that financial information can look two ways. When looking backwards – into the past – it is normal to examine financial accounts, as these are prepared for external use and are based on historical information; they are also required by law. A set of financial accounts will, for example, illustrate the past financial position and financial performance of an organisation.

> **Financial accounting** is the term used to describe the system for recording historical financial transactions and presenting this information in summary form.

However, should a manager wish to be more proactive and examine future trends and issues, they will need to examine more forward-looking (future) accounting information. Such information will not be found in financial accounts, hence there are management accounts, that is, accounts that look forward and are based on providing information for managers to help with the planning, decision-making and control of organisations. Unlike financial accounts, management accounts are not a statutory requirement. It is important that managers understand the distinction between these two types of accounts since they dictate where they should look for information. Financial accounting and reporting are beyond the scope of this chapter because we are only examining tools that you can use to manage event finance. Consequently, we will focus on management accounting and how to plan, make decisions and control event finance.

> **Management accounting** is the term used to describe more forward-looking financial data for planning, decision-making and control purposes.

Event managers should appreciate that they will plan their operations, consider the implications of their decisions and control their organisation in such a way that they reach (in most cases) their organisation's objectives. In order to plan and make effective decisions, a manager will have to adopt the principles of good management accounting, for example budgeting, break-even analysis and cash flow forecasting – some of which will be explored towards the end of this chapter.

Before we continue, it is worth outlining more key terminology that you may encounter when moving through the following sections:

- Income statement or profit and loss account – a summary of financial performance and therefore actual income and expenditure over a period of time.
- Balance sheet – a snapshot of a company's financial position at a specific point in time.
- Cash flow – a forecast of funds coming in and out, presented over a period of time.
- Assets – those things of value that a company owns, such as buildings, equipment and vehicles.
- Debtor – an individual or organisation who owes the company money or service, such as someone to whom you have lent money.
- Liabilities – the opposite of assets, such as credit card debt.
- Creditor – an individual or organisation to which you owe money or service.
- Depreciation – the loss in value of assets over time, for example, a computer will be worth less after it has been used.

6.4 Financial planning and control

The concept behind financial management is not the simplistic idea that you need to manage profit, but, more importantly, how to monitor, evaluate and control income and expenditure for an event. It is vital for event managers to understand the changing values of the events industry and recognise that many events are provided to achieve social objectives, which operate at a loss, and which will normally require a government or local authority subsidy to operate. This does not mean, however, that proper financial planning and controls are not important. It is vital that event managers have an understanding of the costs of the products and services that they offer, in order to operate as effective business entities to generate profits, or ensure that taxpayers' money is not being wasted on frivolous plans or ideas.

Many events will rely on funding from national, regional or local government or quangos (such as Sport England or the Arts Council), sponsorship, or flexible credit terms from suppliers. However, using money from a third party is normally based on the simple assumption that the organisation's future returns will be sufficient to cover the borrowing or meet other objectives. Problems, however, often occur when organisations fail to meet their financial obligations. Consequently, an organisation's ability to pay its debts as they fall due usually means the difference between financial success and financial failure. If event managers are to make effective plans and decisions, they need to control their organisation's finances.

Exercising sound financial planning and control is of fundamental importance in running a successful event. A lack of knowledge regarding the cost of the event will almost certainly lead to failure. It is essential to plan, budget and monitor finances throughout the planning and execution of an event to avoid any implications with cost variation or changing economic conditions.

Before an event progresses too far into the planning process, it is essential to assess its financial viability. This will mean setting out a financial plan to balance the cost of running the event against any existing funds and prospective income. Several draft budgets may need to be compiled before producing the final version. Initially, the budget will be based on estimates, but it is important to confirm actual figures as soon as possible to keep the budget on track and to exercise something resembling financial responsibility (Wilson and Kitchen 2022).

If a decision is made to go ahead with an event, it will be a managerial one and therefore possibly subjective. However, such a decision can be strengthened by a thorough understanding of the finances involved and the ability of the event to meet its financial obligations. What is more, the decision that determines whether an event is financially viable will ensure that effort (and money) is not wasted. Earlier chapters stressed the importance of project management and event design and production, and these stages are vital for the operational success of an event but they will yield success only if they have sufficient financial resources available.

CASE STUDY 6.1

Delivering a stage of the Tour de France

Background

The Tour de France is an annual road cycling race held over 23 days, normally in July. Established in 1903 by a French newspaper, *L'Auto*, the Tour is the most well-known and prestigious of cycling's three 'Grand Tours'. The others being the Giro d'Italia, held in Italy, and the Vuelta a Espana, held in Spain. Typically covering 3,500 kilometres (2,200 miles), passing through various territories and iconic locations in France, the race is broken into day-long segments, called stages. Individual finishing times for each stage are totalled to determine the overall winner at the end of the race.

The course changes every year, but always finishes in Paris and, since 1975, along the Champs-Elysees. The start of the course is known as the Grand Départ which, since the 1950s, has taken place in a different town each year. Since the 1970s it has been common to award the Grand Départ to cities outside France as a way of increasing international interest in the competition and the sport. Since 2010, the Grand Départ has been held in places such as the United Kingdom, Germany and Belgium.

When the Grand Départ was awarded to the United Kingdom, the first two stages (stage 1 starting in Leeds and finishing in Harrogate; stage 2 starting in York and finishing in Sheffield) took place on Yorkshire roads, with stage 3 continuing between Cambridge and London. Over the three days an estimated 4.8 million people lined the route; 3.3 million of those in Yorkshire and the remaining 1.5 million in Cambridge, Essex and London.

Local planning

York City Council (the host of the start of stage 2) agreed the following objectives for the delivery of the event:

- To deliver a safe and enjoyable event in York, which enhanced the reputation of the city.
- To maximise the economic benefit of the opportunity in the short, medium and long term.
- To secure a long-lasting legacy across their communities, culture, cycling infrastructure and health.

Welcoming the Tour de France to York is understood to have captured the imagination of the city. The route was designed to showcase the best landmarks and the racecourse provided a perfect start location. The council provided spectator hubs in Rowntree Park, the Designer Outlet and Monks Cross. The city itself was adorned with yellow bikes (to depict the leader's jersey), banners and bunting.

Event delivery

Ensuring a safe and enjoyable event in York, as well as one that enhanced the reputation of the city, was expected to be complex. The project in York was managed by a core project team of existing council staff, and specialist input was utilised when required. The team had to work closely with the Tour de France Hub Ltd (the delivery organisation set up to coordinate the three stages), Welcome to Yorkshire and UK Sport, because of the need to work across geographical boundaries to ensure the event felt like the same event over three days. Other additional staff and teams were engaged in preparation, business continuity and volunteering with about 1,000 Tour Makers deployed across the city.

Proposals in the build-up to the Grand Départ weekend included the 100-day festival, Grand Soirée, Grand Départ Concert, Bike Stories, city centre street entertainers and big screens, with a range of spectator hubs with family-friendly activities on the day of the event. Planning for the weekend was modelled on the basis of at least 250,000 visitors coming to the city early, with 28,000 heading for the race start at the racecourse and a detailed traffic management programme was put into place months before the event. These plans were tested before that weekend.

To secure a long-lasting legacy, the council also engaged community groups, schools and local businesses through smaller cycling events, children's races and other themed activities, with more than 10,000 people visiting the J'Adore Bishy Rue Street Party on 6 July, which has subsequently been recognised as a national 'Best Street' and won the Local Community Pride award. Additionally, 400 local families were invited to a community event at the Tour de Tang Hall.

For the first time ever the Grand Départ was preceded by a 100-day festival attracting 800,000 people to nearly 1,500 performances across the region. York had highlights of the Yorkshire Festival, including the Bike Story, What's Yours? and the Tour de Brass festival which celebrated Yorkshire's rich history of brass bands. Other examples include:

- Plant the city yellow – 3,000 packets of seeds were distributed across the city to residents, businesses and organisations.
- Dress to impress city walls community banners project – 60 banners representing 50 organisations and 500 participants.
- Bike Story in schools – a theatre education programme that engaged 23 schools and more than 3,000 pupils.
- Road through York – large-scale, 300 square metre community collage, created by more than 200 participants.

A cycling legacy was also high on the agenda with the launch of a Cycle Yorkshire website, Twitter feed, educational pack for teachers and a Cycle Yorkshire ride route being created.

However, the delivery of these activities, and the stage start itself, needed to be paid for, and it is certainly not a straightforward task trying to find out the real costs behind the Tour since the organisations involved pay different amounts.

Costs and financials

The Tour is run by Amuary Sport Organisation (ASO), a commercial operation which charges a staging fee to the towns and cities wanting to host a start or finish stage. The fee varies according to how big the stage is, making the start more or less expensive. York City Council paid £500,000 to host the start of stage 2, with other operating costs and all the activities on top of that. Sheffield, the host of the finish for stage 2, paid £200,000.

In total, according to Tour de France Hub Ltd, local councils on stages 1 and 2 paid £10.6 million to host and deliver the event, with £3.5 million of that being tied up in bid costs. Putting on the Grand Départ stage 1 cost £3.2 million and stage 2 cost £3.9 million. It is possible to break these figures down by delivery partner, however, and establish the direct costs to the City of York.

The York City Council Cabinet set a budget for the Tour de France of £1.664 million to cover the cost of the event, funded from a variety of existing council budgets. When compared against actual delivery costs of £1.815 million the event can be seen to have exceeded its budget. Whether this is good value or not really depends on the success of the non-financial measures and objectives stated by the council. A summary of the full event budget can be found in Table 6.1 (the terminology is explained later in the chapter).

Table 6.1 Stage 2 start, budget

Budget heading	Budget	Actual	Variance
	£'000	£'000	£'000
Event costs	564	568	4
Highways	200	200	0
Project management	221	222	1
Marketing and communications	100	67	−33
Legacy	99	25	−74
Regional contributions	480	481	1
Events and festivals	0	252	252
Total expenditure	1,664	1,815	151
EIF	500	500	0
DIF	200	200	0
Contingency	473	473	0
Capital contingency	200	200	0
TdF grant	291	204	−87
LCR TdF rebate	0	189	189
Total funding	1,664	1,766	102
Balance	0	−49	−49

This demonstrates that the event was broadly managed within budget once the unearned income (funding) is added. The largest item of unplanned expenditure was the additional cost relating to the events and festivals programme, which was not included in the original budget. This includes the cost of a music concert at Huntingdon Stadium (£187,000), the net cost of camping (£33,000) and the cost to support community events (£23,000). This adds up to a total deficit of £49,000 for the event.

6.5 Users of event finance information

Financial information is useful to a wide variety of stakeholders. These will often span several sectors and each will have a slightly different need for the information. For example, the Board of Directors of Intercontinental Hotels Group PLC will want to see how much profit they have made from trading activities and how each arm of the business is performing so that they can make future investment decisions and consider returns to shareholders. A City Council official will want to know how much subsidy they must provide in order to keep all of their leisure services running, so that their council taxpayers get value for money. The Chairperson of the local swimming and water polo club will want to ensure that enough money is being received through subscriptions and funding to cover their running costs.

Generally, information relating to the finance of an organisation is of interest to its owners, managers, trade contacts (for example, suppliers), providers of finance (such as banks and funding bodies), employees and customers. All these groups of people need to be sure that the organisation is strong, can pay its bills, make a profit if it is commercial, and remain in business. An indicative list of users and their areas of interest is illustrated in Table 6.2.

6.6 Budgeting and events

Budgeting is a subject area that takes its roots from the field of management accounting since it helps management to plan, make decisions and exercise control. It can be shown to be part of the overall planning process for a business, by defining it as 'the overall plan of a business expressed in financial terms'. These plans might involve trying to achieve a predetermined level of financial performance, such as a set profit over the year, or having sufficient cash resources

> ### Table 6.2 Users of financial information and their information needs

User groups	Areas of interest
Event managers	Managers require financial information so that they can make present and future plans for the event and see how effective their decisions have been.
Trade contacts (e.g. suppliers)	Suppliers and other trade contacts need to know if they are going to be paid on time by the event organiser.
Providers of private finance (e.g. banks etc.)	Banks and other lenders of finance need to ensure that any loans and interest payments are going to be made on time, both before they lend money and during the repayment period.
Providers of public finance (e.g. government agencies, quangos etc.)	Funding bodies will want to ensure that their funds are being used for the appropriate purpose and that those funds are helping to meet their performance objectives.
Her Majesty's Revenue & Customs (UK), Internal Revenue Service (USA), the Australian Taxation Office etc.	The tax authorities require information about the profits/surplus of the event so that they can work out how much tax the organisation owes. They also need details for VAT and employees' income tax.
Employees/volunteers	Organisations' employees and volunteers often wish to know whether their jobs are safe and that they are going to be paid on time or that the event is likely to run.
Spectators	It is common for spectators to know if goods/services purchased are going to be delivered/provided.

to be able to replace the equipment in a gym. Organisational business planning can be summarised as an analysis of four key questions:

1 Where are we now?
2 How did we get here?
3 Where are we going?
4 How are we going to get there?

To illustrate the link between general business planning and budgeting, the question 'Where are we now?' can be modified to 'Where are we now in *financial* terms?' Similarly, the question 'Where are we going?' can be modified to 'Where are we going in *financial* terms?' To diagnose where a business *is* in financial terms requires the ability to be able to 'read' an income statement (or profit and loss account), a balance sheet and a cash flow statement. It is difficult to predict where a business is going (as it is to predict the future), but techniques such as compiling an expected income statement (profit and loss account), balance sheet and cash flow can help to focus attention on the business essentials. Furthermore, the process of planning ahead using budgets can help to test whether what you wish to achieve and the accompanying financial consequences are compatible or 'internally consistent'. The concept of internal consistency is covered in the next section, but this section closes by clarifying that the meaning of budgeting is the plan of a business expressed in *financial* terms.

6.7 Budgeting as a logically sequenced planning process

A key point about budgeting is that it is an ongoing process rather than a time-limited, one-off event. The mechanics of drawing up the numbers involved in a budget are only a small part of the overall budgeting process. By bearing in mind that budgeting is designed to help an organisation with planning, decision-making and control, it is possible to appreciate that budgeting is a continuous part of business life. This point can be reinforced by viewing budgeting as steps in a logically sequenced planning process, as shown in Figure 6.1.

Figure 6.1 can be reinforced by a commentary on each of the nine stages of budgeting.

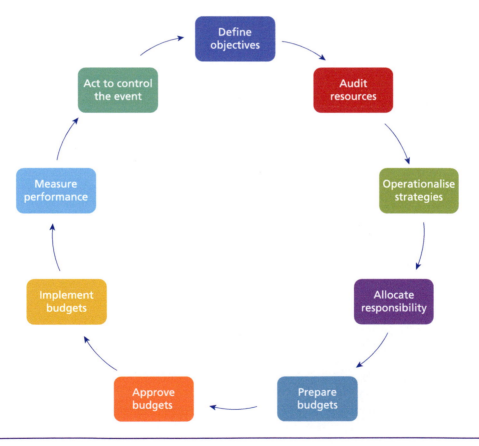

Figure 6.1 The budgeting process

6.7.1 Define your business objectives

The first question to ask when involved with any financial business planning is 'In monetary terms, what are we trying to achieve?' This question should provide a clue that most sane business people would not answer, 'Making a loss'. Losses are made in business but it is inconceivable to imagine that managers set out deliberately to make losses. Losses usually occur when there is a mismatch between what was planned and what actually happened. Organisational objectives vary according to the nature of the business. A community sports club which exists for the benefit of the members may desire nothing more than to break even or to make a small surplus to maintain its existing facilities. A more complex organisation, such as a professional football team, needs to balance the requirements of producing a successful team on the pitch (utility maximisation) with the requirements of being a commercial franchise (profit maximisation). Whatever the objectives of an organisation, they need to have certain qualities that enable them to be measured. These qualities are contained within the MASTER mnemonic.

- **M**easurable – e.g. a profit of £3 million in the financial year, or simply to break even.
- **A**chievable – the organisation must have the capability to attain its objectives; capability means staff, other resources and competitive advantage.
- **S**pecific – objectives must be specific, e.g. £3 million profit, not 'to do well this year'.
- **T**ime limited – objectives must have a stated date for being achieved.
- **E**nds related – objectives must relate to achieving outputs (ends) rather than describing means (how).
- **R**anked – ideally, objectives should be ranked in priority order.

An example of an objective meeting the MASTER mnemonic might be:

> Our first priority is to achieve a net profit of £3 million in the financial year 1 April 20XX to 31 March 20YY. This target is attainable as the organisation has increased its capacity and the market is expanding.

6.7.2 Audit resources

The audit of resources is a 'reality check' on the objectives. Its purpose is to ensure that the objectives and the resources required to achieve them are internally consistent. As an example, Sheffield United need around 15,000 spectators per home match to break even. With a stadium capacity of nearly 31,000, 15,000 people can be accommodated at a home match as long as they can be attracted to the match in the first place.

Where there is a discrepancy between the objectives and the resources available to achieve them, two courses of action are possible. First, the objectives can be changed so that they are compatible with the resources. Second, the gap between the resources available and the resources required can form the basis for prioritising capital investment, such as increasing the capacity of a stadium, or identifying training and development needs to ensure that staff have the skills to deliver what is required of them.

6.7.3 Operationalise strategies

Having defined what you want to achieve and confirmed that you have the resources to deliver the objectives, the budgeting process evolves to consider the day-to-day tactics to be used to meet the objectives. In small-scale events these might include the marketing plans, funding requirements, customer care protocols and opening hours. If organisational objectives can be regarded as *what* we wish to achieve, then operational strategies can be regarded as *how* we plan to achieve the objectives. Thus, a football club aiming for an average match-day turnover of £300,000 might set out to achieve it via operational strategies for spectators, corporate hospitality customers, programme sales, half-time draw tickets, catering, and beverage sales, merchandising sales and car parking.

6.7.4 Allocate responsibility

Successful achievement of objectives does not happen by chance, nor as a result of a mechanical exercise. Events management is primarily a service industry and the most important people in determining the extent to which objectives are met are an organisation's staff. For people to see where their contributions fit into an organisation's overall plan, they need to have agreed responsibility for particular areas of work. Agreed responsibility is particularly important in situations where staff can be rewarded, or indeed penalised, based on their performance. Remember that this could be particularly difficult when managing volunteers. For example, a volunteer responsible for health and safety could be assessed based on the event running smoothly without incident. If it is known and clearly stated who is going to do what and by when, then there is the basis for a meaningful comparison of actual performance with planned or expected performance.

6.7.5 Preparation of budgets

It is worth noting that the actual preparation of budgets does not occur until the mid-point of the budgeting process. This is important because it underlines that budgeting is not an isolated process and is integral to overall business planning. When preparing a budget there are two important considerations: namely *how much* income or expenditure, and *when* will the income or expenditure occur? To illustrate the point, if a major festival is expecting 52,000 admissions at an average price of £25, then the answer to 'How much income will be generated?' is £1,300,000. However, it is unlikely that a festival will average 13,000 admissions per day for four days. There will be peak times, such as during the weekend, and off-peak times, such as on a Thursday when people are at work. Thus, in order to make sure that the appropriate level of resource (for example, staff) is in the right place at the right time, it will be necessary to plan the predicted level of activity on a day-by-day basis. Doing such an exercise will enable event managers to plan for situations where expenditure is greater than income and there is insufficient cash to meet the shortfall. Having identified situations requiring management attention, strategies can be put in place to deal with them, such as negotiating an overdraft facility at the bank, rescheduling expenditure on capital items, or simply arranging late payment to creditors. The important point to note is that the process of budgeting identifies potential problems in advance, so that pre-emptive action can be taken.

It is unlikely that at the first time of asking the figures produced in the preparation of budgets will deliver the outcomes required. Therefore, managers may be asked to revise their budgets in such a way that the desired outcome is achieved. In practice, there are five ways in which a budget can be revised:

1 Increase revenue and keep costs constant. This could be achieved by increasing prices, increasing throughput or a combination of the two methods. The key assumption here is that any increase in price will not be offset by a reduction in demand.

2 Decrease expenditure and keep income constant. This could be achieved by making savings on non-essential expenditure or reducing the quality of the service on offer (for example, fewer staff on duty).

3 Increase income *and* decrease costs, as 1 and 2 above are not necessarily mutually exclusive.

4 Alter the financial outcome required. It may be the case it is not possible to bring the required outcomes and the budget into line by using 1, 2 and 3. Therefore, rather than alter income and expenditure, management may decide to alter the financial outcome required. This approach can work both positively and negatively. If staff provide managers with a budget that exceeds the required bottom line and the assumptions underpinning the budget are correct, then it would make sense to increase the overall budget target accordingly. A much more likely scenario is that the targeted outcome cannot be met by revisions to income and expenditure, so managers decide to settle for a reduced financial outcome; for example, an annual profit of £2.9 million rather than £3 million.

5 Change the overall business objectives. It may well be the case that it is impossible to arrive at an acceptable solution to a budget using steps 1–4. Under these conditions it may be that the required outcomes and the organisation's capabilities are not compatible. The only remaining alternative is to change the organisation's objectives. As an example, private contractors managing local authority events are often required to meet social as well as financial objectives. Occasionally, pursuit of these differing aims may be mutually incompatible, in the sense that programming activities for priority groups at certain times prevents revenue maximisation. Every use of resources has an opportunity cost; that is, the price of the best alternative foregone. Thus, in order to make the budget balance, it may be that some priorities which are no doubt desirable and equitable have to be sacrificed to the cause of wider business interests. For this reason, it is important that where possible objectives are ranked (see 'R' in the MASTER mnemonic in section 6.7.1).

The significance of preparing a budget, comparing it with business objectives and taking corrective action where appropriate indicates the importance of achieving internal consistency. Using the budgeting model described thus far ensures that what an organisation wishes to achieve in overall terms and the financial consequences of doing so are consistent. If potential problems can be identified at the planning (input) stage, pre-emptive action can be taken by drawing up plans to deal with adverse circumstances. Clearly, this approach has a greater chance of success and is more desirable than trying to deal with situations reactively as they materialise, without warning. The process of modelling the financial consequences of various scenarios until an acceptable outcome is achieved is known as an 'iterative' approach, or in less scientific terms 'trial and error'.

6.7.6 Approval of budgets

Once an acceptable match has been achieved between an organisation's business objectives and the financial consequences of those objectives, then a line needs to be drawn under the preparation of budgets stage. The point at which this line is drawn is at the approval of budgets stage, which effectively puts an end to the various iterations of the budget and leads to the formal adoption of the budget the organisation wishes to pursue. It is recognised good practice for the approval of a budget to be formalised in the minutes of a board or committee meeting. Furthermore, budgets should be approved in advance of the financial period to which they relate. The wider significance of a budget being approved formally is that those who have compiled it and those whose performance will in part be judged by it know exactly what their responsibilities are. This, in turn, has two benefits. First, if you know what is expected of you, then evaluation of performance can be objective rather than subjective. Second, expectation generates accountability, which in turn gives managers the focus to concentrate on those things that are important in terms of meeting the organisation's objectives.

6.7.7 Implementation of budgets

As a logical consequence of a budget being approved, it can be implemented with effect from the date to which it applies. For example, if an organisation's financial year operates from 1 April to 31 March, then it would be a reasonable expectation for the budget to be approved by the committee or board at least a month before the new financial year started. A less than ideal situation would be an organisation entering a financial period without an approved budget, which would be the managerial equivalent of a boat sailing without a rudder. However, for one-off events it may be necessary to write up and implement budgets outside normal financial periods so that they reflect the demands of the event itself.

6.7.8 Measurement of performance

To reinforce the notion of budgeting being integral to overall business planning, it is vital to realise that the budgeting process does not end once the preparation and implementation phases are over. When the budget is operational, it is essential that periodically (at least monthly, or weekly in some cases), a check is made between how the organisation is performing compared with how it planned to perform. One of the greatest motivators in life is feedback, and the same is true in budgeting. Management accountants use the mnemonic CARROT as a way of categorising the features of good-quality information for feedback purposes. Each component of CARROT is explained below:

- Concise – information fed back to managers needs to be to the point.
- Accurate – feedback is used for planning, decision-making and control purposes, so it follows that feedback should be error free.
- Reliable – similar to 'accurate', the same results of an actual versus budget comparison should be obtained if different people carried out the analysis; that is, the source information is robust.
- Relevant – different levels of management require different levels of information; therefore, feedback should be presented in terms that are relevant to the intended recipient.
- Objective – feedback should be concerned with verifiable factual evidence and not with individual interpretation of findings.
- Timely – there is a trade-off between timeliness and accuracy, but feedback should be received in sufficient time for it to be of value in terms of planning, decision-making and control purposes.

Measurement of performance is not an end in itself and is only valuable as an exercise if it is used to add value to the process of management in an organisation.

6.7.9 Taking action to control the event

If we accept that rational decisions require information that meets the requirements of the CARROT mnemonic, the final stage of the budgeting process is to use the information to inform the direction of the organisation. It is highly unlikely that there will be a perfect match between budget and actual comparisons, so the first decision to make is whether overall vari-ance is within a tolerable range. If variances are tolerable, then significant changes in policy will be unlikely. By contrast, if variances are so significant that the organisation is 'out of control' (in financial terms), then proactive management action may be needed. On a positive note, if performance is considerably ahead of target, it may be prudent to revise targets upwards. If, however, actual versus budget comparisons reveal a significant shortfall in performance, then corrective action may be needed. Such action might include extra marketing to increase sales, reducing prices to stimulate sales, improving the quality of sales to boost repeat business or, more predictably, cutting costs to try to maintain profit margins.

In concluding this section, it is worth making three points related to the assertion that budg-eting is a logically sequenced planning process.

Budgeting is a process designed to help managers make sensible decisions about running their organisations. It helps to inform decisions, but clearly budgeting is not in itself a decision-making process. Compiling a budget is an iterative process. It is unlikely that the first draft of a budget will produce an acceptable result. Various scenarios will be modelled, and differing assumptions will be tested until an acceptable solution is found. Figure 6.1 is a simple model of an ideal process; in practice, the numerous iterations will result in a more complicated picture. However, the basic point is that each step of the model is a reality check on the previous step, which is designed to ensure that an organisation's overall plans and the financial consequences of those plans are internally consistent.

Although Figure 6.1 implies a step-by-step approach to compiling a budget, some steps are seamless. For example, defining your objectives (step 1), conducting an audit of resources (step 2) and devising operational strategies (step 3) are likely to be interrelated and to occur simultaneously.

6.8 Common methods of budgeting

In this section, 'methods of budgeting' refers to types of budgeting processes and behavioural aspects of budgeting. In terms of budgeting processes, there are two common ways in which budgets tend to be compiled. The most frequently used budgeting process is 'continuation' budgeting (or business as usual), and the other, somewhat rarer, process is 'zero-based budget-ing' (ZBB). Continuation budgeting refers to situations whereby the business objectives of an organisation do not change significantly from one financial period to the next. Under these circumstances, it makes perfect sense to continue with essentially the same business objectives and hence the same approach to budgeting. An example of a continuation budget might be a voluntary swimming club's open meet whose main aim is to break even and to provide a service to the members. These types of budgets will be rarely used for one-off events but may be considered for events that occur as part of an annual calendar of activity. If the club's basic operations lead to a situation whereby the selling price is higher than the cost, then, apart from increasing spectator tickets and secondary spending prices to keep up with inflation, there is no point in wasting time and resources on a more complicated approach to the event's finances.

Continuation budgeting is also referred to as 'incremental' or 'decremental' budgeting. Incremental budgeting refers to a situation whereby an organisation increases its income and expenditure, usually by the rate of inflation, in order to pursue its existing policies. Decremental budgeting refers to a situation whereby an organisation agrees either a standstill level of fund-ing (a cut in real terms) or an absolute decrease in funding. When faced with a decremental budget, managers must deal with the problem of deciding whether to pursue existing policies with fewer resources; to reduce funding to all policies by the same relative amount ('the equal

Table 6.3 Open swimming meet continuation budget

Income	This year	Inflation	Next year
Spectator tickets	1,450	3%	1,494
Other ticket sales	250	3%	258
Sponsorship	1,700	3%	1,751
Catering	220	3%	227
Merchandising	130	3%	134
Total income	3,750	3%	3,864
Expenditure			
Volunteer kit	700	3%	721
Pool hire	2,500	3%	2,575
Marketing activities	136	3%	140
Administration	342	3%	352
Total expenditure	3,678	3%	3,788
Profit/(Loss)	72	3%	76

misery' approach); or to cut funding to some activities in order to preserve the more highly ranked priorities (see R in the MASTER mnemonic). An example of a simple continuation budget for a swimming club's open meet is shown in Table 6.3.

The basic assumptions in Table 6.3 are that the club will pursue the same policies from one year to the next and will increase income and expenditure by the rate of inflation (in this case 3%). Thus, all that has happened to the numbers in the budget is that they have increased by 3%. There are some advantages and disadvantages to using continuation budgeting, which are outlined below.

6.8.1 Advantages of continuation budgeting

- Continuation budgeting is intuitively simple and easy to understand.
- It is an effective use of resources if business objectives, infrastructure and strategies have remained unchanged.
- It is quick and easy to update figures and budget templates that are readily to hand.
- It requires less staff resources and therefore costs less than zero-based budgeting.

6.8.2 Disadvantages of continuation budgeting

- The overall rate of inflation within a country does not necessarily equal the rate of inflation within a particular industry; therefore, the use of the headline inflation figure to increase budgets is somewhat crude.

- Continuation budgeting does not encourage growth in real terms. In Table 6.3, the net position is that the business stands still. Businesses need to grow in real terms to remain competitive and to have the resources to maintain their operating infrastructure.
- Changes may occur within the marketplace that demand a response, such as the application of internet technology and e-marketing. By not taking advantage of business opportunities as they present themselves, standing still may be going backwards, relative to your competitors.
- There is the danger that if income and expenditure budgets are not occasionally challenged, then targets are 'soft' rather than a fair test of an organisation's capabilities. Managers can allow for 'slack' (unnecessary expenditure) in budgets, which can be 'rewarded' when budgets for the next year are confirmed without detailed scrutiny.

Study activity

What are the benefits and drawbacks of using a continuation budget for an annual music festival (such as the Glastonbury Festival)?

6.8.3 Budget, cash budget, continuation budgeting, variance and zero-based budgeting

- Budget – the business or overall plan of an organisation expressed in financial terms.
- Cash budget – an analysis of how the cash available to an organisation is expected to change over a given period.
- Continuation budgeting – budgets compiled based on no change in policies or priorities: business as usual.
- Variance – the difference between actual performance and planned performance.
- Zero-based budgeting – a method of budgeting that starts with the priorities of an organisation and allocates resources to those priorities according to their order of importance.

Although continuation budgeting is by far the most used budgeting technique in all industries (not just events), if an organisation is facing a fundamental change to its operating circumstances or if you are planning a one-off or new event, a more analytical approach may be needed. Rather than starting with last year's budget (or one that you have found elsewhere) and updating it, the zero-based budget starts with a blank piece of paper and challenges every item of income and expenditure. An example of zero-based budgeting questions might be:

1 What is the purpose of this expenditure?
2 On what exactly will this expenditure be made?
3 What are the quantifiable benefits of this expenditure?
4 What are the alternatives to this proposed expenditure?
5 What would be the outcome of cutting this expenditure completely?

For funds to be allocated to a given item of expenditure, a robust defence would have to be made for the expenditure through these five questions. If some expenditure was not defendable, it might be cut and reallocated to more deserving areas of an organisation's activities. As an example, consider the case of the large 'Grand Depart' festival we considered earlier. As part of its agreement with volunteers, it runs its own laundry to wash and iron volunteers' kit. The laundry will make use of staff, space, equipment, energy and consumables – all of which costs money. Furthermore, in the long run, equipment will need to be replaced and service contracts will have to be in place in case machinery breaks down. If commercial laundry facilities were available locally, which could match the quality of service provided in-house at a cheaper price, not only would the club save money, but it could also use the released staff, space and other resources on more important business objectives. Alternatively, it may be even more cost-effective simply to buy additional kit and benefit from discounted prices. Clearly, using the zero-based approach would be a more rigorous way of questioning existing business practices than simply accepting that the club has always provided an in-house laundry and will continue to do so.

The purpose of zero-based budgeting is the allocation of resources in a systematic manner which is consistent with an organisation's wider business objectives. It makes an implicit assumption that people within an organisation act rationally and prioritise business objectives rather than personal agendas. Sometimes this can be an ambitious assumption. Compared with continuation budgeting, zero-based budgeting is resource-intensive and therefore can be wasteful if there has been no significant change in business objectives and operating procedures. Consequently, it is dangerous to make sweeping generalisations about one budgeting process being better than another. As in many instances of using applied management techniques, the best methods to use are the ones most appropriate to the circumstances faced by an organisation. If a business is stable with no major changes on the horizon, continuation budgeting might be the best method to use. By contrast, if a business requires a major strategic overhaul or if you are planning a new or larger event, zero-based budgeting might be the best method to use. Like many things in life, compromise can help to keep most of the people happy for most of the time. Thus, a business could use continuation budgeting most of the time, but once every three or five years a zero-based approach could be used to challenge the status quo and reallocate resources to where they are most needed.

Study activity

What are the benefits and drawbacks of using a zero-based budget for an annual music festival?

In addition to being familiar with methods of budgeting, such as continuation or zero-based approaches, it is important to realise the human dimension of budgeting. Events management is a people business and ultimately the extent to which business objectives are realised depends on the extent of staff motivation towards meeting targets. One of the great de-motivators in life is having targets imposed on you from above (top-down) without consultation. Equally, for management, there is nothing more depressing than letting staff set their own budgets and finding out that the so-called 'bottom-up' budgets do not deliver the organisation's overall business objectives. The compromise approach is for a participatory budgeting style whereby all staff whose performance will in part be judged by meeting the budget have some influence in the compilation of the figures by which they will be judged. There are no hard and fast rules about when to use 'top-down', 'bottom-up' or 'participatory' methods. Good managers need to have a broad range of skills and techniques. Furthermore, these skills and techniques should be used in a context-sensitive manner, contingent upon the circumstances of the business and its operating environment.

6.9 Applying budgeting to worked examples

Event organisers should report a summary of their financial transactions in two, or sometimes three, standard formats:

- The income statement (previously called the profit and loss account, or income and expend-iture statement in the case of non-profit organisations).
- The balance sheet (if the event is running through an established company).
- The cash flow statement.

The income statement is a measure of an organisation's financial performance; the balance sheet is a measure of financial position; and the cash flow statement illustrates how the cash available to an organisation has changed over a given period. In financial terms, the answers to the questions 'Where are we now?' and 'Where are we going?' can be seen by constructing an income statement, balance sheet and cash flow statement to show the change between the start point and the end point. In this section, examples of the income statement and cash flow statement are modelled, and issues relating to them are discussed. (Should you wish to read about the balance sheet, you should follow up some of the additional activities at the end of this chapter.)

6.9.1 The income statement

Table 6.4 repeats the first two columns from Table 6.3 and shows how a swimming club might produce a summary of its income statement for its event. The key message emerging from Table 6.4 is that the club is planning to make a surplus (profit) of £72 during the year (or event).

The problem with Table 6.4 is that a year is a long time, and it is unlikely that income and expenditure will occur at the same rate throughout the year. Indeed, as this statement reflects the event, it is likely that it reflects only the final position, and the budget does not show when profits or losses will occur. Many events are seasonal and will have peaks and troughs in terms of their level of activity. This, in turn, has implications for other areas of management, such as staff scheduling and cash flow management. If the data in Table 6.4 were to be allocated over 12 months based on when such income and expenditure were predicted to occur, the monthly budget would appear like the example shown in Table 6.5. Remember that this is a relatively small swimming event, and you may well have to include much more data – the principles are the same though.

Two important points emerge from Table 6.5. First, simply by looking at the profit or loss per month, the events' position in the calendar is a factor in the events' financial fortunes. Income is received from sponsors in February and again during the event in April in the form of spectator and other ticket sales, while expenditure exceeds income in October, November

> **Table 6.4** An income statement

Income	This year
Spectator tickets	1,450
Other ticket sales	250
Sponsorship	1,700
Catering	220
Merchandising	130
Total income	3,750
Expenditure	
Volunteer kit	700
Pool hire	2,500
Marketing activities	136
Administration	342
Total expenditure	3,678
Profit/(Loss)	72

and December and again in March and May. This negative cash position must be managed. Second, a simple table of figures is not particularly helpful to somebody reading the budget. It would be much more helpful if the numbers were explained by a series of notes such as the examples given below.

- Income: Spectator ticket sales will occur in April, and we expect 580 spectators to purchase tickets at an average price of £2.50 (£1,450). (Last year, 500 sales @ £2.50 = £1,250.)
- Expenditure: Pool hire costs are based on a discounted rate and are paid in May, after the event has taken place. Costs are £2,500. (Last year, pool hire was £3,700.)

In practice, it would be expected that all items of income and expenditure would be qualified by a written explanation. By providing a brief written commentary to the key figures and assumptions that underpin the budget, it is possible for those people who look at it to have a much clearer idea of the organisation's plans. If the club planned to make a profit of £72 (financial performance), it follows that the club's overall financial position would increase by £72.

For most sports managers, budgeting tends to start and end with a budgeted income statement, sub-analysed on a monthly basis (as shown in Table 6.5). This is a perfectly acceptable level of skill for most events managers. However, for those with ambitions to have full responsibility for all aspects of an organisation's financial performance, skills are also needed to be able to produce and act upon budgeted income statements (balance sheets) and cash flow statements.

This review of budgeting concludes with an example of measuring actual performance against budget.

Table 6.5 Swimming meet budget sub-analysed by month

Income	Aug	Sept	Oct	Nov	Dec	Jan	Feb	March	April	May	June	July	Total
Spectator tickets	0	0	0	0	0	0	0	0	1450	0	0	0	1450
Other ticket sales	0	0	0	0	0	0	0	0	250	0	0	0	250
Sponsorship	0	0	0	0	0	0	1700	0	0	0	0	0	1700
Catering	0	0	0	0	0	0	0	0	220	0	0	0	220
Merchandising	0	0	0	0	0	0	0	0	130	0	0	0	130
Total income	0	0	0	0	0	0	1700	0	2050	0	0	0	3750
Expenditure													
Volunteer kit	0	0	0	0	0	0	0	700	0	0	0	0	700
Pool hire	0	0	0	0	0	0	0	0	0	2500	0	0	2500
Marketing activities	0	0	0	136	0	0	0	0	0	0	0	0	136
Administration	0	0	100	100	42	0	0	100	0	0	0	0	342
Total expenditure	0	0	100	236	42	0	0	800	0	2500	0	0	3678
Profit/(Loss)	0	0	–100	–236	–42	–378	1700	–800	2050	–2500	0	0	72
Cumulative	0	0	–100	–336	–378	–378	1322	522	2572	72	72	72	72

6.10 Comparing actual and budgeted performance

The ultimate purpose of budgeting is to assist managers in the planning, decision-making and control of a business. To achieve this aim, periodic comparison of actual performance with planned or budgeted performance is required. Table 6.6 shows how such a comparison might be presented to the managers of an organisation.

The columns in Table 6.6 are explained below:

- 'Actual' income and expenditure refers to entries made to an organisation's accounting system which are supportable by documentary evidence, such as invoices, receipts, staff time sheets and so on. 'Actual' figures are drawn from the financial accounting systems and can be supported by an audit trail of evidence.
- 'Incurred' (or 'committed') expenditure refers to expenditure which relates to the financial period in question that we know has been made but has not yet been billed for. This sort of data can be picked up from such documentation as purchase order forms. In order to produce timely budget reports, it is sometimes not possible to wait until all the paperwork relating to expenditure in a period has been received. Thus, in order to reflect a more realistic picture of events, the 'Incurred' column is used to log known expenditure that is not formally in the account books. The 'Incurred' column tends to be used for expenditure only; it would be unusual to have incurred income.
- 'Total' is simply the sum of the 'Actual' and the 'Incurred' columns.
- 'Budget' refers to the approved budget for a given financial period.

Table 6.6 Actual versus budget comparison

Income	Actual	Incurred	Total	Budget	Variance	Direction	Note
Spectator tickets	1,450		1,450	1,350	100	F	1
Other ticket sales	250		250	0	250	F	
Sponsorship	1,700		1,700	1,800	−100	U	2
Catering	220		220	200	20	F	
Merchandising	130		130	100	30	F	
Total income	3,750	0	3,750	3,450	300	F	3
Expenditure							
Volunteer kit	700		700	600	100	U	4
Pool hire	2,500	0	2,500	3,000	−500	F	5
Marketing activities	136		136	140	−4	F	
Administration	342	50	392	400	−8	F	
Total expenditure	3,678	50	3,728	4,140	−412	F	
Profit/(Loss)	72	−50	22	−690	712	F	6

- 'Variance' is the difference between the 'Total' column and the 'Budget' column.
- 'Direction' is a reference as to whether the variance on any given line of the budget is favourable (F) or unfavourable (U). One characteristic of good information is that it is relevant to the intended recipient. For non-finance specialists, spelling out whether a variance is favourable or unfavourable is a helpful aid to understanding the underlying meaning of the figures.
- 'Note' is a cross-reference to a written qualitative explanation of a variance. Numbers in isolation do not explain a variance, so it is sometimes useful for a written explanation to accompany some of the more significant variances.

To illustrate how qualitative explanations can help to explain the meaning of variances, below are examples of the notes that might have accompanied the actual versus budget comparison in Table 6.6. It is written in the form of a report and can easily be cross-referenced to Table 6.6.

EVENT BUDGET REPORT

To: Swimming Committee
From: Event Manager
Date: 10 September 20XX
Re: Actual v Budget Notes

- Note 1: Spectator ticket sales – Spectator ticket sales (580 at £2.50) were 40 ahead of target (540 at £2.50). More spectator ticket sales have been achieved by encouraging people who attended the event in the past to return this year.
- Note 2: Sponsorship – Following the renegotiation of last year's agreements with our club's partners, we were able to secure £1,700 in sponsorship (£100 below our target). This unfavourable result was due to one company having to reduce its involvement because of market pressures.
- Note 3: Total income – Total income is £300 ahead of target, following strong spectator ticket sales. However, it is not all net gain (see Note 6).
- Note 4: Volunteer kit – The increase in event size necessitated an increase in the number of volunteers and therefore an overspend of £100 against budget. Our club policy is to reward these volunteers for their time with an event T-shirt and we purchased 20 additional items at a cost of £5 per item.
- Note 5: Pool hire – Pool hire costs were £500 below budget due to an improved discount from the facility. We have reached an agreement to pay this set fee for the next five years.
- Note 6: The bottom line – The event had been due to record a loss of £690 following an agreement at the last Annual General Meeting. However, strong ticket sales and a significant reduction in pool hire costs (due to the five-year agreement) mean that the event has made a small surplus of £72. This surplus will be reinvested into the swimming club to provide support for transport costs for away galas.

Signed
Event Manager

Any chairperson/director reading this report would be able to grasp the basic point that the event performed ahead of budget and had secured future discounts for the benefit of the club. At this stage, the actual versus budget comparison would be noted and no action would need to be taken, other than to congratulate and encourage those responsible for delivering the better-than-anticipated performance.

> ## Study activity
>
> Why is it important to compare budgets with actual performance and how frequently should a manager do this for: (1) small events, (2) annual events, and (3) major events?

6.11 Summary

The purpose of this chapter was to demonstrate the importance of financial management within an events management context. While any detailed analysis was beyond the scope of the chapter, provision is made to equip managers with the necessary skills to communicate, in basic terms, the financial sustainability of an event. The cyclical process of planning, decision-making and control, coupled with the analytical techniques that can be applied to management accounting information, should enhance the toolbox of skills that any event manager possesses. The importance of this process should not be underestimated in both profit and not-for-profit events, regardless of size or stature.

The main objective of all events should be to operate within their own resources so that they can be sustainable and so that people can appreciate their value. The tools identified in this chapter, including budgeting, should help this process. Furthermore, using financial and management accounting information as two sides of the same coin – which is rarely acknowledged – will help to provide managers with the necessary discipline and confidence for planning, making effective decisions and exercising financial control.

The income statement, balance sheet and cash flow statement equip managers with information that can determine the financial performance and position of an organisation and demonstrate the difference between profit and the typically scarce resource of cash. In addition, it can be determined whether the event should be held and whether you or your competitors can pay their debts as they fall due.

It is not possible within one chapter to cover all event finance information and budgetary techniques. However, you should have grasped the idea that financial management is important enough to be considered an integral part of any event. Other skills are required to come up with a marketing campaign or a training and development plan, but only those who understand finance can establish whether or not they are financially viable, worthwhile or even necessary in the first place. The best way to ensure that you develop the full range of financial management skills is to achieve a thorough understanding of the theoretical concepts involved and some tangible experience of event finance in practice.

Further reading

Ferdinand, N. and Kitchin, P. (2022) Financing Events. In N. Ferdinand and P. Kitchin (eds) *Events Management: An International Approach* (3rd edn): 142–167, London: Sage. For more information on general event funding and financial planning.

Masterman, G. (2021) Financial Planning and Control. In *Strategic Sport Event Management* (4th edn): 139–160, Abingdon: Routledge.

Stewart, B. (2017) *Sport Funding and Finance* (3rd edn), Oxford: Routledge. For guidance on financial reporting and summarising financial information.

Wilson, R. (2011) *Managing Sport Finance*, Abingdon: Routledge. For guidance on recording and reporting financial information and for more detail on performing a thorough financial health analysis.

Reference

Wilson, R. and Kitchin, K. (2022) Financing Events. In N. Ferdinand and P. Kitchin (eds) *Events Management: An International Approach* (3rd edn): 142–167, London: Sage.

Event marketing

Contents

DOI: 10.4324/9781003102878-7

7.1 Aims

By the end of this chapter, students will be able to:

- describe practical event market analysis methods and considerations and explain marketing planning components
- explain basic customer-focused event marketing terminology and the role of new media in event marketing
- evaluate the relevance of event marketing as an effective relationship-building tool
- describe the role of event sponsorship and understand the process of attracting suitable event sponsors
- explain how to manage the sponsorship process and sponsor relationships as well as current issues facing event managers in relation to sponsorship.

7.2 Introduction

There have been significant challenges for the development of effective event marketing analysis, planning, implementation and control methods. Digital marketing has completely changed the events management industry in the last five years, and we have seen the introduction of new techniques that present considerable opportunities for event marketing managers. Event marketers must fully embrace this new approach and consider digital techniques in their marketing planning. This chapter will highlight the crucial and changing role of the sponsor in modern events, where connection is made between the development of the relevance of the media, and social media to modern events, the scope for communication of sponsorship messages to specific audiences and the significant cost-recovery potential to event managers. In addition to the advantages of sponsorship to events, some of the main challenges facing this important activity will be explored.

It is important to understand what marketing can bring to the discipline of events management and to be clear about what 'event marketing' means. (Event experience is an important part of event marketing, and this was covered in Chapter 3.) Event marketing is: 'the process by which event managers and marketers gain an understanding of their potential consumers' characteristics and needs in order to produce, price, promote and distribute an event experience that meets these needs and the objectives of the special event' (Bowdin *et al.* 2011: 367). Bowdin *et al.*'s definition emphasises the fact that events should be seen as 'special' and that each event merits its own distinct marketing plan. However, this definition does not emphasise the need to build up longer-term relationships with event consumers, who are at the heart of everything to do with selling events.

Marketing should certainly not be seen as a bolt-on activity, nor viewed as merely the creative part of the event planning process. Perhaps an all too familiar view is that marketing commences once the event has been booked and the starting date set; but in this instance, what many event managers understand to be marketing is actually advertising. Advertising is only part of the marketing process. Marketing must be viewed as a discipline that is important *before* the event takes place and as one that is used *during* the event and *after* it has finished, when it is crucial to gauge how well the event was received and to what extent sponsors could see value in the coverage that they paid for. It is also the responsibility of everyone involved with the running of the event, not just of the marketing department or team. Certainly, it is important to make it clear to everybody involved in an event that customer satisfaction should be at the heart of everything that event organisers do, and that this must be captured and used in future planning. Event staff should also be aware of the potential damage to an event caused by expressing their views on social media. Sponsors increasingly look to withdraw from sponsorship contracts when their client brings their brand into disrepute.

The event attendee very often looks for a 'lifestyle experience' (Allen *et al.* 2011) and something that they will remember as interesting, memorable and exciting. This is sometimes known as the '3Es' of event marketing – entertainment, excitement and enterprise (Hoyle 2002). This is still the focus of event marketing and should be the starting point for anybody new to event marketing. The event attendee wants to be entertained by the event, be it live in person or as a digital event, anticipates feeling some excitement as a result of the element of celebration at the event, and expects event organisers to innovate or show enterprise.

Event marketers should differentiate between events that target consumers (B2C) and those that are aimed at business or trades (B2B) as these groups may have different motivations for attending. In B2C, the event attendee is a private consumer who is attending for personal motives, such as to see a favourite musician or to attend a festival. B2B customers are more likely to attend principally for business reasons, such as those who visit an internationally renowned event like the Nuremberg International Toy Fair in Germany. The task of the event marketer becomes more complex when some events attract both business customers and private customers who are interested in the event's theme. For instance, the model train section of a toy fair attracts professional buyers as well as hundreds of enthusiasts who are keen to see the latest developments in their hobby.

7.3 Event marketing planning

The most effective way for an event manager to coordinate the marketing activities for their event is to develop them within a marketing plan. The key purpose of the marketing plan is to identify the current situation in which event organisers find themselves and then to map out a path for the events management team to follow. As with any plan, the event marketing team should then undertake the necessary evaluation to see if they have achieved their goals. Using McDonald's established marketing plan (see Figure 7.1), these main areas of marketing planning are:

- To set goals.
- To analyse the current situation.
- To create the marketing strategy.
- To allocate marketing resources and to monitor or evaluate the plan.

It is critical that the people responsible for marketing an event are clear about the goals that need to be set for it. The event's mission, or that of the events management organisation, should remind the staff working on it exactly what its purpose is. The mission of a corporate event organiser might merely entail becoming a key player in its market. The award-winning Jack Morton Group simply expects its people to 'Be Extraordinary' in its drive to develop Experience Brands'. The simplest mission statements are often the most effective to communicate to an events team. Setting corporate objectives are also targets that the event organisers can use to guide the direction of their business. These might entail being the most recognised

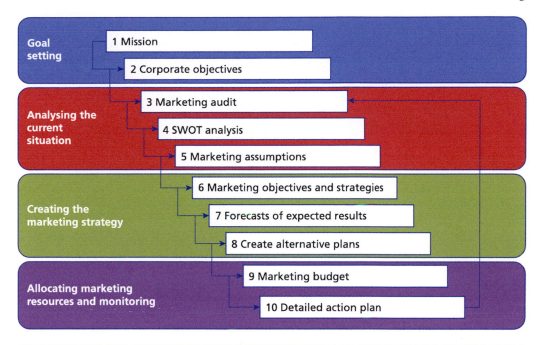

Figure 7.1 McDonald's marketing planning process
Source: Adapted from McDonald and Wilson (2016)

brand in the sector within five years, or to have the highest satisfaction levels of volunteers in the industry. These are better when expressed in numerical terms as it might be easier to set targets to achieve these goals.

After setting the mission statement, the next stage is to analyse the current situation of the event through the use of market research. This looks at the capabilities of the organisers and how they are positioned in the market, and evaluates their marketing strengths. The main tool in this exercise, as shown in Figure 7.2, is a SWOT analysis. The 'internal analysis' shows the strengths (S) and weaknesses (W) of the organisation, while the 'external analysis' illustrates those factors which present the greatest opportunities (O) – such as market data which show increased attendances at music events – and threats (T) – such as the introduction of new safety legislation that might demand increased expenditure.

The next stage is to set marketing objectives in quantifiable terms – for example, using research data to show why people attend an event – which are used to clarify what the marketing team has to achieve. These might specify the levels of customer satisfaction or enjoyment expected at an event, or the level of awareness resulting from marketing activities. A typical example of a marketing objective might be to receive positive feedback about the event from more than 75% of all attendees, or to achieve 40% of sales from previous event attendees. How have the target group responded to social media activity and what are the outcomes of this? Once the marketing objectives have been identified and the budget determined, a detailed action plan will list exactly what needs to be done, by whom and when.

	Strengths	Weaknesses
Internal	1 Established longer than competitors' events 2 Strong brand image 3 High levels of customer feedback 4 High customer loyalty – 60% return to event in following year	1 Low volunteer retention – only 30% 2 Low use of web-based applications
	Opportunities	**Threats**
External	1 To set up an additional event in a new venue 2 To sell 200 more tickets to overseas visitors 3 To increase sponsorship revenue by 20%	1 New safety regulations for events 2 Leading competitor has grown more than current industry average 3 Key target group has reduced spending power

Figure 7.2 SWOT analysis

CASE STUDY 7.1

The Digital Arena, Toronto, Canada

Maple Leaf Sports and Entertainment Ltd (MLSE) launched an exciting new project called the Digital Arena at their sports venue in Toronto, Canada, in recognition of the changing expectations of sports and entertainment consumers. The MLSE own Toronto Raptors (NBA), Toronto FC (MLS) and the Toronto Maple Leafs (NHL), as well as the Argonauts who play in the Canadian Football Leagues and the Toronto Marlies who play in the American Football League. The global pandemic, which forced many events to take place behind closed doors, demonstrated to MLSE and the fans of their teams the importance of their digital arena. Clearly fans who can't attend an event are catered for through television coverage and social media, but the aim of the Digital Arena is to enable their customers to enjoy the event experience in 'real-time'. MLSE saw the need to address this experience and introduced a number of features, including the chance to view multi-cam shots, share statistics about the players taking part and show advanced analytics of the game. They have also concentrated on 'fan interactions' and specifically targeted these fans through a range of competitions, online games and a real-time leader board, which encourages fans to interact with each other as well as with family and friends. These new features have also allowed them to develop new sponsorship and partnership opportunities with brands who want to buy into this audience of younger people. This has helped the club to increase revenue and also develop new partnerships with leading brands, keen to align themselves with this exciting development.

These new ideas should not be seen as 'additions' to their strategy, but as a major strategic development, with extra resources found to support their 'digital team' led by Humza Teherany, a strategist with over 20 years' experience in digital strategy, and who is recognised for his track record in a number of key industries. People are starting to take note of his work at MLSE. Their aim as a division is 'Pushing the boundaries of sports and entertainment by creating extraordinary moments, amplifying our competitive advantage through technology, and fostering a culture of integrity, inclusion and innovation'. This 'belief' is at the heart of everything that they do and has caught the attention of new partners who are keen to share this vision and be part of their new journey.

While the focus is on fan experience, and groups of fans who have different expectations of sport and entertainment, it is the interactive nature of the digital arena which allows partners to promote their products during events, and then be able to measure the impact of these interactions through the purchasing of their products and the levels of interaction with the 'in-game' activities. There are clearly many areas for other event marketers to consider here, even on smaller budgets, where there is an opportunity to share live events with customers who are following the event online.

The live event is still an important part of their business and it is live attendance that also generates income and creates the atmosphere inside the arena, and this is also key to the 'digital fan'. However, MLSE recognise that there are some fans who are exclusively digital and some fans who combine live and digital. What the digital platform allows them to do is to target digital fans in a number of locations and help them grow their international fan base. This represents a significant investment in this new venture, but it is a model that other event managers will follow. A music festival with a sold-out live audience can also be sold digitally, and may be a way of increasing brand awareness and event revenue, while offering something new to sponsors or partners. It will be interesting to monitor their development over the coming years and to see which other sports and events follow their lead.

Source: MLSE (2021)

7.3.1 Expectations of event attendees

As the event market becomes more competitive, and more events take place, it is critical to understand the demands and expectations of attendees. The increased use of 'digital' also presents extra competition for event managers. To what extent has the organiser considered the concept of entertainment inertia, and that a percentage of their target group might choose not to attend because their diary is already full with other events? Can this potential consumer justify giving up time and money to attend another event (Wakefield 2007)? Is this an important event in the lives of those attending, with a reputation for delivering enjoyment or excitement, or is this merely one of a group of events from which some of our target group have to choose?

An attendee's expectation of an event is unlikely to be based solely on the experience of the performer or enjoyment of the event theme. Level of service, or service quality, is also important. The issue of service quality is well established, and researchers such as O'Neill and Wakefield have shown links between service quality and customer satisfaction, even though many of these event experiences are also considered to be 'intangible' and therefore hard to measure (O'Neill *et al.* 1999). However, one can assume that there is a level of expectation of quality of service for most event attendees. In some cases, just asking the question, 'How easy is it for people to get to my event?' might help the organiser to identify factors which could affect attendance (Wakefield 2007). While factors such as availability of parking space, ease of access, social media presence, refreshments, toilets, signage and the helpfulness of event staff might not be considered crucial, it is a straightforward exercise to gauge attendees' attitudes to these points through a carefully constructed questionnaire (O'Neill *et al.* 1999).

7.3.2 Market research for events

The main aim of conducting market research is to try to reduce the risk of running an unsuccessful event and to help meet the objectives of the event organisers (Goldblatt 2011). It is better to spend on market research if it can prevent a failed new event. Without doubt, the main research tool used in event research is the questionnaire, but these can now be administered more effectively through social media accounts and the feedback is instant and easy to analyse. A well-constructed and piloted questionnaire allows a sample of people to give important feedback about all aspects of the event, and it can be the basis for producing meaningful research data to help guide decision-making. The questionnaire should not be seen as the only tool in the armoury of the market researcher, and it has a significant role to play in events management. For the event manager, engaging in market research should become an important part of their role, after all this is the only way of gauging the views of existing customers or potential customers. Published market research reports for the events industry are available, but there is nothing to stop event organisers building up their own market research data. This will not only help organisers to make more informed decisions about events but will be an important aid in attracting sponsorship. It is important to seek feedback that is reflective of attendees' views. Citing a Tweet from an attendee which suggests that this is the best event that they have ever attended is fine if it is representative of the general view of attendees, but should not be used simply because it makes the event organiser look more effective in the evaluative reports that they write.

Event managers can also use market research to help them predict the likely attendance at a new event. Using the Market Breakdown Calculator (MBC), a technique applied by some entrepreneurs to test the validity of their latest venture, is a good way to estimate the likely demand for an event by using market research, and it allows the event manager to input some of their own experience and knowledge of that particular event market. In Table 7.1 the MBC shows how to measure the likely attendance at a wedding fair, which is targeted predominantly at brides-to-be. It is expected that most of the attendees will be female; live within 50 kilometres of the venue; be aged between 18 and 35; have had the opportunity to see four adverts promoting the event; have been in a relationship for more than six months; will be in one of the higher socio-economic groups; and will probably bring at least one other person with them. Of course, these variables will be different for other events. For example, for an event attendee to travel 50 kilometres in the USA is a *local* distance, whereas in other countries this might be considered a long journey.

Using this method, the overall population of the targeted area is calculated and the key criteria for the target group are established. Then, by a process of elimination, the number of those who are unlikely to attend is subtracted. This initial calculation shows that there

Table 7.1 Using the Market Breakdown Calculator to calculate likely attendance at a wedding fair
Source: Holden and Wilde (2011)

Variable	% value	Population	Source of information
Population within 50 km of event venue	100	1,000,000	National statistics
Females	51	510,000	National statistics
Females 18–35	30	153,000	National statistics
Females 18–35 not married, but in a relationship	40	61,200	National statistics
ABC1 – Middle class	65	39,780	Secondary data
Number of people likely to react to adverts (adverts shown four times)	20	7,956	Advertising industry averages
Actual number who will follow up this interest	40	3,182	Industry experience
Likely to bring two other people		6,364	Calculation

are likely to be 3,182 in the target group, each of whom might bring two other people to the event, making a segment size of 9,546 visitors. Of course, this is only one of the likely target groups, and the process can be repeated for other segments, with calculations revised when new research data becomes available. Market research data can be used with the MBC and, while many of the calculations are only estimates, the outcomes are better than complete guesswork. Using a spreadsheet allows the variables to be easily changed. If there is another wedding fair running simultaneously in the area, the event organisers must try to calculate what impact such competition will have on their event. This technique is particularly helpful when it demonstrates that a target group might be only around 9,000 people and the event organiser has in mind that it might be nearer 30,000. It does not mean that the event will not be successful; it just helps to set more realistic targets. If the events are offered via a digital platform, then what is the potential size of the market for this? Having the right equipment in place at the event is critical here.

7.3.2.1 Observation as a research method

Attending an event and taking notes about customer behaviour or their interaction with the event is another way of researching events. This is often called 'participant observation'. To use this research technique, rather than asking attendees about their experiences, researchers attend an event as if they themselves were attendees, record their observations of attendees' behaviour, and then listen for comments made by participants that might give further insight into their views of the event. However, it is important to be aware of the ethical guidelines concerning this type of research, and researchers should not do anything that might impact on people's enjoyment of the event or research in such a way that might endanger those attending or participating.

Researchers who attended the Coca-Cola Masters Surfing Event in Australia as observers were able to capture important information about the event experience. When supported by formal feedback through a questionnaire, this gave a more accurate impression of attendees' levels of satisfaction (O'Neill *et al.* 1999).

7.3.2.2 Secondary research

The key starting point for research data about the events market is published as secondary data in journal or book form. In some countries, this data might be available free through such institutions as business libraries. Industry bodies also produce annual reports on the events industry, and this data can be key in helping to develop marketing plans. Typical secondary reports for the events industry are Mintel's *Leisure Review Germany 2020* (available at www.oxygen.mintel. com) and Key Note's *Online Event Ticketing 2021* (available at www.keynote.co.uk).

7.3.3 Stakeholders

While consumers are the most important group for an event manager, there are other key people to consider – stakeholders. An event stakeholder is any group or individual with influence over the running of an event or someone who might be affected by the event. Allen *et al.* (2011) refer to the most important stakeholders as 'key players'. The event manager should consider what each of these stakeholders is seeking to gain from the event. For an international event, the event organisers will also need to review social media in other countries, where some of their stakeholders may be based.

The importance of stakeholder groups varies from event to event, but many, such as the Planning Department at the local government or council, are important groups for a number of events as they are often required to grant permission before an event can take place. What do we know about social media influencers and the role that they play in our market? It is vital to research these people and consider how to engage with them and their followers. Jess King, known as Rage Darling, an online Twitch gamer and influencer, is invited to international gaming conventions by suppliers, such is her influence in the gaming market. The key to successful stakeholder analysis is not only to identify the most important groups but to manage communication with them and consider which messages are sent to them, as shown in Table 7.2, where some key stakeholders are identified. This list is not exhaustive and serves only to demonstrate how many important stakeholders there are. This table can be adapted to any number of events and new stakeholder groups can be introduced. The local bank, for example, is important for helping the event organiser to secure funding to cope with the high levels of investment needed to launch the event. It helps the bank management to make their decision when they see how much publicity the event is receiving and how much the event is likely to impact on the local economy and community. Event sponsors are also key stakeholders. These are covered later in this chapter.

Study activity

Using the structure in Table 7.2, choose five stakeholder groups (one of which must be attendees) for a new three-day music festival that will take place on the outskirts of your town. At this event, 3,000 people are expecting to see ten bands, with around 1,500 of the attendees arriving by car, and as many as 2,000 camping in a nearby field.

Table 7.2 Event stakeholders

Stakeholder groups	Most appropriate means of communication	Current links with stakeholder (key people or groups)
Local government Planning Department	Written report to the Planning Department and a meeting to discuss the impact of the event in the chosen area	Planning Director Head of Planning Department Director of Cultural and Sporting Events
Governing body for the event	Letter Meetings Report of previous event	Supported by an association – International Festivals and Events Association (IFEA)
Local community	Local newspapers Radio stations Local television station Leaflets, letters and brochures Newsletters	Community leaders representing particular areas of town Police team responsible for local community
The media	Events management journals Local newspapers Local TV Websites Blogs Social media	Journalists in each publication with responsibility for events Specifically named correspondents Radio and TV news departments

7.3.4 Segmenting the events market and why people attend

While it might be assumed that many people are attending an event for the same reason, research shows that attendees often have different motivations and come from a range of backgrounds (Fink *et al.* 2002). How many people are attending an event for the first time, perhaps out of curiosity or as a result of promotional initiatives, and how many are regular attendees? By applying the principles of market segmentation, event managers can divide their attendees into clearly identifiable groups, ideally starting with their motivation for attendance. Capturing data about the social group, age and marital status is basic demographic information, but this is a useful starting point for segmenting events. Kahle *et al.* (1996) looked at the reasons why people attend sporting events, but some of these reasons probably apply to other types of event as well. If event managers are able to identify specific segments and their motivations for attending, it should be possible to send tailored messages to each of these groups.

Kahle *et al.* (1996) discovered that fans attend sporting events because they enjoy the camaraderie of attending with like-minded people, and they sometimes feel obligated to attend as a result of a history of attending. To what extent does this reflect the events that we are marketing? It seems plausible that such reasons will motivate people who attend music or arts events, too. Some of the people who attend an event may well do so just because they like to go to a variety of events – they like to spend time with friends and enjoy the excitement of the build-up and the unpredictability. How is this influenced by the rise in online events? This is a significant segment, so it is important to capture their contact details.

Kim and Chalip (2004) developed a conceptual model to identify why people attend events. Their research focused on 'push factors', such as age, gender, education, income and previous attendance at events, and linked these to 'mediating factors', such as the attraction of the event and interest in the event. They found that both the perceived risk of attending and financial constraints impacted on the intention to attend.

Research will often show important reasons why people attend events and help event managers to make more informed decisions about their events. It is often the case that people attend an event for a new experience, and could potentially be converted into regular event attendees. Event marketers should consider this segment carefully and how to attract new attendees. An international event may be the reason for people to visit the town or city, as well as the event itself.

In many cases, attendees might just come along in order to meet new people. A feature of many developed countries is the mobility of labour, with people taking jobs away from the place where they grew up. Single people will therefore attend events on their own or as part of organised groups as a way of enriching their social lives (Melnick 1993).

7.3.5 Event objectives

Many events have set capacities for attendees and participants. Goal-setting for an event with a stadium capacity of 50,000 people is relatively straightforward and just a matter of working out who these 50,000 people will be. Many event managers use customer relationship management (CRM) databases to manage lists of existing customers. This also includes such areas as loyalty cards for event attendees in order to encourage attendance at future events. Football clubs in England and NFL franchises in the United States often have huge databases, sometimes containing details of more than 400,000 contacts, and these can be important starting points in helping them to sell out their venues.

A simple objective might be to achieve a 70% level of satisfaction with the event, which can be measured by a survey of a sample of those who attended. An event organiser should be careful not to assume that most people who attended were happy if they have no evidence to back up this opinion.

7.3.6 Event marketing mix

The next stage of the event marketing plan – the marketing strategy phase in McDonald's marketing plan structure – is to consider the elements of the marketing mix and break them down into discrete components. For event marketing, these components are usually broken down into Booms and Bitner's '7Ps': product, place, price, promotion, people, process and physical evidence (see Figure 7.3). These include the make-up of the event product and the range of activities built into the event; the place or location which is most appropriate to deliver the right event experience; the pricing levels which represent value for money for those attending while maximising revenue; the promotion or publicity that can be generated in the media to help publicise and make stakeholders aware of the event; and knowing how

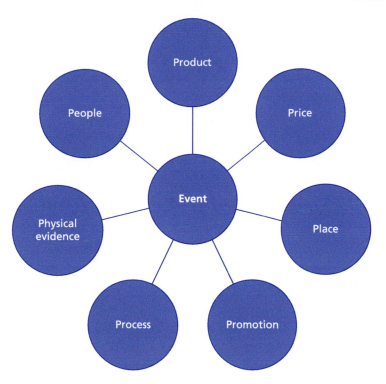

Figure 7.3 Event marketing mix
Source: Adapted from Booms and Bitner (1981)

to position the event in the minds of potential attendees so that they might consider attending it again in the future.

Events also have different characteristics, such as intangibility, inseparability, variability and perishability (Blythe 2009). Research by Lovelock and Gummerson (2004) found that most writers on services marketing referred to the four characteristics of intangibility, heterogeneity, inseparability and perishability. An event is not a physical product – it is intangible – so it is difficult to promote without an understanding of the event experience that appeals to attendees. Booms and Bitner (1981), early researchers in marketing, suggest that the event attendee therefore requires some physical evidence of their event experience. One way of addressing the issue of intangibility is to provide merchandising, such as T-shirts at music events, which act as tangible reminders of the event or the creation of social media content to remind attendees of aspects of the event experience. The event itself is produced and consumed at the same time, so these are inseparable, which means that planning the event experience is also critical. The event production is variable since the experience of the attendee at a music festival or show is not guaranteed, and in a sporting event the outcome is uncertain. Finally, most events are perishable, because empty seats cannot be sold and potential revenue is lost once the event has begun.

7.3.6.1 Event attributes and branding

Developing a recognisable brand and improving brand image are critical for event planners. These should not be seen as separate activities but as parts of the overall marketing plan. Blythe (2009) suggests that a consumer receives the following benefits from a brand:

- self-image
- quality
- cost
- expected performance
- differentiation from competing brands.

Consumers of prestigious events have an expected level of performance and quality, which are usually differentiated from competing events, where its cost reflects the status of the event and the event helps to improve aspects of their self-image. The physical evidence of the brand comes in the form of the brand name, logo and social media presence which are often an attendee's first view of the event in publicity material, so event organisers should invest in the outward appearance of these areas.

7.3.6.2 Event pricing and break-even analysis

Pricing strategies should reflect the objectives of an event organiser and should offer the potential customer value for money, while also taking the pricing of competitor events into consideration. An important starting point for price setting is to establish the break-even point. This is the point at which all the costs of the event are matched by the total revenue. If the total cost of the event is £10,000, and the typical cost of a ticket is £10, the break-even point is the sale of 1,000 tickets. Hitting this target as early as possible will allow the event manager to relax, at least a little.

Consider using 'benefactors' to support an event. Local businesses can be persuaded to support new events if they can see a benefit in being associated with it. The Greenwich and Docklands International Festival in London is supported by local celebrities as well as by major financial institutions, who use the event to reward their staff and families.

Attracting sponsors to cover the costs of running an event is an increasingly important component of event marketing and is an area that appeals to organisations looking to develop firmer relationships with their local communities.

Event marketing managers tend to use Eventbrite for their ticketing and pricing.

It is now seen as a key part of the events industry, a gift to event marketers, where licence holders pay a fee to the company for its use. Eventbrite was launched in the USA in 2006, but did not enter the UK market until 2012. With a turnover of around $300 million and 600 staff, Eventbrite is a leading global brand and synonymous with ticketing and pricing in the events industry.

7.3.6.3 Demand-oriented pricing

Demand-oriented pricing takes into account the various market segments that are attracted to events, allowing the attendee more options to purchase. This requires a more sophisticated approach to pricing and a better understanding of how people buy. The different levels of price might reflect the position of the seats at the event or built-in extras, such as free gifts, discounted refreshments, free car parking and free event literature. Event marketers should always try to add value when they review their pricing, rather than take the riskier option of discounting. Price reductions serve to devalue the event and can ultimately lead to a fall in total revenue, presenting the event manager with the task of investing more money to try to generate new attendees and thereby make up for the resulting shortfall in revenue.

This approach to adding value is also referred to as 'upgrading' (Wakefield 2007). The customer who paid £30 for a ticket to last year's event might be happy to pay £35 this year if they get a better seat, a free drink in the bar and a 20% discount voucher to purchase merchandise. More importantly, this represents another sale to an existing customer and possibly increases their loyalty to the event. Increasingly, consumers expect to be able to purchase tickets online for all events big or small, so these should be made available, but again with added value. Online ticketing is a quicker way of generating extra sales without the cost of employing ticket sellers, and for certain groups of event attendees this is their only purchasing method.

7.3.6.4 All-inclusive pricing

This is sometimes referred to as a 'package price'. It offers the event attendee added value while maintaining revenue levels. For some people, the ticket price might be set at an acceptable level, but they might still be dissuaded from attending if they think they will not be able to buy affordable, good-quality food at the event. Such people's concerns might be alleviated with the offer of an all-inclusive ticket. This is a pricing technique that more event managers should consider, as it makes it easier for event attendees to purchase their 'experience'.

7.3.7 Event distribution channels

'Place' is where the event experience is delivered and also where the distribution of tickets takes place, which in most cases is via their website (Blythe 2009). The main functions of an event website are to remind people about the event experience, to facilitate the sale of merchandise and to make it easier to purchase tickets. For loyal event attendees, the website should manage their expectations and update them with news and developments about the event, performing the role of an online newspaper or magazine, or replacing the products that event managers use to publicise their events. The event manager should also use social media networks and email to disseminate information to potential customers.

7.3.8 Event promotion

A perceptual map is an important technique in the positioning of an event. It requires an understanding of how consumers view events, and also takes into account their attitudes to competitors' events.

In Figure 7.4 the hypothetical Premier Arts Festival (PAF) is positioned using eight variables, which represent the attendee's view of the event experience and also take into account the views of competitors' events. Questionnaires can provide the data needed for this analysis. In Figure 7.4 the PAF ranks lower on all-inclusive tickets and its range of additional services than all of its competitors. These results show the event marketer areas where improvements need to be made.

Advertising on social media or through published media represents an additional cost for an event marketer, so it is essential to understand what impact this has and how its effectiveness can be measured in order that realistic targets might be set. In Figure 7.5 the impact of placing an advert for a wedding fair in a wedding magazine is evaluated. The advert is placed every month for six months. The target group of 60,000 women therefore have six opportunities to see the advert, making a total maximum reach of 360,000, assuming that nobody sees the advert more than once. If only 5% of this group do anything as a result of seeing the advert, then this represents 18,000 people. If the total cost of six adverts is £36,000, the cost of reaching each of these people is £2. Similar calculations can be used for other forms of advertising, but the most important consideration is that advertising does not have the impact that novice event managers often expect it to have.

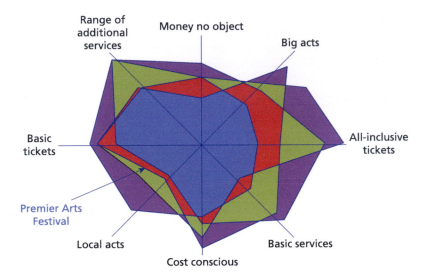

Figure 7.4 Perceptual map for an arts festival

Figure 7.5 Measuring the impact of adverts

Study activity

As the event director for the United Soccer Coaches' Convention, suggest five or six marketing objectives that you would set for next year's convention.

CASE STUDY 7.2

Convention of the United Soccer Coaches, United States

Location: Kansas City, Philadelphia, Chicago, Baltimore, Anaheim USA
Attendance: 8,500

The United Soccer Coaches' Convention, formerly the NSCAA, is one of the biggest events in the soccer (football) calendar. It has been held for more than 60 years. Such is the scale and importance of the event that the dates are already set for the next 15 years, using the same five cities. It has around 12,000 visitors (out of a total of 30,000 registered football coaches), many of whom are actively coaching football teams and are therefore in regular contact with around 500,000 players. The convention attracts over 300 exhibitors, predominantly from the USA, who hire around 700 booths, which has increased yearly over the past ten years. The organisers' aim is to provide an environment where those attending can have fun, excitement and learning opportunities, which involves attracting the most appropriate exhibitors. They create the perfect platform for attendees to observe coaching classes and to mix with important people from the world of football coaching. Usually, at least three high-profile soccer coaches or administrators are recruited to put on shows.

The number of overseas visitors to the convention is increasing, as the rest of the football world starts to wake up to the size of the youth football market in the USA. Trade exhibitors can demonstrate the latest in coaching equipment, footwear and clothing, technological innovations, as well as additional services, such as financial services, insurance and travel. They also run extra events, such as their Hispanic Heritage Month, in recognition of the number of coaches who have a Hispanic background.

The United Soccer Coaches generates additional revenue by selling advertising space in its publications. The *Soccer Journal* is sent to all 30,000 members and exhibitors are also encouraged to join corporate membership programmes, which offer additional benefits and the chance to network with current members, such as Adidas.

Away from the daytime convention, the event attracts sponsors to host evening activities at clubs and restaurants, with partners including hotels, restaurants and bars. Rooms are provided for their committee meetings, and awards ceremonies are hosted to recognise achievement in football coaching.

The convention is usually held during the second or third week in January – in the middle of the traditional break for most clubs based in the north of the USA – which helps to ensure high attendance figures. With increasing numbers of participants, exhibitors and attendees, the convention looks set to continue its growth and enhance its reputation as an important part of the US football market.

7.3.9 E-marketing and internet marketing

It is important to clarify the meaning of the terms 'e-marketing' and 'internet marketing', as they are often used interchangeably. According to Chaffey *et al.* (2006: 252), internet marketing is 'achieving marketing objectives through applying digital technologies', which include websites, email, wireless or mobile and digital television. E-marketing refers to all of these too, but also to 'digital customer data and electronic customer relationship management systems'.

The fast pace of development in e-marketing and web-based technologies continues to present ever more opportunities and threats to event marketers. However, whenever an event manager decides to use any of these applications, they must do so because they see it as a means of improving the overall consumer experience, not just because it is administratively more efficient or a lower-cost option than 'traditional' marketing methods. The challenge for the event marketer is to use these applications to improve overall marketing performance without creating distance from customers (Holden 2008).

The areas that event managers should focus on when developing their e-marketing plan include (adapted from Holden 2008):

- Information strategy – knowing what information the customer needs and providing it.
- Production/delivery strategy – knowing how the product or service (including information) can reach the customer, despite their dealing with the marketing team from a distance.
- Organisational strategy – what needs to happen in the business to enable everything else to happen for the customer.
- Assessment strategy – a way of monitoring success and failure.
- Marketing strategy – focusing on customers to steer all of the above in the direction the company needs to follow in order to achieve its aim.

Managers must ensure that the information needs of attendees are identified, and must then focus on the production and delivery of the event so that customer needs are satisfied. It is also vital to ensure that the whole event team is aware of the benefits of these applications and that evaluation techniques are used to assess the success or failure of the event. The final component is to build e-marketing activities into the overall marketing plan.

For many international event attendees, the internet is usually their first point of contact when seeking information, so it is important for the event organisers to present their event in a professional manner. Web-based applications have built-in measurement tools, such as Google Analytics™, which show how many people have visited a website, the amount of time that each visitor spends on a web page and if any of the site visitors have requested further information or purchased anything. When a website is visited and the contents of a banner advert are accessed, this is called the 'click-through', so the 'click-through rate' is the proportion of website visitors who click on an advert (Chaffey *et al.* 2006).

Google Analytics™ has several other useful features:

- Advanced segmentation – This enables the event manager to segment their visitors by region, by number of visits to the site, by revenue generated per customer, and so on.
- Analytics intelligence – Here, any significant changes in data are noted and automatically pointed out to the site manager.
- Custom reports – All data on Google Analytics™ can be used to produce reports that present data in a more professional format.
- Advanced analysis tools – Extra tools enable the analysis of data using multiple dimensions and features that filter data.

If an event website is used to sell advertising space, payment will usually be based on how many people click-through the advertiser's banner advert. It is important for the event manager to ensure that their website appears near the top of search engines, such as Google, a process called 'search engine optimisation'. The number of adverts that appear online is growing by as much as 20% per year, perhaps encouraged by the built-in feedback that web technology provides (De Pelsmacker *et al.* 2010). Selling sponsorship on the event website is also possible, with the rate paid based on the number of visitors to the site, the time spent on the site and any data that show the type of visitors to the site.

Study activity

How might social media sites, such as Facebook and Twitter, be used to support the activities of an event's marketing manager? You should focus principally on promotion, pricing, brand image and working with stakeholders.

The fact is that the internet helps event managers to sell and distribute their tickets and provide information to stakeholder groups. Consumers now expect events to have their own websites or pages and Twitter feeds and most people are purchasing tickets online. For instance, when the O2 Arena in London announced that 20,000 tickets were available for a Tina Turner concert, they sold out online in less than an hour, with many bought by overseas customers. In total, sales were over £1 million. The Olympic Delivery Authority (ODA) sold the majority of its tickets for the London Olympics online in special auctions, with 1.3 million people applying for only 30,000 tickets that were available for the men's 100-metre final alone (Topping *et al.* 2011). Efficient ticketing systems not only benefit customers but enable the event manager to process money from ticket sales more effectively and give a significant boost to cash flow. How many businesses are able to secure payment for a service that they will not need to deliver in full for at least a year?

7.4 Event sponsorship

The events business provides some of the best examples of how sponsorship works, with some of the biggest sponsorship deals linked to major events. According to Cornwell (2020), sponsorship is: 'an investment in cash or in kind in a property, in return for access to the exploitable commercial potential of association with brands'. According to the International Events Group (IEG) in 2020, close to $1 billion were spent on the sponsorship of festivals, fairs and annual events in the USA; however, these sales are not growing as fast as in sporting events, who are set to increase their overall share.

As more companies research their sponsorship activities, they forge better relationships with their sponsors. Some sponsorship managers have changed their job titles to 'relationship manager' or 'partnership manager', to demonstrate the increased importance of their role. The practice of sponsoring events is well established. For instance, car manufacturers frequently supported early motor races by providing cars, expert mechanics or tyres at reduced cost because their association with the event helped to promote their core business to participants and spectators.

As the events market grows, so event managers must learn about the increasing cost-recovery possibilities that sponsorship presents. While sponsorship is a key function for some companies, the fact remains that the majority have not thought to use it as a marketing tool because they have not been approached by event managers.

7.4.1 Attracting sponsors

The first consideration for event managers who are looking to secure sponsorship is to ask how much money they might secure. Clearly, their goal is to try to get as much as possible in order

Image 7.1 Paralympics, Tokyo 2020
Source: Alex Davidson/Getty Images

to make the event more viable and ultimately more successful. The value of any sponsorship deal is subject to the following:

- How much coverage will the event receive in the media (press, radio, television, social media)?
- Who will be taking part in the event?
- Who will attend the event?
- What, in particular (value), might the sponsor gain by supporting this event?
- What help could be provided to make the partnership a success, such as the number of staff who might be allocated to look after the sponsor at the event?

Finding the answers to these questions will depend on securing data from events through market research and data analysis. Some of this data will be generated by the event organiser's own activities, while the rest might be found in secondary sources.

Sponsors try to reach people by electronic media, and an event organiser who is able to provide a list of contact details for attendees might stand a better chance of securing a deal. Perhaps one of the most important target groups for sponsorship is the media itself, with radio stations likely to be the most cooperative (Skinner and Rukavina 2003). Inviting media partners to be sponsors, even if this is only sponsorship in kind, means that they are much more likely to promote the event. This is invaluable in helping to raise the profile of an event and making it a more attractive proposition for other potential sponsors.

Media coverage is almost certainly the biggest driver of sponsorship deals for events, because it delivers a much bigger potential audience for the sponsor. While 100,000 people might attend an event and see the names of sponsors on billboards, the television audience – numbering in the millions, sometimes across many countries – has a much greater chance of increasing awareness of the sponsor's brand. Consider the size of the TV audience for an event that is shown in several countries with a combined audience of millions. This sort of coverage is important for global brands. However, even without media coverage, and for any size of event, an understanding of how the event audience might be attractive to the sponsor can help to maximise the value of the sponsorship deal.

There are different levels of sponsorship, with the most important being title sponsorship. Here, the sponsor's name is inserted before the event title, such as the BCCI Indian Premier League in cricket. Other levels of sponsorship enable more sponsorship partners to be recruited. In addition to the main title sponsor, different sponsors might be secured for specific parts of the event. These will receive less coverage and fewer benefits. Finally, minor sponsors might provide catering and refreshments, as sponsorship in kind.

An event organiser should always ask the question, 'What can I do for my sponsor(s)?', not 'What can the sponsor(s) do for me?' The organiser of a relatively new music festival is likely to view their 5,000 customers simply as lovers of music, and perhaps as passionate supporters of the event, but these people will have other interests and leisure activities, and they will consume many other products and services. A well-maintained database might highlight that they are predominantly middle class and that they are interested in travel and holidays. These event attendees would therefore be of great interest to a travel company that sells adventure holidays. A mail-out to these music lovers – as an official sponsor of their music festival, with an enclosed discount voucher – might easily generate 50 leads. If the company subsequently managed to sell just five holidays as a result, that would probably more than recoup the money it paid in sponsorship. Of course, this promotion would also increase awareness of the sponsor's core business and might well lead to future enquiries, making it even more financially beneficial. If the event organiser were to provide a hospitality package for the holiday company, enabling it to introduce some of its best clients to one of the bands, this would add even more value to the deal.

7.4.2 Developing the event sponsorship plan

Securing sponsorship for an event starts with a sponsorship plan to highlight what the event can offer a sponsor and the likely cost of the deal. A useful starting point is to produce a list of the costs of the event to see where it might be better to secure sponsorship in kind. Hiring a hall to put on the event might eat into the budget, so securing a sponsorship in kind with an organisation that has the use of a hall would be a good idea.

It is crucial to research potential sponsors. This type of investigation should uncover important information that will enable the event manager to find areas of mutual interest, but it might also prevent potentially embarrassing associations. As the number of sponsorship deals increases, more companies now issue guidelines on what they expect from a sponsorship deal (Stotlar 2005). These guidelines usually show that a company has experience in the sponsorship market, so they are very useful for any event organiser who is in the process of drafting sponsorship proposals.

> ### Study activity
>
> List the key factors that you would need to present to a drinks company if you wanted them to sponsor a musical event that will attract an audience of 5,000 people, mainly female and between the ages of 18 and 30. What would you expect the level of sponsorship to be for your event?

7.4.3 Setting event sponsorship objectives

Having researched potential sponsors, the event manager can begin to develop appropriate objectives for the proposed sponsorship plan, which will outline the benefits of the sponsorship deal. In many cases, the person dealing with the proposal in the sponsor's organisation will not be the ultimate decision-maker, so providing them with a clear list of potential benefits should make their job of convincing their boss to approve the deal that much easier.

Sponsorship objectives must be realistic, and where possible should be measurable. For instance, if the aim is to raise awareness of the sponsor's name, a pre-event survey will show what current awareness levels are, and then subsequent surveys can be carried out during and after the event to provide evidence of the sponsorship's effectiveness.

Some potential sponsorship objectives are:

- To increase awareness levels of a company's products/services (Rines 2002; Cornwell 2020).
- To demonstrate new or improved products to clients in an exclusive environment (Rines 2002; Skinner and Rukavina 2003).
- To improve the company's image (Sneath *et al.* 2005; Cornwell, 2020).
- To incentivise the workforce (Rines 2002; Stotlar 2005).
- To motivate/recruit/retain the workforce (Rines 2002; Skinner and Rukavina 2003).
- To develop better working relationships with distributors (Rines 2002).
- To improve relationships with the press (Rines 2002).
- To increase global exposure (Stotlar 2005; Zaharia *et al.* 2017).
- To increase sales (via product sampling) (Stotlar 2005).

More than one of these can be achieved in one deal. Perhaps the most popular objective is to increase levels of awareness of the sponsor's brand, but sponsors increasingly expect more than just this (Rines 2002).

Attendees are more likely to view a company more favourably as a result of its sponsorship of an event. For example, as many as 57% of attendees said that their opinion of a motor manufacturer had improved after a six-day charitable event in the USA that attracted over 750,000 spectators (Sneath *et al.* 2005). Increasingly, evaluation services are being offered by specialist agencies, who can help to provide the data that event organisers need to provide to potential sponsors, but of course the cost of hiring agencies has to be included in the marketing budget.

7.4.4 Preparing the sponsorship proposal

In order to inform new potential sponsors of what they might gain from sponsoring an event, the management team must draw up a sponsorship proposal. This will communicate to the potential sponsor the precise benefits of sponsoring the event and how much cash or sponsorship in kind they will be expected to provide. It should also explain why they will achieve a much better return on their investment through sponsorship than they would from traditional advertising or sales promotions (Solomon 2002). A survey in the United States showed that around 55% of all new sponsorship deals were secured as a result of a cold call to a potential sponsor (IEG Survey 2001, cited in Stotlar 2005). Ideally, a sponsorship proposal should cover the following areas (adapted from Solomon 2002):

- Exclusivity – Proposed sponsor to be the only one from their product category.
- Television – Specify the minimum amount of TV coverage for the sponsor.

- Signage – State how many signs the sponsor will be allowed to place at the event.
- Entertainment – Indicate how many hospitality options and free tickets are included in the deal.
- Display/merchandise – Indicate which merchandise options are available to the sponsor.
- Promotions/public relations – List the sponsor's access to event promotions and PR activities.
- Advertising – Detail how the sponsor's logo will be used in event advertising.
- Cost – How much the deal is worth and when the money should be paid.

These categories are the minimum that a potential sponsor will require; they should be comprehensive enough to protect both the sponsor and the event organiser; and they will form the basis of the sponsorship contract. Increasingly, sponsors demand exclusivity and are not prepared to share sponsorship with a company from the same industry. A sponsor will pay more for an event with media coverage, so a guarantee of a minimum level of media exposure might need to be specified. Sponsors often insert clauses into their contracts which specify minimum levels of media coverage. Therefore, the amount of space that will be in view of the media must be included, particularly if the names of other sponsors are going to appear in view at the same time. The total number of entry tickets to be included as part of the deal must be clarified in order to enable the sponsor to plan exactly who will benefit from them. Sponsors generally expect to be able to hand out publicity about their company, and in some cases give out samples, so the proposal must state exactly what they will be entitled to do. Using the sponsor's name in any advertising, promotion or public relations activities must be considered so that the sponsor gains more value from the deal.

7.4.5 Creative sponsorship strategies

Some of the biggest sponsorship deals are now struck over naming rights of venues. For instance, the Sheffield Events Arena was sponsored by a local radio station and was called the Hallam FM Arena and the major event arena in Los Angeles is named the Staples Center, after the office supplies company. This is an additional source of revenue for event marketers.

Increasingly, though, companies are looking to develop more innovative sponsorship strategies. When the National Westminster Bank sponsored cricket in England, it used a corporate social responsibility strategy to try to position its brand at the heart of the community. It designed a 'Cricket Community' road show, which invited local children to try cricket for the first time, with research showing 85% of people thought that it had encouraged more children to take up sports. The amount of publicity that these events generated was important, but the fact that the bank was involved in such a project also helped to change the perception of some of its stakeholders.

It is important to manage relationships with sponsors. Early sponsorship deals were secured as a result of personal preferences within the sponsoring company, rather than for commercial reasons. When a local engineering firm sponsored an annual music festival, it was often as a result of a decision made by a director of the company who wished to support his partner's favourite event, rather than for sound commercial reasons. Of course, an engineering firm might receive considerable benefits by sponsoring such an event, but such an investment needs to be made as a result of effective research.

Many successful sponsorship deals now involve 'activation' – an amount of money that a sponsoring company invests above its initial sponsorship payment. According to Performance

Research, after making a £1 million sponsorship payment, a company might find it beneficial to invest another £3 million to promote and support their sponsorship of an event (cited in Stotlar 2005: 38).

Companies often use sponsorship agents to help them to find the best match. Fiona Green, a sponsorship consultant with over 20 years' experience in the field, brokers deal between companies and potential sponsors. When representing an organisation that is interested in sponsorship, she compiles a list of events and compares these with the potential sponsor's objectives. She then contacts the managers of the most appropriate events to see if they can strike a deal. Despite the importance of this process, the roles of sponsorship agents are very rarely mentioned publicly by sponsors and partners once they have launched a new deal.

7.4.6 Evaluating event sponsorship

Evaluating the effectiveness of sponsorship shows sponsors that their main objectives have been met, and, hopefully, exceeded. However, a budget for these activities must be agreed in advance. For larger sponsors, these services are usually provided as part of a comprehensive package by companies like the International Events Group (IEG). Smaller sponsors might also contract out some of their evaluation, but invariably they carry out their own research as part of their overall market research activities.

One of the most important techniques for assessing the impact of a sponsor's activities is to measure the amount of publicity generated, as shown in Table 7.3. The most frequently used measurement is the advertising value equivalency of publicity (AVE). The exposure of the sponsor's brand on television is measured against the cost of buying the same amount of time in a TV advert. If, for example, Euronics sponsors the Ideal Homes Exhibition, which is then featured on television, the amount of time that the sponsor's name appears is recorded. According to the IEG, this is based on the amount of time that the brand name appears in shot, as long as it is at least 75% visible (Lagae 2005). If the brand name appears in a prime-time television show for 30 seconds, then the AVE is the same as a 30-second advertising slot during that programme. If the cost of placing a 30-second advert is £40,000, then the AVE is £40,000. If this appears in five different countries, calculations must be made for each of those markets. Similarly, if the brand name appears in a half-page story in a magazine, and the cost of a half-page advert is £5,000, then the AVE is £5,000. Clearly, the simple appearance of a brand name does not have the same impact as an advert, but it is a recognised form of measurement. Keeping cuttings and files from press articles and social media coverage and presenting them to the potential sponsor is one way of showing them how they will benefit from event sponsorship.

Other evaluation techniques include interviewing important stakeholders, such as participants, to test their view of the sponsorship and their attitude to the brand. For larger groups, a survey will also provide important feedback. Sponsorship packages that direct participants to a website can be measured by the number of visitors to that website and the degree of movement around it.

Cinch, an online motoring sales platform, has agreed to sponsor the English Cricket Board, as part of their overall strategy of increasing brand awareness in their principal markets, with some exposure in overseas markets also guaranteed. Sponsoring cricket events is more affordable than other sports such as American Football or Football, and offers a potential sponsor a particular target group.

Table 7.3 Sponsorship evaluation techniques

Aims of sponsoring events	Techniques for measuring the impact of sponsorship
To increase awareness levels of product/service and company (Rines 2002; Cornwell 2019)	Survey to measure percentage recall of the sponsor's involvement with the event, based on prompted brand awareness Media exposure measurement based on time on television and radio and the number of column inches in publications
To demonstrate new products or improved products to clients in an exclusive environment (Rines 2002; Skinner and Rukavina 2003)	Feedback from participants or attendees to gain their views about new products shown
To improve company image (Cornwell 2019)	Collect press cuttings and record the number of mentions as well as the audience or readership of the media where cuttings appear (Kwon *et al.* 2016)
To incentivise the workforce (Rines 2002; Stotlar 2005)	Staff attitude survey or interviews about proposed sponsorship
To motivate, recruit/retain the workforce (Rines 2002; Skinner and Rukavina 2003)	Staff surveys and interviews as part of appraisal
To develop better working relationships with distributors (Rines 2002)	Formal and informal feedback from distributors who attend the event Measure the increase in sales, or sales leads, as a result of sponsoring the event
To involve the local community	Interview key stakeholders Survey local community
To create a global identity (Rines 2002; Zaharia *et al.* 2017; Cornwell 2020)	Measure the impact of media coverage on a global basis

Study activity

What are the main threats that an event manager will face when trying to secure sponsorship for the first time?

7.4.7 Building loyalty and sponsor networks

Even though the sponsorship market is growing, unfortunately, for event managers, sponsors do not always continue to sponsor the same event. If the principal aim of the deal was to increase awareness of the brand and this has been achieved, a sponsor might choose another marketing communications activity that will help to generate new sales leads. Others do not renew their deals if the sponsorship has not delivered the expected benefits. Event managers must take this into consideration and develop effective working relationships with their sponsors. As a minimum, they should produce an annual report with feedback about the impact of the sponsorship deal, and collaborate with the sponsor throughout the year.

Other, more innovative ideas are to hold a party for the sponsor to celebrate the relationship and to give gifts, such as signed photographs or other tangible mementos of the event (Skinner and Rukavina 2003). It is also important, if possible, to sign long-term agreements with sponsors, or to renew contracts if the partnership has been beneficial. In some cases, encouraging staff and participants to buy the sponsor's products is a simple way of rewarding the sponsor for their investment.

7.4.8 Ethical and legal considerations in event sponsorship

Event organisers are under increasing pressure not to associate with controversial sponsors. When tobacco companies were banned from advertising on television in the 1970s, they turned to the sponsorship of major events, predominantly sports, in an attempt to ensure that their brand names received continued media exposure. However, now, while Formula One teams are still sponsored by tobacco companies, they are not allowed to show the sponsor's name or logo when they compete in France (Stotlar 2005). This legislation also extends to the large fleets of vehicles that are used to transport team equipment from event to event. There is also more pressure on event organisers not to work with sponsors from the booming online betting industry, and there has even been some discussion about accepting sponsorship from fast-food companies. While these companies are not yet affected by legislation, it is important to monitor current opinion and to be clear about how this type of sponsorship impacts on brand image.

Event organisers should also be aware of ethical considerations when choosing their sponsors. While a local school might be happy to receive £20,000 to help in the staging of its annual swimming gala, is it acceptable for a local fast-food outlet to sponsor the event, given the current problem of childhood obesity? It is sometimes difficult to find the right answers to such questions, especially when large sums of money are involved, but the event organiser should always be aware of the danger of negative publicity.

Ambush marketing represents a threat to sponsorship agreements, and event managers must be prepared to protect the interests of their sponsors. An ambush marketer creates marketing communications at or near an event to convince stakeholders that they are an official sponsor, even though they are not. Thus, an organiser must take steps to prevent attendees from displaying the brand names of non-sponsoring organisations. Event personnel might be instructed to confiscate any non-sponsor branded items, to stop them from being filmed by television cameras or photographed by the press inside the venue. This created a stir at the World Cup in Germany in 2006, when Dutch football supporters were instructed to remove branded dungarees that had been handed out by a non-sponsor, leaving the fans to watch the match in just their underpants.

A major computer game manufacturer Nintendo chose not to attend the Nuremberg International Toy Fair, but it ambushed the event by driving a mobile promotional van through the centre of the city during the week of the event. The organisers of the event are not able to prevent this happening.

Industry voice

Mario Zambas, General Manager, Middle East and North Africa

How did you become General Manager at PTI Digital? What was your journey in the events industry?

I started my sporting event career working with Norwich City FC in 1999 as their Head of IT, where I was responsible for writing and delivering an IT business strategy, centred around CRM (customer relationship management). NCFC wanted to get closer to the fans, understand their buying habits around ticketing, retail and partner products and implementing a CRM strategy was a first step towards gaining a better understanding.

After seven years at Carrow Road, I moved to Dubai, where I joined Dubai Sports City as Head of IT. DSC was a multi-use, multi-venue project incorporating football, cricket and indoor venues, as well as a golf course and training academy and mixed use office and residential accommodation. My responsibility was to lead the technology implementation around customer-facing systems as well as infrastructure. Two years later I was offered a position at the Yas Maria Circuit (YMC) in Abu Dhabi. As the Director of IT I was responsible for activating the technology infrastructure in preparation for the first race, the Etihad Airways Abu Dhabi Formula 1 Grand Prix in 2009.

I left YMC in 2011 and then was invited by Deloitte, a management consultancy firm, to help activate the Circuit of the Americas F1 circuit in Austin Texas in 2012. My role there was to lead the implementation of the event and venue management systems, assist with the ERP (financial) system rollout and set up a main operations centre to coordinate the communications between the key internal and external stakeholders, which included police, security and all operational areas of the circuit.

My final F1 role was working as a consultant for the Sochi Autodrom (SA) in Sochi, situated by the Black Sea in the Russian Federation and the location for the 2014 Winter Olympics. The circuit was built around the non-alpine venues, including the Adler Arena (speed skating), ice hockey and ice skating arenas. Logistically, this was quite challenging as we had to coordinate with the IOC in terms of access and also the imposition of a build cessation for almost two months, due to the Winter Olympics/Paralympics taking place.

My responsibility at the SA was to recruit and train an English speaking IT team and act as liaison with Formula 1 management and the Fédération Internationale de l'Automobile (FIA) regarding the technology requirements of the teams and the FIA and their stakeholders.

What is the best thing about working on a major sporting event like a Grand Prix?

If I may I will answer the question in two parts.

Firstly, I have been fortunate to have worked at three F1 circuits – in Abu Dhabi (United Arab Emirates), Austin Texas and Sochi in the Russian Federation – during the build and activation phases. What was exciting about that was that we were working out everything from scratch, without the benefit of what had happened before, because these were the first events. It is the challenge of the unknown and planning for all eventualities.

Obviously, after Abu Dhabi we knew 'what was coming' so to speak, but the challenges that presented themselves in the Middle East, USA and Russia were surprisingly varied.

My roles were also quite different on the three projects. At the Yas Marina Circuit in Abu Dhabi, I was the Director of IT and therefore ultimately responsible for delivering the entire IT infrastructure. At the Circuit of the Americas in Austin Texas, I was employed by the management consultants Deloitte to oversee and project manage the installation of event and management systems and assist in the implementation of a financial ERP system. Upon completion of those projects I worked with the operations team to set up and manage the main operations centre, which was the venue communications hub for all the main internal and external stakeholders and acted as a liaison with the IT and Operational teams on the ground.

At the Sochi Autodrom in the Russian Federation our team was brought in to help the Russian operational teams activate for their first F1 Grand Prix. For me that involved recruitment and training of IT staff, setting up processes and procedures, and acting as liaison with the FIA and FOM (Formula 1 Management). In conclusion, the number of different activities that you can get involved in means that it is 'never a dull moment!'

Secondly, and to the main point of your question, is there is nothing like working to deliver a global sporting event. The responsibility, excitement and adrenaline rush that goes with the build-up to the first event and then the satisfaction that comes after a successful delivery stay with you for a long time.

How important is IT in sporting event management?

You have the opportunity to work with some incredibly talented, knowledgeable and driven individuals from across the event and venue spectrum, and teamwork and communications are obviously of paramount importance.

IT, like all the operational departments, sits at the centre of both the venue and event delivery.

From the venue perspective, taking an F1 circuit or a football stadium as examples, IT is responsible for ensuring that the systems and technology were in place, up and running and checked to make sure they work. My CEO at Yas Marina Circuit Richard Cregan always said that you needed to check, check and check again!

Some of the key systems that are required include:

- Networks and communications infrastructure, including Wi-Fi
- Ticketing and access control
- Retail and catering systems
- Financial, HR, procurement (ERP)
- Media centre, broadcasting
- Main operations
- IPTV
- Distributed antennae systems
- Event and venue management
- CCTV
- Health and safety/security systems, including PA and alarm systems
- Asset management
- Preventative maintenance systems
- Race track management electronics systems (F1)
- Business continuity and disaster recovery, including backup power

From the event perspective, although separating the two, event and venue, is not always black and white, you are drilling down into the detailed requirements for the individual events that are taking place within the venue.

A complex event like an F1 race or a football match obviously is built around what is taking place on the circuit or stadium, whether it is a race or a match.

But around that many other activities are taking place such as media and broadcasting, hospitality, security and many others, all of which have to be supported by IT.

How important is it to develop good working relationships with the event sponsors?

It is important to remember that the sponsors of an event are one of the key stakeholder holder groups and as such need to be managed in a way that delivers the full benefit that they are expecting in return for their sponsorship investment in the event.

When I was working at the Yas Marina Circuit our title sponsor was Etihad Airways, who paid a significant fee to be the naming sponsor at the Etihad Airways Abu Dhabi Formula 1 Grand Prix. We had to ensure that all elements that related to their sponsorship agreement were delivered according to the terms of the agreement. This covered ticket allocations, marketing materials, signage and the LED boards that were positioned over the circuit start-finish line. Etihad also fly a commercial airliner flanked by planes from the UAE air force over the home straight prior to the start of the race, which is both noisy and an impressive sight!

As is usually the case when a high-profile global event takes place at your venue, the sponsors from the day-to-day activities often change when an international televised event comes to town.

So, when F1 or UEFA/FIFA are the promoter for an event their beer or car sponsor might be different to the ones that may be in place for the venue, for example. The venue and event team needs to ensure that they have checked to make sure that everything is in its place.

What do you think are the biggest challenges for sporting event managers?

There are many, due to the fact that there are many moving parts. When you consider that the event takes place in a complex venue and is comprised of the following 'parts', for example.

In F1, you have the sporting and non-sporting elements. The sporting elements include the track, pit wall and pit garages, the media centre and broadcast areas.

Then there are the guest services, marketing, commercial and hospitality areas and finally the operational areas around the venue, incorporating facility management, IT, administration and much more.

The event and venue management team are responsible for the overall event coordination and are a key component to the successful operation of the event within the venue as they act as liaison between the key internal and external stakeholders.

The challenge is trying to keep 'all of the people happy all of the time!' – a big ask!

What advice would you give students who want to work in sporting events? What should they be doing to prepare for this?

Research, network, volunteer now Covid restrictions are being lifted, be prepared for non-standard working hours; job descriptions get stretched, pressure can be overwhelming, preparation and checking are immensely important, and no event or venue works without teamwork, from people across multiple disciplines. Be prepared to understand all of the components and moving parts that exist in a venue and the corresponding events. And step outside your bubble – whether it be event management, venue operations, facilities management, catering, IT services etc.

Because if you understand and connect with all of these stakeholders, it will improve the chances of delivering a successful event. After all it is a team game and requires an enormous collective effort by all.

Last pieces of advice:

- You need comfortable shoes as you will do a lot of walking.
- Grab food and water at every opportunity when you are working at full tilt, so make friends with catering.
- Check, check and check again, I cannot stress it enough.

7.5 Summary

To gain an understanding of what event consumers require from an event experience, it is necessary to investigate what role the event plays in their lives, and which emotions are associated with that experience. Events are about lifestyle, excitement and escapism from day-to-day life; they must be memorable and an important ingredient in the lives of attendees. This requires a new approach to research and marketing planning to ensure that organisers cater for both consumers and key stakeholders, who can contribute to the success of the event. The digital event is an essential part of event marketing and one which requires further research. Event managers must ensure that research is at the heart of everything they do when planning an event. They must work hard to develop the event's brand image and must be willing to improve factors that impact on service quality. More attention needs to be paid to pricing and promotion, as well as to new technologies that can improve overall customer satisfaction. There are a bewildering number of social media options available and these should feature in your marketing activities, and event managers should be fully conversant with how to use them or else employ people who can.

Growing numbers of event managers are now dependent on sponsors for funding, so they must find ways to improve relationships with these companies. An ability to attract sponsorship might well be the difference between success and failure, so more resources must be devoted to sponsorship evaluation and innovative sponsorship strategies that will make potential sponsors even keener to invest in events.

Review questions

1. What are the 3Es of event marketing?
2. What do B2C and B2B mean?
3. What is the purpose of marketing planning for an event manager?
4. Why do event marketers use market research?
5. What are stakeholders and why are they important for event planners?
6. What are the 7Ps of service marketing?
7. Why is all-inclusive pricing attractive to event attendees?
8. How can event marketers attract new sponsors?
9. What are the main objectives of event sponsorship?
10. How can we measure the effectiveness of event sponsorship?

Further reading

Fink, J. S., Trail, G. T. and Anderson, D. E. (2002) Environmental Factors Associated with Spectator Attendance and Sport Consumption Behaviour: Gender and Team Differences, *Sport Marketing Quarterly, 11*: 8–19. This important article explores sports fans' consumption during sporting events and features the previously under-researched area of female attendance at events.

Green, F. (2018) *Winning with Data: CRM and Analytics for the Business of Sports*, Abingdon: Routledge.

McDonald, M., Mouncey, P. and Maklan, S. (2014) *Marketing Value Metrics: A New Metrics Model to Measure Marketing Effectiveness*, London: Kogan Page.

O'Neill, M., Getz, D. and Carlsen, J. (1999) Evaluation of Service Quality at Events: The 1998 Coca-Cola Masters Surfing Event at Margaret River, Western Australia, *Managing Service Quality*, 9 (3): 156–165. This is one of the first articles to consider the importance of service quality as part of an overall marketing plan in events management, with clear suggestions for future research in this area.

Video links

The Best Digital Marketing Strategies for Events: www.markletic.com/blog/the-best-digital-marketing-strategies-for-b2b-events/

Bidding and Hosting Sporting Events 101 – Ottawa Sport Council: https://sportottawa.ca/bidding-and-hosting-sport-events-101/

The Mercedes Benz Arena, Atlanta, USA: www.youtube.com/watch?v=tkVt5MC_AiY

Selling Tickets with Eventbrite Organiser: www.youtube.com/watch?v=VGHoLMxewv4

Seven Top Event Marketing Strategies: https://blogs.constantcontact.com/event-marketing-strategies/

Weblinks

Event Sponsorship: The 2021 Guide: https://blog.bizzabo.com/event-sponsorship

Festival Organisers Guide to Corporate Social Responsibility: www.events-insurance.co.uk/media/Festival-Organisers-Guide-Corporate-Social-Responsibility.pdf

Global Esports – Major Esports Events: www.globalesports.org/events

Russia 2018: The Octagon Guide to Effective FIFA World Cup Sponsorship: www.sportspromedia.com/interviews/russia-2018-fifa-world-cup-sponsorship-octagon-guide

The Ultimate Guide to Securing Event Sponsorship: www.eventbrite.co.uk/blog/guide-to-event-sponsorship-ds00/

References

Allen, J., O'Toole, W., Harris, R. and McDonnell, I. (2011) *Festival and Special Events Management*, Hoboken, NJ: John Wiley & Sons.

BDS (2010) *Sponsorship*. Available at: www.sponsorship.co.uk/in_sponsorship/in_sponsorship.htm [Accessed 27 August 2021].

Blythe, J. (2009) *Principles and Practice of Marketing*, Andover: Cengage Learning.

Booms, B. and Bitner, J. (1981) Marketing Strategies and Organizational Structures for Service Firms. In J. Donnelly and W. George (eds) *Marketing of Services*, Chicago, IL: American Marketing Association.

Bowdin, G., Allen, J., O'Toole, W., Harris, R. and McDonnell, I. (2011) *Events Management* (4th edn), Oxford: Butterworth-Heinemann.

Chaffey, D., Ellis-Chadwick, F., Johnston, K. and Mayer, R. (2006) *Internet Marketing: Strategy, Implementation and Practice*, London: Prentice Hall.

Cornwell, B. (2019) Less 'Sponsorship as Advertising' and More Sponsorship-Linked Marketing as Authentic Engagement, *Journal of Advertising*, 48 (1): 49–60.

Cornwell, B. (2020) *Sponsorship in Marketing: Effective Partnerships in Sports, Arts and Events* (2nd edn), Abingdon: Routledge.

De Pelsmacker, P., Geuens, M. and Van den Burgh, J. (2010) *Marketing Communications: A European Perspective*, London: Prentice Hall.

Goldblatt, J. (2011) *Special Events: A New Generation and the Next Frontier*, Hoboken, NJ: John Wiley & Sons.

Holden, P. R. (2008) *Virtually Free Marketing*, London: A & C Black.

Holden, P. R. and Wilde, N. P. (2007) *Marketing and PR*, London: A & C Black.

Hoyle, L. H. (2002) *Event Marketing: How to Successfully Promote Events, Festivals, Conventions and Expositions*, New York: John Wiley & Sons.

Kahle, L. R., Kambara, K. M. and Rose, G. M. (1996) A Functional Model of Fan Attendance Motivations for College Football, *Sport Marketing Quarterly, 5* (4): 51–60.

Kim, N. and Chalip, L. (2004) Why Travel to the FIFA World Cup? Effects of Motives, Background, Interest and Constraints, *Tourism Management, 25*: 695–707.

Kwon, E., Ratneshwar, S. and Kim, E. (2016) Brand Image Congruence through Sponsorship of Sporting Events: A Reinquiry of Gwinner and Eaton (1999), *Journal of Advertising, 45* (*1*): 130–138.

Lagae, W. (2005) *Sports Sponsorship and Marketing Communications: A European Perspective*, London: Prentice Hall.

Lovelock, C. and Gummerson, E. (2004) Whither Services Marketing? In Search of a New Paradigm and Fresh Perspectives, *Journal of Service Research, 7* (*1*): 20–41.

McDonald, M. and Wilson, H. (2016) *Marketing Plans: How to Prepare Them, How to Profit from Them* (8th edn), London: John Wiley & Sons.

Melnick, M. J. (1993) Searching for Sociability in the Stands: A Theory of Sports Spectating, *Journal of Sport Management, 7* (*1*): 44–60.

Mintel (2019) *Sports Sponsorship*, London: Mintel International Group Ltd.

MLSE (2021) Digital Arena. Available at: www.mlsedigital.com/products/digital-arena [Accessed 3rd August 2022].

Morton, Jack (2021) Jack Morton Agency – About. Available at: www.jackmorton.com/about/ [Accessed on 31 July 2021].

Rines, S. (2002) Guinness Rugby World Cup Sponsorship: A Global Platform for Meeting Business Objectives, *International Journal of Sports Marketing and Sponsorship, 4*: 449–465.

Skinner, B. E. and Rukavina, V. (2003) *Event Sponsorship*, New York: John Wiley & Sons.

Sneath, J. Z., Zachary Finney, R. and Close, A. G. (2005) An IMC Approach to Event Marketing: The Effects of Sponsorship and Experience on Customer Attitudes, *Journal of Advertising Research*, December: 373–381.

Solomon, J. (2002) *An Insider's Guide to Managing Sporting Events*, Champaign: Human Kinetics.

Stotlar, D. (2005) *Developing Successful Sports Marketing Plans*, Morgantown: Fitness Information Technology.

Topping, A., Collinson, P. and Walsh, F. (2011) Olympics: Man Gets £11,000 of Tickets after Bidding for £36,000, *Guardian*, 1 June. Available at: www.guardian.co.uk/sport/2011/jun/01/olympics-man-wins-tickets-bidding [Accessed 12 June 2017].

Wakefield, K. L. (2007) *Team Sports Marketing*, Oxford: Butterworth-Heinemann.

Zaharia, N., Brandon-Lai, S. and James, J. (2017) Show Me the Money: On Predicting Actual Purchases in Cross-National Sponsorship, *International Journal of Marketing Studies, 9* (*4*): 38–53.

Chapter 8

Event law, health, safety and risk management

Contents

DOI: 10.4324/9781003102878-8

8.1 Aims

By the end of this chapter, students will be able to:

- understand the legal environment for events
- understand ownership within the events industry, and the concept of duty of care
- discuss the external legal framework and frameworks that events operate within
- understand key health, safety and risk management terminology
- evaluate the health, safety and risk legal and moral obligations associated with managing events
- explain the process of risk management at events
- analyse in detail three of the key risks associated with events.

8.2 Introduction

Within the events industry, health, safety and risk issues and the legal environment have become a priority. Whilst, in the past, there was a tendency to view health and safety issues as 'red-tape' bureaucracy that merely ticks regulatory boxes whilst creating extra work for the already stressed event manager, these days nobody can run an event without some awareness of the importance of keeping people safe. The importance of health, safety and risk has been highlighted through many high-profile event disasters that could, conceivably, have been prevented if correct health, safety and risk procedures were in place. And of course, events have been the target of many of the atrocious terrorist attacks around the globe, as well as being almost completely shut down by the Covid-19 pandemic. All of these issues, from the health and safety issues caused by poor planning to the unexpected impacts of a rise in terrorism and a global pandemic have brought health, safety, risk and the legal environment right to the forefront of any event management planning.

Balancing health and safety requirements with the provision of exciting events is becoming a significant challenge as laws and regulations grow at the same speed as innovations and experience opportunities. The industry strives to juggle both aspects, driven by the desire to put on a good but safe show. It is important that event managers understand the skills needed to manage health and safety on-site, which should enable them to deliver that wow factor in that vitally important safe environment.

There are three elements to managing health and safety matters correctly: first, the management of health, safety and risk prevents or reduces accidents and near misses on-site; second, correct management prevents litigation, claims, fines, imprisonment and bad press for the event organisation; and third, risk assessment and health and safety compliance are often legal requirements. As governments and industry bodies have realised the potential risks associated with the events industry, they have sought to regulate against future problems by increasing legislation.

8.3 The legal environment

The consideration of and adherence to legalities is seen as the key to securing event operations (Shone and Parry 2010). It is therefore essential that event managers keep abreast of the legal framework and relevant events legislation. Goldblatt (2013: 261) suggest that the 'event planner has both a legal and an ethical responsibility to event stakeholders to design and maintain a safe and secure event environment'. It is also important to comply in order to avoid adverse legal consequences, such as being sued for negligence or losing permits and licences that allow you to operate in the industry.

Legislation changes continually and there are many issues that cannot be fully explored here, so it is essential that event managers keep up to date with the ever-changing legal landscapes. Laws also vary from country to country. However, there are some common legal themes that event managers need to consider. For all aspiring event managers, it's important that you grasp what is a legal requirement in your country – we'd therefore strongly advise you undertake the study activity below.

Study activity

Using the internet, look up the key legislative requirements for event management in your country. Tip: this chapter gives you the broad headings and indicative laws, regulations and licences that will help you to frame your search.

8.3.1 Event ownership and duty of care

'Who owns the event?' is one of the key questions in the legal external environment. As Bowdin *et al.* (2011) point out, establishing who owns the event is a crucial point – whoever owns the event has legal responsibility and is therefore liable; and liability opens up the event owner to potential claims of negligence and costly litigations. The legal owner of the event could be the event manager, the organising body, the event organisation, the event committee or even the client. The question of ownership is vital to establishing outcomes in legal situations, as potentially negligent activities can lead to expensive and drawn-out litigation processes, and can ultimately have disastrous impacts on the event owner. It is therefore important that the answer is established from the outset – ownership of the event should be implicit throughout all pitching, proposals and contractual negotiations. Issues surrounding intellectual property (who owns the idea or concept) should also be established at the start of any event.

Once the ownership of the event is established – and the responsibility (liability) in the eyes of the law is therefore apparent – the event owner is endowed with a duty of care. Duty of care is a fundamental legal principle that, when applied to events, means 'taking all reasonable care to avoid acts or omissions that could injure employees, contractors, users, participants and visitors' (Bowdin *et al.* 2011: 339).

Study activity

In 50 words or less, explain why the principles of duty of care and event ownership are integral to the events industry.

8.3.2 Equality acts

Event managers need to ensure that their event is accessible to all members of society. In the UK, legislation exists in order to ensure that events are accessible. This is known as the Equality Act of 2010, and it legislates against discrimination across a number of protected characteristics. Of the eight protected characteristics (age, disability, gender reassignment, marriage and civil partnerships, race, religion or belief, sex, and sexual orientation), disability is one of the key concerns for event managers. It is unlawful for a service provider to discriminate against a disabled person by refusing to supply any service that it provides for other members of the public (Bowdin *et al.* 2011). In real terms, this means that event managers must consider issues relating to access to venues, ensuring that disabled guests have access to all services offered and fair treatment of disabled employees. Other countries have similar laws and legislations, and it is advisable that event managers keep abreast of these and seek advice on how to adhere to them. In the USA, laws such as the Civil Rights Act of 1964, the Equal Pay Act of 1963 and Title 1 of the Americans with Disabilities Act of 1990 need to be considered. Websites such as www.gov.uk, www.eeoc.gov (US Equal Employment Opportunity Commission), https://humanrights.gov.au/ (Australian Human Rights Commission) and www.india.gov.in (Indian Fundamental Rights) are invaluable tools for the event manager seeking further information.

8.4 Legal requirements

The regulations, laws and legislation that event organisers are required to adhere to vary from country to country, but it is always essential that organisers understand their legal obligations. Bear in mind that an event organiser must understand the laws and regulations in both the country where their organisation is based *and* the country where the event will take place – often, there are marked differences between the two. It is essential that anyone involved in event management is clear on the legal responsibility that they have in relation to compliance with health and safety legislation because, in the majority of cases, this responsibility will rest with the event organiser (HSE 1999: 167).

Legal issues are the foundation of all elements of event planning. The importance of operating within the rules set by government and local authorities must never be underestimated.

CASE STUDY 8.1

Government responsibilities: the Colectiv Nightclub, Bucharest, Romania

On the 30 October 2015, a fire broke out at a Romanian nightclub after a spark from a pyrotechnics show ignited foam décor. Forty-five people died and dozens of others were injured. It is believed that up to 400 people may have been inside the club for the rock concert. Reports from concert goers suggested that there were only two exits and only one of these was initially open, with the audience having to break the second door down to escape.

The club's owners and city hall clerks, as well as the owners of the company that installed the fireworks that caused the fire, were all either arrested or put under investigation.In an unexpected twist, the tragedy sparked protests in Bucharest, and led to the resignation and arrest of the local mayor. Protestors said that the mayor had granted a permit for the club, despite it not being authorised by firefighters. These protests in turn lead to large-scale protests, which claimed the government was corrupt – these protests resulted in the resignation of the prime minister and his government less than a week after the fire.

Sources: BBC (2015), Guardian (2015)

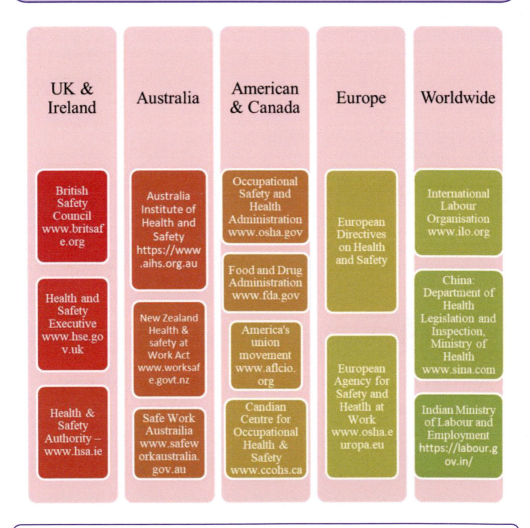

Figure 8.1 International resources for health and safety legislation

Image 8.1 Firework displays often need special permits

Health and safety legislation changes continually, and it is often difficult to keep up to date with the latest amendments and additions to laws and regulations. It is essential, however, that event managers do so. Figure 8.1 gives some useful links to resources that contain the latest health and safety regulations around the world. Please note that these resources change frequently, and so may be out of date by the time of publishing. Up-to-date resources are easily found.

Identify the key health and safety acts for your country. In pairs, discuss the key requirements of these acts in relation to the events industry.

8.4.1 Regulations, licences and permits

No matter which country an event is organised in, there are myriad regulations with which the event manager must comply. These regulations change from country to country, and indeed from region to region (regulations are often governed by local authorities or regional councils). Generally, the larger the event, the more regulations, licences and permits that will be required. It is important to note that the event organiser is legally required to obtain the right permits and licences, and failure to do so may well result in fines and penalties. It should also be noted that authorities have the right to cancel events if the right permits are not obtained.

It is perhaps easier for event managers to consider the event components that need licences and permits, rather than to try to keep abreast of the ever-changing regulations. Therefore, below, we suggest some of the event elements that may need permits or licences. As each event varies significantly, the list is dictated by the event design and the event product. However, once established, this list can act as a standard plan that merely needs revising and evaluating every time the event is repeated. Again, it should be stressed that many of these licences are legal requirements, so event managers should check carefully.

Event managers should consider the following issues and the regulations, permits and licences that might apply to each one:

- Alcohol consumption
- Food handling
- Staffing
- Noise
- Building regulations/standards
- Fire precautions
- Health and safety at work
- First-aid regulations
- Lifting equipment and manual handling operations
- Occupancy levels
- Music and performance rights and licences
- Intellectual property
- Electricity at work
- Environmental protection
- Signs and signal regulations
- Waste disposal
- Street trader or temporary market trader licences
- Street closures

- Public entertainment licences
- Criminal Record Bureau checks (required for events involving minors; similar police checks are required internationally).

As Bowdin *et al.* (2011) suggest, the principal rule is that the event manager should carry out careful research in order to ensure they understand and comply with all regulations that relate to their event. It should also be noted that the amount of time taken to identify and comply with regulations can vary enormously – the process should be started at the earliest point in order to deal with such issues as delays in the granting of licences.

Study activity

You are organising an outdoor music festival for 1500 attendees in your town or city. The venue is a local park, which has a capacity of 1600. Write a list of the key event components that might have regulatory considerations and those which might require a permit or licence. Then, using the internet as your primary resource, research the regulations and obtain information about which permits or licences will be needed.

Many of the regulations, licences and permits relate to environmental issues (such as noise control); licences for temporary or personal activity; licences for premises; fire regulations; ambulance, medical and police provision; highways and traffic control; and general workplace health and safety. In the UK, guides issued by organisations such as the Association of Events Organisers (AEO), the Association of Event Venues (AEV) and the Event Supplier and Services Association (ESSA) are key resources. In particular, *The Purple Guide to Health, Safety and Welfare at Music and Other Events* (www.thepurpleguide.co.uk) and the Guidance for events in UK venues (AEV 2020) should be read by event managers, as should the Health and Safety Executive's 'Events health and safety' (www.hse.gov.uk/event-safety/). The Emergency Management in Australia is a useful tool for event managers operating there, and other countries have similar resources which are equally easy to find. Some of the UK regulations that need to be considered during the build-up, show and breakdown phases of an event are listed below, though note that now the UK has left the EU, some rules and procedures are likely to change (similar regulations exist in other countries):

- Health and Safety at Work etc. Act, 1974
- Management of Health and Safety at Work Regulations 1999
- Workplace (Health, Safety and Welfare) Regulations 1992
- The Licensing Act 2003
- Personal Protective Equipment at Work Regulations 1992
- Provision and Use of Work Equipment Regulations 1998
- Lifting Operations and Lifting Equipment Regulations (LOLER) 1998
- Manual Handling Operations Regulations 1992 (amended 2002)

- Fire Precautions (Workplace) Regulations 1997, as amended 1999
- Health and Safety (First Aid) Regulations 1981
- Reporting of Injuries, Diseases and Dangerous Occurrences Regulations (RIDDOR) 2013
- Electricity at Work Regulations 1989/EVA Regulations for Stand Electrical Installations
- Health and Safety (Signs and Signals) Regulations 1996
- The Control of Noise at Work Regulations 2005
- Building Regulations
- Building Standards (Scotland) Regulations
- Environmental Protection Act 1990/Environment Act 1995
- Health and Safety in Construction – HSE Publications HS(G)150
- Temporary De-mountable Structures Guidance on Design Procurement and Use 1999

Additional codes of practice and guides to consider include:

- *The Purple Guide*
- Guide to Fire Precautions in Existing Places of Entertainment and Like Premises 1990
- *Event Safety Guide* (a guide to health, safety and welfare at music and similar events which has now been turned into multiple webpages)
- NOEA's Code of Practice for Outdoor Events
- Specific local authority regulations (your venue will be able to advise you about these)

This list is not exhaustive, and changes are often made, but it demonstrates the large number of issues that the event manager needs to consider at the start of every event. It should be noted that there is concern that the sheer volume of health and safety regulations is strangling some sectors of the industry – in particular small-scale local community and cultural events. For instance, organisers of local street parties often find the myriad rules, regulations and legalities intimidating. They fear that they might face the cost of acquiring licences and permits, and worry about navigating the legal system, so it is hardly surprising that they frequently come to the conclusion that it is not worth the effort.

8.4.2 Health and Safety at Work etc. (HSW) Act 1974

This is the primary piece of legislation for health, safety and welfare of people at work within the UK and is an example of national legislation that affects the events industry. In Australia and the USA, similar legislation is in the form of the Occupational Safety and Health Acts. If there is no such legislation in the country where the event manager is operating, it is suggested that they follow the procedures and requirements outlined in the HSW in order to develop their own code of practice.

The HSW sets out general principles of managing health and safety at work, and enables the creation of requirements through such regulations as the Control of Substances Hazardous to Health Regulations 2002 (COSHH) and the Management of Health and Safety at Work Regulations 1999 (MHSWR). It therefore explains the general duties that employers have to employees and members of the public, and the duties that employees have to themselves and to each other.

In the UK, this is the most important legislation to which the events industry must adhere. It makes it mandatory for all employees to conduct a risk assessment of their work activity

(Upton 2008). It is therefore essential that each event manager and company has a grasp on the document and its key points. Specialist legal support should be sought, if necessary, and students working or living in other countries should be familiar with their own key pieces of legislation.

8.4.3 The Management of Health and Safety at Work Regulations (MHSW) 1999

The Management of Health and Safety at Work Regulations 1999 generally make employers' legal obligations with respect to health and safety much more explicit. Like the HSW, they apply to every work activity: 'The MHSW regulations have been put in place in order that you take care of all those you work in conjunction with – employees, contractors, clients or customers. The aim of the regulations is to reduce damage by assessing all potential risks and to create action plans for emergencies' (HSE 2003: 2). The regulations require employers to review risk assessments periodically, to ensure that they are familiar with hazards and risks in the workplace, to improve safety procedures at every opportunity, and to ensure work is organised and training is offered (HSE 2003).

The regulations state that organisations have a legal duty to put in place suitable arrangements to manage health and safety. The HSE (2014) advocates a common-sense, practical approach that should be part of the everyday process of running an organisation – as such, they suggest organisations adopt the Plan, Do, Check, Act approach, which integrates health and safety into good management practices, rather than treating it as a stand-alone process. This approach can be summarised as:

- Plan – determine your policy and/or plan for implementation
- Do – identify the risks, organise for health and safety and implement your plan
- Check – monitor the performance and investigate after incidents
- Act – review the performance, act on lessons learnt.

8.4.4 Corporate manslaughter law

Legally, the event organisation often has responsibility for the safety of its employees. In the UK, this is covered by the Corporate Manslaughter and Corporate Homicide Act 2007. Event organisers operating in other countries should check their own laws on corporate responsibility in detail. These laws specify that adequate safety practices and procedures must be in place, and they allow for conviction if it can be proved beyond reasonable doubt that a company was homicidally reckless about risk. During events, this applies to accidental death of both employees and attendees.

In 2008, there was a stampede of 2000 people at the launch of a sale event at a Wal-Mart store in America, and an employee was trampled to death. The employee's family sued Wal-Mart in a wrongful-death lawsuit which claimed that the company had engaged in marketing and advertising techniques specifically designed to attract a large crowd and create an environment of frenzy and mayhem. In America, a wrongful-death case alleges that a person was killed as a result of another's negligence or other form of liability. The lawsuit was settled when Wal-Mart agreed to improve its crowd control for its day-after-Thanksgiving events, and 'the world's largest retailer also agreed to set up a $400,000 victim's compensation fund, donate

$1.5 million to the community and provide 50 jobs annually to high school students in the area' (Robideaux 2009; see also the video sources at the end of the chapter).

Study activity

For non-UK students

Find the relevant corporate responsibility law or act for your country and make a note of its exact name. Now do the same for control of hazardous substances and safety at work legislation. Finally, identify the governing body for health and safety and note any other specific health and safety regulations for your country.

For UK students

What are the major differences between the Health and Safety at Work etc. Act 1974 and the Management of Health and Safety at Work Regulations 1999? Discuss your findings with another student.

8.5 Insurance

Events are susceptible to any number of issues that are often outside the event organisation's control. Natural disasters can have severe effects on an event's performance – in the past outbreaks of contagious diseases like bird and swine flu in Asia and South America, respectively, and foot and mouth in the UK have had severe implications for specific events, and now, of course, we all know about the impacts that a global pandemic such as that caused by the outbreak of coronavirus can have on the events industry. Other natural disasters, such as extreme weather conditions including flooding or blizzards or the bush fires in Australia, can also result in cancelled events and loss of revenue for the entire supply chain. On top of the seemingly increasing number of natural disasters, the events industry has witnessed a shift towards a larger number of claims made from attendees who have injured themselves at an event or who make claims when they perceive the event to be unsatisfactory – perhaps due to the cancellation of the main act or a change of venue. Event insurance is therefore now seen as essential, though it is not always fit for purpose, and that in itself has made it become one of the key issues for the industry.

Study activity

Research how the Covid-19 pandemic impacted on the events industry in your country. Can you identify whether the events industry would be covered for epidemics or communicable diseases?

Event insurance will typically cover such items as cancellation of the event, venue bankruptcy, non-appearance of celebrities, failure to vacate the venue, damage to property or premises, legal liabilities, damage to equipment, and public liabilities (Shone and Parry 2010).

The importance of event insurance was illustrated by the Wimbledon tennis tournament, which had to be cancelled in 2020 due to coronavirus – however, the organisers had taken out an extension to their insurance policy (a communicable diseases extension) which effectively insured them against the pandemic. They were therefore able to claim for their cancellation and are poised to earn a substantial pay-out as a result (Eventsforce 2021). Cancellation is usually the very last option for event organisers, though – often, they will approach their insurance company

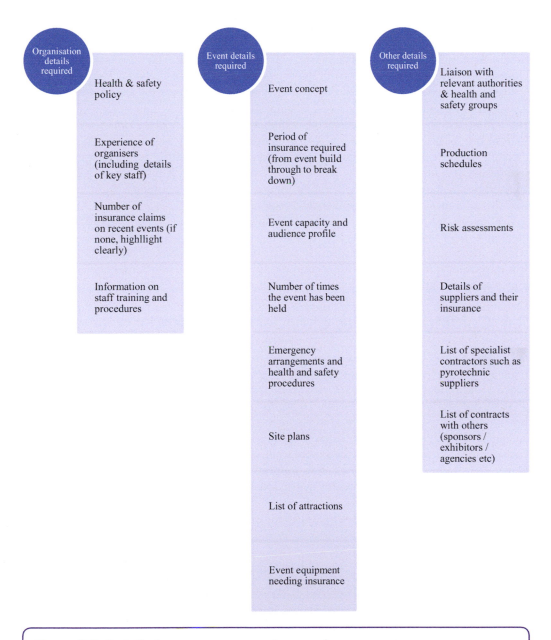

Figure 8.2 Details insurance companies require
Source: Adapted from EventScotland (2019)

to fund preventative action. Insurance companies will often cover smaller amounts that enable the show to go on: for instance, they might make funds available for extra transport to ensure that guests can beat transport strikes, or for a change of venue at the last minute. Both organisers and insurers will obviously explore such options in preference to cancellation of the whole event.

Insurance that covers theft, fire, weather and workers' compensation is also important, as is public liability (sometimes known as personal accident) insurance and property damage insurance. Any special insurance for particular elements of the event should also be acquired (for example, marquees often require special insurance and events that take place outside can sometimes ask for weather insurance) and consideration should be given to event equipment and property cover to ensure that any hired equipment is covered. Many insurance policies exclude terrorist attacks and 'acts of God' (typically defined as acts that are outside of human control, such as natural disasters).

Event managers should also always check that suppliers – such as the artists, venue, audio-visual suppliers, entertainment agencies, staffing agencies and so on – have their own insurance and liability cover and are in compliance with industry and legal regulations.

Insurance policies and the clauses within them are often very specific and should be read carefully. It is also important to give the insurers the right information. Equipment used on-site will need to be detailed carefully: for example, expensive musical instruments are often not covered by standard insurance policies. Figure 8.2 provides a sample checklist of information that the insurance company or brokers will require.

Event insurance should therefore be in place for the entire planning process and, in order to gain the correct cover, insurance requirements should be investigated in good time, preferably with an insurance broker or with specialist event insurance companies (Shone and Parry 2010). It is advisable to aim to confirm event insurance two to three months before and certainly no less than one month before the event date (EventScotland 2006).

8.6 Guiding principles of health, safety and risk

For industry professionals, the essential principle to understand is that health, safety and risk management is a key part of event planning. It should be factored in from the very start of the process and should be considered during every part of the planning process.

There are four key principles relating to health and safety that every event organiser should bear in mind. These are summarised in Figure 8.3.

This textbook demonstrates that every event is unique and needs particular attention and consideration. However, it is useful to note some key areas of event planning that need a particular focus from a health, safety and risk perspective. These can range from significant aspects of event planning – venue and site design – to circumstantial issues, such as refreshments and sanitation (HSE 2014).

Some of the key areas for event organisers to consider can be summarised as:

- control of hazardous substances
- communication procedures
- crowd management
- electrical installations and lighting, including special effects and pyrotechnics
- facilities for people with special needs
- fire safety
- food, drink and water
- noise and vibration
- major incident (emergency) planning

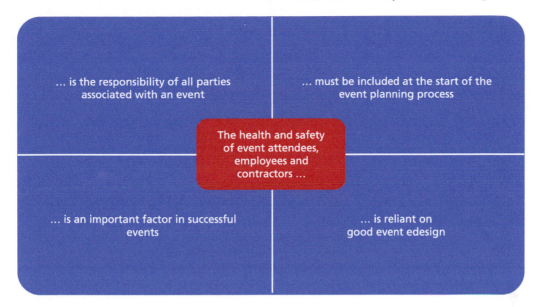

Figure 8.3 The importance of health and safety at events

- medical, ambulance and first-aid management
- performers, TV and media
- sanitary and waste facilities and management
- structures and barriers
- transport management
- venue and site design and management.

(List adapted from HSE 1999: 3)

Later in this chapter, three specific risks of particular interest to event managers will be discussed in detail.

As well as the individual areas that need health, safety and risk management, it is important that event organisers consider the event phases and the safety implications for each. These phases can be represented as the build-up (pre-planning); load-in (set-up of the event); show (the event itself); load-out (dismantling equipment); and breakdown (dismantling the venue or the final processes of leaving the venue, as appropriate). These phases and the safety implications for each can be seen in Figure 8.4.

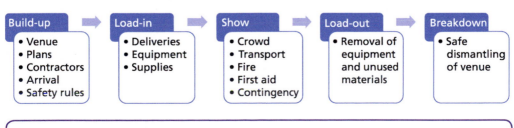

Figure 8.4 Event safety phases

Useful resource

This Eventbrite Blog provides an excellent checklist of Health and Safety Considerations when organising events: www.eventbrite.co.uk/blog/guide-health-and-safety-for-events-ds00/

8.6.1 Impacts of health, safety and risk-related incidents

Health, safety and risk-related incidents at events can have wide-ranging and often disastrous impacts. Without proper attention to health, safety and risk management, event organisers expose their audience, their colleagues and their contractors to injury and loss of life.

A small-scale incident, such as a person tripping and falling, can result in a loss of event focus as the audience is distracted by the incident. This loss of focus will affect the audience's perceptions of the event and may result in issues with stakeholders, who will be unhappy with the shift in focus, away from their key messages. Such small-scale incidents can therefore impact on the future effectiveness of an event, so their importance should not be dismissed.

Study activity

You are an event manager of a small-scale, local event. During the event, a child trips over a cable and breaks her leg. The local newspaper runs the story and questions how safe your event is. Write a list of ways in which you can respond to this incident, which will help you to recover some of your reputation for running a safe event.

Small-scale incidents can have serious ramifications. But it is the large-scale incidents that will cause the most problems for the event organisation. It is important to remember that these health, safety and risk-related incidents can also have devastating and ruinous results. The media may report the incident, resulting in negative publicity, changes in the local mood towards the event and a shift in worldwide perceptions. An example of this was the 2010 tragedy at the Love Parade in Germany, which resulted in 19 deaths, worldwide negative publicity and the eventual dissolution of the event. (For news reviews and footage of this disaster, see the video sources listed at the end of the chapter; see also the further reading for a fascinating article on this disaster.) Another example is that of the Shoreham air show crash that took place in South East Britain in August 2015. A vintage jet aircraft crashed whilst doing a display over land, killing 11 people and injuring 16 others. This tragedy led to the Civil Aviation Authority announcing certain restrictions on displays over land, which resulted in the cancellation of or fundamental changes to displays at airshows across the UK.

A large-scale event disaster occurred when the *Marchioness* leisure boat sank in 1989. The boat was hosting a private party with 131 people on board when it collided with a large dredger. The pleasure boat sank almost immediately and 51 people drowned. According to Hartley (2002), the long-awaited public inquiry blamed almost everyone involved, including the Department of Transport, the captains of both vessels, the companies that managed them and the police. This inquiry eventually led to the Department of Transport carrying out a comprehensive Formal Safety Assessment of River Thames passenger vessels (later extended to all operating environments for domestic passenger ships in the UK), which covered every aspect of their safety, including 'their encounter risk with large ships and bridges, fire risk, stability, subdivision, freeboard, visibility, lifesaving appliances, means of escape, manning, passenger numbers, trading areas and safety management' (Maritime and Coastguard Agency 2005: 1).

8.7 Health and safety management

The information and advice in this section is drawn from the Health and Safety Executive website 'Guidance on Running Events Safely', which is essential reading for all events management students and organisers.

8.7.1 Key elements of successful health and safety management

As we have seen, legislation and regulation of health and safety have become paramount to the successful and safe delivery of any event. Once the event concept is developed, but *before the event manager proceeds any further*, it is essential that they turn their full attention to the management of health and safety before, during and after the event. This process begins with the creation of a health and safety policy.

AEV (Section 3, p. 9 of 2020 edition) advise the following procedures for the creation of a health and safety policy (they are concerned chiefly with exhibitions, but their advice is relevant industry wide):

> A health and safety policy should set out a clear direction for the organisation to follow. It should contribute to all aspects of business performance as part of a demonstratable commitment to continuous improvement. It should specifically set out the following:
>
> 1   The policy statement
> 2   Organisation of health and safety
> 3   The arrangements for the management of health and safety

It is a legal requirement that employers with five or more employees produce a written health and safety policy. For UK students, templates of these policies can be found at www.hse.gov.uk/event-safety.

Even if you are not required to have a health and safety policy, all event organisers should have, as a minimum, a safety plan. A safety plan identifies the following:

- Scale, type and scope of the event
- Type and size of audience
- Location
- Duration of the event
- Time of day and year the event will be held

Using this information, event organisers can create risk assessments (see section 8.9 for details).

> ### Study activity
>
> In groups of three or four, devise your own event concept, and, from that, create a safety plan. You will use this plan to create a risk assessment later in the chapter.

Once a safety plan or policy has been created, the event manager must ensure that it is put into practice. This involves the dissemination of the relevant parts of the policy to all relevant stakeholders, including all staff, the local authorities and government, suppliers, the venue and the customers. Once these stakeholders have been briefed, the event manager must monitor the ongoing delivery and performance of the health and safety policy and ensure that all aspects of it are implemented correctly, efficiently and within all legal requirements and available guidelines. The last part of the management of any health and safety policy happens after the event has finished. At this point, the policy should be fully reviewed and audited, in order to assess its performance and management. The importance of this should not be underestimated. If the health and safety policy is not managed effectively, then the event manager and their organisation may be held liable for any accidents or issues that arose during the event.

8.7.2 Responsibilities

In order to be clear on the importance of ensuring health and safety policies and procedures are in place, it is useful to have an understanding of the responsibilities of both the employee and the employer/event organisation.

8.7.2.1 Employer

An event employer must consult employees or a health and safety representative on (among other things) any changes that affect health and safety at work; the information to be given on the likely risks and dangers arising from event work and the measures to reduce or eliminate these risks; what to do when dealing with a risk; and health and safety planning.

General employer duties also include making the workplace safe; ensuring machinery is safe; and giving the necessary information, instruction, training and supervision for health and safety. In particular, an employer must assess the risks to health and safety and make arrangements for implementing the health and safety measures identified as being necessary by the assessment. They must also appoint a competent person to assist with health and safety responsibilities, and consult the safety representative about this appointment; cooperate on health and safety with other employers sharing the same workplace; set up emergency procedures; provide adequate first-aid facilities; and ensure that the workplace satisfies health, safety and welfare requirements (HSE 1999).

8.7.2.2 Employee

It is important to note that event employees' health, safety and welfare at work are protected by law in most countries. However, an employee also has a responsibility to look after themselves and others around them. This responsibility includes the need to identify potential issues and recognise problems within the health and safety provision. These problems can be small, such as identifying a loose panel on a stage set and informing someone so that it does not cause injury. Or they can be large, such as noticing that the planned layout for crowd flow may cause a crush and ensuring the relevant amendments to the plan are carried out. At the very least, if there is a problem, event employees should discuss it with their employer or safety representative, if there is one.

8.8 Risk management

Risk management involves an organisation or employer looking at risks in the workplace and implementing policies and procedures to minimise them. It is not solely concerned with health and safety. In fact, risks can arise in any area of the business, including financial, business planning and strategies, employee relations and sales and marketing. In events, the management of risk will therefore relate to the overall event strategy, with organisers required to carry out several other forms of risk management based on specific issues, such as finances and return on investment, marketing and PR, sponsorship/ticket revenue strategy, and environmental impact.

In particular, risks are now frequently assessed in terms of the 'triple bottom line' (TBL), which refers to the social, economic and environmental aspects of activities. These aspects are usually assessed in the evaluation of an event to determine the outcome for various stakeholders (Hede 2007), and it is becoming increasingly common to include them in a risk assessment which reviews external risks to the event. In other words, a TBL risk assessment will ask questions relating to the social, economic and environmental risks and impacts associated with the event, will assess how these risks affect the wider public, and will gauge the extent to which the event organisation is accountable for them. (A TBL approach to risk management is also often related to sustainability, which is covered extensively in Chapter 14.)

Another key aspect of risk management is that risk is not solely a negative concept. A good risk management strategy will highlight opportunities as well as potential problems. Risk management theory has moved away from the idea that the process is about crisis management. Instead, it is now widely agreed that the identification of risk can lead to greater understanding of a company's relationships, working practices, decision-making processes and overall output. It is therefore important for the event manager to understand the fundamental purpose of risk management and how it should be used across the events business.

However, the major focus for an event manager when considering risk management in an event context is the consideration of specific risks that usually relate to operational issues. Allen *et al.* (2008: 588) define risk as 'the likelihood of the special event or festival not fulfilling its objective', and from here on this chapter will focus on the operational risks that might result in such an eventuality.

8.9 Risk assessment

A risk assessment focuses on risks that really matter and pinpoints the (usually straightforward) solutions to ensure that risks are controlled. Risk assessments protect workers and businesses and ensure compliance with the law. As the Health and Safety Executive (2011: 1) points out, 'The law does not expect you to eliminate all risk, but you are required to protect people as far as "reasonably practicable"'. Carrying out a risk assessment is an absolute necessity for all event managers, even when the legislation does not require one – it should be noted however that there IS a legal requirement in the UK to carry out a 'suitable and sufficient' risk assessment under the Management of Health and Safety at Work Regulations. In general, your venue will prepare a risk assessment for the space in which your event takes place, but the organiser should produce their own specific risk assessment which details the hazards and controls of that particular event (AEV 2020).

An event risk assessment is an examination of elements that could cause harm to people. In other words, it is the identification of things that could go wrong (Tum *et al.* 2006). Every event will have many elements of risk: for instance, bad weather can create havoc at an outdoor event; overcrowding of one area can cause a crush; heavy consumption of alcohol may result in behavioural problems; a loose piece of wire may cause a trip; and so on. Every event should therefore have a risk assessment which enables the organisers to gauge whether they have taken adequate precautions to prevent harm to employees, visitors and suppliers. Organisers are legally required to assess the risks in the workplace and implement a plan to control those risks (HSE 2011).

As Tarlow (2002) points out, risk assessment is not only a way of identifying potential risks and attempting to eliminate or reduce them – it should also form the basis for contingency plans and emergency procedures.

8.9.1 Definitions

There are several key words that events industry professionals use when referring to health, safety and risk. It is important that the definitions of these words are clear and properly understood.

- *Hazard* – Anything which has the potential to cause harm to people. This could be a dangerous property of an item or a substance, a condition, a situation or an activity.
- *Risk* – The likelihood that the harm from a hazard is realised and the extent of it. In a risk assessment, risk should reflect both the likelihood that harm will occur and the severity of it.
- *Risk assessment* – The formal assessment of the relevant hazards and the potential severity of the outcome.
- *Risk control* – Methods employed to reduce risk to acceptable levels.

8.9.2 Carrying out an event risk assessment

A risk assessment should identify the period of time for which it will remain valid. It should take account of the views of employees and safety representatives and should follow the five steps outlined by the Health and Safety Executive (shown in Figure 8.5). Broadly, in an event context, these steps equate to identifying and assessing hazards and implementing preventative measures.

The record should be retrievable for use by the employer in reviews and for safety representatives, other employee representatives and visiting inspectors (HSE 2003). A risk assessment template can be seen in Table 8.1. Included are some typical examples of potential hazards to illustrate how to complete the form.

Risk assessments should not be overcomplicated. Often, the risks are well known, and appropriate control measures are easy to apply. An event manager usually does not need to be a health and safety expert to complete a risk assessment – they simply need to have a good understanding of what is involved. However, larger and more complex events may require some expert help. A variety of risk assessment organisations can assist here, while local authorities and governing bodies are often able to advise, too.

- **Step 1** • Identify the hazards
- **Step 2** • Decide who might be harmed and how
- **Step 3** • Evaluate the risks and decide on precautions
- **Step 4** • Record your findings and implement them
- **Step 5** • Review your assessment and update if necessary

Figure 8.5 Five steps to risk assessment
Source: HSE (2011)

As Shone and Parry (2010) point out, however, the risk that is inherent in much of events management is not chiefly related to safety. It often relates to whether suppliers will provide their services, whether the audience will turn up, or whether the marketing will deliver the expected results. Such risk factors, often identified during the screening process, do not need to be included in the risk assessment document. However, contingency plans should be in place as part of the overall event plan.

For practical guidance on completing a risk assessment in the UK context, readers are directed to the e-guide 'Guidance for events in UK venues' produced by the Association of Event Venues, and last updated in 2020 (see further reading for details). They provide the following list of examples of common risks associated with an event or exhibition, which may prove a useful starting point for event managers. Remember though that each event is unique and the risk assessment should be conducted in the context of the venue, the type of event and the type and number of visitors expected.

- Multiple contractors working in a single workplace
- Fall from working at heights and working on a live edge
- Slips, trips and falls on a level surface
- Manual handling – lifting or moving of heavy/awkward loads
- Falls on stairs or escalators
- Injury from electric shock
- Objects falling from height or loads falling from vehicles
- Impact injury from moving vehicles
- Injury from use of work equipment, e.g. circular saws
- Hanging wires
- Structural collapse of seating or an exhibition stand
- Outbreak of Legionnaires disease from a water feature

- Food poisoning incident from temporary catering outlet
- Fire and fire related incidents
- Major incident and civil emergency
- Excessive working hours
- Stress
- Alcohol and drug misuse related incidents

Table 8.1 A sample risk assessment document

EVENT NAME				
EVENT DETAILS	Location	Date	Running times	Expected audience numbers
DURATION	Site build	Live event	Break	
PERSONNEL	Organiser	Venue contact	Sponsors/exhibitors	Audio-visual suppliers
	Entertainment/ Artist	Staging/set designers	Catering	Other suppliers
RISK ASSESSMENT	Completed by	Signature	Date	

IDENTIFICATION OF HAZARDS					
What is the hazard?	Who might be harmed and how?	Existing measures to control risk	Level	Further action required	Responsibility
Slippery floor	Staff and visitors might slip on wet floor left by caterers or caused by spillages in food hall.	General good housekeeping. Suppliers and cleaners briefed thoroughly to mop floors regularly, and immediately after a spillage.	Low	Food hall monitored every 30 minutes by nominated personnel.	Event manager
Transportation around site	Movement of vehicles around event site requires transport to use the same pathways as pedestrians. Accidents may occur.	Some designated roads for vehicles. Pathways clearly signposted for pedestrians. Routes positioned to enable easy access to work areas.	High	Separation of pedestrians from transport pathways by fencing.	Site manager/ event manager

What is the hazard?	Who might be harmed and how?	Existing measures to control risk	Level	Further action required	Responsibility
Risk of verbal or physical abuse	Unhappy visitors may abuse staff, entertainment or artists.	Managers on hand to intervene and security to be called if necessary.	Low	N/A	Event manager/ HR manager/ supplier managers
Manual handling of boxes, event material and equipment	During set-up and breakdown of event, staff may be at risk of injury.	Porters employed to do most movement of materials. Materials as far as possible to be delivered to the correct room/ building to avoid second handling.	Low	Staff will not set up on their own – always working in pairs. Trolleys provided to transport material.	Operations manager
Fire evacuation of main room/ building	All	Staff briefed on fire evacuation procedures. Fire evacuation procedures explained to student staff when they first arrive on-site for the event. Basic fire evacuation procedures explained to visitors during the introductory talk.	High	Ensure that all staff running event have received information and training on fire evacuation procedures (usually given during induction).	Operations manager

8.10 Specific event risks

Event organisations are usually concerned with a number of particular risks. It is important to note, however, that the three specific event risks listed here by no means comprise an exhaustive list. Event organisations will certainly need to consider many more issues when compiling a risk assessment. These include the use of volunteers, communication procedures, emergency planning (including medical, ambulance and first-aid management), environmental impacts, recording and reporting of incidents, smoking, the protection of children and facilities for special needs. Of course, each event is unique and therefore demands a particular and individual risk assessment process.

8.10.1 Alcohol and drugs management

The management of alcohol, drugs and smoking makes up an important aspect of the control systems that need to be implemented in order to maintain a safe and comfortable atmosphere at an event. These elements are highly unpredictable, which means they represent a risk, so they should be managed as such. Many events have been cancelled or fined due to problems caused through the provision of alcohol or illegal drug-taking in the audience. Sometimes, even the threat of such activities is enough to disrupt an event. For instance, in 2010, the district administration in southern Goa revoked a 'no-objection' certificate that had been granted to a music festival that was due to take place on Agonda Beach, citing concerns over potential drug-dealing. (See video sources at the end of the chapter.)

For many events, provision of alcohol is part of the organisational plan. Different types of events will, of course, involve different levels of consumption. A weekend musical festival with a primary target audience of 18–25-year-olds will probably need to think carefully about the management of the likely heavy consumption of alcohol, whereas a classical music concert in a park will probably be dealing with much lower consumption. Nevertheless, both events demand consideration and planning.

It is important to note that alcohol is defined as food under the law, so its provision must meet the relevant food safety legislation, regulations and codes of practice. In order to ensure that the provision of alcohol is kept within legal, and safe, limits, Bowdin *et al.* (2011) suggest implementing alcohol risk management procedures that include limiting ticket sales, closing hotels early, increasing security and roping-off certain areas. In addition, the following prevention strategies should be employed:

- Ensure that security is well trained and correctly briefed.
- Ensure that no under-18s are served.
- Serving staff should be fully trained to refuse service, recommend soft drinks and slow down service, if necessary.
- Use a drink ticketing system.
- Provide adequate access to food.
- Implement crowd management procedures.

The risk of drugs at events has increased steadily in line with the proliferation of drugs in society generally. In the UK, much of the current anti-drug legislation and many of the drug policies have their roots in attempts to regulate the illegal raves that were prevalent in the 1980s (Lenton *et al.* 1997). As it happens, this particular cultural moment has seen a resurgence in recent times and there is still a strong correlation between dance events and drug use. Students interested in how drug use impacts upon events will find much of interest in research that centres on rave culture and dance events (a good starting point is the afore-mentioned article by Lenton *et al.* 1997).

It is important to note that many drugs are illegal, so the prevention of drug-taking should be paramount to event organisers. Strategies for searching guests, refusing entry and involving the police, where appropriate, are essential. However, most events in the UK and Europe with a profile audience who may be open to the use of drugs now operate a controlled drug policy, which, as well as putting into place prevention strategies, ensures that harm-reduction measures are in place. Lenton *et al.* (1997) suggest three main strategies to minimise the drug-related harm suffered by youngsters at dance events: information campaigns; guidelines issued to nightclub owners and/or rave promoters; and the employment of outreach workers. Figure 8.6 incorporates these strategies alongside other practical solutions to provide a robust drug control policy that should minimise harm. In addition, Case Study 8.2 discusses a more controversial method for ensuring audience members don't encounter harm from illicit drug use at events.

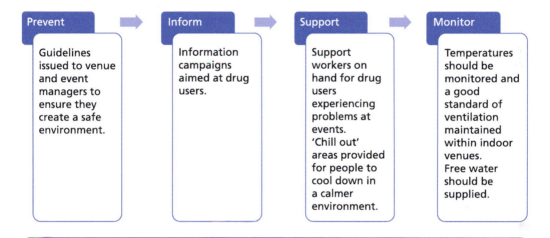

Prevent
Guidelines issued to venue and event managers to ensure they create a safe environment.

Inform
Information campaigns aimed at drug users.

Support
Support workers on hand for drug users experiencing problems at events. 'Chill out' areas provided for people to cool down in a calmer environment.

Monitor
Temperatures should be monitored and a good standard of ventilation maintained within indoor venues. Free water should be supplied.

Figure 8.6 Drug control strategies to minimise potential drug-related harm

CASE STUDY 8.2

Drugs and prohibition: different strategies to prevent harm or death from drugs at events

In Europe, events – and particularly music festivals – have in recent years begun to move towards a hard reduction model at their events. This is not to say that they have stopped trying to prevent drugs entering their events – searches upon arrival are still commonplace at a festival, as are arrests and confiscation of illegal substances – but that they have acknowledged that these preventative measures are largely ineffective and have therefore moved towards creating a safer environment for audience members by minimising the risk of taking drugs. Drugs 'cut' with other, far more dangerous, substances are a leading cause of death at festivals and so festival organisers have attempted to tackle this by offering a drug testing service in which attendees can have their drugs checked for content. Accompanying these testing facilities are 'amnesty bins' in which attendees can dispose of illegal substances without fear of recrimination. These areas also allow festival attendees to discuss drug use in a safe environment, offering the chance to change consumer behaviour at the point of consumption.

In Europe, it is recognised that these strategies which aim to educate attendees and reduce harm are working. In countries such as Australia, where no drug testing service exists, research in 2020 discovered that there is a 63% support level for testing, but the various state governments are still ignoring the calls made by coronial inquest and public feeling.

To find out more, see the following:

Hughes, C. E., Moxham-Hall, V., Ritter, A., Weatherburn, D. and Maccoun, R. (2017) The Deterrent Effects of Australian Street-Level Drug Law Enforcement on Illicit Drug Offending at Outdoor Music Festivals. *International Journal of Drug Policy*, 41: 91–100.

Hurst, D. (2020) Majority of Australian Voters in Favour of Pill Testing, Election Data Shows. *Guardian*, 22 November. Available at: www.theguardian. com/society/2020/nov/23/majority-of-australian-voters-in-favour-of-pill-testing-election-data-shows [Accessed 31 July 2022].

Sources: www.release.org.uk,
SBS News (2020)

8.10.2 Fire safety

Uncontrolled fire at events can cause problems that range from minor injury or property damage to panic, stampedes and death. Fire prevention and evacuation procedures are therefore essential parts of the risk assessment process.

In 2003, the heavy-metal band Great White started a fire with their stage pyrotechnics. These pyrotechnics ignited the highly flammable soundproofing in the club where the band was performing, and 96 people died as a result. The band's tour manager, Daniel Biechele, pleaded guilty to 100 counts of involuntary manslaughter and spent four years in prison. One of the club's owners received a similar sentence, while the other received a ten-year suspended sentence, three years' probation and 500 hours' community service. In 2008 it was reported that a total of $175 million had been offered to the victims' families by various defendants (*USA Today* 2008; Challis 2009). Another example of fireworks creating a tragedy at an event can be seen in Case Study 8.1.

Events are subject to fire prevention regulations. In the UK, this is covered by the Regulatory Reform (Fire Safety) Order 2005. Event managers need to ensure that they understand the fire regulations and requirements of whichever country is hosting their event. These regulations usually establish minimum requirements that will provide a reasonable degree of safety from fire in buildings or other structures. They cover such areas as the number and functionality of fire exits, the storage of flammable liquid, the extinguisher or sprinkler systems, and the use of open flames and cooking devices (Silvers 2004). They also outline the regulations relating to safe capacity of spaces and evacuation procedures.

In order to understand the provision of fire safety, it is essential that event organisations follow these general principles:

- People can walk unaided to safety; particular provision should be in place for those less able to walk unaided and for disabled visitors.
- The route out of the venue should be clearly recognisable and accessible no matter where the fire breaks out.
- When fire breaks out, people often try to leave the way they entered. Where this is not possible (perhaps because the fire has broken out there or smoke is causing visibility issues), people should be able to find an alternative route to safety (HSE 1999: 22).
- Stewards and staff must be trained to usher people to safety. There is often resistance from guests who have underestimated the risk and do not want to use another exit.

Large-scale events or those involving pyrotechnics or other designed elements that present a fire hazard will require a site inspection by a fire warden or fire marshal. The event manager will be present during this inspection, and they might be asked to install extra fire extinguishers or fire exit signs. Equipment may need to be moved and venues may be required to install sprinkler systems (Silvers 2004) or to make provision for extra fire wardens on-site during the event.

Finally, whilst it is much less likely that people will be trapped by fire at an outdoor event, the risks should still be managed and controlled as they are for indoor events. Fire warning systems are required for outdoor structures, such as marquees, campsites should have fire watchtowers, and campers should be provided with safety advice.

Study activity

Remember the event you created in groups earlier in the chapter? Revisit the safety plan, and using the information provided above, carry out a risk assessment which considers all the major hazards your event might encounter. Use a template from the internet to create your risk assessment.

8.10.3 Managing crowds safely

As Abbott and Abbott (2000) suggest, crowd management and crowd control are two distinct but interrelated concepts. The former relates to the facilitation and movement of crowds during the normal circumstances of an event, whilst the latter relates to the steps that must be taken when a crowd starts to behave unexpectedly. Therefore, crowd management is proactive, whilst crowd control is reactive. Crowd management is carefully planned and implemented via the risk management and risk assessment processes prior to an event, and 'a well-conceived crowd management plan hopefully will eliminate the need for extensive crowd control' (Abbott and Geddie 2001: 269).

8.10.3.1 Key issues of crowd management

CROWD ANALYSIS

The most important of aspect of crowd management involves making an accurate estimate of the number of attendees (Bowdin *et al.* 2011; Silvers 2004). When doing this, event managers need to bear in mind the capacity of the venue, and they should be able to forecast expected turnout. This forecast should be based on several factors: attendance in previous years, numbers who visit similar events, proposed level of publicity, number of advanced ticket sales, and so on. Allowance should always be made for much larger numbers turning up on the day, especially for events that are not based solely on advanced ticket sales.

At the end of the 1990s, the Glastonbury Festival suffered a few years of over-attendance, and these additional attendees (who gained entry without tickets) caused numerous safety problems. These problems became so severe that the festival was prosecuted in 2000 for having too many people on-site, and the local authority felt that it could no longer issue a public entertainment licence. The following year, the festival took a year off to review the

Image 8.2 Crowds watch the Metamorphosis show at Glastonbury Festival

situation and its organisers devised workable solutions that complied with safety regulations, allowed proper crowd management and did not impact on Glastonbury's core philosophy and creativity. They set up a Licensing Working Group and liaised closely with industry experts, the police and the local authorities to implement various highly effective measures. A copy of Glastonbury's 2019 event management plan, including details on how they manage crowds, can currently be found at Mendip Council (see citation for Mendip Council 2020).

CROWD BEHAVIOUR

It is important to have an understanding of the type of attendee the event will attract. A rock concert that encourages dancing and generally boisterous behaviour will have a very different crowd management plan from that of a toy exhibition, which will attract mainly families. The Health and Safety Executive (HSE 2000) therefore advises that it is important to know the age range and social mix of attendees, which will allow event managers to anticipate likely behaviour and make appropriate arrangements for it.

Abbott and Geddie (2001) highlight the importance of circumstances that may trigger crowd problems. Their list includes cancellation, no-shows, congestion, lack of parking, the use of special effects, and the presence of obscene or violent performing acts. Other factors, such as weather, noise levels and the presence of rival groups, should be carefully considered in the crowd risk management process.

So, event managers need to have a good understanding of the type of event they are staging and how their audience might react. This is not as simple as deciding that a concert for 70,000 young adults will need detailed crowd management plans whereas a classical music event for 15,000 middle-aged adults will not – a loss of crowd control can occur in the most unlikely places, as the Wal-Mart stampede tragically proved in 2008. Similarly, religious festivals often suffer crowd-related tragedies. For instance, 147 worshippers died in a crush in a Hindu temple in 2008 (BBC 2008); and at least 340 people died in a stampede at a water festival in Cambodia two years later (Masis and Siddique 2010). There have also been many serious incidents during the Muslim Hajj: in 1990, 1400 pilgrims died in a stampede in a pedestrian tunnel; in 1994, 270 people were crushed to death; in 1997, 350 people died in a fire; in 1998, 180 pilgrims died in a crush; in 2004, stampedes resulted in the deaths of 250 people; and in 2006, at least 362 people died in a similar fashion (Al-Bab.com 2011; BBC 2001; and see Case Study 8.3).

However, a key point for organisers to remember is that crowd disasters are usually created because of management issues, and not because of the way a crowd behaves. In order to militate against crowd disasters, event organisers should be planning for crowds not to be too tightly packed. Work by the Fire Safety Engineering Group at the University of Greenwich (FSEG 2020; Benedictus 2015) indicates that moving crowds with a density of up to four people per square meter are safe, because individuals within them have room to make decisions and the crowd will not move like a fluid. However, when the density of the crowd becomes higher – around six people per square meter – bodies are too tightly packed together and individuals can no longer choose where they go. This creates pressure waves which can travel through the crowd, resulting in a loss of control. When the crowd is this dense, they become prone to two types of accident – a progressive crowd collapse, where one person falls and adjacent people fall on top due to the sudden gap and the pressure from the other sides. This often happens when crowds are moving through confined spaces (see Case Study 8.3). The second type of crowd disaster is when people are 'squeezed' to the extent that they can no longer inflate their lungs, and die gradually of asphyxiation. This is known as a 'crowd crush' and happens when people push into a confined area – Hillsborough is an example of this, as is the disaster at the Love Parade in Germany.

> Crowd forces can reach levels that are almost impossible to resist or control. Virtually all crowd deaths are due to compressive asphyxia and not the 'trampling' reported by the news media. Evidence of bent steel railings after several fatal crowd incidents show that forces of more than 4500 N (1000 lbs) occurred.
>
> (Crowd Dynamics 2011)

Silvers (2004) provides a useful list of definitions to explain potential reactions of a crowd in unforeseen circumstances:

- *Crowd crush* – The crowd is compressed into ever-smaller areas due to an absence of a portal or escape, and this compression quickly becomes critical. An example was the Hillsborough Stadium disaster in 1989 (see video sources at the end of the chapter).
- *Crowd collapse* – Individuals at the front of a crowd fall over, and those behind consequently lose their balance and fall on top. An example of this is the 2015 Hajj tragedy.
- *Crowd craze* – This is rarer than other crowd reactions and typically occurs when the crowd rushes or pushes forward, towards an individual or a desired object.
- *Crowd panic* – The frenzied desire to escape a real or perceived danger. Panicking crowds often trample those who have fallen and are lying on the escape route. In the aforementioned Cambodian water festival disaster, the crowd seems to have panicked because of rumours that people were being electrocuted and that the bridge on which they were standing was starting to collapse (see video sources at the end of the chapter).
- *Crowd surge* – This often occurs at concerts. In the 2009 Mawazine Festival in Morocco, the 70,000-plus crowd surged forward to see singer Abdelaziz Stati. This resulted in at least 11 deaths and 40 injuries.

The general principles are that the event manager must know their crowd and must have the right precautionary (and often calming) measures in place before the event starts. These measures can range from ensuring the visibility of security staff and personnel to removing audience members who are displaying inappropriate or unruly behaviour. No two crowds are the same, so it is difficult to predict how one will behave in unexpected circumstances, but event managers should still have an understanding of a crowd's basic sociological behaviour and how it might react. For further information on this topic, see numerous relevant articles in the journal *Events Management*, Abbott and Abbott (2000), Abbott and Geddie (2001), the HSE's *Managing Crowds Safely* (2000) and Crowd Dynamics (2011). A particularly valuable resource is the Fire Safety Engineering Group (2020).

Study activity

In pairs, read the following article and discuss the key findings. Do you think that the use of technology to model crowd behaviour is useful? Explain why.

Zhao, H., Thrash, T., Kapadia, M., Wolff, K., Holscher, C., Helbing, D. and Schinazi., V. R. (2020) Assessing Crowd Management Strategies for the 2010 Love Parade Disaster Using Computer Simulations and Virtual Reality, *The Royal Society*, 17 (*167*). https://doi.org/10.1098/rsif.2020.0116

8.10.3.2 Crowd control planning

In order to implement a successful crowd management plan, event managers also need to assess the factors that make up a crowd control plan. This will consist of the steps and procedures that should be taken once a crowd has lost control, and it will outline the measures that should be implemented at different stages of the event (Abbott and Geddie 2001).

Abbott and Geddie (2001) suggest that there are three stages in a crowd control plan – pre-crisis, crisis and post-crisis. During the pre-crisis stage, the event manager will consider certain preventative tactics to avoid crowd control problems (such as staff training, facilities management and the use of a control centre to aid communication). A crowd-related risk assessment will be produced at this stage. To help with this, the event manager should consider what might go wrong, who might be harmed and what the best response would be (see Table 8.2).

The second stage – the crisis stage – begins when the preventative measures fail. During this stage, practical crowd control measures, such as clear evacuation procedures and calm personnel, are essential – as is a proactive response before the situation escalates. For instance, overcrowding should be dealt with before the crowd starts to panic.

CASE STUDY 8.3

Crowd safety: The Hajj

Image 8.3 A crowd perform the 'tawaf' around the Kaaba inside the Masjidil Haram (the Grand Mosque), Mecca, Saudia Arabia
UnSplash.com, photographer: Adli Wahid

Muslims consider pilgrimage to the holy city of Mecca, Saudi Arabia – known as the Hajj – as the most significant demonstration of their faith and unity; as the world's largest annual pilgrimage, the Hajj attracts more than two million people every year. The size and scale of the event have resulted in a string of major accidents which have raised serious concerns over the management of the annual pilgrimage.

The worst accidents have occurred near Mina, where the pilgrimage traditionally ends with the 'Stoning of the Devil' ceremony. All pilgrims must pass through a small area in a single day in order to participate in the symbolic stoning of the devil – and this has caused major crowd safety implications.

At the event in 1990, panic broke out among the crowd inside a tunnel – more than 1,400 people died. In 2006, a stampede after the lunchtime prayers led to the deaths of 362 people. After this tragedy, the Saudi Arabian government took steps to manage crowds at this crucial point in order to reduce the risk of future fatalities. Their plan included the construction of a further two levels, resulting in a total of three balconies from which pilgrims could throw their stones, enabling freer and faster passage. Tens of thousands of personnel were hired to promote safety and provide stewarding and safety-related services to attendees. Hundreds of closed-circuit television cameras were installed along the route to monitor crowd movement, allowing the timely correction of bottlenecks of pilgrims as soon as they arose, and to enable stewards to clear groups of people as they gathered.

In addition to improving safety at the 'Stoning of the Devil' ceremony, the organisers have focused on the health of attendees. Over 40 ambulances are now on hand to attend to victims of heatstroke, those experiencing breathing problems due to overcrowding and poor ventilation, and those who have been hit by rebounding stones. Cooling equipment has been installed inside the galleries on each balcony to maintain air circulation and reduce the temperature.

These modern measures, designed to reduce the risk of death and injury, were implemented in order to bring one of the world's oldest festivals into line with both health, safety and welfare legislation and the progressive practices of the modern, international events industry. However, in 2015, panic broke out when two groups of pilgrims preparing for this last major rite of their trip collided at the intersection of two narrow streets. Eyewitness reports suggest that this crush resulted in the crowd continuing to 'surge' behind, with more and more people being pushed into the tragedy. As the problems became apparent, more issues were created by people attempting to escape in a variety of directions. Official numbers from the Saudi government suggest over 700 people died. The Associated Press count indicates the death count was actually 2,177. Early indications suggest that this disaster was a progressive crowd collapse (see section 8.7.3 for details).

To find out more, please see: Alaska, Y. A., Aldawas, A. D., Aljerian, N. A., Memish, Z. A. and Suner, S. (2017) The Impact of Crowd Control Measures on the Occurrence of Stampedes during Mass Gatherings: The Hajj Experience. *Travel Medicine and Infectious Disease, 15*, January – February: 67–70.

Sources: Mackay (2015), France-Presse (2015)

> **Table 8.2** Crowd management risk assessment checklist

Are the numbers controlled and predictable?

Are visitors likely to be familiar with the venue?

What are the characteristics of the predicted crowd – age/gender/family structure?

Is the event likely to generate high emotions?

How will performers affect this?

Might there be aggressive behaviour/drug/alcohol use?

Are gatecrashers likely?

The final stage – the post-crisis stage – involves the review and evaluation of the strategy after the event. A full review should be completed by the organiser to ascertain whether security and personnel all responded effectively and efficiently, and to identify key issues or problems that may arise again in the future.

Study activity

The 'Stoning of the Devil' ceremony requires the organisers of the Hajj to balance religion, culture, tradition and safety. In pairs, discuss what you think the organisers' priorities should be and pinpoint five of the key challenges they face in managing this crowd.

Industry voice

David Strafford, TechIOSH, Director of Hopper Events Ltd and Hop Forward Training

I've been working in the events industry since my second year at university. I started running my own club nights and live gigs and was soon hooked. The club nights got bigger however – and *a lot* cheesier – when I joined the Entertainment Department at Sheffield University Student Union in 2002 as their new Special Projects Manager.

Part of my role at the Student Union was to 'House Manage' the club nights, which was a kind of duty manager. This is where I learned a great many lesson about why health and safety is important at events. I ran a number of club nights every week, and the Wednesday night ROAR in particular used to attract the sports teams, who let's say, used to enjoy themselves in the bars of Sheffield before arriving at the Union. It can be challenging dealing with drunk customers, but managing weekly club nights in a Students Union is certainly a good place to learn. The main arguments I seemed to have were with drunk girls who had taken their shoes off and were walking around the club barefoot, with broken bottles and glasses on the floor!

Risk assessing the audience at club nights and live gigs essentially requires you to understand the customers, on a really deep level. On the surface our club nights may have seemed similar, but we knew that the crowds were very different for each night. They would behave differently, due to the nature of the audience. They might arrive at different times, drink different drinks, respond differently to different music, take different drugs. Some nights involved big groups of mates and other nights were more about pulling. For me, it was this type of qualitative insight that helped me – with the help of a great in-house security team – to manage the crowds effectively.

Talk to any security guard who has worked in mosh pits and they'll tell you that mosh pits are actually pretty friendly places; the crowd tends to look after each other really well. If someone falls down, they'll be picked up again and protected. There's an unspoken bond between moshers that you have to look after each other. Crowd-surfing is a different matter though – those pesky flying boots are uncontrollable and often cause injuries! Black eyes and unexpected kicks round the head aren't pleasant. Before each gig at the Student Union, I would sit down with the Security Manager and talk him through what to expect at each show – who were the band, what sort of music they played, what their crowd was like, what the crowd liked to do at the live shows, when they arrived, when they'd leave, that kind of thing.

These insights would dictate how we managed the show: how many security we needed, did we need extra drugs searches on entry, how many pit crew, how many on stage, how many roaming. For bigger name DJs or famous celebrities, we might need extra security to walk them through the crowd. One famous DJ we booked insisted on playing in a boxing ring 'in the round' meaning the only access to the stage was through the crowd – which was a nightmare for the security when he'd finished his set. Another famous band's front man we booked decided to stage dive off the front of the stage mid-set, but the pit crew didn't recognise him and threw him out the venue for causing trouble! That story made the front page of the NME, which was a bit embarrassing.

Eleven years working with drunk students was a good training ground for my company Hopper's first big job – organising children's events with BBC Learning and CBeebies. Drunk students are a little bit like toddlers in many ways! We had to make signage and crowd management instructions super clear, with no room for misinterpretation. However, I also had to start thinking about the event from a toddler's perspective, thinking of hazards at 'toddler height'. I'm not a parent, but baby proofing your house takes on a whole new meaning when you are running outdoor events for 20,000 customers for the BBC. We would put hazard tape on everything! Anything that could fall over in the wind (or be pulled over) was pegged or weighed down. We would wrap everything at knee height in packing foam and bright tape to prevent injuries. Clearly, we were desperate to avoid any kind of injuries to the children, as not only would this in itself be a bad thing, but we were keen to avoid any front page headlines here. In the events industry your reputation is everything.

So ultimately I think there are three key reasons why health and safety is so important for us event managers. Firstly, financial – our reputation is so important to us. Our safety record is often what helps us win contracts, especially with high profile clients and organisations, and we don't want to risk that. We're also keen to avoid being sued!

Secondly, legal – we obviously have a legal responsibility as event managers to write risk assessments, method statements, evacuation plans, wind action plans, staff training sessions, event safety plans, alcohol codes of practice, drugs policies, the list goes on. We have a legal duty of care for our staff, workers, contractors and audience members and it's critical we follow the law to keep people safe and avoid being prosecuted by the HSE.

And finally of course, we have a moral duty of care. Aside from the financial incentives and the legal obligations, we should feel responsible for everybody on our event sites if we're in charge. A good event manager will take good care of their team, their suppliers, their audience. Even the drunk students with no shoes on!

David Strafford is a Director of Hopper Events Ltd (www.hopper.uk) and Hop Forward Training (www.hopforwardtraining.com), offering the one-day IOSH-approved *Working Safely at Events* course.

8.11 Summary

This chapter has demonstrated the centrality of health, safety and risk issues in the event planning process. The guiding principle is that health, safety and risk management should be built into the planning process from the very start. The health, safety and welfare of event attendees, employees and contractors are the responsibility of all parties associated with events and should be paramount in all decision-making.

Health and safety is governed by much legislation and regulation, and event managers need to be confident that they understand the myriad licences, permits and regulations required to stage an event (no matter what size) and that they are operating within the relevant laws. Professional advice should be sought if there is any doubt.

This chapter has also focused on the management of health and safety, particularly on the design of an event, to ensure that hazards and risks are minimised. Without due care and attention to the management of health and safety, and the assessment of potential risks, event organisers expose themselves to potential claims, fines and even criminal prosecution should things go wrong. And when things go wrong at events, they often do so with catastrophic results. Identifying what may be a hazard, and the likelihood of that hazard causing problems for the staff or attendees, is therefore an essential part of the risk management process. The risks associated with event management are wide-ranging and atypical – every event is unique and should be assessed as such. This chapter has outlined the key risks and has looked at some of them in more detail, but a successful event manager will understand that the information presented here is far from exhaustive.

Whilst health, safety and risk management can cause some restrictions to event design, the experience will not be compromised if it is handled skilfully. Consequently, the delivered event will be both excellent and safe.

Review questions

1. Who owns an event? Explain event ownership and the duty of care.
2. What is the guiding principle for health and safety management in the events industry?
3. Many events have difficulties with making their events accessible to all members of society, in accordance with legislation such as the Equality Act of 2010. What accessibility issues might the following events pose, and what solutions are there to ensure that events do not discriminate in terms of who can and can't attend?

   - A three-day music festival, with camping.
   - A live concert in a music venue.
   - A corporate networking event with a keynote speaker.

4. What are your views on drug testing at events?

Further reading

Sharma, D., Bhondekar, A. P., Shukla, A. K. and Ghanshyam, C. (2016) A Review on Technological Advancements in Crowd Management, *Journal of Ambient Intelligence and Humanized Computing*, 9: 485–495. A really useful article that summarises recent technological advances in crowd planning and monitoring techniques.

Worksafe Victoria (2007) *Crowd Control at Venues and Events: A Practical Occupational Health and Safety Guide* (2nd edn), Melbourne: State Government Victoria. A useful 44-page guide that will help both crowd control agencies and host employers (venues and events) to fulfil their responsibilities in relation to the Occupational Health and Safety Act 2004. It identifies common safety problems and suggests solutions to ensure crowd control is conducted as safely as possible. Finally, it provides numerous recommendations and tools to ensure the health, safety and welfare of crowd control staff as well as other staff and patrons. Access it here: www.worksafe.vic.gov.au/resources/crowd-control-venues-and-events-practical-occupational-health-and-safety-guide

Zhao, H., Thrash, T., Kapadia, M., Wolff, K., Holscher, C., Helbing, D. and Schinazi., V. R. (2020) Assessing Crowd Management Strategies for the 2010 Love Parade Disaster Using Computer Simulations and Virtual Reality. *The Royal Society*, 17 (167). Available here: https://royalsocietypublishing.org/doi/full/10.1098/rsif.2020.0116

Video links

Case Study on Crowd Management at the Hajj (multiple videos and further reading): www.workingwithcrowds.com/hajj-pilgrimage-2000-dead-crush-near-mecca/

Deputy Collector Revokes Permission Granted for Chakraview Music Festival in Agonda: www.youtube.com/watch?v=Yevh3NNYnmI

Drug Use at Festivals across USA (multiple videos): https://oneedm.com/columns/drug-use-in-music-festivals-across-the-united-states/

German Love Parade Raw Video Footage from Associated Press (content warning: video shows crowd crushes and the images and comments may be disturbing): www. youtube. com/watch?v=4WnV74PW4bo&feature=related

Health & Safety: Plan Do Review Act. Brodies LLP – Scottish Solictors (UK context but relevant worldwide): www.youtube.com/watch?v=1TZWkX3KplI

Official Documentary of the Love Parade (content warning: video shows crowd crushes and the images and comments may be disturbing): www.youtube.com/watch?v=8y73-7lFBNE

Risk, Safety and Emergency Management for Events and Festivals. Hear from Joseph Pred, who has worked with Glastonbury and Burning Man (among others) in a health and safety event management role: https://youtu.be/ksX4fsYuPt4

Sky Sports News: Hillsborough Disaster 20th Anniversary (content warning: video shows crowd crushes and the images and comments may be disturbing): www.youtube.com/watch?v=pPAD1Q2jzVI

Stampede Kills 378 during Cambodian Festival (content warning: video shows crowd crushes and the images and comments may be disturbing): www.youtube.com/watch?v=3_VqI2TY-H0

Using Crowd Psychology to Boost Public Safety: https://youtu.be/J-YgfM55DII

Wal-Mart Stampede Death Lawsuit (content warning: video shows crowd crushes and the images and comments may be disturbing): www.youtube.com/watch?v=Wsa4BYcwII0

Will Pill Testing at Music Festivals Save Lives? ABC News (Australia): https://youtu.be/6rKzL_KZ_XQ

Weblinks

AEV (Association of Event Venues) (2020) E-guide Guidance for Events in UK Venues: www.aev.org.uk/e-guide. The eGuide brings together guidance for achieving common standards of health, safety and operational planning, management and on-site conduct for events at all participating AEV member venues. The scope and development of the eGuide follows extensive consultation with operations professionals within the exhibition and events industry in order to ensure an overall approach that remains broadly acceptable to the community. The status of the eGuide is similar to that of an Approved Code of Practice. It is an industry-specific guide developed by authorised professionals from the UK event venues. It incorporates health, safety and operational practices that represent compliance with building regulations and health and safety legislation.

BizBash Blog – How Can Event Planners Prepare Employees for Active Shooter Incidents? A very interesting blog piece, from an American perspective but with international relevance, which looks at an experiential agency's new event initiative that involves site-specific safety plans, mandatory employee training and a threat intelligence system. You can read it here: www.bizbash.com/production-strategy/strategy/article/21083289/momentum-worldwides-event-safety-initiative

Bucharest nightclub fire: www.bbc.co.uk/news/world-europe-34684973; www.theguardian.com/world/2015/nov/07/romanian-prosecutors-arrest-local-mayor-over-bucharest-nightclub-fire

Event Safety Guide: www.hse.gov.uk/event-safety/running.htm

EventBrite Blog on Event Insurance Explained. This blog gives an excellent introduction to event insurance in a UK context; read it here: www.eventbrite.co.uk/blog/event-insurance-explained-ds00/

Health and Safety Executive (2016) *Managing Crowds Safely*: www.hse.gov.uk/event-safety/ crowd-management.htm. This aims to provide practical guidelines on managing crowd safety in a systematic way by setting out an approach which can be utilised by organisers of any event or venue. Guidance is targeted at all owners and operators in all public venues where the HSW Act applies. The venue may be used regularly (e.g. shopping centres and sports grounds), or occasionally (e.g. fireworks displays and agricultural shows). The guide is aimed at organisers, but will also be of interest to venue staff and contractors.

Shoreham Airshow Crash (2017) *Anniversary of Shoreham Airshow Crash*: www.shoreha mairshow.co.uk

The Purple Guide to Health, Safety and Welfare at Music and Other Events: www.thepurple guide.co.uk. An essential resource for any event manager. This guide goes beyond the compliance with the Health and Safety at Work Act and covers not only legislation and good practice for health and safety, but other legislation and good practice across the industry including the Licensing Act 2003, the Civil Contingencies Act 2004, the Regulatory Reform (Fire Safety) Order 2005 and others.

References

Abbott, J. L. and Abbott, S. M. (2000) The Importance of Proper Crowd Management and Crowd Control in the Special Events Industry. In J. Allen, R. Harris, L. K. Jago and A. J. Veal (eds) *Events Beyond 2000: Setting the Agenda, Proceedings of the Conference on Evaluation, Research and Education, Sydney, July 2000*, Sydney: Australian Centre for Event Management, University of Technology.

Abbott, J. L. and Geddie, M. W. (2001) Event and Venue Management: Minimizing Liability through Effective Crowd Management Techniques, *Event Management*, 6: 259–270.

Al-Bab.com (2011) The Hajj Pilgrimage to Mecca. Available at: www.albab.com/arab/back ground/hajj.htm [Accessed 9 June 2011].

Allen, J., O'Toole, W., Harris, R. and McDonnell, I. (2008) *Festival and Special Event Management* (4th edn), Brisbane: John Wiley and Sons.

Association of Event Venues (AEV) (2020) E-guide Guidance for Events in UK Venues. Available at: www.aev.org.uk/e-guide [Accessed 10 February 2020].

BBC (2001) Hajj Perils, Ancient and Modern. Available at: http://news.bbc.co.uk/1/hi/world/ middle_east/1203697.stm [Accessed 9 June 2011].

BBC (2008) Scores Die in India Temple Crush. Available at: http://news.bbc.co.uk/1/hi/world/ south_asia/7643373.stm [Accessed 9 June 2011].

BBC (2015) Bucharest Nightclub Fire Leaves Romania Stunned. *BBC News*, 31 October. Available at: www.bbc.co.uk/news/world-europe-34684973 [Accessed 31 July 2022].

Benedictus, L. (2015) How Crowd Disasters Happen. *Guardian*, 3 October. Available at: www.theguardian.com/world/2015/oct/03/hajj-crush-how-crowd-disasters-happen-and-how-they-can-be-avoided [Accessed 7 January 2016].

Bowdin, G., Allen, J., O'Toole, W., Harris, R. and McDonnell, I. (2011) *Events Management* (3rd edn), Oxford: Butterworth-Heinemann.

Challis, B. (2009) After the Great White Tragedy: Where Now with the Crowd Safety Legislation? *Music Law Updates*, December. Available at: www.musiclawupdates. com/?p=116 [Accessed 10 February 2020].

Crowd Dynamics (2011) Homepage. Available at: www.crowddynamics.com [Accessed 14 February 2011].

EventScotland (2019) A Practical Guide to Managing Your Event: Chapter 8: Insurance. Available at: https://www.visitscotland.org/events/advice-materials/management-guide [Accessed 30 September 2022].

Eventsforce (2021) Covid-19 and Event Insurance: What You Need to Know. Available at: www.eventsforce.com/blog/covid-19-and-event-insurance-what-you-need-to-know/ [Accessed 4 February 2021].

Fire Safety Engineering Group (FSEG) (2020) Homepage. https://fseg.gre.ac.uk/ [Accessed 10 February 2020].

France-Presse, A. (2015) 2015 Hajj Stampede Deadliest Ever as Foreign Governments Put Toll at 1,849. *Guardian*. Available at: www.theguardian.com/world/2015/oct/20/2015-hajj-stampede-deadliest-ever-as-foreign-governments-put-toll-at-1849 [Accessed 2 August 2022].

Goldblatt, J. (2013) *Special Events: Creating and Sustaining a New World for Celebration* (7th edn), New York: Wiley Global Education.

Guardian (2015) Romanian Prosecutors Arrest Local Mayor over Bucharest Nightclub Fire. *Guardian*, 7 November. www.theguardian.com/world/2015/nov/07/romanian-prosecutors-arrest-local-mayor-over-bucharest-nightclub-fire [Accessed 31 July 2022].

Hartley, H. (2002) A Party on the River: The 1989 *Marchioness* Disaster: Regulation of Safety on the River Thames and the 'Political Economy' of Risk, *World Leisure Journal*, 44 (4): 30–43.

Health and Safety at Work Act (1974) Available at: www.legislation.gov.uk/ukpga/1974/37/contents [Accessed 9 June 2011].

Health and Safety Executive (HSE) (1999) *The Event Safety Guide*, Norwich: HSE.

Health and Safety Executive (HSE) (2000) *Managing Crowds Safely: A Guide for Organisers at Events and Venues*, Norwich: HSE.

Health and Safety Executive (HSE) (2002) *COSHH: A Brief Guide to the Regulations*, Norwich: HSE.

Health and Safety Executive (HSE) (2003) *Health and Safety Regulations: A Short Guide*, Norwich: HSE.

Health and Safety Executive (HSE) (2009) *Working with Substances Hazardous to Health: What You Need to Know about COSHH*, Norwich: HSE.

Health and Safety Executive (HSE) (2010) Example Risk Assessment for a Village Hall. Available at: www.hse.gov.uk/risk/casestudies/villagehall.htm [Accessed 12 February 2010].

Health and Safety Executive (HSE) (2011) *Five Steps to Risk Assessment*, Norwich: HSE.

Health and Safety Executive (HSE) (2014) *Managing for Health and Safety*, Norwich: HSE.

HSE (2022) Guidance on Running Events Safely. Available at: www.hse.gov.uk/event-safety/ [Accessed 10 August 2022].

Hede, A. (2007) Managing Special Events in the New Era of the Triple Bottom Line, *Event Management*, 11: 13–22.

Lenton, S., Boys, A. and Nothcross, K. (1997) Raves, Drugs and Experience: Drug Use by a Sample of People who Attend Raves in Western Australia, *Addiction*, 92 (10): 1327–1337.

Mackay, M. (2015) Hajj Stampede: 5 Things You Need to Know. *CNN*. Available at: https://edition.cnn.com/2015/09/24/middleeast/hajj-deadliest-disasters/index.html [Accessed 2 August 2022].

Maritime and Coastguard Agency (2005) *Formal Safety Assessment & Research Projects of Domestic Passenger Vessel Standards*, London: HMSO.

Masis, J. and Siddique, H. (2010) Cambodia Water Festival Turns to Tragedy in Phonm Phenh. *Guardian*, 23 November. Available at: www.theguardian.com/world/2010/nov/23/cambodia-water-festival-phnom-penh [Accessed 10 February 2020].

Mendip Council (2020) Glastonbury Festival Licensing and Event Management Information. Available at: www.mendip.gov.uk/article/7467/Glastonbury-Festival-Licensing-and-Event-Management-Information [Accessed 10 February 2020].

Robideaux, C. (2009) Wrongful Death Suit Settled Involving Wal-Mart 'Black Friday' Stampede. Available at: www.youtube.com/watch?v=Wsa4BYcwII0 [Accessed 10 February 2020].

SBS News (2020) More than 20 festival goers hospitalised after using drugs. Available at: www.sbs.com.au/news/article/more-than-20-festival-goers-have-been-hospitalised-after-drug-use-this-weekend/5h2h426cu [Accessed 2 August 2022].

Shone, A. and Parry, B. (2010) *Successful Event Management* (3rd edn), Andover: Cengage Learning.

Silvers, J. (2004) *Professional Event Coordination*, Hoboken, NJ: John Wiley and Sons.

Tarlow, P. E. (2002) *Event Risk Management and Safety*, Chichester: John Wiley and Sons.

Tum, J., Norton, P. and Wright, J. N. (2006) *Management of Event Operations*, Oxford: Butterworth-Heinemann.

Upton, M. (2008) Safe Event Management, paper presented at Theatre Managers Association Conference, 10 June. Available at: www.crowdmodelling.com/2008_upton.pdf [Accessed 4 November 2011].

USA Today (2008) RI Club Fire Released from Prison. Available at: www.usatoday.com/news/nation/2008-03-19-4281531984_x.htm [Accessed 9 June 2011].

Sporting events

Contents

DOI: 10.4324/9781003102878-9

9.1 Aims

By the end of this chapter, students will be able to:

- review the development of the sports industry to its present role
- understand the processes involved in sporting event business management
- discuss the challenges posed by current issues affecting sporting events
- understand the legacies of particular sporting events.

9.2 Introduction

This chapter will highlight the specific nature of sporting events and their major contribution to the development of events management as a worldwide industry. The issues of political influence, legacies, economic impact and how to bid for sporting events will also be discussed, in light of the current difficulties facing a number of sports, as will the extent to which the event manager can prepare to deal with these issues. The motivation of attendees at sporting events, the development of sponsorship and the role of television and social media in sporting events will also be reviewed. Particular practical emphasis will be placed on the management of participants, event safety in relation to challenges of crowd behaviour and management of such issues as violence, racism, drugs and alcohol.

The history of sporting events is unclear, as the first events began more than 2,000 years ago. There is evidence of these occurring in ancient Greece, China and Egypt, with the first Olympic Games held in 776 BC (Masterman 2014). The first modern Olympics took place in Athens, Greece, in 1896. Football – now perhaps the biggest global sport – was first played in its current format in Sheffield in 1860, when Sheffield FC, the oldest football club in the world, met Hallam FC, the second-oldest club in the world, at Sandygate Lane, the oldest football stadium in the world. They competed for the Youden Trophy, sponsored by Thomas Youden, a local theatre owner, at a cost of £2 (equivalent to £170 today; Hallam FC 2021).

That first football game in Sheffield exhibited some of the key components of a modern sporting event. The sport of football was given a set of rules by the Sheffield FA, which enabled competition to take place within a clearly laid-out formula. Each team or participant had the opportunity to win a prize – donated by a benefactor or sponsor – and they were overseen by a referee. Spectators either paid to watch or were invited to attend, hospitality and catering were laid on for them, and the media – at this stage simply the local newspaper – was present to record the event. In the following years, as the number of teams grew, so did the competition, the number of spectators and the revenue from the sale of refreshments.

9.3 Overview of the sports industry

The scale of sporting events varies from the small local event, attracting only a handful of competitors and in some cases no spectators at all, to the mega-event that is open to billions of people around the globe. As illustrated in Table 9.1, sporting events vary in terms of number of participants, total media coverage, value of sponsorship deals, total running costs, management type and the distance travelled by the participants. However, all of these events, whether a one-day local wrestling competition or a one-month international basketball tournament, usually feature an individual or team winner, some form of prize and arbitration of the event.

Table 9.1 Typology of sporting events

Size of the event	Characteristics of the event
Local	For example, school sports day
	Restricted to local entrants
	Usually well established
	Small-scale sponsorship and local media coverage
	Costs are usually covered by entrants and donations of facilities made by the local community
Regional	For example, regional baseball tournament
	Restricted to counties or states
	Usually linked to a regional sports organisation
	Sponsorship usually offered by a sponsor with direct interest in sports
	Media coverage might (occasionally) include television
	Most costs are covered by entrants and/or their sports team
National	For example, national ice-skating championships
	Open to all clubs/individuals based in one country
	Organised by a national sports body and financed by the entrants
	Sponsorship linked to a recognised national brand
	More media coverage than a regional event
International	For example, Berlin Marathon
	Open to a number of countries but cost to entrant determines the level of international involvement
	Majority of participants come from host country and nearest neighbours
	Organisers mainly part time, with support from volunteers
	More media interest but still mainly national media coverage
Global event (mega-event)	For example, Olympic Games
	Participants travel from many countries, so most cover considerable distances
	Organising committees are usually full time or on long contracts, with high volunteer involvement
	Sponsorship is high due to increased media coverage on a global basis
	Revenue-generating opportunities are considerable

In all events, it is the spirit of sport and taking part that are the most important factors, and, as Masterman (2014: 3) points out, there is 'wider significance to society than just the staging of a sporting event'. Such are the growth and increasing value of the sporting events industry that continuing political intervention and political comment in the future are almost inevitable. Governments have long used sporting events to make political statements, such as the US government boycotting the Moscow Olympics, and many people are prepared to stake their political and personal reputations on bidding for lucrative sporting events. Even in the 1980s, a sporting mega-event might generate a few million pounds in revenue, but now the bidding process alone can easily stretch into the tens of millions. This has led to accusations of bribery and corruption being levelled at both those who wish to host events and members of awarding committees. This has escalated to such a level at FIFA that the very future of the organisation has been brought into question. Following an investigation, brought on by an FBI investigation, many key people have been banned from sporting organisations, with the threat of prosecution for fraudulently syphoning money out for personal gain.

All of this illustrates that the sporting events industry is a fast-growing and lucrative business, but also presents considerable financial and reputational risk to the organisers. Sporting events management is an important academic research area, with several key publications covering the topic. There are increasing numbers of events management degrees offered at university level, and a growing number of Masters' level degrees. While more academic journal articles have been written on the subject, many of these tend to focus on the US sporting events industry, but there are opportunities for researchers in other geographical regions to embark on this type of research. In 2016, according to Visit Britain (2021), 800,000 tourists attended football matches in England, spending £684 million during their stay.

This industry continues to grow. The Global Sports Market is estimated to be worth $471 billion (Statista 2020) and is expected to grow more. In the United States, the overall sports market – which includes participation in sports, taking part in events and attending as a spectator – was estimated at $71 billion and is expected to grow to $83.1 billion in 2023 (Statista 2020). This not only establishes sport as an important contributor to the general economy in terms of employment and revenue generated but suggests that sport, and sporting events, impact on the lives of a significant number of people. A key turning point in this development of sport as a profitable business was the 1984 Olympic Games in Los Angeles – the first modern Games not to incur a huge loss for the host city. Profits were achieved through the greater involvement of sponsors, lucrative broadcasting contracts and other outside investment. All of this was in stark contrast to the Montreal Olympics in 1976, which incurred such huge losses that the city government was still paying off the debt 30 years later.

There is frequent discussion about European football leagues and the fact that just a handful of teams in most countries win the majority of the league titles and cup competitions, and that these leagues and cups are not competitive for most teams as they lack outcome uncertainty. American sporting events organisers take this problem very seriously, to such an extent that they have devised a system to overcome it. In order to maintain competitive leagues and retain the interest of all fans throughout the season, the National Football League (NFL) manages professional teams' recruitment of new players by ensuring that the best college players sign for the teams that finished lowest in the divisions. This 'draft pick' was introduced in an attempt to ensure that all teams are competitive and have a chance of winning at least their regional division (Cousens *et al.* 2001). Not only does this help to regulate sport, but it has also become a key sporting media event in its own right, with many millions tuning in to see the results of the draft pick. The draft itself is also a major event and is televised live.

9.3.1 The impact of sporting events

Considerable emphasis is now placed on sporting events' impact and legacy. These topics will be covered in more detail in Chapter 14, but their importance in the sporting events industry merits further attention here.

9.3.1.1 The social impact of sporting events

There are a number of ways in which a sporting event can impact on a local community, either positively or negatively. The key negative impact is inconvenience for local residents (Small 2007), with specific problems including increased traffic congestion, extra people in the area during the event and the possibility of crowd disorder or even hooliganism. These have been issues for decades, but recently more individuals and communities have started to argue that the benefits of hosting sporting events outweigh the negative aspects. An example follows that illustrates this change in attitude.

In the 1970s, Sheffield United Football Club applied to Sheffield Council to redevelop part of its ground. The proposal included building a hotel, expanding leisure facilities, increasing the overall capacity of the stadium and introducing new corporate hospitality viewing areas. These extensive plans were rejected by the city council, which ruled that an increase in traffic and numbers of people attending the stadium would affect the quality of life of local residents. The latter were already unhappy about the disruption caused by sporting events in the area, which numbered only about 25 each year. Forty years later, the football club submitted much-revised plans, but with the same aim of developing the stadium to include more facilities. They were accepted and the development has begun, and it is hoped that it will regenerate what has now become a rundown area of the city. It will certainly create much-needed jobs for a local community with high unemployment. The current stadium already has a hotel and several office suites that are rented out to local companies, and these have created jobs and have generally improved the local environment.

Obviously, objections from the local community can seriously threaten the success of a sporting event. The London Olympics drew fierce opposition from the residents of Greenwich – an important stakeholder group – who felt that the equestrian events – which were held in their Royal Park – would cause disruption for at least six months before the main event in August 2012 and that the park would be closed during this time. This is a far from unusual reaction and this was further emphasised when pictures appeared in the national press of banners with the word LOCOG printed on them, displayed outside local business, which is the logo of the London Organising Committee of the London Games, with the slogan 'Licence to Kill Off Greenwich', as a protest at the amount of business that they lost during the equestrian events held in Greenwich. While governments generally promote the positive social impacts of major sporting events, local residents are still often sceptical (Preuss and Solberg 2006).

Some sporting event organisers attempt to overcome such opposition by claiming that local residents will have the opportunity to meet people from other countries and other cultural backgrounds, and that the event will benefit other local cultural activities. For instance, a car-racing event in Florida was promoted as a sports tourism event, because it was expected that attendees would stay on after the race and take part in local cultural activities. However, research found that most people who attended the main event did not take part in other events in the area, so there was no significant social benefit (Pennington-Gray and Holdnak 2002; Maennig and Zimbalist 2012).

9.3.1.2 The economic impact of sporting events

The economic impact of a sporting event is usually a key part of the bidding process for staging it. Barget and Gouguet (2007) estimated the net social benefit of hosting a prestigious new tennis tournament in France. After deducting all of the costs associated with the tournament, and measuring the reactions of local people, the net social benefit was €215,000 (£195,000).

There are two schools of thought, and much debate, among sports economists and event planners about the economic impact of sporting events. For instance, some researchers have highlighted 'time switchers' – people who are displaced when an event takes place in a major location (Preuss 2005). If an event takes place in Barcelona in August and attracts many visitors, other people who would normally visit the city in the summer might well avoid it because they have no interest in the sporting event. Their revenue is not only 'displaced' for that year, but they may never return in the future either. Event planners often ignore this consequence of hosting a sports event. They are more likely to make a calculation based solely on the number of visitors to their event multiplied by the average amount of money that those people will spend when they are in the city. To that can be added the jobs created by building the new facilities. For example, the Olympic Village in London was used to provide housing for local people after the event, and regenerated what was deemed to be a deprived area. However, those opposing the event might well suggest that the government should build houses and regenerate the area anyway, as part of their general responsibility to the community, without the need for an Olympic Games. The organisers also built into their calculations the impact of increasing property prices. If for example they built 1,000 apartments that increased in value by £10,000, then that would represent a profit of £10 million, further justification for hosting the event.

To sum up, a city will usually gain some social and economic benefits from hosting a sporting event. However, there will almost certainly be considerable costs, too, and these should always be considered when planning such an event.

Image 9.1 Mercedes Benz Arena, Atlanta, USA
Source: Getty Images

9.3.2 Sporting event legacies

The legacy of a sporting event is now one of the key criteria for sporting events bids, and it is frequently discussed by politicians and the media. Barcelona gained improved transport links and benefited from other regeneration projects as a direct result of hosting the 1992 Olympics. However, the Olympic Stadium stood empty for a number of years. It was handed over to the football club Español after the Games, but they have now moved to their own purpose-built stadium. The future of London's Olympic Stadium has been the subject of much legal wrangling and challenges in the courts, with several rival football clubs bidding to make it their new permanent home. The stadium was eventually taken over by West Ham United, but the cost of remodelling what was a new stadium added an extra £200 million to the bill, and the rent that West Ham pay has also caused considerable discussion and is not without controversy. Manchester City Football Club's move into the city's Commonwealth Games Stadium was less problematic and ranks as one of the more successful conversions of a mega-event stadium after a games. There is also a view that hosting major sporting events has a positive impact on the host city and that this presents an opportunity for the host nation to improve its image. Research by Tasci *et al.* (2019) considered the impact of hosting the 2016 Summer Olympics in Brazil. While there were some changes in the image of the country, there were no significant changes in the destination image of the Olympic city itself.

> **Study activity**
>
> You are advising one of your national sporting organisations to bid for a prestigious sporting event. What would be the advantages and disadvantages of hosting this event?

9.3.3 Bidding to host sporting events

In the previous sections dealing with the impact and legacy of sporting events, reference was made to the potential social and economic benefits of hosting a sporting event, as well as the influence of local and national governments. There is now increasing competition to host such events, with governments from all over the world making bids. The competition is so fierce for events such as the Olympics, the European Football Championships and the FIFA World Cup that several million pounds have to be invested in the bidding process alone. New bidding procedures have emerged in an attempt to guarantee fairness in the selection of hosts, and therefore bidding teams should pay more attention to making successful bids.

Countries now set up organising committees to prepare complex bids for high-profile events, while multi-venue events – such as the FIFA World Cup – also generate strong *internal* competition between cities who want to host some of the games. This means that sports clubs and their local authorities now invest heavily in trying to become a designated host venue. When the Football Association (FA) in London coordinated its bid to host the 2018 or 2022 World Cup, 15 potential host cities tendered bids to host matches, meaning that three were likely to be unsuccessful if England were awarded the competition. These were complex bids requiring teams of experienced people from football clubs, sporting associations, local councils, area development agencies, industry figureheads and sponsors, each of whom spent up to six months working on the project. (For further information, see the FA website: www.thefa.com.)

Of course, the vast majority of bids for sporting events end in failure for the bidding committee (Emery 2002: 317). It is estimated that the Football Association spent as much as £10 million on the bid for the 2018 and 2022 World Cups, which many consider to have been an unnecessary waste. Not hosting a World Cup meant that deprived areas are not regenerated and the region does not gain a reputation as a major sporting venue. As a result of the high failure rate of bids, any people who have been involved in successful bids are highly sought after and rewarded, not only in their host countries but overseas. For instance, the late Mike Lee was part of the successful bid teams for both the 2012 and 2016 Olympics, and then helped Qatar secure the 2022 World Cup.

Given the increase in the number of bids to host sporting events, bidding teams need to look closely at the factors that contribute to a winning bid, and need to incorporate these elements, where possible, in their own bid. Of course, it could be argued that the bidding process varies according to the sporting event, but a review of the literature suggests that a number of factors are universally helpful to all bids. Some successful bids have hired well-known personalities in an attempt to influence the key stakeholders that make up the team which awards the event. For instance, the British government recruited footballer David Beckham to lobby individual members of the International Olympic Committee (IOC) during the 2012 bidding process. Gold medal-winners Dame Kelly Holmes and Sir Steve Redgrave were also part of the lobbying group, but Beckham was the key weapon. Prime Minister Tony Blair introduced him to individual IOC members who had not yet decided how they would vote, and many of these men and women were said to have been 'star-struck' in Beckham's presence. With the final vote so close, Beckham's influence may well have helped to secure the Olympics for London.

In a survey of 135 people from 21 countries who had been involved in bidding for a variety of 'hallmark' sporting events, eight key factors for success were identified (Westerbeek *et al.* 2002; see Table 9.2). These provide a useful starting point for any group that is interested in compiling a bid for a sporting event.

Table 9.2 Key success factors when compiling a bid for a sporting event
Source: Adapted from Westerbeek *et al.* (2002)

Success factors	Issues to address
Accountability	To what extent does the bid represent the views of the community whose tax revenues will be spent on the event, and how strong is the reputation of the bidder in this sport?
Political support	Are the key decision-makers in the sporting bodies, local council, local government and national government known? Does the event promise to leave a legacy for the bid city?
Relationship marketing	Are there enough people with influence in their sport, or established event managers, who can influence key stakeholders?
Ability	What evidence is there to show that the bidder can successfully manage this type of event? Experience counts.

(continued)

Table 9.2 (Continued)

Success factors	Issues to address
Infrastructure	Where will all the spectators, competitors and employees stay during the event, and how good are the arrangements for transporting them to and from the venues?
Bid team composition	Can a bid team be assembled that represents the sport and will be able to deal comfortably with important decision-makers?
Communication and exposure	How well known is the potential host city and does it have a reputation for hosting events?
Existing facilities	Given the escalating costs of providing new facilities for events, are there existing facilities that can be utilised for the event?

Study activity

To what extent do you think that Westerbeek *et al.*'s (2002) success factors for bidding for an event are still relevant? Are there any areas that you think should be added to their eight key factors? What about your own country, are some factors more important than others?

A bidding host city or sporting body must address all of these issues when making a presentation. They comprise a checklist not only for the bidders but also for the committees charged with choosing the successful applicant. While the cost of facilities is not necessarily the most important factor, it is becoming harder for countries without a strong infrastructure to be successful in bids, as the costs of providing the necessary facilities are unlikely to be covered by sponsorship revenues and government grants. The typical cost of a new stadium for a mega-event can easily reach £750 million, but some of this outlay can be recouped if it is handed over to a new owner or tenant once the event has finished. This also has the benefit of making the venue available for future bids for other events.

While this research was conducted into bidding for mega-events, those wishing to host smaller events can learn from it, too. The principal reason for staging a sporting event should be to promote and develop sport, so this should always be stressed in a bid. This could help to secure the support of local politicians who wish to promote healthy lifestyles among the community. In turn, this might persuade other key stakeholders to offer their support or funding. Any potential benefits to the local economy should also be calculated and presented to stakeholders, as should any research which indicates that the local community is in favour of the event (Hautbois *et al.* 2012).

Byun *et al.* (2020), in their research into the importance of joint-bidding for sporting events by stakeholders, found that collaboration in bidding increases the chances of success in securing events, as this enables each party to exploit their strengths and reduce overall expenditure by playing to these strengths. This was emphasised in the Euro 2020 Football Tournament, where the games were played in a number of different countries.

9.3.4 Venue design

If a bid has been successful, the first thing to consider is the design or development of the stadium (or stadiums) where the events will take place. Over the last ten years, greater emphasis than ever before has been placed on venue design. The economic viability of a stadium has become a key factor in this design process, with owners keen to ensure that their investment continues to generate revenue on a regular basis.

Table 9.3 provides some examples of recently built or redeveloped sports stadiums that now operate as multi-purpose event arenas. These innovative approaches have generated considerable additional revenue for the stadiums' owners. Charlton Athletic and Leyton Orient secured public funds for their redevelopment projects by incorporating a school and a health centre, respectively, in their new facilities. The New York Yankees' new stadium is another wonderful example of a multi-purpose stadium. With 1.3 million square feet, it can cater for a range of non-sporting events that generate additional revenue on an almost daily basis. The Staples Center in Los Angeles is home to four sports franchises and hosts a number of high-profile concerts and other key events. It is not uncommon for four different events to take place every weekend and the event organisers pride themselves on their ability to switch from one key event to another in just a few hours.

> **Table 9.3** Features of new and redeveloped sports stadiums

Club or organisation	Country	Extra features at venue
Arizona Diamondbacks	USA	Replaceable stadium floor to cater for events that cannot take place on grass or AstroTurf
Wembley Stadium	England	Sliding roof to reduce the impact of inclement weather, and hosts a full-time sports university
Sapporo Stadium	Japan	Sliding roof and interchangeable floors to suit different sporting events
Emirates Stadium	England	Assisted housing for local people employed in key services, conference facilities and museum
Phoenix Suns	USA	Nightclub, café and shops
Leyton Orient Football Club	England	Apartment blocks in corners of the stadium, medical centre and training facility shared with local community
Sheffield United Football Club	England	Offices that can be converted into hospitality areas on match days, car parks used for the city's Park and Ride scheme, new hotel and conference facilities
Charlton Athletic Football Club	England	School/college that converts to hospitality area for events, including gym and crèche
New York Yankees	USA	Extra space for non-sporting major events, including conference facilities and hospitality
Mercedes-Benz Stadium, Atlanta	USA	Multi-purpose stadium hosting three different sports teams

Study activity

Design a new stadium with multiple uses
How would you design a new stand to hold 10,000 in a new stadium in your home market, which is not only a sports venue, but that which can also be used to increase revenue-generating opportunities? List and justify the additional features that you would incorporate, say how much they are likely to cost, and then show how these new features will add to the weekly turnover for the venue. For example, turning the hospitality area into a wedding venue might cost £1000 per event, but it could generate £10,000 in additional revenue. State what the advantages and disadvantages of each feature are.

CASE STUDY 9.1

The design of a new multi-purpose stadium in the Gujarat province in India by StadiArena

Location: StadiArena, Gujarat, India
Event venue: Sporting and other events
Attendees: Up to 25,000

This case study looks at the design of a new multi-purpose stadium in Ahmenabad, Gujarat, India, using StadiArena's innovative design to convert part of the outdoor stadium into an indoor arena using the latest technology.

It is believed to be the first venue of its kind in the world and the first ever multi-purpose stadium to be built in India. While this sort of design incurs additional costs, compared to a traditional-style stadium, the flexibility that this conversion allows the venue means that they will be able to use it every day of the week and it can accommodate a range of different activities. By being able to section off one end of the main stand, the football stadium can still be used, while the other end of the stadium can host a sporting or cultural event. The designers of the stadium have also made use of the stadium roofs, by placing tennis courts on top of one of the stands. According to Paul Fletcher, the founder of StadiArena, the brief for this stadium was to 'create a sporting arena with the potential to generate revenue 365 days a year'. The StadiArena patented technology means that the stadium can be converted from an outdoor to an indoor arena at the push of a button and the seats from one end of the stadium start to retract to create additional space.

This multi-purpose stadium will host a range of both sporting and cultural events, and will also feature retail outlets, offices, banquet halls and a hotel.

9.4.3 Crowd management

One of FIFA's guidelines on stadium safety states that 'the match organiser must take all reasonable measures to ensure that the consumption of alcohol does not interfere with the spectators' safe enjoyment of the match' (FIFA 2013: 69). Clearly there is a dilemma, as some sports benefit from the sale of alcohol at events but have to ensure that attendees do not consume so much that it negatively affects their behaviour.

Of course, the problem of alcohol consumption at sporting events is not restricted to football. It presents a serious dilemma for the majority of sporting event managers, particularly as sponsorship revenue may well come from major brewers. For instance, InBev signed a six-year sponsorship deal with the NFL that was reputed to be worth as much as $1.2 billion. To counteract criticism of such links with brewers, some sporting event organisers have introduced alcohol-free areas in an attempt to isolate any drink-related problems that might arise.

9.4.4 Violence and racism at sporting events

While the majority of sporting events take place without any spectator violence, organisers must always be sensitive to the threat of it. As far back as 1910, Swedish fans invaded the pitch to attack opposition players (Andersson 2001), and since then there have been numerous examples of violence at football matches throughout Europe, although the number of incidents has fallen significantly over the past ten years. There are still serious problems at football matches in Argentina, where the *Barras Bravas*, the name given to hooligan gangs, are responsible for vicious assaults on rival fans (Duke and Crolley 1994). Such is the level of violence that the Argentinian government has frequently suspended the football league in order to penalise the clubs, who otherwise seem to have little interest in rectifying the problem. While many event organisers will argue that hooliganism is a societal problem rather than a sporting problem, they need to be aware that people often cite violence at football matches as a reason for not attending some live sporting events.

Another recurring problem at some sporting events is racism. Black footballers are still subjected to racist chants and taunts from opposition supporters, especially in Eastern Europe. This problem appears to have escalated as people are able to use social media platforms, without the need to register their real identity. Nor is this problem confined to football in Europe. Tennis players Serena and Venus Williams suffered racist abuse at the Indian Wells Tournament, California, in 2001. As a result, they refused to play in the event for the next two years – a boycott that had a significant impact on the success of the tournament (Spencer 2004).

Many clubs and organisations are taking positive steps to tackle this issue through anti-racism campaigns. The 'Kick It Out' campaign is English football's attempt to convince fans to reject racism and the racist groups that have long tried to recruit new members at matches. Meanwhile, Atlético Madrid has specifically encouraged immigrants from South America to support the club, thereby broadening the ethnic mix of its fan base. It is estimated that up to 500,000 people have arrived in Madrid from South America in the past few years, and a television advertising campaign has urged these new arrivals not only to come along to Atlético's matches but to integrate with the wider community.

CASE STUDY 9.2

The new Mercedes Benz Arena, Atlanta, USA

Location: Atlanta, USA
Event type: American Football, soccer and general-purpose
Attendees: 75,000

When the Mercedes-Benz Arena in Atlanta hosted the NFL Super Bowl in 2019, the world witnessed one of the most advanced sporting arenas. Opened in 2017, at a cost of around $1.5 billion, the new stadium incorporates many of the requirements of a modern stadium and addresses the key issue of sustainability as well as allowing the stadium owners to maximise income, due to the multi-purpose design of the arena. Not only is this a stadium for the future, it is also aesthetically pleasing and adds to the appeal of Atlanta as a major city. The stadium is stunning and has already won a number of important awards. Built with the support of the State Government of Georgia, the new stadium is expected to have a significant economic impact on the region, and will encourage more business to consider this location as a venue for their events.

The stadium has been built with customer experience in mind, and has a number of important features. It features what is perhaps the first 360 degrees screen built by Daktronics, which means that wherever fans sit in the stadium, they will always have a view of the screen. Event organisers in the USA are aware that they might lose fans who prefer to watch games at home, so this screen is an attempt to replicate the experience of an 'at home' fan. Fans at the stadium will never miss out, and the new screen encourages the teams to provide extra entertainment in the stadium.

The retractable roof means that the stadium can be turned into an indoor venue and weather-proof, and means that the owners can run a number of indoor and outdoor events, making it perfect to deal with weather extremes.

Naming the stadium after one of the biggest global brands Mercedes-Benz also adds to the stadium's image, and the design features represent the design qualities of Mercedes-Benz. While the exact details of the deal are not shared, it is reputed to be around $10 million a year, which over ten years would amount to $100 million, a contribution of around 10% of the overall building costs. They have been able to sell other sponsorships within the stadium and these have generated as much as $200 million. Hosting concerts in a 70,000-seat venue can generate as much as $7 million per night. Companies are also invited to purchase personal seat licences (PSL), with some costing $350 per game, and in some cases people pay as much as $40,000 per set over a given period. This is estimated to have brought in $250 million. These are not insignificant amounts of money, and show the value of association with sporting brands, as well as the potential to generate revenue with key events.

While developing the stadium, the main focus was on fan satisfaction, and there are several important hospitality areas, as many as 600 in total, where speed of service and convenience are key drivers for the stadium owners. The focus for the owners is service excellence, which encourages spectators to spend more time at the stadium before the event, which increases revenue significantly. Their pricing structures ensure that their refreshments are affordable and 'contactless payments' also speed up service delivery.

While this stadium has cost a significant amount of money and involved buy-in from several key stakeholders, a multi-purpose venue allows for more events to be held and means that revenue can be generated on a daily basis. Atlanta have set out a template for other cities to follow, while also raising the expectations of sports consumers, have opened up new markets in events and exhibitions, and ultimately should give their investors a return on their investment.

9.5 Sporting events marketing

Sporting events marketing attempts to unravel what motivates people to attend sports fixtures, matches and tournaments. While there are examples of research into sporting event attendees which date back to the 1970s and 1980s, it was only during the late 1990s that the first specialist publications in sports marketing started to appear. This fact always surprises people in the sports industry, who assume that this is a well-established and thoroughly researched subject. Perhaps 90% of all research papers on sports marketing focus on US sports, such as baseball, American football, ice hockey and basketball, and they look at collegiate as well as professional events. The Sports Marketing Association was launched in the United States in 2002, in recognition of the growing importance of sports marketing among practitioners and as an academic subject.

The main difference between the marketing of normal goods and services and the marketing of sporting events is that the outcome of the latter is uncertain, meaning that the attendee could view it as either the best or the worst event ever. However, the focus remains the same, with the aim of the organiser being to satisfy a range of customers in the expectation that satisfied customers will choose to return in the future. A sports event marketer must therefore identify the service needs of attendees, understand those needs, and continue to satisfy them. The organisers must be aware of their relationship both with customers, who pay to attend the event, and with other stakeholders, such as sponsors and broadcasters who pay for television rights.

In trying to understand why people attend sporting events, factors influencing attendees can be broken down into three broad categories: front room, back room and circumstantial, as shown in Table 9.4 (Tomlinson *et al.* 1995). Using these various factors, researchers attempted to gauge the attitudes of sports fans attending events. It is important to consider all of the reasons why people attend such events in order to satisfy their needs and requirements. While it is assumed that the main reason for attending an event is love of the sport, Table 9.4 shows that many other factors also influence attendance. This table therefore provides a useful checklist for sporting event organisers. When Tomlinson *et al.* (1995) carried out their research, they found that back-room factors had the largest negative impact on attendance.

> **Table 9.4** The factors that affect attendance at a sporting event
> Source: Adapted from Tomlinson *et al.* (2005)

Front room	Back room	Circumstantial
Does the general atmosphere appeal to the attendee?	Is there a tradition of going to games?	Are they attending with family or friends?
Are the right food and drinks available?	Is it an evening game? (May have different atmosphere to a daytime game)	Are they interested in live sporting action?
Is the venue clean?	How easy is it to get to the stadium?	Do they prefer to attend at certain times of the season?
Is the stadium well-designed?	What is the parking like?	Does the team have a chance of winning?
Is there any pre-match entertainment?	Is the game live on television?	Has the team played well recently?
Is there off-field entertainment?	Will star players be appearing?	Are there other games on television?
How will the other fans behave?	Is there community support for the team?	Are there other sports teams nearby?
Is there a band?	Are there facilities for children?	Is the weather good for this event?
How good are the seats?	What is the transport like for the event?	Has the team won a high percentage of their games? Is this game a special event? Is the opposing team successful?

While seeing their team win is important for sporting events customers, the other factors are equally important – and perhaps even more important – to compensate for the team losing. A typical example is the quality and value of the food and drink that are available. Clearly, with attendances of over 50,000 people, and at an average of around £4 per head in additional expenditure, the potential revenue from refreshments alone can be as much as £200,000. Kruger and Saayman (2019) researched the live event experience and focused on understanding how people are attracted to 'action events', using an 'experience-based typology' of event aficionados, entertainment seekers and crowd pleasers.

One of the key challenges for sporting event marketers is to ensure that customers receive high levels of service and that the issue of queuing is taken seriously. Research undertaken in the United States has found that service quality, the physical environment and waiting times all affect attendees' enjoyment of the event (Hightower *et al.* 2002). At the very least, then, sporting event managers should look for innovative ways to reduce attendees' queuing times. For instance, upgraded tickets could include food and drink in the purchase price, and these items could then be delivered to the attendee's seat during the event. Consequently, that person would not have to waste time queuing for food, and the queue would be shorter for those who did not choose to buy the upgraded ticket. A number of organisations have also developed

Image 9.2 Saudi International Golf Tournament
Credit: Ross Kinnaird/Getty images

apps which allow attendees at events to order and pay for their food and drink before the intervals, which reduces the queues.

Tomlinson *et al.*'s (1995) research challenges the traditional view that fans' motivation to attend is based primarily on the performance of their team. Other researchers, such as Wakefield and Sloan (1995), also challenge this view, suggesting that people are motivated by the experience of the event, being with similar people and pure escapism. Given the competition with televised sports events, it is even more important for sporting event managers to research the reasons why people attend their sporting events.

Fan festivals and events prior to the start of an event are innovative ways to attract more attendees. For instance, the Women's United States Soccer Association held an interactive fan festival – 'Soccer Sensation' – in which fans were able to meet players and take part in soccer activities (Jowdy and McDonald 2003). The main objectives of this type of 'experiential branding' are to raise customer awareness and to improve relationships between players and supporters. On this occasion, the event also raised cash through sponsorship, which meant it was able to sell tickets for future matches at discounted prices.

Study activity

To what extent does the televising of sporting events affect attendance at live sporting events? Consider two sporting events that are televised and list the main area where you think that this might impact on live attendance at the event.

9.5.1 Types of attendees at sporting events

The crowds at sporting events are often made up of groups of like-minded people, and a sporting event organiser should be able to identify these distinct groups using the principles of market segmentation. Most of these people will insist that they are unique individuals and do not resemble any of their fellow attendees, but research has shown that that is rarely the case.

As can be seen in Table 9.5, there are four broad categories of sports attendee: the most devoted, who attend frequently; the moderates, who attend an average number of games; the less frequent, who attend occasionally; and the 'new fans', who are relatively recent attendees at sporting events. All of these fans might claim to be loyal, but they consume sporting events differently, so attempts to communicate with them should be different, too. This basic level of segmentation is a starting point for developing marketing strategies. For instance, those fans who attend only three or four games each season, out of a possible 25, might be encouraged to attend just two more games each year. Meanwhile, those who already attend every game could be offered the opportunity to upgrade their tickets. Different marketing techniques might then be devised to increase the attendance of those who usually watch events from private hospitality boxes, the increasingly important family market and the growing number of female sports fans. Compiling a database of attendees will help sports event organisers to categorise them more accurately, and will therefore enhance the efficiency of their marketing initiatives.

Table 9.5 Classification of sports fans by frequency of attendance

Type of fan	Author/researcher
Most loyal: high or vested, devoted, fanatical, dysfunctional, frequent, season-ticket holders, hard core, old, genuine, traditional, strong emotional tie	Branscombe and Wann (1991), Sutton *et al.* (1997), Hunt *et al.* (1999), Arnett and Laverie (2000), Tapp and Clowes (2002), Malcolm (2002), Amato *et al.* (2005), Stewart *et al.* (2003), van Driel *et al.* (2018)
Fans showing average support: medium or focused, local, enthusiast, moderately frequent attendance	Branscombe and Wann (1991), Sutton *et al.* (1997), Hunt *et al.* (1999), Arnett and Laverie (2000)
Occasional fans: low or social, temporary, casual, infrequent, sporadic spectator, don't follow enough	Branscombe and Wann (1991), Sutton *et al.* (1997), Hunt *et al.* (1999), Tapp and Clowes (2002), Amato *et al.* (2005), Arnett and Laverie (2000), van Driel *et al.* (2018)
New fans: usually watch major teams/stars, corporate, temporary	Redhead (1997), King (1997), Giulianotti (2002), Sandvoss (2003), Tanaka (2004), Stewart *et al.* (2003), Hunt *et al.* (1999), Crespo *et al.* (2003)

Study activity

How does an economic downturn affect the running of a major sporting event, such as the Olympic Games?

CASE STUDY 9.3

The rise of eSports events

Location: Online
Event type: Online with multiple entry points
Attendees: Depends on the scale of event

This case study looks at the rapid growth of the eSports market and the increasing importance of eSports events. While there is considerable debate as to whether eSports should be considered to be a sport (Hallmann and Giel 2018), the eSports market continues to grow with significant global reach. Not only are these events that attract millions of players, there is also a growing number of eSports spectators who tune in to watch major eSport tournaments. There are a number of eSports associations and perhaps three of the most important currently are NASEF (North America Scholastic Esports Federation; www.nasef.org), the British Esports Association (www.britishesports.org) and Esports Europe (www.esportseurope.org). In fact, the British Esports Association states that they promote eSports 'not to rival traditional sport', but to show it is a 'credible activity in its own right, with positive cognitive and other eSports benefits, such as teamwork, communication, developing communities and providing jobs'. Citing the Ovum Market Research Report on eSports, the British Esports Association stated that the global eSports market in 2022 will be around $2 billion, an increase of 20% from 2021.

Esports Charts monitor eSports events and produce key statistics that are used to attract sponsors and media coverage. In 2021 the ONE Esports Singapore Major 2021, one of a number of eSports events that are staged globally every year, was played for a prize find of $500,000. It attracted around 225,000 viewers, who watched around three million hours, which equated to 21 hours of airtime. With such figures, it is easy to see why eSports tournaments are attractive to sponsors, and also attract media coverage.

Event managers who stage eSports tournaments can leverage higher sponsorship deals by presenting viewership statistics and the profile of the people attending eSports events. Sponsorship revenue for tournaments also continues to grow and new sponsors are attracted to the benefits of sponsoring global events. Consider the World Connected Series, hosted by Global Esports (www.globalesports.org), which in 2020 attracted participants from 75 different countries, with as many as 5,000 registering to compete in the tournament. They managed to draw 530,000 spectators online with as many as 2.2 million across social media platforms.

There would appear to be increasing opportunities for more eSports events and there would appear to be a place for them within the existing event market landscape. There are more examples of professional sports clubs that are investing in eSports, and event managers who are looking for new events should research the opportunities that eSports presents.

> ## Study activity
>
> Choose a sport, such as football, American football or cricket, and identify six key market segments that you think a club should target. You should indicate what percentage of the total supporter base each segment might represent.

Industry voice

Javier Doña, Stadia and Sports Management Advisor, based in Spain

Javier is an experienced sports management consultant based in Spain, who specialises in the design and construction of new sporting stadia. In the course of his career, he has been recognised for his expertise in stadium design and is a Visiting Professor at the highly acclaimed Real Madrid Graduate School in Madrid, where their MBA draws students from all round the world and partners UCLA, among other prestigious universities. He also teaches at FC Barcelona, as well as on other sports management degrees. He shares his views here on designing venues for sporting events, based on his experience and research of worldwide sporting venues.

Briefly summarise your experience of the sports industry

It was 21 years ago when I first started working in professional sports management, having learned my trade working on consumer goods for multinational brands. When I first started to work in the Spanish sports sector, it seemed like we were starting from scratch.

From that moment, the growth has been exponential, especially in the last seven or eight years. Today the sports sector is mature, but there is still significant growth potential, in terms of sporting experiences, entertainment and leisure time.

Tell us about your career in sporting events and stadia design and about your teaching at Real Madrid School and FC Barcelona

The strategy in the first few years was to learn about the good practice in the North American market, looking at the main stadia and arenas in the various American leagues and how they were managed. This allowed me to have a vision of the best management methods and how to be effective in sport management. My goal then was to take what I learned there and apply some of these principles in other markets, putting my own take on this.

First my main role was that of sports consultant. However, we wanted to take this further and we decided then to invest in our own projects. We became project specialists, and we agreed that with our own finance and our designs, we could build and sell premium products.

We decided to specialise and worked out that with our own finance and our design, that we could build and market premium facilities in some of the most important sectors in the market. For about ten years we worked with major international events companies, and were able to deliver a product from start to finish.

We also entered many design competitions, such as the remodelling of the Santiago Bernebeu stadium in Madrid for Norman Foster and Partners and Rafael de La Hoz.

At the same time, I have developed my career as a Professor of Stadium Design and Management on MBA programmes. It is a privilege to be able to share my experience with so many students in universities such as Real Madrid Graduate School and FC Barcelona, among others.

How important is customer experience for people attending events and how important is this when you are designing a stadium?

The heart of a stadium is its fans, and without this there is no experience. This should be the only objective of building a stadium. In order to ensure that a stadium is successful, the first step is to identify the different types of customers. After this, we then look at the profile of the venue and the business model.

When you have all the necessary data, then the most important part of the process is to design the experience that your customers need. It is important to design a personalised experience and then work out the right pricing strategy. Customers are looking for unique experiences and increasingly demand more so that our product is going to compete with all the requirements of leisure and entertainment.

In your opinion, which are the best stadia for sporting events? (Give some examples of why you like them.)

The best stadium is the one with the right business model and the best fan experience. The ones that stand out are the Veltins Arena in Germany, which combines the passion of its core fans with corporate facilities, and the Stade Pierre Mauory in France, a two-in-one, which combines an indoor arena inside the main stadium.

The Tottenham Hotspur Stadium stands out because the design has incorporated the profile of its customers, that is the design and symmetry of the stands, which makes it perfect for their fans.

In the United States, I always recommend that people visit the ballparks, with the most impressive fan experience in the market, built for the duration of a baseball game and its particular rhythm of play. My favourites are Minute Maid Park, City Field and of course Fenway Park.

In the NFL and NBA there are some extraordinary venues, where the stands are segmented to suit the fans. The Mercedes-Benz Stadium in Atlanta or the Lucas Oil Stadium in Indianapolis are also worth visiting, with different but very successful designs. In the NBA, there is probably the most holistic experience with their excellent calendar of events. My personal recommendation would be the Madison Square Garden.

The new designs of the MLS are very interesting where they combine the excellent design of an American stadium with the atmosphere of a European stadium such as Allianz Field and the TQL stadium in Cincinnati.

How important is it for sporting organisations to design facilities that can be used when there are no sporting events in the stadium?

This is the most critical aspect of venue design. The average use of a football stadium is 28 games per season, or 7.6% of the year, with 92.4% of the time spent empty.

An average investment is €250 to 300 million, taking up a minimum space of 4/5 hectares, which represents a significant opportunity cost, and there are a number of 'white elephant' stadia around.

This is why the decision to build should be based on the right business model. In the Bernabéu design, it was betting on the development of a bigger corporate section, but the inclusion of a hotel in the design was discouraged because of the requirements of the arena.

What advice would you give a student who wants to work in sporting events?

There is a general rule that decisions should be taken after listening to the needs of customers. This is no different for stadia and events, so that when you design a stadium experience or event, you are designing a product.

However, we can't ignore the fact that stadia have an emotional component that is very special. The fans, who are in effect the client, feel like they are the owners, as if they are at home, and from that point of view the stadium experience is clearly emotional for them. These people are the heart of the stadium and create the atmosphere in the stands, and so any decision must take into consideration their feelings, as to not do so might increase the chance of failure.

Javier, you talk a lot about how to include extra features in a stadium, but where are the best examples of this type of stadium?

A stadium must be multi-functional and these additional features should be included in the design of the stadium. It should also be a personalised design. As an example, the proposal for the TIAA Bank Field in Jacksonville, with a swimming pool on the open terrace, is perfect for Florida, but might not be suitable in less clement areas.

In Europe there are several good examples of a commercial design, such as the Johan Cruyff Arena, Allianz Stadium and Alvalade XXI Friends Arena. . . all with a wide range of retail outlets built into the design.

In the United States we can find designs such as the Gillette Stadium in Foxborough with a wide range of commercial activities and a hotel included. There is Camden Yards in Baltimore, which includes retail outlets and restaurants. Of course the Sofi Stadium in Inglewood is a good reference point, but some of its projects are not transferrable for other stadium designers.

The corporate profile is one of the most important factors, with multifunctional spaces such as Ford Field, Detroit, Stadium MK in Milton Keynes or the Wanda Metropolitan in Madrid. They are very different in many ways, but they share a similar business model. It shows how much analysis is required when trying to design the right stadium or venue for your client.

9.6 Summary

This chapter has highlighted the significant growth in the sporting events industry; in terms of participation, media attention, overall revenue generation and the importance of staging events to local and national governments. Consideration has been given to the impact of sporting events and the legacies left by some of them, as well as the process involved in making a successful bid for an event. Politicians' involvement and influence have also been discussed, as has the relationship between sports and politics.

The chapter has shown that sporting event arenas have changed significantly over the past 25 years to meet higher consumer expectations and to compete with other events. More emphasis is being placed on comfort and additional services, both for fans and for those using the facilities when the main sporting event is not taking place. Examples of good practice in stadium design have been given, as have suggestions for how sporting event managers might incorporate these into their future plans. We have seen that significant improvements have been made in customer care and event safety in recent years, but also that crowd violence may still pose problems for event organisers. Managing the experience of participants has also been identified as an important consideration for staging events in a more competitive sporting event market. Finally, we have highlighted the need for more research into why people attend sporting events. What remains clear is that the sporting events industry is vibrant, with increasing revenues, rising attendances and ever-expanding television viewing figures.

Review questions

1. How can you categorise 'types of sporting events?'
2. What is the difference between an international sporting event and a global sporting event?
3. How do you measure the impact of sporting events?
4. What are the key success factors when bidding for a sporting event?
5. Can you name three multi-purpose stadia?
6. How can sporting event organisers make their events more attractive to participants?

7. What 'front room' factors should event managers be aware of when organising a sporting event?
8. How can you classify event attendees?
9. How big is the global eSports market?
10. Why do people attend sporting events?

Further reading

Masterman, G. (2014) *Strategic Sports Management* (Olympic edn), Oxford: Butterworth-Heinemann. This is the leading book on sporting events management from a European perspective.

McGilivray, D. and Turner, D. (2018) *Event Bidding: Politics, Persuasion and Resistance*, Oxford: Routledge.

Tomlinson, M., Buttle, F. and Moores, B. (1995) The Fan as Customer: Customer Services in Sports Marketing, *Journal of Hospitality and Leisure Marketing*, 3 (1): 19–36. This article, one of the first to focus on customer service in the sporting events industry, used research to identify the most important service factors from a spectator's perspective.

Video links

Bidding and Hosting Sporting Events 101 – Ottawa Sport Council: https://sportottawa.ca/bidding-and-hosting-sport-events-101/

How Tottenham Moves Its Pitch – Changing the Stadium for NFL: www.youtube.com/watch?v=SsQZnyCH37M

The Mercedes Benz Arena, Atlanta, USA – An Introduction to the Iconic Mercedes-Benz Arena, from Concept to Build, Showing the Versatility of the Stadium: https://mercedes benzstadium.com/the-stadium/

The Olympic Congress and Country Bids: www.olympic.org/130th-ioc-session

Tokyo 2016, Leaving a Legacy: Mega-Sporting Events, World Economic Forum: www.you tube.com/watch?v=X1bUaYn9Vp0

Weblinks

FIFA Stadium Safety and Security Regulations: https://img.fifa.com/image/upload/xycg-4m3h1r1zudk7rnkb.pdf

Global Esports – Major Esports Events: www.globalsports.org/events

The MasterCard Stadium Concept – Smart Cities and stadia of the Future: www.mas tercard.com/news/europe/en-uk/newsroom/press-releases/en-gb/2019/april/maste rcard-report-reveals-how-football-fuels-smart-cities/

Olympic Guidelines – Host City Contract Operational Requirements, International Olympic Committee: https://stillmed.olympic.org/media/Document%20Library/OlympicOrg/Documents/Host-City-Elections/XXXIII-Olympiad-2024/Host-City-Contract-2024-Operational-Requirements.pdf

Sport England – Clubhouses and How to Design Them: www.sportengland.org/how-we-can-help/facilities-and-planning/design-and-cost-guidance/clubhouses

References

Amato, C. H., Okelshen-Peters, C. L. and Shao, A. T. (2005) An Exploratory Investigation into NASCAR Fan Culture, *Sport Marketing Quarterly, 142*: 71–83.

Ambrose, P. J. (2004) Drug Use in Sports: A Veritable Arena for Pharmacists, *Journal of the American Pharmacists Association*, 44 (4): 501–516.

Andersson, T. (2001) Swedish Football Hooliganism 1900–1939, *Soccer and Society*, 2 (1): 1–18.

Arnett, D. B. and Laverie, D. A. (2000) Fan Characteristics and Sporting Event Attendance Examining Variance in Attendance, *International Journal of Sports Marketing and Sponsorship*, 23: 219–238.

Barget, E. and Gouguet, J.-J. (2007) The Total Economic Value of Sporting Events: Theory and Practice, *Journal of Sports Economics*, 8 (2): 165–182.

Beckett, A. H. and Cowan, D. A. (1979) Misuse of Drugs in Sport, *British Journal of Sports Medicine*, 12: 185–194.

Branscombe, N. R. and Wann, D. L. (1991) The Positive Social and Self-Concept Consequences of Sports Team Identification, *Journal of Sport and Social Issues*, 152: 115–127.

Byun, J. Ellis, D. and Leopkey, B. (2020) The Pursuit of Legitimacy through Strategic Alliances: The Examination of International Joint Sport Event Bidding, *European Sport Management Quarterly*, 21 (4): 544–563.

Cousens, L., Babiak, K. and Slack, T. (2001) Adopting a Relationship Marketing Paradigm: The Case of the National Basketball Association, *International Journal of Sports Marketing and Sponsorship*, 2: 331–355.

Crespo, A. H., Garcia de los Salmones, M. M., Agudi San Emeterio, A. and del Bosque, R. (2003) Analisís de los Factores de la Calidad Percibida en los Espectaculos Deportivos Aplicación al Fútbol Professional, paper presented at the Congreso Mundial de Gestión Económica del Deporte, Barcelona, 14–15 May.

Dickie, J. F. (1995) Major Crowd Catastrophes, *Safety Science*, 18: 309–320.

Duke, V. and Crolley, L. (1994) Argy-Bargy at the Match: Football Spectator Behaviour in Argentina, European Studies Research Unit Working Paper, University of Salford.

Emery, P. R. (2002) Bidding to Host a Major Sports Event: The Local Organising Committee Perspective, *International Journal of Public Sector Management*, 15 (4): 316–355.

FIFA (2013) *FIFA Stadium Safety and Security Regulations*. Zurich: FIFA.

Giulianotti, R. (2002) Supporters, Followers, Fans and Flaneurs: A Taxonomy of Spectator Identities in Football, *Journal of Sport and Social Issues*, 261: 25–46.

Hallam FC (2021) *Our History*. Available from: www.hallamfc.co.uk/index.php/our-club/our-history [Accessed 3 August 2022].

Hallmann, K. and Giel, T. (2018) eSports – Competitive Sports or Recreational Activity, *Sport Management Review*, 21 (6): 14–20.

Hautbois, C., Parent, M. M. and Seguin, B. (2012) How to Win a Bid for Major Sporting Events? A Stakeholder Analysis of the 2018 Olympic Winter Games French Bid, *Sport Management Review*, 15 (3): 263–275.

Hightower, R., Brady, M. K. and Baker, T. L. (2002) Investigating the Role of the Physical Environment in Hedonic Service Consumption: An Exploratory Study of Sporting Events, *Journal of Business Research*, 55: 697–707.

Hunt, K. A., Bristol, T. and Bashaw, R. E. (1999) A Conceptual Approach to Classifying Sports Fans, *Journal of Services Marketing*, 136: 439–452.

Jenny, S. E, Keiper, M. C, Taylor, B. J., Williams, D. P. Gawrysiak, J., Manning, R. D. and Tutka, P. M. (2018) eSports Venues: A New Sport Business Opportunity, *Journal of Applied Sport Management*, *10* (*1*): DOI:10.18666/JASM-2018-V10-I1–8469.

Jowdy, E. and McDonald, M. A. (2003) Relationship Marketing and International Fan Festivals, *International Journal of Sports Marketing and Sponsorship*, 4: 295–312.

King, A. (1997) The Lads' Masculinity and the New Consumption of Football, *Sociology*, *31* (2): 329–346.

Kruger, M. and Saayman, M. (2019) Kick-Starting the Experience: An Experience-Based Typology of Spectators at a Live Action Sport Event, *Annals of Leisure Research*, *22* (5): 679–698.

Maennig, W. and Zimbalist, A. S. (2012) *International Handbook on the Economics of Mega Sporting Events*, Cheltenham: Edward Elgar Publishing.

Malcolm, D. (2002) Football Business and Football Communities in the Twenty-First Century, *Soccer and Society*, *1* (*3*): 102–113.

Pennington-Gray, L. and Holdnak, A. (2002) Out of the Stands and into the Community: Using Sports Events to Promote a Destination, *Events Management*, 7: 177–186.

Preuss, H. (2005) The Economic Impact of Visitors at Major Multi-Sport Events, *European Sport Management Quarterly*, *5* (*3*): 281–301.

Preuss, H. and Solberg, H. A. (2006) Attracting Major Sporting Events: The Role of Local Residents, *European Sport Management Quarterly*, 6 (4): 391–411.

Redhead, S. (1997) *Post-Fandom and the Millennial Blues: The Transformation of Soccer Culture*, London: Routledge.

Rodriguez, D., Wigfield, A. and Eccles, J. S. (2002) *Changing Competence Perceptions, Changing Values: Implications for Youth Sport*. Research report, National Inst. of Child Health and Human Development (NIH), Bethesda, MD.

Sandvoss, C. (2003) *A Game of Two Halves: Football, Television and Globalization*, London and New York: Routledge.

Small, K. (2007) Social Dimensions of Community Festivals: An Application of Factor Analysis in the Development of the Social Impact Perception (SIP) Scale, *Event Management*, *11*: 45–55.

Spencer, N. E. (2004) Sister Act VI: Venus and Serena Williams at Indian Wells: 'Sincere Fictions' and White Racism, *Journal of Sport and Social Issues*, *28* (2): 115–135.

Statista (2020) *Size of the Global Sports Market 2018*. Available at: www.statista.com/statis tics/1087391/global-sports-market-size [Accessed 3 August 2022].

Stewart, B., Smith, A. C. T. and Nicholson, M. (2003) Sport Consumer Typologies: A Critical Review, *Sport Marketing Quarterly*, *12*: 206–216.

Sutton, W. A., McDonald, M. A. and Milne, G. R. (1997) Creating and Fostering Fan Identification in Professional Sports, *Sport Marketing Quarterly*, *61*: 15–22.

Tanaka, T. (2004) The Positioning and Practices of the 'Feminized Fan' in Japanese Soccer Culture through the Experience of the FIFA World Cup Korea/Japan 2002, *Inter-Asia Cultural Studies*, *51*: 52–62.

Tapp, A. and Clowes, J. (2002) From 'Carefree Casuals' to 'Professional Supporter', *European Journal of Marketing*, *3611* (12): 1248–1269.

Tasci, A. D. A., Hahm, J. and Breiter Terry, D. (2019) A Longitudinal Study of Olympic Games' Impact on the Image of a Host Country, *Journal of Travel and Tourism Marketing*, *36* (4): 443–457.

Tomlinson, A. (2005) *Sport and Leisure Cultures*, London: University of Minnesota Press.

van Driel, I. I., Gantz, W. and Lewis, N. (2018) Unpacking What It Means to Be—or Not Be—A Fan, *Communication Sport*, *7*(5): 611–629.

Visit Britain (2021) *Visit Britain Research Highlights Football's Importance in Boosting Inbound Tourism*. Available at: www.visitbritain.org/visitbritain-research-highlights-footballs-importance-boosting-inbound-tourism [Accessed 3 August 2022].

Wakefield, K. L. and Sloan, H. J. (1995) The Effects of Team Loyalty and Selected Stadium Factors on Spectator Attendance, *Journal of Sport Management*, 9 (2): 153–172.

Westerbeek, H. M., Turner, P. and Ingerson, L. (2002) Key Success Factors in Bidding for Hallmark Sporting Events, *International Marketing Review*, 19 (3): 303–322.

Chapter 10

Mega-events

Contents

DOI: 10.4324/9781003102878-10

10.1 Aims

By the end of this chapter, students will be able to:

- define and categorise mega-events
- analyse individual mega-events across different periods of their existence
- evaluate the relationship between mega-events and urban regeneration
- evaluate the relationship between mega-events and tourism.

10.2 Introduction

Mega-events, like the Olympic Games and the World Expos, have become increasingly important in the global economy as governments compete to bring them to their cities to catalyse economic, social and cultural change. These events attract attendances in the millions and the largest of them command television audiences that number in the billions. This chapter is intended to introduce the concept of the mega-event and to highlight key challenges in successfully managing this diverse group of events. A definition and typology of mega-events will be given which shows that the 'mega' category can relate to audience size, economic impact, visitor numbers and/or socio-cultural significance. Emphasis will be placed on understanding the pre-, during- and post-event periods and the relationships between mega-events, tourism and urban regeneration.

10.3 Defining mega-events

The term 'mega-event' refers to those events that take place for a global media audience and/or that have significant, long-term impacts on economies and societies.

For the purposes of distinguishing between different kinds of events and for moving on to think about how these events are planned and delivered, we can place mega-events on a scale of large events, depending on their socio-economic and media impacts.

Mega-events are distinguished by the immense scale of their audiences and their social and economic impacts, as shown in Figure 10.1. Included in the total audience are both large numbers of attendees at the 'live' event and even larger numbers of people who watch the event via various media, especially television. Increasingly, these media audiences are being extended and developed through the use of streaming media and media archives. The cumulative broadcast audience for the FIFA 2018 World Cup in Brazil was 3.572 billion, of which 309.7 million watched on digital platforms (FIFA 2018).

Events on this scale are infrequent but usually periodical. The Summer and Winter Olympic Games, for example, take place on four-yearly cycles. The World Expo, a global cultural fair, moves between countries on a five-yearly basis, and the 2015 Expo in Milan, Italy attracted 22 million visitors, following investment of more than €3.2 billion (see Case Study 10.1).

Mega-events are the largest scale of planned event. They can be sporting, cultural or political in character and have a significance that comes from their vast audiences and impacts, judged in terms of visitor numbers, media audiences or the changes that they cause to society

Mega-events

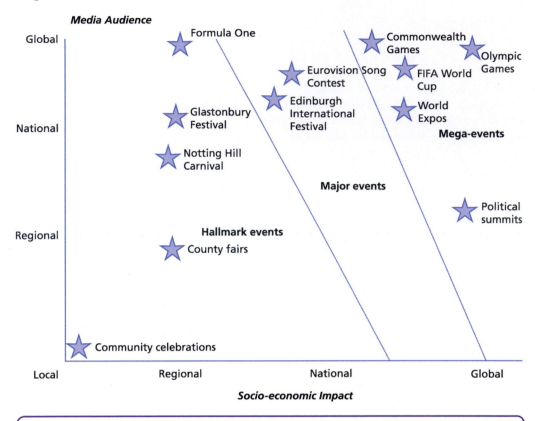

Figure 10.1 Media and socio-economic scales of large events

The Milan Expo 2015

Location: Milan, Italy
Event type: Mega-event
Attendees: 22,000,000

Expo Milano was held in Italy from 1 May to 31 October 2015. The theme of the World Exposition was 'Feeding the Planet, Energy for Life'. One hundred and forty-five countries participated in the Expo, as well as 17 NGOs, the European Union and the United Nations, and corporate sponsors. Within the 2.9 square kilometre site of the event, each country had a pavilion showcasing their own cultures and achievements relating to the theme of the expo. Additionally, five theme pavilions were developed by the hosts to promote the theme, which included a biodiversity park and a hyper-technological supermarket.

Image 10.1 Expo 2015 Village, Milan, Italy
Source: Unsplash: https://unsplash.com/photos/mZBVSxayxtI

The total investment in the 2015 World Expo was €3.271 billion, of which €1.252 billion came from the public sector, with the rest coming from corporate partners or international participant countries and agencies.

or economies. Roberts (2004) emphasises the stand-alone character of mega-events, suggesting that they are out-of-the-ordinary events, discontinuous in character and remarkable for their size.

Discontinuity and drama are undoubtedly two key elements of mega-events that help us to understand their appeal and significance. However, these are relative concepts that vary between locations and cultures. Events such as the Glastonbury Festival, an annual UK music festival, stand out within their host communities as dramatic and a break from the normal routine, but Glastonbury's 2019 TV audience of just 23 million viewers suggests that it is on a different scale to the Olympic celebrations in Rio de Janiero in 2016, which attracted an estimated worldwide audience of 3.6 billion. Getz and Page (2016: 59; emphasis added) incorporate this relativity into their definition of the mega-event, explaining that they are 'those that yield extraordinarily high levels of tourism, media coverage, prestige, or economic impact *for the host community, venue or organisation*'.

Within the category of mega-events, three major kinds can be identified that are characterised by their audience and/or significance at the global level: cultural, political and sporting mega-events.

10.3.1 Cultural mega-events

These mega-events focus on the development and/or promotion of regional or national culture. Typically, they involve the designation of an area or region as the event hub for a specific period of time and include a wide programme of cultural events across a variety of cultural forms. Examples include the Eurovision Song Contest, which involves a series of regional and national events and finally a single international event, and the European Capital of Culture programme.

Plovdiv, in Bulgaria, was selected as the European Capital of Culture 2019, in 2014, along with the Italian city of Matera. During 2019, Plovdiv hosted 600 events for domestic and international audiences, involving more than 130 different organisations from across Europe. More than 1.2 million Bulgarians participated in a cultural event in Plovdiv during this year, and international tourism to the city grew by 27% during this period, with more than half of these being visitors coming from the European Union. In 2019, the city of Tartu in Estonia was announced as a European Capital of Culture for 2024. The organisers have the following objectives, which demonstrate ambitions to achieve the wide-ranging impacts that are characteristic of mega-events:

- The project is designed to be carried out by our today's and tomorrow's cultural operators: artists, organisers, institutions and creative entrepreneurs.
- During and after the ECoC preparation period and title year it is possible to evaluate the impacts of the ECoC process: the increase in the goodwill of the residents who are engaged as audiences and creators, the attractiveness of the city in the eyes of talents, investors and entrepreneurs, and the improvement of connections to and from Europe.
- A well-organised ECoC will greatly benefit the region's economy. Direct benefit will come from the increased number of daily and overnight visitors but also from increased investments from national and international stakeholders.
- The bidding process supports solving major challenges stated in Tartu and Southern Estonian development and cultural strategies. In addition, a successful candidacy will benefit all the important stakeholders: educational institutions, companies, non-profit organisations etc. (Tartu2024 2019).

10.3.2 Political mega-events

Political mega-events take place on the world stage, bringing together governments and other political actors to consider political issues of global importance. These events have increased in frequency and size with the progress of globalisation. Now, more than ever, political delegations and NGOs from the developed and developing world meet to debate and harmonise policies on global trade, security and the environment. These events, like the World Economic Forum, the Asia Pacific Economic Cooperation summit and the G20 have a global significance that transcends visitor numbers and budgets that would normally be associated with a major event, such as a cultural or sport event.

The United Nations Climate Change Conference Copenhagen 2019 (COP25) was an example of this new kind of mega-event. Held during the Covid-19 pandemic, this event brought together participants from 197 countries, 1,049 NGOs and 127 international bodies and organisations, as well as journalists from 844 media outlets. In total, 22,354 people participated in nine days of discussions aimed at driving forward implementation of the Paris Climate Change agreement that had been signed at a previous event in 2015, COP15. Key to understanding the position of COP25 as a mega-event is its political and environmental significance. The event brought together political leaders and decision-makers with global levels of influence. Millions more participated in the event at a distance through protests and demonstrations in other countries, with the aim of influencing the proceedings.

An increasingly common feature of these events is the large number of protesters and demonstrators who attempt to disrupt or influence them. At COP15, around 100,000 protesters took to the streets, provoking a large and costly police response. Despite this, the event made a contribution of around £80 million to the local economy. In 2021, the G7 conference was held in Cornwall in the UK, with the policing costs alone estimated to be in the region of £70 million.

10.3.3 Sporting mega-events

Sporting mega-events such as the Olympic Games and the FIFA World Cup stand alone in terms of their attendance, media audience and commercial activity. New technologies of communication and digital media have played a part in the development of sporting mega-events as the world's premium media events. Since 1960, the amount paid by US broadcasters for the rights to broadcast from the Summer Olympics has grown from $390,000 for Rome to $894 million for Beijing, and the broadcaster NBC has paid $7.75 billion for the rights to broadcast the games from 2021–2032. The budget for the Beijing Olympics in 2008 – by far the largest and most visually spectacular games yet seen – reached $40 billion and involved the creation of six new Olympic venues and the reconstruction of a large area of the city.

The huge costs associated with bidding for and staging a sports mega-event means that they are increasingly justified to the public in terms of the impacts they will have in the host destination and the legacy that they will leave for future generations. This legacy will normally include post-games uses for the venues, improved infrastructure in the host city and an improved destination brand for the city in the international tourism market. Four years after hosting the 2006 Winter Olympics, Torino, in northern Italy, was the country's fourth most visited city, after Rome, Florence and Venice. This was achieved through the development of the local tourism industry during and following the Games period, the use of the Games as a catalyst for urban renewal and the increased media profile of this largely industrial town. This demonstrates the potential power of the Games to rebrand a host city through harnessing the vast investment and media audience that the world's largest mega-events generate.

Study activity

What events in your country would you class as mega-events? What are the impacts of these events at the local, regional and national levels?

10.4 Mega-event periods

Like all events, mega-events have a planning stage and can have impacts that extend beyond the life of the event itself. When analysing mega-events, we can talk about the pre-event period, the event period and the post-event period.

10.4.1 The pre-event period

10.4.1.1 Competitive bidding

The first stage in the pre-event period is when the decision is made to stage a mega-event or, more commonly, to *bid* to stage a mega-event. Recent years have seen the emergence of a trend of prosperous economies from the Global North reducing their bidding activity, or withdrawing from bidding processes at a late stage, due to concerns over costs or public perceptions, but an increase in bids from developing countries and the Global South (Graeff and Knijnik 2021). A few mega-events are intimately linked to particular places (such as Munich's Oktoberfest),

Figure 10.2 The Olympic host city selection process for London 2012
Source: Adapted from Theodoraki (2007)

but this process usually begins with the event owners – for example, the International Olympic Committee or the International Expositions Bureau – announcing that they will accept submissions from potential hosts. There are then several competitive stages during which the number of potential hosts is reduced until a winner is chosen. The stages include the submission of bid documentation, visits by the event owners and formal presentations. Each city will develop a bid file, or 'bid book' (McGillivray and Turner 2018) that will normally include:

- Guarantees from the host city to the event owner.
- A profile of the host city, including:

  o demographic information
  o information on the environment
  o economic information
  o political information.

- Plans for the content of the event.
- Plans for facilities, accommodation and transport.
- Plans for associated celebratory and educational events.

The period of competitive bidding will start well in advance of the actual event itself. The level of planning required to stage a mega-event and the resources required to make it a success mean that an eight- to ten-year lead-in period is not uncommon for successful Olympic bids (Girginov and Parry 2005). At the start of this period, a Bid Committee will be formed that brings together political figures, Olympic experts, planners, media professionals and a range of stakeholders in the Olympic planning process. This Bid Committee will eventually hand over to an Organising Committee for the Olympic Games (OCOG), which will then be the lead body for the delivery of the Games themselves. Figure 10.2 gives an overview of the host city selection process for the London 2012 Olympic and Paralympic Games.

It is not only the Olympic city candidature process that generates a frenzy of bureaucratic activity. The successful bid of Umeå, in Sweden, to become European Capital of Culture in 2014 took ten years from start to finish and involved 350 people and collaborations with six other European cities.

CASE STUDY 10.2

Controversies over mega-event bids: the 2022 FIFA World Cup in Qatar

Location: Qatar
Event type: Mega-event
Attendees: 1,000,000+ (predicted)

Ever since FIFA awarded Qatar the right to host the 2022 World Cup, there have been controversies about this decision aired in the press, discussed by researchers and even heard in court. Before the decision was taken, two members of the 24-man awarding committee were sacked after being filmed offering their votes for cash. An internal FIFA-led investigation cleared the committee of any potential corruption, but legal investigations are ongoing in France and Switzerland, and a US court indicted three further committee members for allegations of taking bribes to back Qatar's bid. FIFA, however, maintain that the bid was awarded mainly due to Qatar's plans to develop a football culture in a region where football participation is historically low.

Qatar's plans to host the FIFA World Cup were already controversial for a number of reasons. The climactic conditions in that region meant that the event had to be moved from its traditional time in the summer to a winter schedule. This has had impacts on the scheduling of professional football leagues around the world. Additionally, Qatar has imported more than one million immigrant workers, mostly from South Asia and Africa, to work on $300 million of infrastructure projects associated with the event, including eight entirely new stadiums. Investigations by journalists have led to allegations of widespread mistreatment of these workers, including human rights abuses. Since the World Cup was awarded to Qatar, more than 6,500 immigrant workers have died in the country, many of whom were working on World Cup infrastructure projects.

In order to reassure the public of the integrity of its processes, FIFA have launched a guide to the bidding process for future World Cup events. This document sets out the following key principles:

- Transparency
- Objectivity
- Participation
- Commitment to Human Rights and Sustainability

Study activity

Review the FIFA document 'Guide to the Bidding Process for the 2026 FIFA World Cup'. What evidence can you find in the document that FIFA understand the concerns raised about previous controversial bids? Do you think this document will reassure the public?

Document link: https://digitalhub.fifa.com/m/5730ee56c15eeddb/original/hgopypqftviladnm7q90-pdf.pdf

10.4.1.2 Resources

A major task facing any city planning to host a mega-event is assembling the required resources to make it a success. It is estimated that the costs of hosting the Athens 2004 Olympic Games rose to $12 billion, far in excess of the possible contribution from the Olympic movement of $4.3 billion. South Africa initially planned to spend around $2.4 billion on hosting the 2010 FIFA World Cup, and this rose to $3.9 billion. This has serious implications for our understanding of the pre-event period, during which mega-event hosting cities must seek to acquire sufficient resources to produce the event. Although host cities aim to achieve significant benefits and produce a legacy from hosting these events, assembling adequate resources is a key task of the pre-event period. This funding typically comes from two sources: direct public investment, and partnerships with the private sector.

Hosting a mega-event requires large amounts of public investment. From the beginning of the bidding and planning process, the potential host city begins to accrue costs for something which, at this stage, may not even take place. The cost of bidding includes marketing, PR, staffing, premises, travel and lobbying. If a bid is successful, the host city must identify and acquire the land required for developing the mega-event location and begin the long and costly processes of planning and consultation. This is followed by the huge capital investments required in infrastructure development to improve travel networks to cope with visitors and the construction of venues for the event. In addition, the human and organisational capital required to coordinate and manage these processes places a drain on state resources at both the local and the national levels. In the majority of cases, these upfront costs will be met through direct taxation and sometimes a special levy on residents, with the justification that the benefits of hosting the mega-event will outweigh the costs, especially once its legacy is taken into consideration. Politicians and event organisers frequently justify the decision to host a mega-event using the 'public good' argument.

Getz and Page (2016) set out the three criteria of the 'public good' that have to be satisfied in order to justify the massive public sector commitment to hosting a mega-event:

- Events fit into accepted policy domains (culture, health, economics etc.).
- Public benefits are substantial (it is worth our while to get involved), inclusive (everyone gains), and can be demonstrated or proved.
- There are rules and accountability for money spent and other actions taken.

Within these three points, the most contentious is the second – demonstrable public benefit. Assuming that the benefits can be anticipated, planned for and measured, then the decision to host a mega-event becomes a matter of performing a simple cost–benefit analysis: will the benefits of hosting the event outweigh, or at least match, the costs of producing it? The assumption that is implicit in all mega-event bids is that they will, but the dispersed and diverse impacts of mega-events make this difficult to assess. Mega-events always have a number of specific effects that occur at different points in the life of the event, as is shown in Figure 10.3.

The problem caused by this distribution of event impacts is that the tangible benefits of hosting a mega-event are predicted to take place during the event itself or after it. (The exception to this is the area of tourism, which will be dealt with in a later section of this chapter.) The very long planning period for mega-events and the huge public resource commitment involved during the pre-event stage can therefore cause significant political difficulties for host cities and governments. (The issue of the public perception of mega-events is also addressed below.)

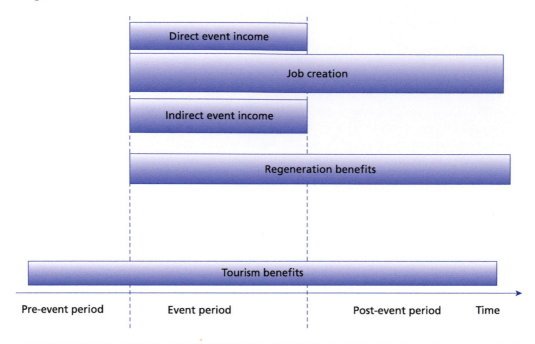

Figure 10.3 The distribution of mega-event impacts over time

Two categories of partnership are important for understanding the planning and resourcing of mega-events. First, there are the partnerships required between different agencies, departments and companies in the public and private sectors that are involved in delivering the event. Second, there are the partnerships between the event owners and hosts, on the one hand, and private companies, on the other, which take the form of sponsorship arrangements. The most significant sponsorship deals often allow companies to brand themselves as 'official partners' of the mega-event. These two types of partnerships can be termed *delivery partnerships* and *commercial partnerships*, and both help to generate the resources needed to stage a mega-event. Delivery partnerships generate extra resources for a mega-event during the pre-event period in two distinct ways: through planning and construction.

Planning partnerships tend to be embodied in particular organisations or forums. A planning partnership makes use of resources that are dispersed through different public bodies and other organisations. In particular, it brings additional organisational resources, experience and in-kind benefits to the planning of a mega-event, as well as additional human capital in the form of experts and administrative support. An example is the partnership agreement between the Organizing Committee for the 2028 Olympic and Paralympic Games in Los Angeles, USA, and Deloitte, one of the world's largest consultancy, accountancy and auditing firms. The seven-year partnership will see Deloitte become the official professional services partners of the event:

> 'As we prepare to welcome the world to Los Angeles, we are thrilled to collaborate with Deloitte on our journey as we explore and evolve what the Olympic and Paralympic Games experience can be', said Kathy Carter, LA 2028 Chief Revenue Officer.

'Leveraging Deloitte's abilities across numerous industry sectors, we're looking at the fan journey like never before and connecting the experience in ways that will completely transform the Games.

Deloitte has been an incredible sponsor for Team USA and the Olympic and Paralympic Movement in the United States and we couldn't be more proud to extend their involvement to LA28'.

Stacy Janiak, Managing Partner, Chief Growth Officer, Deloitte LLP, added: 'Deloitte is proud to be the Official Professional Services Provider of the LA28 Olympic and Paralympic Games, building upon our long-standing sponsorship with Team USA, which has been in place since 2009.

'As part of our relationship, over the next seven years, we will be supporting LA28 with management and business consulting services as both a trusted advisor and sponsor, helping the Games organisers in their efforts to deliver an unparalleled Olympic and Paralympic experience for athletes, fans and the community'.

(International Paralympic Committee 2021)

Construction partnerships are typically made between public and private sector bodies, to contract in the experience, capabilities and capital of the private sector to support the construction of venues and improvements to infrastructure as well as other capital-intensive projects that would be difficult for the public sector to fund on its own. For example, the $600-million Cape Town Stadium for the 2010 FIFA World Cup in South Africa was constructed by Murray Roberts and WHBO, who were contracted in by the Organising Committee. The project was not directly managed by the state, and the management of the stadium during the event and in the post-event period was handled by a consortium of partners from the private sector with specific stadium-management experience.

Commercial partnerships add capital and commercial support to a mega-event, usually through sponsorship deals that offer a promotional benefit to the event partner. The highest category of these partnerships is that of 'official partner'. Official partners of mega-events are often granted permission to use the event logos and branding materials as part of their own promotional activity.

Liverpool08 had twelve official partners, each making a cash or in-kind contribution to the event. For example, Hill Dickinson LLP was the first official partner announced for Liverpool's Capital of Culture programme, taking on the responsibility for 'all legal and contractual dealings with sponsors, partners, suppliers, event organisers and the myriad of other businesses involved in the multi-year programme building up to 2008 and in the legacy years following' (Hill Dickinson LLP 2009). Virgin Trains paid £2 million for the right to become an official partner of Liverpool08, additionally agreeing to promote the mega-event on its trains and through its services.

Potential sponsorship deals began at £20,000 and were marketed by Liverpool08 as a portfolio of opportunities:

Depending on the level of investment, companies can get access to a spectrum of Culture Company assets, including:

- intellectual property (logos, designations, 'Look of the Capital of Culture')
- category exclusivity
- corporate use (letterheads, business cards, B2B promotions, website)
- consumer use (TV, radio, print, direct mail, outdoor, website, database use)
- sponsor recognition (banners, advertising, website links)

- tickets and hospitality (complimentary allocation and access to purchase additional)
- event creation and involvement upgrades.

(Liverpool08 2008)

10.4.1.3 Public perceptions of mega-events

As mentioned above, the public perception of mega-events is affected by the distribution of event impacts. With the majority of the benefits of hosting a mega-event occurring late in the life of the event itself and often well into the future, beyond the event and into the legacy period, it is not surprising that public reaction to plans to host a mega-event based on predictions of these long-term and often intangible benefits can often be negative or hostile. There is a widespread belief that the 'true' costs of a mega-event are often hidden from the public in order to avoid widespread alarm, an assumption that is supported by facts like the dramatic 300% rise in costs of the Sydney 2000 Olympics in the 12 months before the Games were held (Girginov and Parry 2005). Farmaki *et al.* (2019) found that while residents of Pafos, Cyprus, were generally positive about the city hosting the European Capital of Culture event in 2017, the degree to which they actively supported the event depended on how involved they were with the local tourism industry, and whether they thought increased tourism would affect them positively or not.

A key element of the management of mega-events in the pre-event period, then, is the marketing of the event – not to potential event tourists and attendees, but internally, to the population of the host city and country. This internal marketing is a key activity of the bidding team for any mega-event and, once the event has been won, it becomes a significant task for the Organising Committee.

For the London 2012 Olympic and Paralympic Games, this involved extensive consultation through roadshow and drop-in events in East London, focusing on the local employment and regeneration benefits of the Games. More widely across the UK, the focus was on the celebratory aspects of the Games, the increased tourism opportunities they would provide and the increase in sporting participation that they are expected to drive, especially among young people. Research into UK citizens' willingness to pay (WTP – a measure of the amount that individuals think is a reasonable contribution for them to make to the staging of an event) for the 2012 Olympics found that this decreased with distance from London, with Londoners' WTP at £22 per annum, Mancunians' £12 per annum and Glaswegians' just £11 per annum (Atkinson *et al.* 2008). With the vast majority of sporting activities taking place in one area of the country, the Cultural Olympiad programme of events associated with the Games was promoted as a way of spreading the benefits of hosting the Olympics around the country (Kennell and Macleod 2009).

It is important to note that public perceptions of the decision to host a mega-event are changeable and will be influenced by the actual manifestations or otherwise of benefits associated with the event. Research carried out by Guala (2009: 25) shows that public opinion regarding the Torino 2006 Winter Olympics was representative of that measured for similar events: 'pride and optimism at the beginning, then uncertainties and concerns two or three years before the games . . . then happiness and success during the games and shortly after; one year after the games a more realistic judgement is registered, but always positive about the experience and [the future]'.

Look at the websites of the IOC, the International Expositions Bureau and FIFA. Examine the successful bids of the most recent host countries. To what extent did the bids discuss how to involve and support host city communities? Which of the bids do you think was strongest in this regard, and why?

10.4.2 The event period

During a mega-event, the organisers will be required to carry out a vast number of functions. The Athens Organising Committee identified 53 separate areas of responsibility during the 2004 Olympic Games. Broadly, these functions can be broken down into a number of interrelated areas common to all mega-events (see Figure 10.4). The Beijing Organising Committee for the Olympic Games (BOCOG) had 25 departments, each with a separate management function.

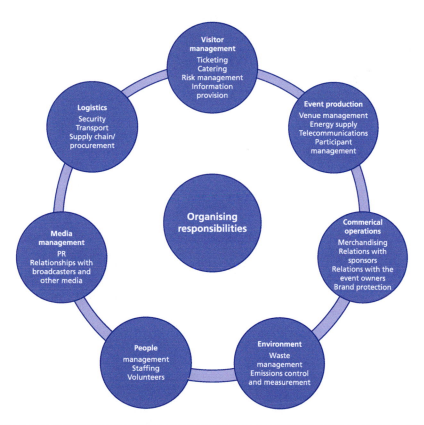

Figure 10.4 Mega-event organisers' responsibilities in the event period

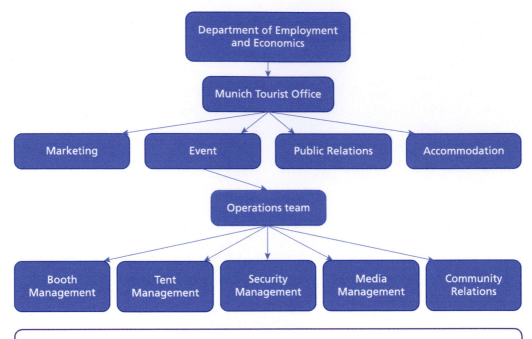

Figure 10.5 The functional structure of the Munich Oktoberfest
Source: Adapted from Shulenkorf (2005)

It is not only host cities of the Olympic Games that have to deal with this sort of logistical complexity. Munich's annual Oktoberfest beer festival attracts an average of 7 million visitors over 16 days each year. There are 700 booths or small stalls and 14 large tents, each capable of holding 10,000 people. Each Oktoberfest contributes approximately $1.4 billion to the regional economy of Munich and Bavaria. To deliver such an annual mega-event successfully, there is a need for a complex functional structure that integrates political oversight, departmental responsibility and management functions (see Figure 10.5).

We look at the management issues associated with all events elsewhere in this book, but it is useful here to look at three areas of management that are of particular significance to mega-events during the event period: volunteers, global media and security.

10.4.2.1 Volunteers

Mega-events make use of volunteers on a huge scale. Without their contributions, mega-events as we have come to understand them could not take place due to the huge investment in human capital that would be required to employ a paid workforce. During the Rio 2016 Olympic Games, the organisers made use of the skills and experience of 50,000 volunteers, chosen from around 240,000 applicants. Although Winter Olympics are smaller events, Sochi 2014 relied on 19,200 volunteers and the 2018 edition in Pyeongchang, Korea made use of a further 13,500. The organisers of the 2006 Melbourne Commonwealth Games recognised the important contribution made by volunteers by nominating all 14,500 of them as 'unsung heroes' of the event. Everyone was named individually in the official event documentation.

During a mega-event, volunteers can be used in all aspects of staging. These volunteers will be drawn from diverse sections of the population and, although the headline-grabbing volunteer programmes for mega-events often publicise opportunities to meet famous people or to become part of the media-spectacle, the majority of volunteer opportunities will be in customer-service or behind-the-scenes roles. Many mega-event hosts seek to link volunteer programmes to skills development and the creation of employment opportunities, both to attract applicants and to contribute to local economic development in the host community. Although it is unrealistic for every volunteer to expect to move directly from the event into paid employment, large-scale, long-term volunteering programmes aim to provide opportunities for citizens to develop their skills and to gain basic qualifications and work experience.

Employment growth is a key element of the justification given by cities for hosting mega-events. Given the huge public investment involved, the success of this is a major factor in influencing public opinion. During the pre-event period of the 1992 Olympic Games in Barcelona, unemployment in the city halved, mainly thanks to the creation of 59,382 jobs that were directly connected to the Games. Immediately after the Games, unemployment rose again by 21,000, before falling back in 1995 (Brunet 2009). The investment generated by hosting the Olympic Games contributed significantly to the strong relative performance of Barcelona's employment market in the legacy period, but the city's experience demonstrates that the employment benefits of hosting a mega-event are not always straightforward or immediate.

This suggests that people must volunteer for reasons other than the hope of gaining direct employment. Indeed, volunteer motivation is a much-researched topic in events management literature. Getz (2007) highlights the most important motivating factors for volunteers:

- altruism
- social benefits
- career benefits
- a sense of challenge
- volunteering as a form of 'serious leisure'
- community pride.

Bladen (2009) conceptualises the motivations of mega-event volunteers within a model of repeat volunteering. This model suggests that first-time or one-off volunteers are motivated primarily by altruism, while repeat volunteers are driven by the quality of the volunteering experience, and career volunteers see the intrinsic benefits of volunteering itself. So there is a progression from altruistic volunteering motivations to egoistic motivations, as shown in Figure 10.6, which implies that different management strategies will be necessary for managing different volunteers successfully. The sheer scale of the volunteer contribution at a mega-event means that event managers will be working with large groups of individuals at different points on this motivational journey.

Figure 10.6 Bladen's developmental stages of volunteering
Source: Bladen (2009)

10.4.2.2 Global media

Horne and Manzenreiter (2006) claim that the growth of mega-events can be understood only by reference to a 'sports – media – business alliance', based on the development of new communications technologies, the professionalisation and commercialisation of sports and the economic opportunities offered to host cities by successful mega-events. This alliance is encapsulated in the relationship between the Olympics and global media. As Roche (2000) points out, the media audience for other mega-events is dwarfed by that of the Olympic Games; and indeed, for mega-events such as the World Expos, whose aim has always been to show-case global culture, the rise of television and new media has provided increased competition for their natural audiences. In contrast, the growth of visual media has helped to extend and deepen the sporting mega-event audience.

For the Olympic Games, broadcasting rights are sold by territory. In the United States, media companies bid competitively for the right to broadcast the Olympics inside North America. For the 2008 Games, NBC paid $894 million. European rights are sold to a collective entity, the European Broadcast Union, which then re-sells them at the national level. For Beijing 2008, European broadcast rights were sold for $443 million. Broadcast rights account for 53% of total income for the Olympic Games, with sponsorship in second place at 34%, ticketing at 11% and merchandising at 2%. Table 10.1 shows the growth in broadcast deals for the Olympic Games in the US from 1960 until the present day.

As well as broadcast rights, the media presence at the Olympic Games is managed through the use of an accreditation system. Individual journalists and media organisations are given

Table 10.1 US broadcast rights for the Summer Olympic Games

Year	Host city	Network	Amount $m
1960	Rome	CBS	0.39
1964	Tokyo	NBC	1.5
1968	Mexico City	ABC	4.5
1972	Munich	ABC	7.5
1976	Montreal	ABC	25.0
1980	Moscow	NBC	72.0
1984	Los Angeles	ABC	225.0
1988	Seoul	NBC	300.0
1992	Barcelona	NBC	401.0
1996	Atlanta	NBC	546.0
2000	Sydney	NBC	705.0
2004	Athens	NBC	793.0
2008	Beijing	NBC	894.0
2012	London	NBC	1181.0
2016–2020	Rio de Janeiro, Tokyo	NBC	4380.0
2024–2032	Paris, Los Angeles, Brisbane	NBC	3120.0

official permission to report from inside the Games, are granted access to secure areas and are able to use an accredited media centre, which will have been specially constructed and equipped so that journalists can plug directly into global media networks.

The growth of new media and the diffusion of journalism into non-traditional networks, such as blogs and other forms of social media, have complicated the relationship between the organising committees for each Games and the media, and, at the same time as traditional broadcast deals have grown, reporting of the Olympic Games has become less and less controllable. In response to this, the Sydney 2000 Games was the first to include a non-accredited media centre, and this has been repeated in every Games since. These spaces provide facilities for *any* journalist and they are often used by those reporting on the non-sporting aspects of the Games, such as the cultural programme, local-activity and human-interest stories (Garcia and Miah 2004). During Beijing 2008, more than 12,000 journalists used the non-accredited media centre. The incorporation of these reporters provides two main benefits to the organisers of each Games, and to the Olympic movement as a whole. First, it creates a space in which new media realities of citizen journalism and online democracy can be brought into the organisation of the event in a managed way. Second, it helps to legitimise the system of charging for accredited media access to the Games by creating a tiered system of privileged access to athletes, officials and facilities.

10.4.2.3 Security

In order to understand the security implications of hosting a mega-event, it is necessary to examine why events are often targets for acts of terrorism or protests. Tarlow (2002) provides four reasons for why events become targets:

- *Location* – Events are necessarily held close to major transportation routes and population centres.
- *Economic* – Disrupting events can cause significant damage to tourism and other business activity.
- *Media* – The media will already be present on-site, leading to increased reporting of any attack.
- *Anonymity* – The presence of large numbers of attendees at an event makes it likely that terrorists can remain anonymous in a crowd.

These criteria are all present to extremes at mega-events, so it is likely that they will continue to be significant targets for terrorism and other forms of political protest.

The most infamous security breach at a mega-event took place at the 1972 Olympic Games in Munich. Palestinian terrorists killed 11 Israeli athletes during the Games and the tragedy was given widespread and instantaneous media coverage thanks to the presence of vast numbers of journalists at the Olympic site. The location of this terrorist attack had been chosen for precisely this high symbolic value.

Mega-event planners are increasingly conscious of the possibility of a terrorist attack at one of these high-profile, urbanised, global media events. Between the Los Angeles Games in 1984 and the Tokyo Games in 2021 security costs rose from $79.4 million to $1.5 billion. Additional costs associated with providing health security measures associated with the Covid-19 pandemic mean that Tokyo may yet prove the most expensive Games ever, surpassing Beijing 2008. This is not a uniquely Olympic issue: planning for the FIFA World Cup in South Africa in 2010 made provision for the use of 40,000 police officers, 50,000 reservists and thousands of private security staff (Giulianotti and Klauser 2009). In 2009, an al-Qaeda plot to attack the Munich

Oktoberfest was detected in advance by the security services, leading to the imposition of a 3.7-kilometre no-fly zone around the site and enhanced physical security in 2010.

In common with urban security management generally, attempts to manage the risk of terror are becoming more dispersed and anticipatory, with host cities relying heavily on techniques such as surveillance, behaviour and attendee profiling, as well as the increased use of private security firms. One of the legacies of Beijing 2008 for the mega-events field has been its security innovations, including the use of official protest areas and unprecedented levels of monitoring and security clearance that were implemented to reduce the negative impacts of political protest and terror at the event. Although the presence of the Games in China has been hailed by some as helping to create a climate in which limited protest was allowed, in contrast to the pre-Games period in China, these protests were very tightly controlled. It is likely that future Games will follow this model of licensed protest. The 2010 Winter Olympic Games in Vancouver, Canada, saw an unprecedented level of security, with a security budget that rose from an initial estimate of $175 million to more than $1 billion by the end of the event. This money was spent on 17,000 security staff, a network of nearly 1000 CCTV cameras and the establishment of secure zones for channelling both spectators and protesters. A newly formed Vancouver Integrated Security Unit brought together 20 different law-enforcement agencies, armed with semi-automatic weapons, including border police, who carried out spot checks of citizens' immigration and citizenship status during the Games period (Boykoff 2011).

Cultural and sporting mega-events are high profile and require significant political support to take place, which situates them within the political arena. However, political mega-events acquire their significance through their political impact, and this impact also generates significant security concerns in their management. Protests associated with the meeting of the group of 20 industrialised nations (G20) and the World Trade Organisation (WTO) have contributed to the high profiles of these mega-events in the global consciousness and have proved extraordinarily expensive to police. Much of the publicity generated by such gatherings is negative, on account of the often violent security operations that are associated with them. The 2009 meeting of the G20 in London prompted the largest security operation seen in the UK for over a decade, with total security costs estimated at upwards of £10 million for the two-day event.

Study activity

How can mega-event organisers balance security concerns with the need to create exciting, dynamic events? As an attendee at a mega-event, what inconveniences would you be prepared to accept in the name of security and at what point would these deter you from attending?

10.4.3 Event legacies

The concept of 'legacy' refers to those long-term impacts of an event that continue to be felt long after the event has concluded. Typically, these are measured over years or decades. When planning for very large and mega-events, the potential legacy benefits are often used to convince licensing authorities and investors to commit to the event. Gold and Gold (2009) note that in Olympic circles 'legacy' has acquired almost magical status in its ability to convince and persuade. Indeed, the majority of the supposed benefits of staging a mega-event tend to be expressed in terms of legacy. In 2007, the Olympic President Jacques Rogge said: 'Legacy is our *raison d'être*. It ensures that the Olympic Games are more than metres and medals. . . Values, partnership and legacy are all required to turn the Olympic Games into an enduring celebration of the human spirit. Once an Olympic City, always an Olympic City. Wherever the Games have appeared, cities are changed forever' (quoted in Gold and Gold 2009: 16).

It is tempting to view legacy in purely positive terms, but, of course, the impacts of any event can be positive or negative. The social and human rights implications of the developments associated with mega-events have become more controversial in recent years, with researchers and journalists drawing attention to problems associated with (for example) displacement, disempowerment, exclusion and the marginalisation of host communities (Duignan and McGillivray 2019). Preuss (2007) sets out a series of positive and negative, tangible and intangible legacy effects associated with staging an event (see Table 10.1).

10.4.4 The post-event period

The post-event period is the longest and most complex to analyse because it has no definitive end point, and because the impacts attributable to mega-events, or claimed by host cities, are numerous. It is therefore necessary to differentiate three separate timeframes within the post-event period (see Figure 10.7).

Immediately following the mega-event period, a number of short-term effects will occur. These will not necessarily be reliable indicators of the long-term impacts of hosting a mega-event, but they can include: a sudden and dramatic drop in local employment as event-related jobs, and volunteering opportunities, are wound up; problems of over-supply in the tourism market as the increased capacity developed for the event period is no longer needed; and the under-utilisation of expensively constructed mega-event venue and infrastructure projects. These consequences alone can make assessing the impacts of a mega-event problematic in the immediate post-event period. There will also be a period of delay in the winding-up of the event organisation, the processing of statistical information and the movement of capital

Table 10.2 Legacy impacts
Source: Preuss (2007)

Legacy impact	Tangible	Intangible
Positive	New infrastructure	Destination image/reputation
	Urban realm improvements	Renewal in community spirit
	Increased tourism	Increased regional cooperation
	Urban regeneration	Formation of popular memories
	Additional employment	Educational opportunities
	Inward investment and company relocation	Production of new ideas and cultural forms
Negative	Debts from construction	Opportunity costs
	Debts from delivery	Socially unjust displacements
	Redundant infrastructure	Unjust distribution or resources
	Increases in property costs	

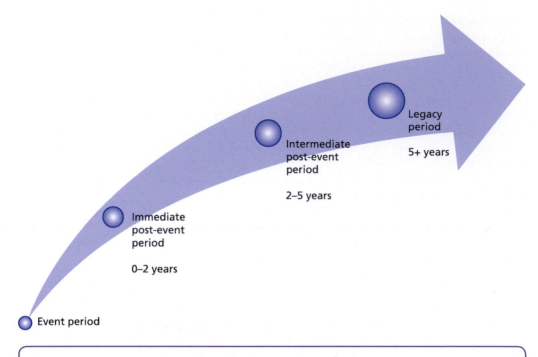

Figure 10.7 The post-event period

flows associated with hosting the event, such as sponsorship money, merchandising income and ticket revenue.

The intermediate post-event period is when the impacts of hosting a mega-event can become clear. Within this timeframe, host cities can develop post-event management arrangements for facilities and governance frameworks for former mega-event sites. It is not uncommon for there to be large-scale political changes within a host nation or city during this period, as the post-event period will extend beyond standard political electoral cycles. This will also have an impact on the post-event impacts of a mega-event as the financial, physical and social aspects of the event become part of the political discourse in the host city. Five years after the 2004 Athens Olympics, all but one of the 22 Olympic venues were unused, and one of the core venue complexes had become notorious for hosting not prestigious sporting events but large groups of illegal squatters. It is now possible to assess the impacts of the Athens Games accurately, especially in comparison with its successor event in the Olympic calendar, the 2006 Winter Games in Turin, which successfully handed its venues to a management company and has integrated them into its regional and sporting development strategies. Following the 2012 Olympic and Paralympic Games in London, the Olympic Stadium was leased to a Premier League football club, West Ham, to run commercially, but this still attracted subsidies from local government of more than £8 million per year to make it commercially viable.

The legacy period is the most politically charged aspect of the post-event period for a mega-event. Planners and politicians alike view the hosting of a mega-event as a way to fast-track processes of urban development and economic restructuring that would normally take place over much longer timeframes (Andranovich et al. 2001). Hosting mega-events now provides a stimulus for the redevelopment of cities, the creation of new urban areas and the diversification

> **Image 10.2** The empty canoe/kayak slalom centre at Helliniko Olympic complex
> Source: Getty Images

of economies. Alongside these instrumental legacies of a mega-event are the intrinsic legacies that hosting high-profile examples of sporting and cultural practices is supposed to deliver: an increase in sports activity within the population, for example, or a rise in cultural participation. Set alongside further socio-economic targets, such as rises in employment, educational achievement and social cohesion, it is worth considering why these mega-events, if they are so beneficial to society, have not become the norm, rather than the exception, in development planning. A look at the history of some of these development goals associated with mega-events shows that these potentially high-impact events are also high risk: for every high-profile success story (such as Barcelona: see Case Study 10.3), there is a parallel story of cost overruns, poorly managed legacies and political problems. Issues of event impacts and legacy are dealt with in detail in Chapter 14. The main area in which the long-term benefits of mega-events are anticipated by planners is regeneration.

10.4.5 Mega-events and urban regeneration

As outlined above, many of the positive impacts claimed for hosting mega-events in the legacy period are linked to the concept of urban regeneration. This is a 'comprehensive and integrated vision and action which leads to the resolution of urban problems and which seeks to bring about a lasting improvement in the economic, physical, social and environmental condition of an area that has been subject to change' (Roberts 2000: 17). Mega-events, by virtue of the massive investment they attract and the policy focus that they generate, can provide a major stimulus to regeneration programmes and, in many cases, can become the main element of major regeneration schemes. This phenomenon is not limited to mega-events; increasingly city administrations have come to see and promote the benefits of a range of types events for urban regeneration (Smith 2012).

Strategies of regeneration have been explicitly employed throughout the UK and Europe since the Second World War as the need for physical reconstruction provided an opportunity for the reconsideration of urban form in response to new economic and social conditions. In the UK, successive governments have produced regeneration and development frameworks that have prioritised different economic sectors, institutional actors and policy outcomes. Table 10.3 summarises the variety of approaches to regeneration that have been adopted in the UK since the 1950s.

We can see from this historical overview that events have begun to take on a role in regeneration only since the 1980s. This period was one of major economic restructuring in Western economies as industrial production moved globally south and east to areas of lower costs, and the manufacturing bases of many cities were lost. This period of globalisation left many derelict industrial sites in its wake and, with this, a legacy of unemployment, skills loss and social problems. Increasingly, governments in the UK, the US and Europe turned to major projects, such as the hosting of mega-events, as means for regenerating these former industrial areas and addressing their associated cultural, social, political and economic problems.

The contributions that a mega-event can make to regeneration are manifold. Although the tendency is to look to an increase in tourism as the main socio-economic impact of a mega-event, we can identify three strategies of integrating mega-events into urban regeneration, in a development of Evans's (2005) categorisation of cultural regeneration.

10.4.4.1 Mega-event-led regeneration

This strategy places a mega-event at the core of a regeneration strategy, as a catalyst for all other developments in the area. Such schemes use the event to brand the regeneration scheme and to promote its uniqueness and value. An example of a city that has pursued this policy consistently is Barcelona, which used the 1992 Olympics and then the 2004 World Forum of Cultures to drive the regeneration of the city (see Case Study 10.3).

10.4.4.2 Mega-event within regeneration

This category describes regeneration strategies where the event is embedded into a broader regeneration strategy, being only one element amid other, equally important components. An example of this is the role that the 2002 Commonwealth Games played in the regeneration of Manchester in the north-west of England. Although hosting the Games became a major impetus for the deepening and continuation of regeneration in the east of the city, their potential to contribute to existing regeneration policy in the city was identified by planners and politicians at the bidding stage (Carlsen and Taylor 2003). Hosting the Games provided an opportunity to leverage additional external funding into an area that has been undergoing significant regeneration developments since the 1980s (Smith and Fox 2007).

Table 10.3 The evolution of British regeneration policy

Sources: Roberts (2000), Bianchini (1993), McGuigan (1996), Diamond and Liddle (2005), Morgan (2002)

Period	1950s	1960s	1970s	1980s	1990s	2000s onwards
Policy type **Major strategy and orientation**	Reconstruction Post-war reconstruction and extension of older areas and cities, with some suburban growth	Revitalisation Continuation of 1950s themes	Renewal Focus on in-situ renewal and neighbourhood schemes; mainly peripheral new developments	Redevelopment Many major high-profile schemes; events begin to be incorporated into regeneration strategies	Regeneration Move towards more integrated and holistic policy approaches	Imagineering Flagship projects and mega-events play key roles in regeneration policy
Key actors and stakeholders	National and local government	Greater balance between public and private sectors	Growing role for private sector	Emphasis on private sector and special agencies and quangos	Partnership the dominant approach	Partnership approach continues
Funding	Majority public sector	Majority public sector with growing private sector	Resource constraints on public sector; greater private sector investment	Private sector dominant, often with public sector funding	Greater balance between public, private and third sector activity	Emphasis on the 'leveraging' of public sector funds to produce large impacts
Social content	Improvement of housing and general living standards	Social and welfare improvement	Community-based action; increase in empowerment	Community self-help, with selective state support	Emphasis on the role of the community	Neighbourhood empowerment and management become key policy concerns
Physical emphasis	Replacement of inner areas and some peripheral development	Continuation of 1950s themes	More extensive renewal of older urban areas	Major schemes of replacement and new developments; growth of flagship schemes	More modest than 1980s; growth of heritage approaches	Urban centre and fringe renewal
Environmental approach	Landscaping and some greening	Selective improvements	Environmental improvement with some innovations	Growth of environmental concern	Broader idea of environmental sustainability introduced	Climate change drives sustainability agenda forward

10.4.4.3 Mega-event added to regeneration

This category describes a situation in which a mega-event becomes an addition to an existing regeneration strategy but is not fully integrated within it. In this category of mega-event planning, the benefits of the event will not be fully leveraged for regeneration purposes. Increasingly, the legacy benefits of hosting a mega-event are viewed as central to successful bidding and to gaining public support for the event, so contemporary events rarely fall into this category. The two most recent Olympic Games to be hosted in the United States, Los Angeles 1984 and Atlanta 1996, can both be identified with this planning style, however. Both host cities emphasised the financial sustainability of their bids, with Los Angeles generating a $200 million profit that was then used to endow a sporting trust, but its Games had no positive impact on the overburdened mass-transit, housing and education sectors of the city. Although contemporary mega-events are less likely to suffer similar criticism, due to the recently developed expectation that all mega-events should contribute to sustainable development, events with poor legacies might fall into this category through bad planning or management. For instance, the Athens 2004 Olympics were poorly integrated into development planning and left the country with a debt of £7 billion (Baim 2009).

Smith (2007) offers ten key principles for the use of events in regeneration:

1 Embed event strategies within wider regeneration programmes.
2 Use the event as a coherent theme and effective stimulus for other regeneration projects.
3 Incorporate regeneration planning into the initial stages of event planning.
4 Promote shared ownership and understanding of the regeneration plans amongst all partners in the event and legacy planning process.
5 Design effective management and functional relationships between event managers and regeneration managers to deliver joint goals.
6 Allocate sufficient human and capital resources throughout the lifetime of an event to achieve its goals.
7 Design event regeneration projects that engage with, and meet the needs of, the most deprived members of a community.
8 Plan for an even geographical distribution of positive impacts across areas targeted for regeneration through an event.
9 Integrate physical and infrastructure developments with social and economic regeneration targets.
10 Ensure community representation from the planning stage onwards in the event management process.

CASE STUDY 10.3

Events and the regeneration of Barcelona

Location: Barcelona, Spain
Event type: Mega-event

Barcelona offers a high-profile example of the role that mega-events can play in strategies of urban regeneration. Potential host cities often cite its success to justify their own bids for mega-events, with many of them lauding the 'Barcelona Model' (Balibrea 2001).

Until the 1970s, Barcelona was a major European industrial city, with a large Mediterranean port and manufacturing services for the automobile, pharmaceutical and textiles industries. Global economic restructuring in the 1970s, coupled with the restructuring of the Spanish state in the post-Franco period, led to a series of industrial and economic crises in the city, leaving it in a 'post-industrial' state, with many derelict former industrial spaces and buildings.

In 1991, in response to this period of decline, the Mayor of Barcelona, Pasquall Maragall, articulated his vision for a city that would be globally competitive: 'in urban competition, factors like the environment and cultural and education infrastructures count more and more. In a strategic sense we can say that cities are like businesses which compete to attract investments and residents, selling places which are suitable for industry, commerce and all kinds of services' (cited in Balibrea 2001: 213). Maragall oriented the city to a mega-event-led regeneration strategy. In 1986, the city was awarded the 1992 Summer Olympic Games, and this became the key driver of Barcelona's attempts to reinvent itself for the post-industrial era.

The Olympic Village was constructed in the disadvantaged port area of Poblenou and the construction of the Olympic venues and public spaces was integrated into a major physical development programme. This included waterfront developments, a new ring-road for the city, the reclaiming of brownfield sites and the demolition of redundant industrial buildings. Figure 10.8 shows the distribution of investments made in Barcelona during this period. The new developments associated with this period of change were polycentric, with the aim of 'Monumentalising the outskirts and revitalising the historic centre' of the city (Balibrea 2001: 212) to produce a more sustainable arrangement of urban form. Tourism development was encouraged through the construction of new hotels as well as rail and airport improvements. Between 1986 and 2000, Barcelona's hotel capacity increased by 300%.

The cost of producing the Games themselves was $1.3 billion, but the associated physical investment totalled $8 billion, demonstrating the contribution made to the development of the city through hosting this mega-event (Brunet 2009).

Alongside these significant physical developments, a process of rebranding and managing the symbolic representation of the city took place during this period (Garcia 2004). Barcelona's local government seized on the opportunity to promote the city as a leisure and tourism destination, promoting Catalan culture and refurbishing key architectural landmarks, as well as implementing an ambitious cultural development programme, capitalising on the opportunity to reposition itself in the global tourism market. By 2006, Barcelona was voted Europe's most attractive city, and was the continent's fourth most-visited.

In 2004, Barcelona hosted the Universal Forum of Cultures, another global event, in this case under the umbrella of the United Nations. Although this drew only 3.5 million visitors against an expected target of 5 million, and cost $2.3 billion to produce, it provided an opportunity for the city to maintain the mega-event-led strategy of urban regeneration and to continue to develop through event-associated investments in infrastructure and tourism.

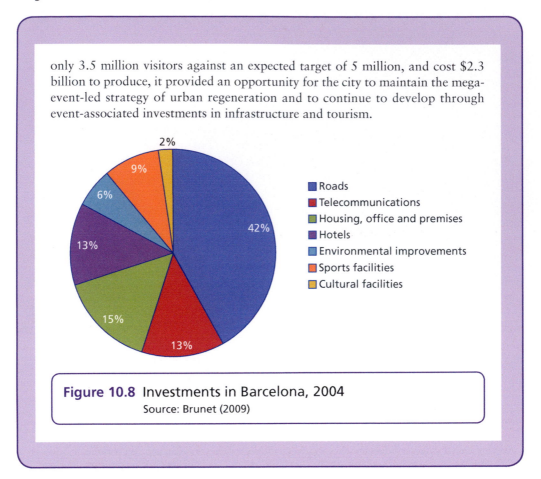

Figure 10.8 Investments in Barcelona, 2004
Source: Brunet (2009)

Legend:
- Roads
- Telecommunications
- Housing, office and premises
- Hotels
- Environmental improvements
- Sports facilities
- Cultural facilities

Study activity

What steps can mega-event organisers take to win public support for hosting the event when the legacy benefits may not be immediately apparent?

10.5 Mega-event tourism

Mega-event tourism can be defined as tourism activity generated either directly or indirectly by the presence of a mega-event within a location.

The major direct economic driver associated with mega-events, and the most obvious manifestation of their impact in the event period, is tourism. The planned increases in tourism that accompany mega-events are related to the increased exposure that an event location will gain in the three event periods and also the opportunity that a mega-event provides for a host city to reposition itself within the global tourism marketplace. Forecasts for the Osaka 2025 World Expo in Japan predict that an estimated 28 million tourists will visit the city, compared to average tourist arrivals of just 4.7 million, clearly indicating the significance of mega-events in the tourism marketplace.

Tourism that is directly generated will include attendance at the event itself and visits in the pre- and post-event periods that are motivated by a desire to encounter the event in its development or legacy phases. From 2009, it was possible to book excursions and visits to the 2012 Olympic site in London, and this increasingly formed part of tourist itineraries in the British capital in the run-up to the Games.

Indirectly generated tourism activity will be related to the increased media profile of the host city and promotional campaigns mounted by both the city and the host nation to maximise the benefits of this increased global exposure. Typically, these campaigns will include the promotion of other events during the event periods, as well as other destinations in the host nation.

10.5.1 Pre-event period tourists

These tourists have been attracted to the destination due to the increased media coverage of the destination resulting from it becoming a mega-event host. Pre-event tourists may be motivated to experience the planning period of the event – perhaps to visit an event location or to participate in pre-event activities, such as hand-over ceremonies or cultural celebrations.

10.5.2 Event period tourists

Tourism flows in the event period can be positive, negative or neutral. Weed (2008) makes use of Preuss's (2005) nine categories of 'event affected people' to categorise movements of people associated with the mega-event period. These are summarised in Figure 10.9.

This figure shows the complexity of mega-event tourism flows. The scale of the event means that it has implications for understanding the behaviours not only of event tourists directly but of all potential tourists to and from a host city during the event period. In fact, minimising the impacts of negative tourism flows associated with mega-events can be as crucial to the overall economic success of the event as maximising positive flows.

10.5.3 Post-event period tourists

Hosting a mega-event generates both tangible and intangible tourism legacies. The intangible tourism benefits include enhancing or developing the image of the city, and increasing and improving tourism industry skills within the local economy. The tangible benefits for the tourism industry include an increased accommodation supply, improved visitor facilities and transport infrastructure, and new visitor attractions. Many mega-event tourists are cultural tourists who seek new cultural experiences associated with a mega-event; many of these experiences come after the event thanks to the creation of new districts and cultural facilities. For example, the main attraction at the 2005 World Expo in Aichi, Japan, was a life-size reconstruction of a house inhabited by the characters of Miyazaki's animated children's film *My Neighbour Totoro*. This was reopened in 2006 and continues to be the most popular tourism attraction in the park that is the legacy of the event, which attracts around 1.6 million visitors per year. In 2022, the house will be the centrepiece of a new theme park based on the movies of *Studio Ghibli*, demonstrating that the resources left by a mega-event can form part of a long-term tourism legacy.

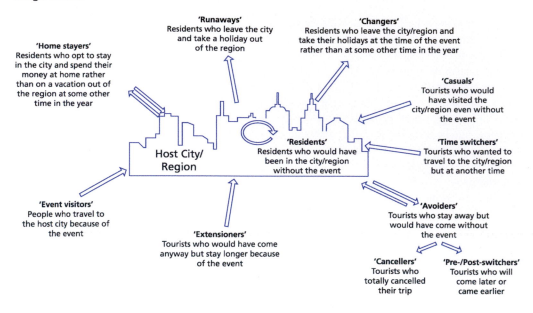

Figure 10.9 Mega-event tourism flows
Source: Weed (2008), adapted from Preuss (2005)

The tangible and intangible tourism benefits of hosting a mega-event can deliver a significant uplift in visitor numbers through enhancing the image of the destination, increasing its media exposure and enhancing the visitor experience.

CASE STUDY 10.4

The tourism impacts of the 2018 Winter Olympic Games

Location: Pyeongchang, Korea
Event type: Mega-event
Attendees: 1,070,000

The 2018 Winter Olympics was hosted in Pyeongchang, Korea. This was only the second time that this event had been held in Asia, after Japan 1972. In the bid for the event, the city forecast that costs would range from $3.5 billion to $9.5 billion, and it is estimated that the final costs came in at around $12.9 billion.

Ninety-one countries participated in the games, which took place from 9 to 25 February 2018. There were 102 events held over 15 disciplines, which is a record number of events, across 12 venues in the Alpenisa Sports Park (The Mountain Cluster of events) and Gangneung Olympic Park (The Coastal Cluster of events).

Economic growth, and the economic impacts of mega-event tourism, were a key reason why Korea bid to hold this mega-event. Planners hoped that as well as the direct economic benefit of event tourism, benefits would also occur in other sections such as construction and transportation. Wood and Meng (2020) used input – output modelling (see Chapter 14) to estimate the economic impacts of the tourism associated with the 2018 Winter Olympics, to evaluate whether the outlay of so much money by the Korean government provided a good return on investment for the public.

They found that:

- 11.5 trillion South Korean Won (SKW) were invested into providing new infrastructure for the games, or upgrading existing infrastructure – this is approximately $10 billion.
- 321,411 international tourists arrived in Korea to watch the Winter Olympics.
- The main industries where tourism had an impact on economic growth were the trade, restaurants and hotel sectors.
- The impacts of tourist spending for the event led to:

  o 2 trillion SKW of new economic output
  o 324 billion SKW of income
  o 744 billion SKW of added value
  o 19,097 new jobs.

Study activity

How can tourism agencies maximise the benefits of positive tourism flows and minimise the impacts of negative tourism flows during a mega-event period?

Industry voice

Lude JI, Head of Theme Development Department, Bureau of Shanghai World Expo Coordination, 2010 Shanghai World Expo, Shanghai, China .

The ten stages of theme development for a world Expo

In July 2006, in the pre-event period, the Bureau of Shanghai World Expo Coordination established its Theme Development Department (TDD), and I was appointed as the head of this department. The TDD was established at the request of the Bureau of International Expositions (the owners of the World Exposition events) to promote the delivery of the Shanghai World Expo in all its aspects.

At that time, the Bureau of Shanghai World Expo Coordination had three understandings of what the theme development process was for in relation to the event: first, it related to background research and concept development; second, it referred to planning and organising the activities and events associated with the Chinese Pavilion and the Theme Pavilion; finally, the theme of the Shanghai World Expo should be expressed in all aspects of the event.

The basic function of the TDD is to deliver these three parts of the process, but because the divisions between the functions of departments involved in a mega-event is not always clear, we also became involved in a large number of other projects for the World Expo. In general, the work that took place for Theme Development can be divided into roughly ten stages. The following are some very brief introductions to these.

The first stage was the determination of the overall theme of the Shanghai World Expo from 1999 to 2002, as part of the bidding process for the event. This was the prelude to the whole theme development. In May 1999, the Development Research Center of Shanghai Municipal Government set up a theme research group. At the end of 2000, the theme statements were identified.

The second stage was the background research and deepening the development of the theme from 2004 to 2005, which led to the production of the third chapter of the Shanghai World Expo's registration report, 'Deepening the Theme of Shanghai World Expo and Classification and Introduction of Activities in the Expo Site'.

The third stage was the first round call for exhibition proposals for the China Pavilion and Theme Pavilion, from April 2005 to November 2005. This round of the process involved a lot of organisation, interaction and communication with planning agencies and companies making proposals, and agreeing on the exhibition standards to develop experience for future planning.

The fourth stage was the second round call for exhibition proposals for the China Pavilion and Theme Pavilion, from the end of 2005 to July 2007. Although, at this stage, the proposals were still judged as not satisfactory, after more than a year of research and further development it did indeed lead to enriched ideas for the China Pavilion and Theme Pavilion, which became the basis for all future planning of the event.

The fifth stage involved further study of the theme framework, from the middle of 2006 to the beginning of 2007. This was mainly a theoretical and reflective study, which did not involve specific projects, but it provided a new basis for future project planning, taking into account the success and developments that had taken place on the project up to this point.

The sixth stage was the third round of calls for planning proposals for the China Pavilion and Theme Pavilion, from June 2007 to July 2008. One of the reasons that this stage was important was that national and local planning systems change frequently and the TDD had to become a common platform, connecting all stages and all departments, and communicating these changes and what they meant for the Expo.

The seventh stage was the planning, implementation and management of the China Pavilion project, from August 2008 to the opening of the World Expo. In August 2008, after the completion of the joint study of the Bureau of the World Expo and the enterprises shortlisted for the China Pavilion planning, an innovative working system and mechanism was established, which was led by the China Central Academy of Fine Arts, and joined by the Bureau of the World Expo, enterprises and experts. After that, the theme development of the China Pavilion was soon complete in all aspects, including its conceptual framework and the main exhibition designs. Finally, the China Pavilion became the highlight of the entire Expo.

The eighth stage was communicating about the theme development to all of China's provinces, municipalities and autonomous regions, which began in September 2007. Through the work of the Domestic Exhibition Department of the Bureau of Shanghai World Expo Coordination, representatives' discussion, on-site communication, theme promotion meetings and other kinds of events were held to promote the exhibition to domestic audiences and partners.

The ninth stage was communication about the theme with the official exhibitors, which began in September 2006. This stage was very complicated. Each participant must submit a "theme statement" which explains the concept and basic content of their part of the exhibition. We have the right to put forward our opinions, but there are not any enforcement measures that we can use to ensure alignment with the general theme. Under the leadership of the General Representative of the Chinese Government, the TDD, together with other departments of the Shanghai World Expo Coordination, took part in a lot of coordination and liaison work during this stage.

The tenth stage was participation in communication about other projects in the Expo that were linked to the theme. The theme of the World Expo has an impact in three areas of the Expo, namely, exhibitions, forums and events. The TDD, which I led, was not deeply involved in the detail of all of these, although our work was very influential on them.

10.6 Summary

This chapter has defined and categorised a mega-event as a special kind of large-scale event that delivers global media and/or socio-economic impacts.

The timeframe of the mega-event has been split into three periods. The pre-event period is characterised by huge levels of speculative public investment and the battle to win public approval. The event period itself requires sophisticated organisation and functional apparatus to respond to the complexity of managing one of the world's largest events. Finally, the benefits of perhaps a decade of investment must be leveraged in the post-event period.

Mega-events have the potential to generate massive benefits for host cities and nations, but they can equally encumber both city and state with massive burdens. Embedding mega-events into broader strategies of urban regeneration and tourism development helps to increase the likelihood of positive outcomes whilst reducing the risk of negative impacts.

Further reading

Frawley, S. (2015) *Managing Sports Mega Events*, Abingdon: Routledge. This book gives an excellent overview of the many strategic and operational issues faced by managers working in mega-events.

Video links

COP25 Summary Video: www.youtube.com/watch?v=wbn-kd8e_ZY
Presentation of the Award of the 2018 and 2022 FIFA World Cup Tournaments: www.youtube.com/watch?v=YfyPi5MnPSY
The Tokyo 2022 Olympic and Paralympic Games Opening Ceremony Highlights: www.youtube.com/watch?v=y2B_5lTU3Rk

Weblinks

Beyond the Games: https://olympics.com/ioc/beyond-the-games
Eurovision Song Contest: https://eurovision.tv/
International Paralympic Committee: www.paralympic.org
The website of the International Bureau of Expositions, which is responsible for the awarding and regulation of World Expos: www.bie-paris.org
The website of the International Olympic Committee, which contains archived information on all previous Olympic and Paralympic events: www.olympic.org

References

Andranovich, G., Burbank, M. and Heying, C. (2001) Olympic Cities: Lessons Learned from Mega-event Politics, *Urban Affairs*, 23 (2): 113–131.
Atkinson, G., Mourato, S., Symanski, S. and Ozdemiroglu, E. (2008) Are We Willing to Pay Enough to Back the Bid? Valuing the Intangible Impacts of London's Bid to Host the 2012 Summer Olympic Games, *Urban Studies*, 45 (2): 419–444.

Baim, D. (2009) Olympic-driven Urban Development, in G. Poynter and I. MacRury (eds), *Olympic Cities: 2012 and the Remaking of London*, Farnham: Ashgate.

Balibrea, M. P. (2001) Urbanism, Culture and the Post-industrial City: Challenging the 'Barcelona Model', *Journal of Spanish Cultural Studies, 2* (2): 187–210.

Bianchini, F. (1993) *Cultural Policy and Urban Regeneration: The Western European Experience*, Manchester: Manchester University Press.

Bladen, C. (2009) Towards an Olympic Volunteering Legacy, in J. Kennell, E. Booth and C. Bladen (eds) *The Olympic Legacy: People, Place Enterprise: Proceedings of the First Annual Conference on Olympic Legacy, 8 and 9 May 2008*, Greenwich: Greenwich University Press.

Boykoff, J. (2011) Anti Olympics, *New Left Review, 67*: 41–59.

Brunet, F. (2009) The Economy of the Barcelona Olympic Games, in G. Poynter and I. MacRury (eds) *Olympic Cities: 2012 and the Remaking of London*, Farnham: Ashgate.

Carlsen, J. and Taylor, A. (2003) Mega-events and Urban Renewal: The Case of the Manchester 2002 Commonwealth Games, *Event Management, 8* (1): 15–22.

Diamond, J. and Liddle, J. (2005) *Management of Regeneration*, Abingdon: Routledge.

Duignan, M. B. and McGillivray, D. (2019) Disorganised Host Community Touristic-Event Spaces: Revealing Rio's Fault Lines at the 2016 Olympic Games, *Leisure Studies, 38* (5): 692–711.

Evans, G. (2005) Measure for Measure: Evaluating the Evidence of Culture's Contribution to Regeneration, *Urban Studies, 42* (5/6): 959–983.

Farmaki, A., Christou, P., Saveriades, A. and Spanou-Tripinioti, E. (2019) Perceptions of Pafos as European Capital of Culture: Tourism Stakeholder and Resident Perspectives, *International Journal of Tourism Research*, 21 (2): 234–244.

FIFA (2018) More than Half the World Watched Record-Breaking 2018 World Cup. Available at: www.fifa.com/tournaments/mens/worldcup/2018russia/media-releases/more-than-half-the-world-watched-record-breaking-2018-world-cup [Accessed 31 July 2022].

Garcia, B. (2004) Urban Regeneration, Arts Programming and Major Events: Glasgow 1990, Sydney 2000 and Barcelona 2004, *International Journal of Cultural Policy, 10* (1): 103–118.

Garcia, B. and Miah, A. (2004) Non-accredited Media, the Olympic Games, the Media and the Host City: The British Academy 2004 Project, *Culture @ The Olympics,* 6: 1–7.

Getz, D. (2007) *Event Studies*, Oxford: Butterworth-Heinemann.

Getz, D. and Page, S. (2016) *Event Studies*, 3rd Ed., Oxford: Butterworth-Heinemann.

Girginov, V. and Parry, J. (2005) *The Olympic Games Explained*, Abingdon: Routledge.

Giulianotti, R. and Klauser, F. (2009) Security Governance and Sport Mega-events: Toward an Interdisciplinary Research Agenda, *Journal of Sport and Social Issues, 34* (1): 1–13.

Gold, J. R. and Gold, M. M. (2009) Future Indefinite? London 2012, the Spectre of Retrenchment and the Challenge of Olympic Sports Legacy, *The London Journal, 34* (2): 179–196.

Graeff, B. and Knijnik, J. (2021) If Things Go South: The Renewed Policy of Sport Mega Events Allocation and its Implications for Future Research, *International Review for the Sociology of Sport*, https://doi.org/10.1177/1012690220981342.

Guala, C. (2009) To Bid or Not to Bid: Public Opinion Before and After the Games: The Case of the Turin 2006 Winter Olympic Games, in J. Kennell, E. Booth and C. Bladen (eds) *The Olympic Legacy: People, Place Enterprise: Proceedings of the First Annual Conference on Olympic Legacy, 8 and 9 May 2008*, Greenwich: Greenwich University Press.

Hill Dickinson LLP (2009) Official Partners. Available at: http://www.08business connect.com/detail/Hill_Dickinson_LLP/45/80.aspx [Accessed 16 January 2010].

Horne, J. and Manzenreiter, W. (2006) An Introduction to the Sociology of Sports Mega-events, *Sociological Review, 54* (2): 1–24.

International Paralympic Committee (2021) LA 2028 Announces Seven-Year Collaboration Agreement with Deloitte. Available at: www.paralympic.org/news/la-2028-announces-seven-year-collaboration-agreement-deloitte [Accessed 31 July 2022].

Kennell, J. and Macleod, N. (2009) A Grey Literature Review of the Cultural Olympiad, *Cultural Trends, 18* (1): 83–88.

Liverpool 08 (2008) *Commercial Support*. Available at: www.liverpool08.com/commercial [Accessed 16 January 2010].

McGillivray, D. and Turner, D. (2018) *Event Bidding: Politics, Persuasion and Resistance*, Abingdon: Routledge.

McGuigan, J. (1996) *Culture and the Public Sphere*, Abingdon: Routledge.

Morgan, K. (2002) The New Regeneration Narrative: Local Development in the Multi-level Polity, *Local Economy, 17* (3): 191–199.

Preuss, H. (2007) The Conceptualisation and Measurement of Mega Sport Event Legacies. *Journal of Sport and Tourism, 12* (3–4): 207–228.

Preuss, H. (2005) The Economic Impact of Visitors at Major Multi-sport Events, *European Sport Management Quarterly, 5* (3): 281–301.

Roberts, K. (2004) *The Leisure Industry*, London: Palgrave.

Roberts, P. (2000) The Evolution, Definition and Purpose of Urban Regeneration, in P. Roberts and H. Sykes (eds), *Urban Regeneration*, London: Sage.

Roche, M. (2000) *Mega-events and Modernity: Olympics and Expos in the Growth of Global Culture*, Abingdon: Routledge.

Shulenkorf, N. (2005) *Oktoberfest Munchen: The World's Largest Public Event*, Nordestet: Grin Verlag.

Smith, A. (2012) *Events and Regeneration: The Strategic Use of Events to Regenerate Cities*, Abingdon: Routledge.

Smith, A. (2007) Large-scale Events and Sustainable Urban Regeneration: Key Principles for Host Cities, *Journal of Urban Regeneration and Renewal, 1* (2): 1–13.

Smith, A. and Fox, T. (2007) From Event-led to Event-themed Regeneration: The 2002 Commonwealth Games Legacy Programme, *Urban Studies, 45* (5): 1125–1143.

Tarlow, P. (2002) *Event Risk Management and Safety*, New York: John Wiley and Sons.

Tartu2024 (2019) Objectives. Available at: www.tartu2024.ee/objectives [Accessed 31 July 2022].

Theodoraki, E. (2007) *Olympic Event Organisation*, Oxford: Butterworth-Heinemann.

Weed, M. (2008) *Olympic Tourism*, Oxford: Butterworth-Heinemann.

Chapter 11

Events in the public and third sectors

Contents

DOI: 10.4324/9781003102878-11

11.1 Aims

By the end of this chapter, students will be able to:

- analyse the differences between the private, public and third sectors in the events industry
- evaluate the particular considerations associated with the planning and delivery of public sector events
- evaluate the particular considerations associated with the planning and delivery of events in the third sector.

11.2 Introduction

Our understandings of events often rely on management analysis and academic research with a 'for-profit' focus. However, a large proportion of UK events are carried out by and on behalf of the third sector of the economy and the public services. Such events, whilst often high budget and carried out by cash-rich organisations, do not usually embody the same characteristics of planning, design and management as their for-profit sector counterparts. Building on the key aspects of events management that are applicable to events in all sectors of the economy, this chapter highlights the particular characteristics of third sector and public sector events and the different nature and style of managing their success.

Getz and Page (2019) discuss three different groups of event organisers, in terms of their ownership of legal status: private, non-profit and government/partnership groups. However, this categorisation does not adequately account for the important role of social enterprise in the events industry (explained below), especially the ways in which events can form a part of the commercial activities of otherwise charitable or public organisations, or businesses with a social mission. Figure 11.1 demonstrates the bridging role that social enterprise can play between these different groups.

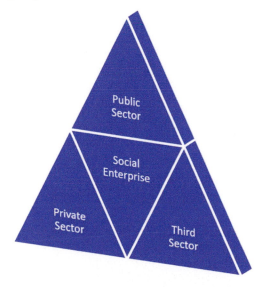

Figure 11.1 The event-producing sectors

The private sector has been the focus of the majority of event management textbooks, dominating the literature with discussions of profitability and revenue management. In this chapter, we will explore events in the public and third sectors, both of which are increasingly using events in order to achieve their social, political and cultural aims, and to develop new revenue streams through social enterprise.

11.3 The public sector

The public sector refers to those organisations that are either in the direct control of government at the national, regional or local levels, or receive their core funding from public finances. This sector, despite being encouraged to be more businesslike, is fundamentally different from the private sector when it comes to managing events in one major respect: accountability is to local citizens and the electorate rather than shareholders and/or investors (Wood 2009), notwithstanding that financial accountability and offering value-for-money on public investment is a central feature of modern local government, especially when considering the large amounts of money required to attract, promote and deliver large-scale events in a destination (Getz 2019; Ormerod and Wood 2020).

The main impacts of this difference are seen in terms of how public sector organisations justify their involvement in events management and in how the events themselves are evaluated. Although it is tempting to suggest that public sector events will differ fundamentally from events in other sectors in terms of their content and design, recent moves towards greater private and third sector involvement in what have traditionally been areas of public sector monopoly – such as health, education and welfare – have blurred these distinctions. In much events research, the public sector is viewed as a key stakeholder in the events industry, but this perspective can see the public sector in a very passive way, either as a partner to be consulted with when considering event impacts, or as playing a legislative or regulatory role on the fringes of events. However, in recent years, the public sector has become more active in creating, delivering and funding events of all kinds, with events increasingly being seen as fundamental to achieving strategic goals of policy-makers and governments (Cho *et al.* 2019; Nordvall and Brown 2020).

CASE STUDY 11.1

The role of governments in the events industry

Event name: Singapore: Passion Made Possible
Event category: Various
Venue and location: Singapore
Date: Year round
Website: www.visitsingapore.com/mice/en/

'Passion Made Possible' (PMP) is the slogan for the support offered to the events industry, with a focus on the MICE sector, by Visit Singapore, the public sector-funded tourism board for the dynamic island state. Visit Singapore is involved in long-term strategic planning for event tourism, growing international markets and attracting investment to the sector.

PMP offers public sector support to the events industry through three main schemes:

- Approved International Fair (AIF): A programme to endorse and accredit trade fairs in Singapore, offering tax breaks to events with significant international and commercial appeal.
- Business Events in Singapore (BEIS): Through this programme, event businesses can receive funding, help with securing appropriate venues, and introductions to key event stakeholders.
- Singapore Mice Advantage Programme (SMAP): This is a suite of discounts and incentives offered to event organisers who choose to hold events of a certain size in Singapore, including complimentary welcome desks at the national airport, discounts on event spaces and discounted flights for delegates.

Source: Visit Singapore (2020)

Study activity

Carry out some background research on the Visit Singapore website at www.visitsingapore.com/mice/en/. What can you find out about why the Government of Singapore is so supportive of the MICE sector? Consider the following two questions:

1 Why do you think the organisers of international events in Singapore might need these kinds of support services?
2 What benefits do the citizens of Singapore get from the public money that is being spent on this service?

There has been a huge recent growth in the use of events by local and regional governments, although most government involvement at the level of the city or region remains overwhelmingly operational and ad hoc, and lacks coherence (Ziakas 2019). However, despite these concerns, in some more progressive localities, events strategy has become a new form of public policy, with the public sector involved in events that range from local, interactive gatherings to mega-events like the Olympic Games (Richards 2017a). Recently, public authorities have begun to use the concept of the event portfolio to develop holistic programmes of events in destinations, where the cumulative effect of hosting events produces increased benefits for the destination, and the relationships between the events are leveraged to enhance both value for money in public investment and the capacity of the local events industry to deliver ever more impactful events (Ziakas and Getz 2020).

Despite the portfolio approach becoming more common, especially in the drive to create 'eventful' destinations with year-round programmes of events (Richards 2017b), it is still the case that the public sector is mostly involved in the events industry in a less strategic way, but across a diverse range of activities. The sections below will look at the relationship between the public sector and the events industry in more detail, using international examples. The model in Figure 11.2 categorises the different roles that the public sector plays in the events industry, and these are used to structure the remainder of this section.

11.3.1 Venue ownership

In many locations, especially outside regional metropolitan centres, event venues can be publicly owned. Local government is often the owner of theatres, arts centres, community facilities, and parks and streets where events are staged. Public ownership of event venues usually either reflects historical patterns of ownership in an area or is a legacy of public sector investment that has been necessary to develop large event facilities. Increasingly, these venues are operated by specialist event organisations that are able to maximise return on the state's investment through the application of specialist management techniques in promotion, human resources and artist management.

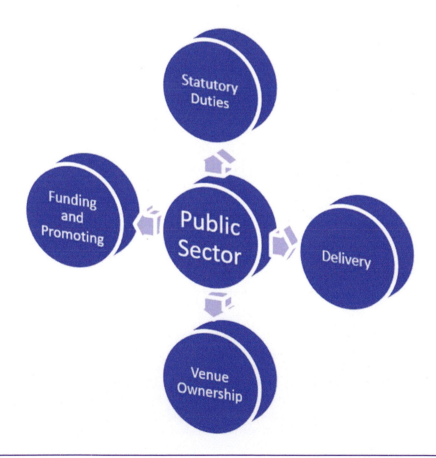

Figure 11.2 The role of the public sector in event management

For example, in Nashville, Tennessee, in the United States, the Bridgestone Arena is owned by Davidson County and the Sports Authority of Nashville, who invested approximately $155 million in its construction (Metro Government of Nashville 2020). The day-to-day management and promotion of the venue have been contracted out to a specialist management company, Powers Management, which has the specialist arena and events management skills required to make a success of this 20,000-capacity venue – which is one of the most well-known event venues in America, having welcomed more than 13 million visitors since it opened (Bridgestone Arena 2020). In Krakow, Poland, the ICE Krakow Convention Centre received more than €91 million in public funding as part of a significant investment in both regional economic development and support for the growth of the events industry in Poland. The Centre now receives more than 250,000 delegates per year and is managed on a day-to-day basis by KBF, a specialist events organisation from outside of the public sector, who have the expertise and experience to operate a significant venue of this kind (ICE Krakow 2020; KBF 2020).

11.3.2 Statutory duties

Governments and, in particular in this context, local governments who become involved in the events industry have a series of duties that they are legally obliged to carry out in the public interest, known as their statutory duties. The exact duties will vary from country to country, but typically relate to areas such as environmental protections, education, policing, refuse collection and public health and safety. In exercising their statutory duties, public sector agencies frequently engage with the events industry.

Image 11.1 Iggy Azalea at the Bridgestone Arena
Source: Getty Images

For example, the public sector also often has a statutory duty to monitor and regulate some of the negative impacts of events, which it does through licensing and the enforcement of statutes on, for example, noise pollution. In addition to this, the public sector is able to incentivise or disincentivise particular forms of activity through taxes. This can be done by central government through the manipulation of nationwide taxes, or through changes in local taxation by local government. Using funds raised from taxation, local government will be responsible, to a greater or lesser degree, for the maintenance of public space, transport, utilities provision and the emergency services – all of which must be in place for the smooth running of an event. Liaising with local government departments on these issues is a key aspect of the management of large events and event venues. In 2017, the policing costs for the UEFA Champions League final in Cardiff were estimated to be £5.7 million, with more than 90% of these costs being met by the public sector (BBC 2018).

Exercising their statutory duties in regard to public health during the global Covid-19 pandemic, governments around the world introduced restrictions relating to public gathering, social distancing and travel, which led to the cancellation or postponement of many events, including the interruption of in-progress sporting competitions (Ludvigsen and Hayton 2020). In recognition of the devastating impact of the pandemic on the events industry, many governments announced specific support packages to help to re-start the industry. For example, in Germany, €150 million of the government's €1 billion economic stimulus package was allocated to support the music events sector (The Ticketing Business 2020).

11.3.3 Funding and promotion

The public sector can make direct and indirect funding contributions to events. Direct funding involves the finance necessary for the production of an event. For example, the Australian Government provides funding of approximately AU$1.5 million per year to support the creation of work for Australia's major international festivals. This is delivered through the *Major Festivals Initiative*, which has the aims to:

- increase access for Australian audiences to new high quality Australian performing arts productions of scale
- support the development of new Australian works that grow audiences
- expand appreciation of new Australian performing arts productions
- promote international awareness of the quality of Australian performing arts productions and Australian stories
- strengthen Australia's reputation as a sophisticated and artistic nation with a confident, outward-focused arts sector
- increase overall levels of presentation of new Australian performing arts productions of scale.
         (Department of Communications and the Arts 2016: Major Festivals Initiative)

Indirect financial support to the wider events industry is provided through state support for training for events professionals (for example, through higher education programmes) and business support services.

Where events receive direct support from the public sector in terms of marketing, this is normally related to destination marketing and tourism promotion. Competition to attract high-value events, such as association conferences, has intensified as their economic impacts have been increasingly acknowledged as important to the work of Destination Management Organisations (DMO) (Nolan 2020). Governments make use of events for destination branding by public sector bodies concerned with inward investment and tourism, as well as to support other goals, such as the promotion of social cohesion and civic identity (Raj *et al.* 2013). Events, especially cultural events and festivals, have become core elements in destination marketing (Richards and Palmer 2010), and many towns and cities now include events in their marketing strategies. A specific approach to attracting, supporting and developing events involves the use of Convention Bureaus. Although these are sometimes part of a DMO, they are an established feature of public sector support for events in many destinations. In Thailand, the Convention and Exhibition Bureau was established by the government in 2002, and in 2019 the estimated contribution made by its work to the Thai economy through the support of MICE events was $9.3 billion, 1.65% of GDP (TCEB 2019).

11.3.4 Delivery

In some cases, public sector organisations are directly responsible for producing events. Although this function is often contracted to specialist event organisers, some celebratory and commemorative events are still delivered directly by public sector bodies. As Pugh and Wood (2004: 61) state, 'the majority of local governments in Britain now have a substantial and varied events programme', but these events are usually supported only by departments with limited, non-specialist resources in terms of staff, funding and time (Wood 2009).

The fundamental test of whether the public sector should be involved in events, and whether their involvement has been constructive, is based on the 'public good' argument (O'Sullivan 2020). This asks whether the contribution of government to an event will produce benefits for society as a whole or for targeted groups within it. This argument can be tested in the pre-event and post-event phases by asking the following three questions:

1 Does the event fit into the accepted policy domain of government?
2 Are the public benefits significant and inclusive?
3 Is the event managed sustainably in economic, social and environmental terms?

CASE STUDY 11.2

Public sector support for a new festival in Mexico City

Event name: Day of the Dead
Event category: Cultural
Venue and location: Mexico City, Mexico
Date: October/November, annually
Attendance: 1,200 participants plus c.300,000 attendees
Sponsors: Mexican Tourism Board
Website: www.visitmexico.com/en/

La Día de Muertos, or Day of the Dead, festival is a primarily Mexican festival associated with the Catholic religious traditions of All Saints' Day and All Souls' Day. It is a celebration of remembrance for family members and friends who have died, that has been inscribed on the UNESCO list of worldwide intangible cultural heritage. Over the last century, the festivities have become popular outside of Mexico with both Hispanic and non-Hispanic communities, and features of the Day of the Dead, including skeletons, bright colours and Mexican music, have been used in films, music and product branding.

The Day of the Dead Parade in Mexico City has only existed since 2016, when the Mexican Tourism Board sought to capitalise on the popularity of the recent James Bond film, *Spectre*. The film featured an imaginary parade in the city, which had never held one before, in its opening sequence, creating expectations in Mexico and abroad that the city would host one. Seeing the huge commercial potential of the event, the Mexican Tourism Board funded and supported the creation of a new parade, which has been held every year since 2016.

In 2019, the festival in Mexico City involved a number of connected events, in addition to the parade itself. These included a night tour and light installation in the city's Chapultepec Park, a sound and light performance using video mapping at the Monument to the Revolution, and performances and installations, often focusing on the public inauguration of ceremonial altars in the city. In total, more than 300,000 tourists visited for the event, with local hotels at 100% occupancy during the festival, which generated more than US$140 million for the economy.

Image 11.2 The Day of the Dead Parade in Mexico City
Source: Getty Images

11.4 Public sector-specific events

Governments can use events to gain control of specific agendas in the public eye, build support for policies and programmes, and deliver on specific policy objectives. National governments take responsibility for major international and political events, occasions of state and national celebrations (Allen *et al.* 2010). Local government has responsibility for place-making, destination-branding, generating inward investment, reducing out-migration and community cohesion, and it makes use of events to fulfil these duties.

Local authorities deliver a wide range of events for their communities, business and visitors, which may include:

- networking events
- conferences
- festivals and other celebratory events
- cultural events
- information and consultation events.

The first four of these are covered in the chapters on corporate and cultural events (Chapters 12 and 13, respectively). However, information and consultation events are specific to the public sector and have specific characteristics that are explored below.

11.4.1 Information and consultation events

These events are used by the public sector to inform the public about new projects or initiatives and to produce a dialogue with citizens that can inform the development of these areas. They can occur on a variety of scales, from small neighbourhood-level meetings to touring information roadshows.

It is generally recognised that, when government aims to develop a new project, or create a new policy, they should consult with the public in a participatory way (Saab *et al.* 2018). This is especially important in the planning of large and mega-events as, even though the members of the community around an event are often conceived as key beneficiaries of its positive impacts, the idea to stage the event rarely comes from within the community, and the project may face objections and resistance. As part of the preparations for the 2022 FIFA World Cup, the government in Qatar organised a series of consultation events that visited five different shopping malls across the country, which were attended by around 30,000 people. The aim of the events was to learn more about progress in delivering the event, but also to listen to residents' opinions about the 2022 mega-event (Supreme Committee for Delivery and Legacy 2016).

Community consultation events can take any one of the four forms illustrated in Figure 11.3.

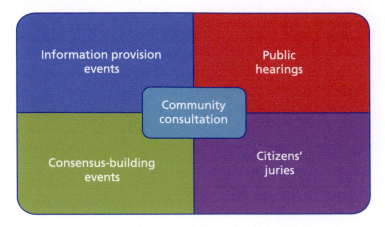

Figure 11.3 Forms of community consultation events

Information provision events are the most common form of community consultation. Limited forms of interaction are offered, but these events are useful for conveying large amounts of information to a wide audience. They can be repeated and can be mobile, at a low cost. For example, in Malta, proposals were put forward in 2017 for significant developments, involving €3 million of public funding, for the township of Paola. An exhibition of the proposals, and development options, was held over three days, which saw almost 900 local citizens then case votes for their preferred way forward for the area (URBACT 2017).

At public hearings, evidence is presented to the public, along with expert advice, and at the end decisions are taken by a representative body, such as a court or council. An example of this kind of consultation event was the public hearings that began in September 2020, in Brazil, to decide on the outcome of a case brought against the Federal Government by a coalition of political parties, seeking to compel the government to act on climate change and to enforce policies on sustainable development in the country. The hearing heard evidence from 66 experts: scientists, environmentalists, indigenous people, representatives from the agribusiness and financial sectors, economists, researchers, parliamentarians and representatives of the federal and state governments (LSE 2020).

In consensus-building events, the public are brought into the decision-making process and can influence the outcome of the decision. In 2019, the Department of City Planning in New York, USA, invited residents to a 'Planning Camp', to become involved in decisions relating to the development of the 520 miles of waterfront areas in the city. The event involved arts organisations, government departments, marine charities and professional facilitators, with the aim of creating a participatory planning process (NYC Planning 2019).

In a citizens' jury, selected members of the public are asked to represent the views of the community as part of the decision-making process. These have been used more widely in the United States and Germany than elsewhere (Carson 2001), but they are being utilised increasingly in a range of contexts as a cost-effective way of gauging public opinion. This form of consultation was used in 2019 in Leeds, UK, to deliberate on how the city should respond to the climate crisis. The citizen's jury took place over 30 hours and nine sessions, involving 25 randomly selected citizens from across the city, who heard evidence from 22 experts. The process led to 12 recommendations which then informed the City Council's Climate Emergency Strategy (Leeds Climate Commission 2020).

11.4.2 The impacts of public sector events

Public sector events share sets of outcomes with all other forms of events (see Shone and Parry 2019), but these have particular implications in the public sector due to governments' responsibilities towards, and accountability to, their citizens (see Figure 11.4).

11.4.2.1 Economic implications of public sector events

Any event can have either positive or negative impacts. However, a private sector event normally has a direct economic impact – one way or the other – only on the event company that produces it. By contrast, a public sector event can have significant economic consequences, sometimes for many years after the event has taken place. In the case of small-scale events, these economic implications may be limited to individual departments or public bodies, but with large and mega-events, the consequences can be much more significant, sometimes affecting national economies and the future delivery of public services. Among the potential negative impacts of a mega-event are consumer price and land price inflation, tax increases, the mismanagement of funds and the costs associated with corruption.

11.4.2.2 Developmental implications of public sector events

The public sector will normally be engaged in the development of particular locations when it supports or delivers events, ideally guided by the principles of sustainable development. However, although developmental goals – such as poverty reduction, educational attainment and public health improvements – often form part of the bid for hosting an event, there are ongoing controversies and debates over the perceived and actual benefits of hosting events requiring large public investments (Smith *et al.* 2018).

Figure 11.4 Aspects of public sector events

11.4.2.3 Political implications of public sector events

Staging or financing events to support a particular policy or political agenda can work in favour of the public sector or against it, depending on the success or failure of the event. In addition, a non-political event can have political implications if it is seen not to have produced good value for money in terms of public investment or to have caused controversy that reflects badly on the political decision to back it. Especially for major and mega-events, hosting always has political implications when there is public sector involvement.

Barker *et al.* (2001) analysed the impacts of hosting the America's Cup, a sailing competition and the oldest sporting trophy competition in the world, in Auckland, New Zealand. There were high expectations of the potential positive impacts of this event, to such an extent that the government appointed a minister to maximise them. The event was judged to have improved international trade relations, to have increased the potential of the country to attract overseas investment, and to have enhanced New Zealand's international image and reputation, which would strengthen its bids for future major events.

11.4.2.4 Social/community implications of public sector events

Many events are produced or supported by the public sector because of the positive impacts that they may have in such areas as community cohesion, social inclusion, local pride and identity. However, events can also have negative social impacts (as set out in Chapter 14), and these can lead to both financial problems for governments and reputational problems with political implications.

11.4.3 Public sector event financing

Governments around the world are becoming commissioners of services from the private and third sectors, meaning that they increasingly commission specialist event producers to deliver their events. This is in line with the more strategic marketing orientation in local government that was identified by Pugh and Wood (2004) when they looked at local authority events. These developments form part of a changing public sector paradigm in which government is seen as enabling and facilitating, rather than directly delivering the full range of public services.

CASE STUDY 11.3

Private companies delivering public sector events

Event name: United Nations Global Compact Leaders Summit
Event category: Public sector event
Venue and location: Online

Audience: 23,000
Website: https://registration.unglobalcompact.org/website/12559/home/

This 20th anniversary event for the United Nations brought together thousands of leaders from around the world to decide how businesses can support governments and communities to recover from the three crises of health, inequality and climate. The United Nations explained that:

> Our 20th anniversary Leaders Summit will virtually convene leading voices from Business, Government, the United Nations, Civil Society and Academia for a 26-hour conversation about how we can rebuild more inclusive economies and societies to set a new course for a socially just, low-carbon and climate resilient world, where no one is left behind.

The United Nations commissioned a private events agency, Catapult, to design and deliver the event, which took place virtually for the first time. Since 1999, Catapult have produced international events for diverse clients and have offices in Ireland, Los Angeles and New York. Catapult explain their value clearly to their clients:

> We believe in creative collaboration. We love working with our clients, designers, producers and innovators to nail the overall strategy. We share responsibility from initial brief all the way to final analysis. And we firmly believe that building great relationships creates the best outcomes no matter what the project demands.
>
> We have over 20 years of experience in the industry. We execute live event experiences across a multitude of sectors, nationally and internationally. Captivating live experiences creating moments of magic with real meaning is what we do. Our deliberate design shifts behaviours to deliver bottom-line results. We understand that great events do not happen in isolation. Their success is firmly rooted in your wider business and marketing objectives. Experiences have to be more than just wow – they need to impact on behaviour.
>
> (Catapult, 2022)

For this innovative event, Catapult's involvement included:

- Full technical management
- Speaker advancing
- Technical rehearsals with speakers
- Live studio production
- Digital content creation
- Live broadcast and stream management
- Run of show

11.5 The third sector

Between the private and public sectors, and often bridging the two in practical terms, is the third sector. Known historically as the 'charitable' or 'voluntary' sector (Shone and Parry 2019), when it comes to events management, contemporary third sector organisations often still contain a strong voluntary and/or charitable component, but they may act in entrepreneurial, businesslike ways that do not conform to older stereotypes of village fête committees and well-meaning volunteer organisations. Many third sector organisations channel public sector funding to the community level, delivering services in communities, and increasing numbers of them engage in forms of social enterprise – generating profitable business for socially sustainable ends. Such businesses have often evolved from charitable and voluntary groups that wished to avoid the constraints imposed by the regulation of charities and sought to develop a more entrepreneurial attitude to social change.

Although these definitions can vary between countries, we split third sector organisations into three groupings. The first of these are *charities*. These are organisations which are set up for a specific cause. Charitable organisations rely on fundraising and donations for their income, and have very formal management structures. Normally, these involve boards of trustees who have a stewardship role for the organisation, with day-to-day running of the charity often being carried out by volunteers or, in some cases, by a small number of paid staff. In many countries, being registered as a charity denotes a certain privileged status, which may include tax benefits. Because of this, charities are often very limited in the scope of their activities and are very tightly regulated, entailing annual reporting and high levels of public accountability. A less formal organisational form is a *community group*. These groups exist to provide a service for people, and although they may take specific legal forms such as Community Interest Companies, or Unincorporated Associations, they are less limited in what they can do, and are subject to less regulation than charities. However, they do not have the same status, financial or moral, as charities, and are often more local in their scope.

A third form of third sector organisation is a *social enterprise*. Social Enterprise UK, a representative body for social enterprise in the UK, states:

> Social enterprises are businesses that are changing the world for the better. Like traditional businesses they aim to make a profit but it's what they do with their profits that sets them apart – reinvesting or donating them to create positive social change. Social enterprises are in our communities and on our high streets – from coffee shops and cinemas, to pubs and leisure centres, banks and bus companies.
>
> By selling goods and services in the open market, social enterprises create employment and reinvest their profits back into their business or the local community. This allows them

to tackle social problems, improve people's life chances, provide training and employment opportunities for those furthest from the market, support communities and help the environment.

(SEC 2020)

Adrenalin is a full-service events agency in Singapore that was founded as a social enterprise. Adrenaline began as a two-person business, and now employs 30 people, managing more than 100 events every year, with an annual turnover of more than $2 million. Adrenalin believe that any event can be used to support a social purpose, through methods such as hiring other social enterprises to deliver parts of their events, by improving sustainability, or by becoming involved in events which spread positive messages. Founder and Managing Director Richard Chua is very clear that what has driven their success in working for client such as Shell, Changi Airport and Citibank is not just their social mission, but being a 'sustainable and strong events agency [who are] bringing something fresh to the audience'. Adrenalin specialises in creative projects and events with a social mission, helping their clients to design events that give back to their communities. Adrenalin's recruitment strategy has also been designed to bring under-represented groups into the events workforce, with 30% of their staff classified as deaf, wheelchair-bound or youth-at-risk (Business Times 2018).

11.6 Events in the third sector

Third sector organisations operate in the same social and economic climate as any other form of business, so it should come as no surprise that the third sector has embraced the growth in the planned events sector as vigorously as its private and public sector counterparts. However, third sector organisations often face constraints to their work in events that do not affect their private sector counterparts. The legal status of some third sector organisations can prescribe the activities that they can and cannot become involved in, especially when it comes to formal charitable status, meaning that some organisations find it difficult to innovate in this area. Additionally, the decision-making process within some charitable and community groups can be quite bureaucratic. This is a necessary governance role for the responsible management of organisations who have charitable purposes and make use of public money and donations, but it can make it difficult for these groups to engage with the commercialised environment of event venues and agencies, or to respond quickly to changing event trends. When third sector groups are in receipt of funding for their work from trusts and foundations, or from government agencies, this funding can sometimes be very prescriptive about how it is used. For example, funders may specify which groups or individuals should benefit from the funding, or locations where it should be spent.

Third sector organisations carry out three main roles in the events industry, as shown in Figure 11.5.

11.6.1 Venue management and ownership

Third sector organisations, such as charities, community organisations and social enterprises, can own and/or manage event venues. In the UK, local government will often retain legal ownership of a range of possible event venues, but the day-to-day management of these venues will be provided by a third sector organisation. This system ensures that the venue is run in accordance with the public sector's commitment to public value, but it removes many of the costs and complications of management from the public sector.

Figure 11.5 The roles of the third sector in events

Image 11.3 The Hub, Cape Town, South Africa
Source: Gallo Images/Getty Images

Other third sector organisations own venues outright and use them to generate income to help them meet their social, cultural or environmental goals. An example is the Impact Hub, in Johannesburg, South Africa. This venue was set up to support local third sector groups and to encourage innovation in social enterprise. It does this by providing networking, meeting and work space for social enterprises, along with an exhibition and event space with catering facilities. The Hub makes its spaces available for private hire to generate income, and also hosts its own events on such topics as climate change, social entrepreneurship and new technologies. They describe their activities with the following statement, clearly showing the entrepreneurial, international outlook of many contemporary social enterprise projects:

> Impact Hub Joburg forms part the world's largest network of inspiring workspaces, vibrant learning communities, and entrepreneurial incubation programs – from startup to investment ready and beyond. We foster social innovation through collaboration to create sustainable impact.
>
> From Amsterdam to Johannesburg, Singapore to San Francisco, Impact Hub has evolved into a rapidly expanding, diverse global network of over 15000+ members in 81 Impact Hubs in 50 countries on 5 continents. Each community is a wealth of innovative programs, events, and cutting-edge content.
>
> (Impact Hub Johannesburg 2016)

11.6.2 Service provision

Third sector organisations can be involved with both indirect and direct service provision for events. Within communities, third sector groups can provide services relating to neighbourhood management, crime reduction, the maintenance of public space and youth work that help to create a stable and secure environment for events. In addition, they can provide direct services, such as catering, volunteers, and advice and consultations. In Manchester, UK, Good Mood Food provides catering services for the local events industry, mainly for small- to medium-size business events and private functions, but also larger events such as award ceremonies and annual meetings. They also hire out watering and catering staff, as well as providing crockery hire. The firm is a social enterprise that offers training, employment and volunteer opportunities for individuals suffering from mental health problems, and it also campaigns to highlight the links between good food, health and mental well-being (Good Mood Food 2021).

11.6.3 Event organisation

Third sector organisations stage events to gain publicity for their social goals, to raise funds, and/or for training and networking purposes. The third sector is very diverse, including everything from international non-governmental organisations to small local campaign groups. Because of this diversity, third sector organisations are involved in staging a wide range of events, including:

- Cultural events
- Networking events
- Conferences
- Community festivals
- Fundraising events

The last two categories in this list are characteristic of third sector events activity. Festivals are discussed in depth in Chapter 13, but fundraising events have a specific and prominent role within the third sector, so are explored in more detail below.

11.6.4 Fundraising events

Fundraising events, of which there are many different types, are extremely common within the third sector. Events that are often used to raise funds for charitable causes can include:

- Celebrity or 'legend' sports events
- Themed concerts
- Entertainment shows
- Dinners and 'after-dinner' events
- Online streaming events
- Challenge events
- Auctions

CASE STUDY 11.4

A mass-participation challenge event for Cancer Research

Event name: Race for Life
Event category: Third sector event
Venue: Across the United Kingdom
Date: 1994 – present
Audience: More than 8 million participants
Website: www.cancerresearchuk.org/get-involved/find-an-event/charity-runs/race-for-life

Every year since 1994, Cancer Research UK has been organising an annual multi-site challenge event to raise money for research into all 200 types of cancer. These events have raised more than £547 million to fight cancer, and have involved more than 8 million participants, who fundraise individually and donate the money to the charity.

There are three separate challenge events that form the 'Race for Life'. These are a 5-kilometre run, which is the most popular event, a 10-kilometre run, and an obstacle course event. Originally, the event was only open to women, with a strong focus on female cancers, but the event is now open to men and children, a decision made in 2019 to help to widen the appeal of the event, which had seen its fundraising success falter slightly in previous years.

A local event organiser for one of the hundreds of events that take place simultaneously across the country explains the event's appeal:

> Our events are fun, colourful, emotional and uplifting. You don't need to be sporty to take part. You don't have to train, and you certainly don't need to compete against anyone else!
>
> By taking part and raising money, participants will play a crucial role in helping to turn discoveries made in the lab into new, better treatments for patients across Devon and throughout the UK. That's why every person and every penny raised counts.

Webber (2004) provides a categorisation of fundraising events which helps to explain their various objectives (see Table 11.1).

However, as Webber goes on to show, such events, in themselves, are not very efficient in terms of income generation (see Table 11.2). Instead, they should be seen as part of a more strategic approach to fundraising that includes relationship-building and increasing awareness if their potential for charitable giving is to be fully exploited.

Table 11.1 Types of fundraising events
Source: Webber (2004)

Fundraising event	Objective
Donor development	To generate additional income from existing supporters
Rewarding current supporters	To maintain the enthusiasm and engagement of current supporters
New support generation	To attract new supporters
Networking	To increase networking opportunities between supporters and potential supporters
Awareness raising	To develop awareness of the cause for which funds are being raised; to maintain awareness of the cause in the minds of supporters, public and the media

> **Table 11.2** Productivity of different fundraising methods
> Source: Webber (2004)

Fundraising method	Income raised per pound spent
Legacies	43.3
Committed giving	3.7
Memberships	2.7
Local fundraising	2.3
Fundraising events	2.2
Direct marketing	2.0
Not from individuals	
Trusts	9.9
Corporate	4.7

CASE STUDY 11.5

Charity concert events during the Covid-19 pandemic

Event name: Together at Home
Event category: Third sector event
Venue: Facebook
Date: 18 April 2020
Audience: More than 19 million viewers in the United States, but also syndicated worldwide
Website: www.globalcitizen.org/en/media/togetherathome/

Together at Home was an online, live streamed fundraising event in support of the World Health Organisation, held during the Covid-19 pandemic. The event was organised by the Global Citizen organisation, and curated by Lady Gaga. As well as raising money, the event also aimed to promote the virtues of social distancing.

The event was hosted by celebrity presenters including Jameela Jamil, Matthew McConaughey, Danai Gurria, Becky G, Laverne Cox and Don Cheadle and featured appearances by numerous celebrities. As well as being broadcast on television, the event was live streamed on Apple TV, Facebook, Instagram, Twitch, YouTube and TenCent, amongst other platforms.

The event raised nearly $128 million, making it the joint most successful charity concert in history, alongside Live Aid in 1985. The event also set the world record for the most money ever raised by a remote music festival, and the most musical acts to perform at a remote music festival.

Industry voice

Jo Tilley-Riley, Director of Communications, Hestia, www.hestia.org

 When most people think of events in the charity sector, the first thing that comes to mind are probably the fundraisers – from glamours galas to mass participation fun runs. But for charities such as Hestia, events are also a vital tool for influencing change.

Last year, Hestia marked 50 years of supporting people in crisis. We started out as a small group of volunteers responding to rough sleeping. Today we support over 15,000 people to recover from crisis – whether they have endured domestic abuse, been a victim of modern slavery or are dealing with challenges to their mental health. But we no longer only want to respond to crisis. We want to take the lived experiences of the people we work with and use them to change the systems and prevent crisis.

Over the last few years, we have had a focus on bringing the lived experiences of survivors of domestic abuse to the fore, primarily through the campaign that we host (UK SAYS NO MORE) and centred on the opportunity to influence legislation through the Domestic Abuse Bill. One of the most successful early elements of this was an event we held to engage parliamentarians. In coming up with the concept for the event we were lucky enough to have pro-bono support from public affairs agency Interel. Billed as a "rally", it was held in Portcullis House, directly opposite the Houses of Parliament. Recognising the fast-changing pressures on the diaries of parliamentarians, we decided to schedule the event over two hours with a mixture of opportunities to listen to speakers (from across the political spectrum and adults with lived experience), network and have a photo opportunity.

This format secured high engagement and enabled us to sign up over 100 parliamentarians to a charter calling for the impact of domestic abuse on children and the role of employers in tackling domestic abuse to be enshrined in the new Bill. We leveraged the charter to generate media coverage and the photo opportunity also meant we got high levels of visibility for the event on social media. The Rally was high impact and low cost (we just paid for some printing and coffees) and provided a strong foundation for our subsequent advocacy around the Domestic Abuse Bill. We were able to follow up with one-to-one conversations and many of the parliamentarians who attended that Rally have gone on to table key amendments as the Bill has progressed through Parliament.

However, in the past year, with the social distancing restrictions due to the pandemic, events such as the Rally have not been possible. Yet the need to ensure policymakers hear and understand the experiences of our service users has never been greater. And so our events have migrated to Zoom. Early on we were concerned that the digital format would fundamentally undermine the critical interpersonal relationships formed and fostered through events normally. To counter this, we have been focused on designing events that remain about engagement and conversation, not broadcast. For example, we had originally planned one large event to launch some new research we had done into criminal exploitation in modern slavery. We redesigned this event as a digital summit with three separate panel discussions with a variety of experts discussing key areas of the report. This format enabled genuine participation and lively Q&A segments throughout. Hosting the summit online also brought a wider mix of people together, without the challenges of travel to act as a barrier.

As social distancing restrictions ease, we hope to be able to return to face-to-face events where we can bring a diverse range of people together on key topics. However, I am sure that we will also continue to have a greater use of online events and build on the benefits of these which we might not have otherwise discovered.

11.7 Summary

In this chapter, we have seen that the rapid recent growth of the events industry in the private sector has been matched by that in the public and third sectors. The public sector carries out a range of roles in the events industry – from regulation, taxation and oversight through to event production and marketing. Increasingly, however, the public sector seeks to commission specialist event managers and event production companies to deliver events on its behalf. Meanwhile, the third sector is growing in importance, both socially and economically, as the relationships between the state, the private sector and citizens develop in advanced economies. Organisations such as social enterprises and charities are active in the events industry, producing events and providing services for them. Other forms of not-for-profit event have their own specific characteristics and do not fit into the neat categories of private, public and third sectors. In this chapter, we have looked briefly at political, state and faith events as examples of these.

Future event managers will need to develop relationships not just with other private sector organisations but with public bodies and those in the third sector. Increasing numbers of events management students will work in these sectors after graduation. In this area, both nationally and internationally, there are complex relationships of regulation, partnership and funding that impact on successful events management. Keeping abreast of local developments and national trends will therefore be a key skill for future event managers in all kinds of organisation.

Further reading

Raj, R. and Morpeth, D. (2015) *Religious Tourism and Pilgrimage Management* (2nd edn), Oxford: CABI. Covers an important area for events management in terms of visitor numbers and global reach that is currently under-researched in the events management literature.

Ridleyduff, R. (2015) *Understanding Social Enterprise: Theory and Practice*, London: Sage. This is a very useful introductory text for anyone seeking to understand or work within the growing field of social enterprise.

Shone, A. and Parry, B. (2014) The Events Business: Supply and Suppliers. In *Successful Event Management: A Practical Handbook* (4th edn): 116–149, Andover: Cengage Learning. Provides a useful analysis of the different sectors involved in delivering events and the relationships between them.

Video links

Cancer Research Race for Life TV Advert: www.youtube.com/watch?v=Nyiemg9vuqA

Journey through the Premium Levels at Bridgestone Arena: www.youtube.com/watch?v=YPBGbdWKXtE

United Nations Food Systems Summit: www.youtube.com/watch?v=NAPd8-FGXIs

Weblinks

Arts Council Malta: Event Support Scheme: www.artscouncilmalta.org/pages/funds-opportunities/restart-schemes-2021/event-support-scheme/

Organizing a Voluntary Event: A 'Can Do' Guide: www.gov.uk/government/publications/can-do-guide-for-organisers-of-voluntary-events/the-can-do-guide-to-organising-and-running-voluntary-and-community-events

Shanghai Convention Bureau: www.meet-in-shanghai.net

References

Allen, J., O'Toole, W., Harris, R. and McDonnell, I. (2010) *Festival and Special Event Management* (4th edn), Oxford: John Wiley and Sons.

Barker, M., Page, S.-J. and Meyer, D. (2001) Evaluating the Impacts of the 2000 America's Cup on Auckland, New Zealand, *Event Management*, 7: 79–92.

BBC (2018) Policing Champions League Final in Cardiff Cost £5.7m. Available at: www.bbc.co.uk/news/uk-wales-south-east-wales-43410104 [Accessed 31 July 2022].

Bowdin, G., Allen, J., O'Toole, W., Harris, R. and McDonnell, I. (2011) *Events Management* (4th edn), Oxford: Butterworth-Heinemann.

Bridgestone Arena (2020) Home Page. Available at: http://www.bridgestonearena.com/ [Accessed 18 February 2020].

Business Times (2018) Turning Any Event into a Force for Good. Available at: www.businesstimes.com.sg/life-culture/turning-any-event-into-a-force-for-good [Accessed 31 July 2022].

Catapult (2022) About. Available from: www.thisiscatapult.com/about/ [Accessed 8 August 2022].

Cho, B. S., Lee, J., Lee, W. and Min, H. (2019) Changing Management Strategies of a Government-Hosted Festival: The Case of Hi Seoul Festival, South Korea, *International Journal of Event and Festival Management*, 10 (2): 174–188.

Department of Communications and the Arts (2016) Major Festivals Initiative. Available at: https://australiacouncil.gov.au/investment-and-development/multi-year-investment/major-festivals-initiative/ [Accessed 16 April 2016].

Getz, D. (2019) Event Evaluation and Impact Assessment: Five Challenges. In J. Armbrecht, E. Lundberg and T. Andersson (eds) *A Research Agenda for Event Management*: 48–65, Cheltenham: Edward Elgar Publishing.

Getz, D. and Page, S. (2019) *Event Studies: Theory, Research and Policy for Planned Events* (4th edn), Abingdon: Routledge.

Good Mood Food (2011) Good Mood Food. Available at: http://www.goodmoodfood.org/ [Accessed 18 February 2011].

ICE Krakow (2020) About ICE Krakow. Available at: http://icekrakow.pl/en/about-ice-krakow [Accessed 31 July 2022].

Impact Hub Johannesburg (2016) About. Available at: https://theimpacthub.co.za/. [Accessed 16 April 2016].

KBF (2020) History. Available at: http://icekrakow.pl/en/about-ice-krakow [Accessed 31 July 2022].

Leeds Climate Commission (2020) Leeds Climate Change Citizen's Jury. Available at: www.leedsclimate.org.uk/leeds-climate-change-citizens-jury [Accessed 31 July 2022].

LSE (2020) First Climate Case Reaches Brazil's Supreme Court. Available at: www.lse.ac.uk/granthaminstitute/news/first-climate-case-reaches-brazils-supreme-court/ [Accessed 31 July 2022].

Ludvigsen, J. A. L. and Hayton, J. W. (2020) Toward COVID-19 Secure Events: Considerations for Organizing the Safe Resumption of Major Sporting Events, *Managing Sport and Leisure*, 27 (1–2): 135–145.

Metro Government of Nashville (2020) Bridgestone Arena. Available at: www.nashville.gov/Sports-Authority/Bridgestone-Arena.aspx [Accessed 31 July 2022].

MIA (2021) UK Agency and Planner Research, March 2021. Available at: www.mia-uk.org/COVID-19-Recent-Industry-Findings [Accessed 10 March 2021].

Nolan, E. (2020) Modifying the Conceptual Model of Site Selection in the Organisation of Association Conferences, *Journal of Convention & Event Tourism*, 21 (5): 438–457.

Nordvall, A. and Brown, S. (2020) Evaluating Publicly Supported Periodic Events: The Design of Credible, Usable and Effective Evaluation, *Journal of Policy Research in Tourism, Leisure and Events*, 12 (2): 152–171.

NYC Planning (2019) Press Release: City Planning Invites New Yorkers to Help Shape the City's Next Comprehensive Waterfront Plan, Starting with 'Waterfront Planning Camp' for All Ages on Governor's Island on August 17. Available at: www1.nyc.gov/site/planning/about/press-releases/pr-20190807.page [Accessed 31 July 2022].

O'Sullivan, D. (2020) Public Events, Personal Leisure? In S. Page and J. Connel (eds.) *The Routledge Handbook of Events* (2nd edn): 57–75, Abingdon: Routledge.

Ormerod, N. and Wood, E. H. (2020) Regional Event Tourism Funding Policies: A Strategic-Relational Critique of Current Practice, *Journal of Travel Research*, 60 (4): 860–877.

Pugh, C. and Wood, E. (2004) The Strategic Use of Events within Local Government: A Study of London Borough Councils, *Event Management*, 9: 61–71.

Raj, R., Walters, P. and Rashid, T. (2013) *Events Management: An Integrated and Practical Approach* (2nd edn), London: Sage.

Richards, G. (2017a) From Place Branding to Placemaking: The Role of Events. *International Journal of Event and Festival Management*, 8 (1): DOI:10.1108/IJEFM-09-2016-0063.

Richards, G. (2017b) Emerging Models of the Eventful City. *Event Management*, 21 (5), 533–543.

There has been little research into what motivates audiences, or delegates, to attend conferences, because, as Getz and Page (2016) suggest, it is widely assumed that people attend primarily to fulfil part of their business or job description. While this assumption is partially correct, the major motivation for attending conferences could be divided into 'content' (the information attendees are given) and 'networking' (the information and people they meet). The idea that networking is a key reason to attend a conference is supported by research by Hahm *et al.* (2016) and Wei and Miao (2017) which discovered that there is a significant link between the sense of belonging and feelings of community to both intention to revisit and positive conference experiences respectively.

Meetings are less formal gatherings but they are still an important component of the business events industry. They are usually held off-site, with a chairperson and a specific agenda, focused on a very specific issue. They involve attendees from various organisations, all of whom share similar business interests. Meetings tend to be smaller in scale than conferences, which gives each attendee a greater opportunity to contribute to the agenda, debate or discussion.

Study activity

For the past 30 years, the Confederation of British Industry (CBI) has hosted an annual conference that attracts around 1,200 attendees, including senior government ministers, shadow ministers, global and UK business leaders and key principals from public bodies. In 2020 it was a virtual event, but it is usually face to face.

The Enlit Asia event is an example of what Bauer *et al.* (2008) call a 'megabusiness event'. After co-locating POWERGEN Asia and Asian Utility Week in 2019, the organisers decided to create a unifying brand which brings the two (already huge!) events together. In 2019 when the events were co-located, they attracted more than 11,000 attendees and 350+ exhibitors at MITEC, Kuala Lumpur Malaysia, over the course of the three-day event.

Look at the websites of both of these conferences (www.cbi.org.uk/events/annual-conference-2020/ and www.enlit-asia.com/the-enlit-purpose) and identify who organises the event, and what the key aims and objectives might be. Identify five reasons why delegates attend these events. What lessons can you, as future event managers, learn from these high-profile and successful events?

12.4.3 Key issues

There are four key components in the organisation of successful conferences and meetings, as outlined in Figure 12.1.

In order to deliver a successful meeting or conference, the organiser must first have a clearly defined concept and a robust programme. A conference programme includes details of the keynote speaker(s), a list of contributors with brief annotations of their subject areas, information

Figure 12.1 Key components for conference and meeting events management

on breakout sessions and workshops, plans for networking opportunities and full conference timings, including food and beverage breaks. The importance of getting the content of the programme right cannot be overstated – it is this content that provides one of the two key motivations for the target market to attend.

Once the programme has been established, finding a venue that suits the event becomes a priority. The importance of this aspect of business event planning is explored in more detail later in this chapter.

Another consideration is the target market – clearly identifying who will attend and why they should want to is pivotal to the success of any conference or meeting. As conferences are fee-generating, they are often deemed successful only in terms of their return on investment (ROI) and the income that they generate from delegate fees.

Creating and implementing an effective marketing plan is crucial to any event's success (see Chapter 7 for more information). Securing sponsorship is another vital component of conference delivery, as revenue from sponsorship often funds the event and drives budgeting (see Chapters 6 and 7).

CASE STUDY 12.1

Cvent CONNECT, Las Vegas, USA

Event name: Cvent CONNECT
Event type: Conference
Venue: Caesars Forum, Las Vegas
Date: 1–4 August 2021
Attendance: Over 2,000 planners, hoteliers and industry experts
Website: www.cvent.com/en/cvent-connect

Cvent CONNECT is an annual conference where group business, corporations and associations come together to connect, learn and engage with like-minded professionals from the meetings and events industries. In 2020 the event was held virtually, and in 2021 it is a hybrid event, that blends in-person and virtual gatherings, bringing together thousands of people from around the globe.

The event features 200+ exhibitors at the tradeshow, 100+ educational break-out sessions running alongside the full conference agenda, an award ceremony (the Plannies) and opportunities to undertake hospitality and event professional training. There is also a programme of delegate networking events, including drinks receptions, dinners and celebratory nights out. The event typically starts on a Sunday with a full conference programme of educational sessions followed by a sponsored dinner and reception. There are then three full days of conference programming, including a range of plenary and breakout sessions. Each day has a breakfast, lunch and dinner for all delegates.

The event also normally features the Plannies awards and a celebratory night out. On the final day, there is a closing session and a number of breakout sessions, including classroom training and tech talks. The event ends at lunchtime with 'grab and go' box lunches.

The event features talks from 50+ globally recognised industry consultants, executives and influencers, which are designed for delegates to learn best practice from peers and gain actionable insights into improving current processes. In addition, the event features an industry pavilion, which allows delegates to walk through the entire life cycle of an event, learning how each piece of the platform helps you achieve your goals and create an ideal event experience. This includes hands-on training and question-and-answer sessions from the community of experienced customers and industry peers. The event also offers training and certification in event-related areas and offers excellent networking opportunities, as well as the chance to experience Las Vegas.

Source: Cvent (2021)

12.5 Incentive events and performance improvement

12.5.1 Definition

The term 'incentives' covers a wide range of events, including trips and travel, training, away-days and team building. The incentives branch of the events industry has long been seen as a particularly lucrative one (Bowdin *et al.* 2011), and whilst it became less popular in the early 2000s, incentive travel programmes are now firmly back on companies' radar as they gain a deeper appreciation of how effective they can be in motivation and rewarding staff (BVEP, 2020). The BVEP value incentive travel and performance improvement at £1.2 billion in direct spend and The Society for Incentive Travel Excellence (SITE) suggest that incentive travel is the fastest growing sector of the business events industry, with – in America – the highest capita spend and the widest supply chain (SITE 2021). They suggest that the incentive travel industry is estimated to be worth around $75 billion globally.

12.5.2 Characteristics

Incentive events are defined by Davidson (2019: 7) as 'A reward event intended to showcase persons who meet or exceed sales or production goals'. They are exceptional travel trips that employees receive from their employer as prizes for winning a competition related to their jobs. The purpose of such trips is to encourage staff to meet certain business objectives. However, a more comprehensive view of the sector shows that, while incentive trips are still the largest component of incentive events, the sector has grown to include a wider range of activities. A more relevant term, 'incentive travel', is becoming prevalent, as it relates to incentive trips *and* to destination management and exploration and familiarisation trips – journeys arranged by external agencies in order to allow stakeholders to experience specific destinations, activities or venues.

Other incentive events are event-based activities that focus on staff development. Training events, away-days and team-building activities all have motivational experiences for partici-pants as their primary focus in order to achieve specific organisational goals or to increase performance levels. This side of the industry is growing steadily, with a proliferation of such incentives as 'It's a Knockout' days – in which co-workers form teams and complete huge inflatable obstacle courses, often in fancy dress – or 'Olympiad' days – where col-leagues compete in their own mini-Olympics. More often, incentive trips that work towards building the motivation of attendees take the form of cooking days, treasure hunts and visits to zoos!

As the economy grows and contracts, the incentives market usually follows suit. In boom times, spending tends to increase, with trips organised to more distant and exotic locations; during recessions, cost-cutting often leads to shorter trips to cheaper destinations (Davidson 2010). In 2019, in the USA, before the pandemic hit, 44% of incentive travel buyers were reporting an increase in budgets and the average per-person spend was $4000 (Smart Meetings 2019 and IRF 2018). As the effects of the pandemic ease, it is hoped that the industry will enter another boom time, as companies realise the link between incentive travel programmes and increased corporate revenues (BVEP 2020). And of course, the Covid-19 pandemic has also created the desire for many organisations to place increased importance on well-being and the importance of connecting staff. Incentive travel programmes are potentially excellent solutions to these challenges as they can have an impact beyond encouraging employees to sell more – they can also bring about real change in terms of building communities within the workforce and creating long and lasting bonds between employees.

12.5.3 Key issues

Incentive events are widely recognised as useful management tools since they are effective means of recognising, motivating and rewarding employees (Davidson 2019). However, offering incentive events is not the only way to reward employees: cash bonuses, promotions, gifts and profit-related pay are all frequently used by the corporate sector. Given the number of alternatives, and the high cost in financial and human resource terms that incentive events represent for organisations, the question is: why do companies continue to rely on such events? The answer lies in the reward economy and the motivational needs of potential attendees. In order for an incentive event to succeed, the venue, location and event programme must all be attractive to the potential attendees; organisers must also strive to communicate the offering effectively – building up awareness and anticipation is key (Severt and Breiter 2010).

An important consideration for organisers of incentive events is the demographic make-up of attendees. While there may be some commonalities, these are not necessarily related to age, gender, education or cultural background – the only real commonality is the sharing of a job or working for the same organisation. This makes planning for an incentive event that will appeal to a target market of various demographics both complicated and delicate.

CWT Meetings & Events (2021) organised the annual incentive travel package for their client, a global leader in the capital goods sector. The trip is an incentive to reward the top-selling dealers of their equipment and vehicles. CWT Meetings & Events designed a week-long incentive programme in Thailand to reward 37 of the organisation's top selling delegates – the main objectives were to design an activity programme that was both exciting and memorable. The trip involved five-star accommodation, traditional cuisine and an activity every day, including visits to temples; elephant rides; swimming in waterfalls; kayaking; Thai massages; cooking classes and a spectacular gala dinner and beach party. For more information on what they did, and how they did it, see www.cwt-meetings-events.com/uk/en/insights/case-studies/incentive-trip-thailand/.

12.6 Networking events

12.6.1 Definition

Over the years, the focus of business events has shifted from a return on investment viewpoint to a concentration of outcomes. Business people have become more selective in the events they attend, and the motivation for attendance is no longer solely focused on the content of the event but also, and importantly, on the quality and relevance of the other attendees to the guests' corporate objectives. The importance of face-to-face meetings with colleagues, associates, consumers and/or potential clients has never been more strongly emphasised by event participants. HubSpot conducted a survey of 750 professionals and found that 41% of them wished they could attend events more frequently, demonstrating that networking is considered a crucial factor in professional success (Bizzabo 2021).

Many organisations see business networking as a low-cost marketing method to develop sales opportunities and contacts. Others see it as an environment in which they can share ideas and keep abreast of industry developments, or as an essential tool in career development that provides an opportunity to forge key business relationships through personal interaction. The events industry has responded to these developments by providing event spaces that facilitate opportunities to meet and greet interested and interesting parties in a networking-enabled environment.

All events can provide networking opportunities for attendees but here we focus specifically on the events that are held with networking as one of their primary purposes and functions. These networking events include small-scale lunches and dinners, drinks receptions, product launches, conventions, congresses, awards ceremonies and symposia. The main focus is on providing networking opportunities – for sponsors to meet potential new clients; for large brands to raise awareness among a particular audience; for companies to demonstrate their new products to potential purchasers; and for association members to share ideas and innovations as well as to keep abreast of industry developments.

12.6.2 Characteristics

There are a number of different types of networking events – this section explores association events, award ceremonies and B2B networking events.

Association events are organised by trade bodies and professional/industry associations to communicate with their members. They provide opportunities for associations to discuss key issues and to share relevant information with their respective audiences (Allen *et al.* 2011). Attendance is usually voluntary, so the member organisations market them through exciting destinations or locations, and with programming that has a broad cross appeal and is affordable for the association's members. The purpose of these events is often to educate or to inform, as well as to connect with other association members of businesses (Getz 2021).

Association events include conventions, congresses, symposia, summits and awards ceremonies. The first four of these are similar in form to conferences, but are usually larger in size and are often repeated annually. They can be held on a regional scale, such as the annual regional events run by the Motor Neurone Disease Association in the South, North and East regions of the UK; a national scale, such as the Anxiety and Depression Association of America Conference; or an international scale, such as the G8 and G20 summits, held in different places around the world each year, and attracting at least 700 high-profile guests (mostly politicians).

Other forms of association events are familiar to many of us – for example, award ceremonies such as the internationally renowned Oscars. A large and robust industry specialises in corporate award ceremonies; usually (though not always) these are run by or for professional and industry associations. Examples include the high profile MTV Video Music Awards, the Teen Choice Awards, the BRIT awards and the Golden Globes; as well as smaller scale events, aimed at specific industries or sections of the population, for example the Women of the Future Awards, Professional Beauty Awards, the Chemical Industry Association Awards and the Outdoor Industry Association Awards. In the events industry itself, there are also a wealth of awards from association bodies such as the EVCOM awards, the M&IT awards, the Eventex Awards and the BizBash event awards.

Study activity

Make a list of all the associations dedicated to the events industry in your country. What do they offer for their members? Do you think there would be benefits for being a member of any of these organisations?

Uniquely, these association events often have the same audience at each event. The priority is to ensure that audiences are kept abreast of developments in their professional fields and given ample time to network with colleagues and associates (Allen *et al.* 2011). For a full understanding of the history of associations, the range of activities they undertake, and their conferences, we recommend reading Davidson (2019).

The other side of the networking events industry is typified by events run *by* business *for* business (B2B). The primary goal of these events is to encourage business networking or the promotion and marketing of a specific product or brand. They tend to be less formal than other business events, and often concentrate on the social side of networking. Examples include intimate lunches, dinners, drinks receptions, private members club events and product launches. The Supper Club, founded in 2003 by the entrepreneur Duncan Cheatle, is attended by a group of UK entrepreneurs who share knowledge, contacts, best practice and experiences. Its primary function is to encourage peer-to-peer learning, and it actively excludes any organisation that may try to use the network for self-promotion. The Supper Club offers its members a range of events, from intimate roundtables to expert-led webinars, welcoming socials and social events – both digitally and in-person. They also allow members to crowdsource answers to the problems they have with a 'give and get' ethos. It hosts over 200 events every year and has thousands of members, all of whom have founded businesses and get together to share knowledge and inspiration from their peers (The Supper Club 2021).

12.6.3 Key issues

Networking event managers have to be forward-thinking, giving their participants new experiences and unique opportunities to meet colleagues and associates. The industry has recognised the need to drive networking forward as well as the reluctance of some participants to participate in traditional networking, which is often seen as a contrived and jaded concept. Successful organisers continue to devise new ways to ensure that target markets will want to attend their events and that participants will interact when they attend them. There is often a multitude of interests in one room, with guests from a variety of demographic backgrounds, though participants will usually share a common focus. This, coupled with the negative connotations of the word 'networking', has resulted in a need to try innovative ideas.

Bizzabo (2021) report on a number of new, innovative networking events that range from annual conferences for Social Media Marketing World, which involves a bingo networking icebreaker, and the Forbes Under 30 Summit, which includes a Day of Service within the weekend-long event, which focuses on networking and building partnerships among attendees. Bizzabo also tell us about an event run by CoinDesk called Consensus. This is what they say:

> With a $30,000 prize on the line and the chance to convene with top blockchain developers, Building Blocks Hackathon at CoinDesk's Consensus is more than just a competition for engineers. CoinDesk cements Consensus as a networking event by creating an online space for attendees to connect pre, during and post event by encouraging participants to form teams through an **event networking app**.
>
> Giving attendees an opportunity to coordinate with one another prior to the event resulted in a more rewarding networking experience overall. Perhaps just as importantly, the event itself – a prize competition – motivated attendees to get to know one another prior to the event. As a result, participants felt like it was in their best interests to communicate with others beforehand. **Key Takeaway**: Creating an online community can

facilitate a better networking experience during the event. If you can, consider adding prizes that will incentivize team-building and communication between attendees.

(Bizzabo 2021)

In recent years and advancing at warp speed during the Covid-19 pandemic, organisations have turned to technology to support and deliver their networking events. The use of Wi-Fi at all venues of course helps, as will the full arrival of 5G – as parts of the world move towards high-speed connectivity, networking at events will become easier and easier. There are also now a number of tools that have been developed specifically to support networking at events – Eventbrite (2018) reports on the use of apps such as Double Dutch, which helps attendees to identify potentially useful connections by allowing them to select networking tags that represent their interest and areas of expertise, and Grip, which is an AI-powered event networking tool that encourages and supports quality interactions through the use of language processing, advanced algorithms and deep neural networks that learn about the professional goals and interests of visitors, exhibitors and sponsors.

While there has been a strong move towards incorporating technological innovation into networking events, the industry generally remains convinced that interpersonal relationships and face-to-face opportunities are still the best networking tools. Networking events therefore still tend to follow the formula of: a corporate objective (usually a brand, product or key issue that needs promoting or discussing); the participant's objective (to meet colleagues or associates, increase business interaction or gain awareness of new developments in their field of interest); and a networking opportunity (an event that allows all parties to interact face-to-face). These three segments can be viewed (as in Figure 12.2) as the base and centre of a pyramid, building towards the key motivation behind the event (the outcome).

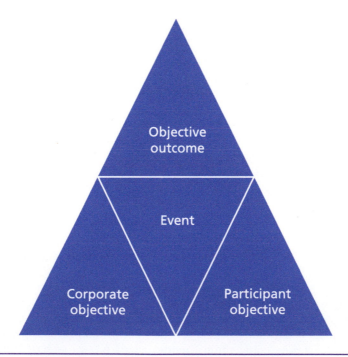

Figure 12.2 Achieving outcomes at networking events

12.7 Corporate hospitality

12.7.1 Definition

Corporate hospitality events – also known as corporate entertainment or B2B hospitality (Davidson 2019) – have as their focus the entertainment of key clients in order to improve or cement business relationships. These events, therefore, involve an element of networking. However, they should not be confused with networking events – there is a clear difference between the two. A corporate hospitality event is a hosted event that forms part of another public live event; in essence, it is an event within an event. Key clients are invited, at no charge, to one event by a particular 'host' organisation. When they arrive at that event, the host organisation will have a hospitality suite for the private use of these invited guests. This suite will offer a premium view of the event itself, plus complimentary food and drinks. As Davidson (2019: 267–268) suggests:

> The general aim of such invitations is to help the host companies to deepen their relationships with existing customers or to start to bond with potential new customers. When companies and the guests interact in a social setting. . . they can relate to each other much more readily as human beings, and discuss business in a low-threat environment.

12.7.2 Characteristics

In the past, corporate hospitality events happened mostly at sporting events, such as the Olympics, the French Open Tennis Championships and the Super Bowl. However, in recent years, there has been a move towards alternative corporate hospitality events, with an increasing number of cultural events providing opportunities to host key clients. Examples of these are boxes at large arenas to watch music concerts, premium seats at the theatre and movie premieres, tickets for opening days of flower shows and VIP areas at festivals. Corporate hospitality events are, by their very nature, one-offs, although corporate clients may well rent the same box at a sporting ground or return to the same festival with different clients every year. They usually last one day or less, and the hosting organisation covers all costs.

A typical corporate hospitality event involves a welcome drink, premium views of the event, usually from a box, complimentary drinks throughout the event and food – sometimes a seated meal, sometimes canapés. There is often a gift for guests to take away at the end of the event.

The corporate hospitality organiser Keith Prowse has various video clips of such events on its website, www.keithprowse.co.uk.

> **Image 12.2** Tom Hiddleston, Sophie Hunter, Benedict Cumberbatch and Katherine Jenkins attend Men's Finals Day of the Wimbledon Tennis Championships at the All England Lawn Tennis and Croquet Club on 14 July 2019

12.7.3 Key issues

The corporate hospitality events industry places great importance on the guest experience. The success of a corporate hospitality event is largely dependent on the success of the hosting at the event itself, aided by a smooth invitation and acceptance process. The hosting at the event therefore has to be carefully planned and managed, with all of the guests' needs catered for by the event organiser so that the host can concentrate on cementing business relationships and potentially creating new opportunities. As Davidson (2019: 266) states:

> most companies, recognising that their dependence on short-term transactional marketing alone may not be enough to enable them to compete successfully in the marketplace, have also adopted a relationship marketing approach, centred on engaging with their customers in order to retain them and develop mutually satisfying, long term, ongoing relationships with them.

The role of brand association is also important: the choice of event is informed by the impression that it will make on the host organisation's key clients. A brand such as Cartier hosts its key clients at various international polo events because it wishes to be associated with high-end experiences. (The relationship between sponsorship of events, corporate hospitality hosting and brand association is discussed in detail in Chapter 7.)

The Bureau of Investigative Journalism conducted an investigation into the effectiveness of corporate hospitality in 2010, and whilst it is now over ten years old, it is still an interesting investigation to read today. It revealed that the UK's most senior civil servants were wined and dined by major corporations and interest groups on more than 3,100 occasions over a period of three years. The accountants PricewaterhouseCoopers and KPMG were the most active hospitality providers, although Fujitsu, BT, Deloitte and arms giant BAE were significant players, too. In an article about the investigation, Curtis and Evans (2010) noted that David Hartnett – the Permanent Secretary for Tax at HM Revenue & Customs (HMRC) – accepted invitations to eat and drink 107 times over the three-year period:

> Hartnett sat down with representatives of the 'big four' accountancy firms 27 times . . . Corporate hospitality is part of Hartnett's approach to raising tax from big firms. Rather than confronting them, he has relied on persuading them to pay their share of tax.

HMRC defended Hartnett's activities by saying that he engaged with

> people from all sectors of the economy in meetings which take place inside and outside office hours. The relationships that Dave has forged have enabled HMRC to transform its relationships with business and other taxpayers. This has made a significant contribution to the increased tax yield HMRC has achieved in the period.
>
> (Curtis and Evans 2010)

12.8 Exhibitions and trade shows

12.8.1 Definition

At the most basic level, exhibitions and trade shows involve a large number of manufacturers and retailers displaying a selection of their products to potential buyers and/or the general public. Exhibitions can therefore be for a consumer target market or for business purposes (the latter events are also known as trade shows). They take place in large, purpose-built venues – such as the ExCel Centre in London, the Vietnamese National Convention Centre or the San Diego Convention Center – are usually held on an annual basis and often attract an international audience.

It is important to note that the typologies 'fair', 'convention' and 'exposition' are sometimes used to describe exhibitions and trade shows (see, for example, Bowdin *et al.* 2011 and Allen *et al.* 2011). Conventions tend to be organised by associations or professional bodies for their members, and the term 'exposition' (expo) tends to be applied to larger-scale exhibitions. The primary difference between a fair and an exhibition is that fairs place more emphasis on entertainment by including live demonstrations related to the industry as well as live music, celebrity guest appearances and so on. Exhibitions, on the other hand, are likely to host accompanying conferences or seminars, which enable visitors to meet and speak to individuals from the companies and organisations in the relevant industry. This obviously increases opportunities for networking and allows influential figures from the industry to present their latest innovations and policies on a more intimate scale than at the exhibition itself.

In recent years, there has been increasing use of the term 'confex' to describe a conference and an exhibition taking place simultaneously at the same venue, with the same overall purpose and content. These events might prioritise the conference, with a small accompanying exhibition; or they might lead with the exhibition and run a small-scale conference alongside. International Confex is a leading UK event that delivers a comprehensive showcase of UK venues and event services and promotes the best of the international events industry during an exhibition that is attended by over 1,000 exhibitors. The 10,000 visitors to the exhibition are invited to attend the accompanying conference and delegates can also participate in an association events forum and the AEO sales conference. This features keynote addresses from industry specialists and seminar sessions that explore key areas of industry debate, marketing and business skills (International Confex 2021).

12.8.2 Characteristics

The key characteristic of any exhibition or trade show is that it is a marketing or communication tool. The benefits of these events are that they allow direct customer contact, provide a platform for products and services and create marketing opportunities by allowing the media to focus on companies or products (UFI 2021).

Exhibitions and trade shows can be divided into two categories: those that communicate primarily with a consumer target market (the general public); and those that focus on a specific business or trade. It is useful to explore these two areas separately, as the management of each kind of event requires significantly different approaches.

Consumer exhibitions and shows are open to the general public. They charge an entrance fee and are centred on such themes as cars, electronics, gardening, travel and other hobbies (Getz and Page 2016). They sometimes move around the country, but, more often than not, they return to the same venue each year. Competition in this sector is fierce, and there are usually a number of exhibitions vying for the same target market.

Consumer-led exhibitions are seen as beneficial for all stakeholders as 'manufacturers test new products at shows, retailers try to sell and the consumer is searching for both ideas and entertainment' (Getz and Page 2016: 138). Examples of consumer exhibitions are The Michigan International Women's Show – a consumer goods fair held annually in the USA; Grand Designs Live – a homebuilding exhibition for the general public, held annually in the UK; and the Good Food and Wine show, held annually in Australia. These events regularly attract hundreds of thousands of visitors every year, and each will have hundreds of specialised exhibitors.

As Getz and Page (2016) suggest, trade exhibitions and shows are usually invitation only and are staged for a specific business purpose or related to an association membership. Their primary function is, therefore, to promote or sell a product from a particular area of business. They allow visitors to evaluate products side-by-side, keep abreast of industry developments and meet suppliers directly.

The Consumer Electronics Show (CES) is the largest trade show in America, hosting 2,500 exhibitors every year. It is not open to the general public, and visitors must work in the consumer electronics industry to attend. The event attracts 126,000 of these industry professionals annually. In addition to being invited to the exhibition, they can attend a conference that runs alongside it and enjoy numerous entertainment options, such as competitions, concerts and celebrity guests (CES 2021).

A growing number of exhibitions and trade shows are now targeting a cross-sector market. Their main target market may be the professionals from a specific industry, but they realise that their content will be of interest to the general public as well. In order to maximise their potential audience (and therefore their profit), they stage events that will appeal to both.

An example of this type of exhibition is Tattoo Jam, a three-day tattoo convention, which was held at Doncaster Racecourse, UK. It featured 300 working artists and traders in the Lazarus Exhibition Hall and had separate function rooms for workshops, seminars and live entertainment. Two days of the exhibition were open to the general public, while the third was reserved for registered tattooists, piercers, guests and associated traders. Tattoo Jam was run by the publishers of *Skin Deep* and other magazines and the organisers of other tattooing events, Tattoo Freeze and the Great British Tattoo Show (Tattoo Jam 2016).

12.8.3 Key issues

Staging an exhibition is a very complex events management skill. A daunting array of operational planning is required when dealing with such a large-scale event. In fact, lead times, from the original concept development through to delivery of the event, can be as long as two years. The exhibition event manager can be dealing with anything from 100 to 3,000 separate exhibitors as well as sponsors, caterers, venue, client, audiovisual providers and so on. The build-up and breakdown of an exhibition are particularly complex and need to be managed with tight control. At the same time, exhibition event managers must comply with a number of regulations, laws, permits and licences, including various Health and Safety Acts (1974, 1981, 1999), Electricity at Work Act 1998, Building Standards and Regulations, Lifting Operations and Lifting Regulations and so on (see AEV 2020 (www.aev.org.uk) or *The Purple Guide* (www.thepurpleguide.com) for more details).

CASE STUDY 12.2

WTM Africa

Event type: Exhibition
Venue: Cape Town, South Africa
Date: Annually (around April usually)
Sponsors: Gauteng, in partnership with SAACI, the South African Association for the Conference Industry
Website: www.wtm.com/africa

The World Travel Market (WTM) events consist of six annual business-to-business events across four continents. The focus of the exhibitions is for travel industry professionals to connect, learn and do business. The events vary in size but all aim to bring global travel professionals in order for them to connect together and to build a global community.

WTM Africa was established in 2014, as part of Africa Travel Week. It is a three-day event, held in Cape Town's International Convention Center (CTICC), and it is the only inbound and outbound business-to-business travel show on the African continent. Over 6,000 travel industry professionals attend each year in order to engage with the exhibition (the show floor) which now includes a travel technology exhibition. There is also a host of seminars and workshops, an award ceremony and a mix of hosted buyers, buyers' club members and media representatives offering pre-scheduled appointments, on-site networking and evening functions. The event is part of a well-established and well-known brand, and is therefore very similar to other WTM events, such as WTM London.

(WTM 2021)

12.9 Experiential business events

As mentioned in previous chapters, businesses have been focusing on experiential marketing and the 'experience economy' for quite some time (Pine and Gilmore 1999). Companies seek to influence their potential consumers through the provision of memorable and enjoyable experiences, leading to a growth in a newer form of business event that can often appear to be cultural or non-corporate in nature, but which actually promotes specific products and services. 'Smirnoff Experience' is a set of music events and music releases and other cultural events that were created to promote the traditional Smirnoff Vodka brand in new markets and to a new generation of consumers. In Bangalore, India, a Smirnoff Experience event was held to market the drink in a region where spirit brands are prohibited from direct marketing. EDM artists, including Nero and Rusko, performed to audiences of more than 5,000 people in a convention centre in an event that also featured the world's first ever projection-mapped stage. The event was successful in generating more than 2 million social media impressions for the brand and 50,000 new Facebook fans, as well as extensive mainstream media coverage (Vice 2014). A variety of Smirnoff Experiences ran all around the world using a variety of agencies to support them, all aimed at creating a unique brand experience of the vodka. See the agency Brand42 for some of their highlights (https://brand42.co.uk/article/smirnoff-experience).

Traditional corporate venues, such as shopping centres and megastores, are also now animated through the staging of pop-up events in order to enhance the retail experience, promote products or attract new markets. For example, Disney used a series of pop-up events in shopping centres in the UK to promote their film *Home*. The events were held at 15 shopping centres and included 53 days of activities that were enjoyed by 53,000 children. The events included themed kids-club activities, character appearances and branded fixtures and fittings (Intu 2016). At the extreme end of this is the Dubai Shopping Festival which launched in 1996 and was initially to promote the economic development of the Gulf state, but eventually became a tourist attraction. It is organised by the Dubai Department of Tourism and, during the month-long event, thousands of shops across the city centre and at least six shopping malls offer discounts and raffle prizes, and events such as family activities, live shows and firework displays take place across Dubai. It has become a major feature of the global corporate events calendar, attracting more than 5 million visitors every year (Visit Dubai 2021).

This combining of events with shopping centres is a growth area in business events and has started to receive academic attention. Strafford *et al.* (2018) published their research on The Gruffalo Experience – a three-week pop-up experiential children's event which was held in destination shopping centres around the UK in 2015 and 2016. Their findings demonstrated that events held within destination shopping centres have the potential for both short-term return – in terms of increased footfall and the interlinking of event attendance and shopping – but also longer-term payback due to increased revisitation intentions expressed by the event customers.

12.10 Key logistical issues for business events

12.10.1 When do business events take place?

Business events have peak and off-peak seasons. Traditionally, few business events took place in December, July or August, as organisations' employees were often on long Christmas or summer holidays. However, as consumption and demand have grown over the past five years, and as the recession has resulted in a drive towards businesses working harder to attract and retain clients, the peaks and troughs have flattened out, with the peak season now stretching

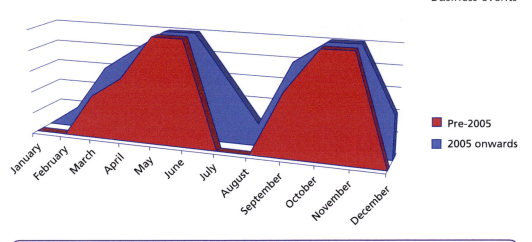

Pre-2005
2005 onwards

Figure 12.3 Peaks and troughs of an event season

from the very start of February right into July and commencing again in the first week of September. Figure 12.3 illustrates the changes that have occurred in the peaks and troughs of a typical event season.

The day of the week on which a business event takes place is a key decision for the event manager. Choosing the wrong day impacts on the number of attendees registering and severely jeopardises the success of the event. With the notable exception of corporate hospitality, business events with businesses as their target market (B2B) tend to take place during the working week. Mondays and Fridays are less popular, as business guests are often away from the office (on long weekends) or are unwilling to attend an event that has elements of socialising at the start and end of the week. The majority of B2B events therefore take place on Tuesday, Wednesday or Thursday. They are often run during business hours: attendees tend to view them as work, so they are usually unwilling to give up their free time to attend.

The notable exception to these unwritten rules of timings are corporate hospitality events, which take place throughout the year, on any day of the week, including weekends, and usually outside office hours. Attendees tend to view these events as entertainment and enjoyable, so they are willing to give up their free time to attend. Events run for members of associations or for consumers are also less stringent about avoiding Mondays and Fridays and often take place over weekends – the perception being that guests are interested enough in the product or in the activities of their association that they will happily invest their spare time in attending an event.

It is essential that event managers check calendars for the relevant industry. For instance, there would be little point running an event aimed at university academics in August, when they take time away from the office to write and prepare for the following year. Similarly, if possible, business events should not be scheduled to clash with major sporting events. Sometimes, however, this is unavoidable. One of the authors once held an event on FA Cup Final day. Three-quarters of the invited audience stated they would not attend if they could not watch the match, so screens were erected around the venue, and the entire programme was rearranged to ensure that guests could see the whole game, if they so desired.

Event managers should also keep track of national holidays. Bank holidays, school holidays, religious festivals and related holidays should all be avoided, unless the event has a specific and related theme.

The key is to choose a date that maximises the potential target market – event managers should identify the best date with the least number of obstacles for their invited guests.

12.10.2 Where do business events take place?

In this section we concentrate on face-to-face business events – please see section 12.13 for discussions on virtual and hybrid events.

As we have seen earlier in this chapter, business events come in many shapes and sizes. They can be local, national or international, and while some of them (conferences, meetings, conventions, exhibitions and trade shows) take place in purpose-built conference and exhibition centres, many others (especially networking and incentive events) might be held in high-end restaurants, museums, art galleries, golf clubs, vineyards or hotels. There is an ever-increasing number of venue finders – organisations whose sole aim is to locate a venue that perfectly complements the event's content and objectives.

Of course, the venue must fit the general event requirements of size, capacity, location and so on (all of which are explored in detail in Chapter 4). However, beyond these logistical requirements, the business event manager will choose the venue on the basis of their perception of stakeholders and target market. The image that the venue projects and the message that it sends to the target market are key considerations in business events, where image is a large part of the whole event concept. A venue such as the Ritz Hotel in London gives an event an air of formality, wealth and top-class service with first-class food, whereas the Moulin Rouge in Paris is more risqué, with an image of informality, entertainment and fun. These images do not just reflect on the event itself, but send deeper messages about the organisers, their products and their work philosophies.

Moreover, the choice of venue often relates to the type of event that is being staged. Business events sometimes rotate around regions (or even countries), so the choice may be limited to a certain location. Similarly, they are often staged alongside other, more established events. For example, the number of business events will mushroom whenever a mega-event is in town, as skilful event managers attempt to exploit the sudden proximity of their target markets by inviting them to smaller-scale events. For instance, there is always a city- or nationwide peak in business events just before, during and immediately after the FIFA World Cup or the Olympics.

For these reasons, it is unwise to stick to a standardised, inflexible checklist of venue criteria. Each venue choice is so specific to the event that a new checklist should be devised every time a venue search is launched. Choosing the correct venue is the most important decision a business event manager can make.

Study activity

A key client has commissioned you to produce a business event. The client runs a high-level accountancy firm specifically for entrepreneurs turning over at least £1 million a year. The entrepreneurs all currently run their own businesses in a diverse range of industries. The brief is given below:

- Event: evening networking drinks reception.
- Attendees: 50 of our most important customers. They are all entrepreneurs and each of their companies generates over £1 million a year. They are mostly men in their 40s and 50s.

- Location: The capital city of your own country.
- Date: A Tuesday, Wednesday or Thursday in May.
- Budget: £100 per head.
- Additional notes:

  o We would like a unique venue, preferably one that our customers will not have visited before.
  o As our customers are high earners, the venue should be high-end and glamorous.
  o We will require canapés and cocktails on arrival, plus drinks throughout the evening.
  o There should be room for 25 staff members, in addition to the invited guests.
  o We will need to be able to make speeches.

Visit www.uniquevenuesoflondon.co.uk or www.venuefinder.com and identify the best venue for the event. In a small group, prepare a five-minute pitch for your venue proposal, clearly showing how your choice will add value to the event.

12.11 The business event customer

The term 'customer' can be confusing when applied to events. For business events, the customer can be either internal or external. Internal customers are people who work for the organisation arranging the event: for example, a meeting for a board of directors or a training day for a team from the shop floor. External customers come from outside the organisation. They are people with whom the organisation already does business, or with whom it would like to do business, or with whom it wishes to communicate in order to satisfy corporate objectives. This distinction between internal and external customers is important for the event manager, as they must identify the target market clearly in order to deliver an event successfully.

Uniquely in business events, the customer is not only the customer of the event (the delegate in a conference or the visitor to the trade show) but the customer of the corporation organising or hosting the event. In this sense, business events have a dual purpose: they must satisfy the wants, needs and demands of the *event* customer, but their primary purpose is to satisfy the wants, needs and demands of the *corporate* customer.

Business events allow organisations to maintain and develop business relationships, close deals and make sales, meet with competitors' clients and work towards the overall corporate objective. Business event managers therefore need to develop an understanding of the customer's desires in order to ensure that the event meets their expectations and perceptions from both event *and* corporate perspectives (see Figure 12.4).

These events focus on the recruitment and retention of corporate customers. Business events are designed to build, increase and protect corporate loyalty. This is a driving force in business events, which in turn form part of a wider continuum of business communication and marketing. The need to impress, entertain and get to know customers in order to build loyalty explains why business events place considerable emphasis on providing networking opportunities.

Internal customers
- Message communication
- Relationship development
- Business opportunities
- Financial sustainability

External customers
- Positive experience
- Timings and convenience
- Food and beverage satisfaction
- Networking opportunities

Customer satisfaction

Figure 12.4 Business event customer satisfaction model

The hosts of business events are responsible for ensuring that the networking is effective, but it is the event manager's responsibility to ensure that the logistical and operational aspects are right. Everything that happens at these events is a direct reflection on the host organisation. Any impressions that are made will ultimately inform the customer's business decision. Will they want to do business with an organisation that serves bad food or allows an event to run over the advertised finish time?

These impressions also relate to the corporation's brand, product or message. As Allen *et al.* (2011) suggest, events aimed at external customers measure their success through, among other things, a change in attitude or perception. This is echoed by a study conducted by Nguyen and Leblanc (2001: 227), in which the authors discovered that 'the degree of customer loyalty has a tendency to be higher when perceptions of both corporate reputation and corporate image are strongly favourable'.

Consideration should also be given to another form of business event customer – the sponsors who are often involved in such events. Satisfying these people, along with other external stakeholders, such as associations and media partners, can be as important as pleasing the event customers, as they often provide the revenue and/or the promotion for the event. (Sponsorship is considered in more detail in Chapter 7.)

While the global pandemic and subsequent economic downturn has resulted in a change in the business events sector – with lower budgets and less extravagance in evidence – the building of corporate loyalty through the perceptions that are created at events continues.

CASE STUDY 12.3

MIPIM Asia

Event category: Global Summit

Venue: Grand Hyatt Hotel, Hong Kong
Date: 29–30 November 2016
Attendees: 812 CEOs and top executives and 89 speakers and keynotes
Sponsors: A range of sponsorship opportunities, with one platinum sponsor, five gold sponsors and six silver sponsors
Website: www.mipim-asia.com

MIPIM Asia is a two-day global leaders' summit that explores Asia Pacific inbound and outbound investment flows, regional development opportunities and projects and retail real estate trends. It consists of the Asia Pacific Real Estate conference and tailor-made networking opportunities, including social events, topic-based luncheons, targeted breakfasts and the conference dinner and an awards ceremony.

Study activity

Comic-Con usually takes place in a large (460,000-square-foot) exhibition hall and features 5,445 exhibitors from comic-book and mainstream publishing, film studios, computer game companies and music companies. The first Comic-Con, in 1970, focused on comics and science-fiction novels and had a small, specialist audience. It is now the most visited exhibition-style event in the United States, reflecting the fact that comic-book characters have moved into the mainstream, with such films as the Batman and Superman franchises and the recent Marvel releases. The event combines a major exhibition with a range of conference sessions attended by movie stars, writers, film producers and artists. In addition, there are a number of interactive sessions where attendees can collect autographs, play games involving their favourite characters, attend workshops and buy products.

Explore the Comic-Con website at: www.comic-con.org

1 List the main features of the event. How would you categorise it: as a conference, an exhibition or a confex? Is it primarily B2C or B2B? Explain your answer.
2 What features of the event make use of experiential marketing techniques? How important are these to the success of Comic-Con?
3 Who do you think are Comic-Con's key market? Name some ways that the organisers appear to be marketing to people outside their expected demographic.

12.12 Business event evaluation

As with all event typologies, evaluating the success of a business event is essential. Without measures in place that reveal the return on investment (ROI) and the satisfaction levels of internal and external stakeholders (often known as return on objectives (ROO)), the value of the event will remain undetermined and no lessons can be learned or advantages exploited.

Event evaluation for business events takes two forms. First, the 'hard' factors should be assessed. This mainly involves looking at the budget and final costings to decide if the event has been a financial success. However, the second form of evaluation is perhaps more important for a business event. This involves evaluating the 'soft' factors, such as enhancing loyalty among customers, aligning individual goals with corporate goals, and strengthening relationships (Hall 2009).

Business event evaluation typically begins with some form of financial modelling to ensure the 'hard' factors are assessed effectively, while a survey or questionnaire might be handed out for completion by delegates either at the event or immediately after it. Thereafter, focus groups might be held to evaluate success; reports might be carried out that can quantify increased business as a direct result of the event; 'wash-up' meetings with key stakeholders, such as sponsors, might be held; and in-depth monitoring of the level of PR or marketing for a set time after the event might be employed.

Some, or all, of these methods are used to create a final report that reflects the success (or failure) of the entire event in terms of how well it met the client's objectives and investment goals, and its legacy.

12.13 Future trends in business events

Future trends are difficult to predict for such a fast-paced industry, particularly given the damage caused by the coronavirus pandemic. As the 2021 C&IT state of the industry corporate report confirmed, the number of B2B events organised by corporates fell by 82%, from an average of 74 events in 2019 to just 13 in 2020. That said, corporate event planners spent much of 2020 and 2021 pivoting to digital meetings and events – normally fairly uncharted waters for them. So the pandemic acted as a catalyst for the growing importance of digital and hybrid events (C&IT 2021).

> **The meetings show – an example of an event pivoting to navigate through the pandemic.**
>
> A large exhibition and conference event that runs annually in the UK, and brings together the events, meetings and incentive industry to learn, network and source suppliers. In 2019, they had over 12,000 pre-scheduled meetings take place on the show floor and 5000 meeting and event professionals attended. In 2020, during the pandemic, the meetings show ran as a virtual event and in 2021 the event ran as a hybrid event, which took place at ExCel London and virtually. Details can be found here: www.themeetingsshow.com/welcome.

Taking events solely online (virtual or digital events) was something that was talked about often in the industry, but rarely done until the pandemic struck and these events were the only ones left available to corporate event planners. In the state of the industry report, just under 94% of companies who took part had run either virtual or hybrid events. Hybrid events – where events are run with a mixture of face-to-face and online access – seem set to remain for the future, as attendees continue to face barriers to attending face to face and organisers realise that it opens up new marketplaces to them, given people from around the globe can attend without attending in person.

As Bowdin *et al.* (2011) note, technological innovation affects many aspects of events management. However, some recent technological developments, especially in the fields of emerging technologies, such as drones, artificial intelligence and facial recognition, are likely to have a significant impact on the design, marketing and delivery of business events. As the use of personal technology continues to increase and more and more people work from home, organisers now have to think creatively and offer something more than the traditional conference formula.

In addition to the increased opportunities offered by technology, external factors, such as environmental concerns (Getz 2005), and major international incidents, such as the terrorist attacks in Brussels and Paris and various conflicts and wars, have changed how, why and under what circumstances people are prepared to travel (Allen 2008). However, ultimately the business events industry centres on face-to-face interaction, the sharing of ideas, and networking with like-minded individuals. Organisers have to work hard to ensure that the programming of their conference or meeting offers something that cannot be captured through technology alone. The programme has to convince the target market that they have to *be* there, or else they will miss out (Haug 2010).

UFI, the Global Association of the Exhibition Industry, published its 26th Barometer Survey in January 2021 (UFI 2021). This report was clearly largely concerned with the recovery of the exhibition industry which has been so badly hit by the global pandemic. Whilst the report gave some stark figures in terms of the severe impact of the Covid-19 pandemic on the global exhibition industry, it also showed some positive signs of an expected rebound of activity in 2021.

The 2021 report concludes that:

Overall:

- 44% of companies benefitted from some level of public financial support, and for a majority of them it related to less than 10% of their 2019 overall costs.
- 54% of companies had to reduce their workforce, half of them by more than 25%.
- 10% of companies state they will have to close down if there is no business for the next 6 months.

As expected, 'Impact of Covid-19 pandemic on the business' is considered as the most important business issue (29% of combined answers, a 2% increase compared to 6 months ago). 'Impact of digitalisation' (11% of answers) and 'Competition with other media' (7%) are also increasing (by respectively +1% and +2%), while 'State of the economy in home market' (19%) and 'Global economic developments' (16%) decrease but remain among the top 3 concerns.

In terms of the evolution of the format of exhibitions in the coming years, global results indicate that:

- 64% – compared to 57% 6 months ago – are confident that 'Covid-19 confirms the value of face- to-face events' anticipating that the sector will bounce back quickly (26% 'Yes, for sure' and 38% 'Most probably'), but 32% are 'Not sure' (31% 6 months ago).

- 63% – compared to 57% 6 months ago – believe that there will be 'Less international 'physical' exhibitions, and overall, less participants' (10% 'Yes, for sure' and 53% 'Most probably'), and 34% are 'Not sure'.
- 80% of companies – close to the 82% from 6 months ago – consider that there is 'A push towards hybrid events, more digital elements at events' (32% 'Yes, for sure' and 48% 'Most probably').
- A minority of 14% – close to the 17% from 6 months ago – agrees with 'Virtual events replacing physical events' (3% 'Yes, for sure' and 11% 'Most probably'), and 44% are 'Not sure'.

(UFI 2021: 129)

Industry voice

Thiago Ferreira, MICE Events Manager, Co-Founder of Talas Travel and TEMMS Consulting

As an events manager from Brazil who has been living and working in Serbia for over a half decade, I have often been faced with challenges. Before becoming one of the founders of two companies who have successfully developed the MICE industry in Serbia and the Balkans, I was born and raised in Rio de Janeiro, Brazil. When I left my hometown in the year of 2012, optimism ruled the country as it was getting ready to host two of the biggest events in the world – the 2014 FIFA World Cup and the 2016 Olympic Games. What would make a sane tourism and events manager leave Brazil and all its momentum to go to Serbia – a country of which many people are not even aware? Some people would call it a reckless move, but ever since I visited Serbia for the first time, I saw that there was a huge opportunity to develop its MICE industries.

Serbia is a landlocked country that suffered a lot in the 90s during the break-up of the former Yugoslavia. Nowadays, even though most of the visible consequences of the war are a thing of the past and the numbers of foreign visitors in the region has been growing every year, a significant number of people around the world still have prejudices about the country. In a scenario like this, those who are willing to work in the MICE industry need to be able to over-look the problems of the past and find ways to get over the poor image of the destination in order to attract delegates to their events or corporate clients to organise their events there.

One of the best things about the MICE industry is its dynamism and constant evolution. The change in the demands and expectations of event planners and delegates worldwide turned out to be useful for Belgrade and other off-the-beaten-path event destinations in the Balkans. As more and more people travel to attend corporate meetings, trade shows, conferences and other events worldwide, it is harder to organise an event that will impress them. Increasingly, the authenticity and uniqueness of a destination plays an important role in the process of choosing a destination for an event that will give delegates the 'Wow effect'. One of the best features of Belgrade that caught my attention when I started my business here is the fact that it is so close to the major European cities and, yet, so different from them. A delegate has the opportunity to visit a place where they will have a unique experience without having to waste too much of their valuable business time travelling to the event.

Authenticity and uniqueness are not only a crucial aspect of the destination, but also of the venue where an event will take place. The idea of organising meetings in standardised, closed-up places with no windows so participants have no distractions is outdated. Belgrade might not have huge congress centres with the most modern technology, but it does have an increasing number of 'boutique' venues in old factories, warehouses and even in catacombs that date from the time of the Roman Empire. The added value that such a venue gives to an event is priceless, because they will keep the participants entertained and satisfied with the event, which will means that they will spread the word about the event through the photos they have taken and posted on social media, and encourage them to stay in the venue and network with delegates after the main event has finished. Overall, the uniqueness of the venue will encourage them to share their good emotions online and offline, which will contribute to building a good general image of the event among participants and non-participants.

When starting my business in the competitive MICE industry, I knew I would need to keep innovating and follow the latest technology trends in order to succeed, but that was not all. It took me a while until I realised that the latest event apps and the best speakers do not mean much if there is no quality face-to-face interaction between people in the venue. When organising a conference, leaving enough time for participants to network is essential, even if that means reducing the time of lectures or the number of speakers. Some delegates come from far-away countries to attend your event, just to exchange ideas and experiences with each other, so giving them time to do so is highly important. Moreover, to multiply the networking possibilities, you should not forget the value of a social gathering after the main event – this could be a dinner or a party for the participants, for example. That interaction in a relaxed environment may be life-changing and can help them engage in deeper conversations without feeling pressure because of the limited time available in a formal event. For some people, that is the easiest and fastest way to get inspiration and meet new people who could be potential clients or partners with whom they could expand their businesses.

My job as a MICE event manager is to put all of these elements together to create the best possible event, but doing so in a developing destination like Belgrade sometimes requires me to look at the big picture and go beyond the Serbian border. In fact, international cooperation is one of the most powerful tools that we can use to increase the power of an event and that is a big opportunity for the Balkans. Every one of the Balkan countries has unique features, from buzzing cities to beautiful landscapes, warm hospitality and excellent cuisine. When combined, the result is a diverse event or incentive trip that people cannot wait to experience. By engaging in international partnerships, we add value to our events or incentive trips, increasing the chances of attracting more people than we otherwise would.

The MICE industry has the power to change the way people do business, but also the way people experience destinations they never thought they would visit. I learned valuable lessons in the time I spent in Serbia, and regardless of how successful or not an event is, I am particularly proud of seeing participants of corporate events I organised coming back to Serbia on their vacations just because they loved it. My mission is complete.

12.14 Summary

This chapter has provided an overview of a diverse and dynamic sector of the events industry. It has focused on a broad sweep of business events, and noted the significance of technological and business developments for the sector. Business event managers face challenging times in the short to medium term as the world economy recovers from the global pandemic and the recessions that have followed around the world. However, events have become central to the way that many companies do business in the twenty-first century, and this, along with innovations in emerging technologies, the increased connectivity that reaches across borders and the desire to maintain face-to-face human contact, means that it is likely that opportunities will continue to present themselves in the business event marketplace. All areas of business events – from exhibitions to corporate hospitality – are, and will continue to be, an important, vibrant and exciting part of the events industry.

Review questions

1. The business event sector was badly affected by the coronavirus pandemic of 2020/21. What happened in your country and has the industry started to recover?
2. Business events place networking at the heart of what they do. Discuss different approaches to networking.
3. Reflect on the variety of events that sit under the umbrella term of 'business events'. Does it surprise you how many events there are, and the wide diversity of events that can take place in the B2B and B2C environment?
4. Have you ever considered things like the Oscars and the MTV Music Awards to be business events? Explain why they might be considered within this typology.

Further reading

Davidson, R. (2019) *Business Events* (2nd edn), Abingdon: Routledge. The most comprehensive textbook on business events available; it offers both a practical and theoretical overview of all key aspects of business events and is a must read for anyone interested in learning more about the sector.

Hahm, J. J., Breiter, D., Severt, K., Wang, Y. and Fjelstul, J. (2016) The Relationship between Sense of Community and Satisfaction on Future Intentions to Attend an Association's Annual Meeting. *Tourism Management*, 52: 151–160. DOI:10.1016/j.tourman.2015.06.016. This paper reviews motivations to attend annual association meetings, which they suggest are imperative to associations because they are the biggest revenue source outside of membership dues. The study concludes that a sense of community is what drives people to attend an association meeting every year, rather than overall satisfaction with the event.

Mitchell, V., Schlegelmilch, B. B. and Mone, S. (2016) Why Should I Attend? The Value of Business Networking Events, *Industrial Marketing Management*, 52: 100–108. DOI:10.1016/j.indmarman.2015.05.014. A research study that looks at the types of value individuals identified when attending business events. A really useful and insightful read, especially given the increasing use of technology potentially reducing the need for people to meet in person.

Video links

2019 Los Cabos Incentive Trip Recap: www.youtube.com/watch?v=TE7EU6_ZKaE

Beyond the Lockdown – the Recovery of the Mice Industry with Rob Davidson: https://youtu.be/5SYEqRPrfHE

The Future of Hybrid Events: www.youtube.com/watch?v=fVAgCuRgVpo

Monaco Grand Prix Corporate Hospitality: www.youtube.com/watch?v=gZqrd7pSxaE

What Is a Fam Trip? www.youtube.com/watch?v=pREE_xiY0mE

Weblinks

Business Visits and Events Partnerships: www.businessvisitsandeventspartnership.com/. The Business Visits & Events Partnership (BVEP) is an umbrella organisation representing leading trade and professional organisations, government agencies and other significant influencers in the business visits and events sector. BVEP's vision is to support sustainable growth for the United Kingdom's Events Industry.

CEMA: https://cemaonline.com/. The Corporate Event Marketing Association advances strategic event marketing and marketing communications for senior-level event marketers and industry professionals. Their website has information about events in the news and a wide range of useful resources.

International Association for Conference Centres (IACC): www.iacconline.org. IACC is a global community of passionate people and companies delivering innovative and exceptional meeting experiences. Their mission is to bring together the brightest industry minds to promote the best meeting venues, which deliver exceptional meeting experiences.

Meeting Professionals International (MPI): www.mpi.org. MPI is the largest meeting and events industry association worldwide. The organisation provides innovative and relevant education, networking opportunities and business exchanges, and acts as a prominent voice for the promotion and growth of the industry. MPI has a global community of 60,000 meeting and event professionals including nearly 14,000 engaged members. It has nearly 70 chapters, clubs and members in more than 75 countries worldwide. 'When we meet, we change the world'.

UFI: www.ufi.org. UFI is the global association of the world's leading tradeshow organisers and fairground owners, as well as the major national and international exhibition associations, and selected partners of the exhibition industry. Their website contains useful case studies, reports and research/blogs. Read the UFI Global Exhibition Barometer here: www.ufi.org/archive-research/the-global-exhibition-barometer-january-2021/

References

Allen, J. (2008) *Event Planning: The Ultimate Guide to Successful Meetings, Corporate Events, Fund-Raising Galas, Conferences, Conventions, Incentives and Other Special Events*, Sydney: John Wiley & Sons.

Allen, J., O'Toole, W., Harris, R. and McDonnell, I. (2011) *Festivals and Special Events Management* (5th edn), Milton: John Wiley & Sons.

Association of Event Venues (AEV) (2020) E-guide Guidance for Events in UK Venues. Available at: www.aev.org.uk/e-guide [Accessed 10 February 2020].

Bauer, T., Law, R., Tse, T. and Weber, A. (2008) Motivation and Satisfaction of Mega-Business Event Attendees: The Case of ITU Telecom World 2006 in Hong Kong, *International Journal of Contemporary Hospitality Management*, 20 (2): 228–234.

Bizzabo (2021) Networking Event Examples. Available at: https://blog.bizzabo.com/networking-event-examples [Accessed 11 March 2021].

BVA BDRC (2022) Meetings & Events – State of the Nation. Available at: www.bva-bdrc.com/projects/meetings-events-state-of-the-nation-report/ [Accessed 8 August 2022].

BVEP (2020) *The UK Events Report*. Available at: www.businessvisitsandeventspartnership.com/news/bvep-press-releases/801-bvep-launches-report-focused-on-70bn-events-industry [Accessed 10 March 2021].

BVEP (2021) The Shape of Events: A Report by the Business Visits & Events Partnership. Available at: www.businessvisitsandeventspartnership.com [Accessed 8 August 2022].

C&IT (2021) *State of the Industry: Corporate Report*. Available at: www.cit-world.com/2021-state-of-the-industry-corporate-report [Accessed 31 July 2022].

Consumer Electronics Show (2021) Homepage. www.ces.tech/ [Accessed 12 March 2021].

Curtis, P. and Evans, R. (2010) Tax Boss Most Wined and Dined Mandarin, *Guardian*, 17 June.

CVENT (2021) Cvent Connect. Available at: www.cvent.com/en/cvent-connect [Accessed 10 March 2021].

CWT Meetings & Events (2021) Incentive Trip to Thailand. Available at: www.cwt-meetings-events.com/uk/en/insights/case-studies/incentive-trip-thailand/ [Accessed 10 March 2021].

Davidson, R. (2010) Trends and Market Report. Available at: www.eibtm.com/page.cfm/T=m/Action=Press/PressID=5 [Accessed 5 August 2010].

Davidson, R. (2019) *Business Events* (2nd edn), Abingdon: Routledge.

Eventbrite (2018) Top Tools to Get People Networking at Your Event. Available at: www.eventbrite.co.uk/blog/top-tools-to-get-people-networking-at-your-event-ds00/ [Accessed 15 March 2021].

Eventia (2009) The UK Market Trends Survey. Available at: www.eventia.org.uk/html/article/uk-market-trends-survey-research [Accessed 2 August 2022].

Getz, D. (2005) *Event Management and Event Tourism*, New York: Cognizant.

Getz, D. (2008) Event Tourism: Definition, Evolution and Research, *Tourism Management*, 29 (3): 403–428.

Getz, D. (2021) *Dictionary of Event Studies, Event Management and Event Tourism*, Oxford: Goodfellow Publishing.

Getz, D. and Page, S. (2016) Event Studies: *Theory, Research and Policy for Planned Events* (3rd edn), Abingdon: Routledge.

Hahm, J. J., Breiter, D., Severt, K., Wang, Y. and Fjelstul, J. (2016) The Relationship between Sense of Community and Satisfaction on Future Intentions to Attend an Association's Annual Meeting. *Tourism Management*, 52: 151–160. DOI:10.1016/j.tourman.2015.06.016.

Hall, A. (2009) ROI: Measured, Guaranteed, *Corporate Meetings and Incentives*, September: 19.

Haug, L. (2010) Lift Lab. Available at: http://liftlab.com/ [Accessed 28 July 2010].

HubSpot (2021) 15 Surprising Stats on Networking and Face to Face Communication. Available at: https://blog.hubspot.com/sales/face-to-face-networking-stats?__hstc=199273009.9940848 3ce5c4b1985907a37eb905005.1613053446183.1613053446183.1615465117987.2&__ hssc=199273009.1.1615465117987&__hsfp=4071611151 [Accessed 10 March 2021].

ICCA (2021) Events and Education. Available at: www.iccaworld.com/evps/ [Accessed 4 October 2011].

International Confex (2021) Homepage. Available at: www.international-confex.com/ [Accessed 13 March 2021].

Intu (2016) Sponsorship and Brand Immersion. Available at: www.intugroup.co.uk/intu-expe riences/sponsorship-and-brand-immersion/ [Accessed 15 June 2016].

IRF (2018) Incentive Travel Industry Index. Available at: https://theirf.org/research/incentive-travel-industry-index-powered-by-site-index-irf-outlook-and-ficp-released/2578/ [Accessed 10 March 2021].

Masterman, G. (2004) A Strategic Approach for the Use of Sponsorship in the Events Industry: In Search of a Return on Investment. In I. Yeoman, M. Robertson, J. Ali-Knight, S. Drummond and U. McMahon-Beattie (eds) *Festival and Events Management: An International Arts and Culture Perspective*: 260–272, Oxford: Butterworth-Heinemann.

MIA (2021) UK Agency and Planner Research – March 2021. Available at: www.mia-uk.org/ COVID-19-Recent-Industry-Findings [Accessed 10 March 2021].

MIPIM Asia (2016) MPIM Asia Summit. Available at: www.mipim-asia.com/ [Accessed 6 February 2017].

Nguyen, N. and Leblanc, G. (2001) Corporate Image and Corporate Reputation in Customers' Retention Decisions in Services, *Journal of Retailing and Consumer Services*, 8 (4): 227–236.

O'Toole, W. and Mikolaitis, P. (2002) *Corporate Event Project Management*, New York: John Wiley & Sons.

Pine, B. J. and Gilmore, J. H. (1999) *The Experience Economy*, Cambridge, MA: Harvard Business Review.

Severt, K. and Breiter, D. (2010) The Anatomy of an Incentive Travel Program, Research Funded by the Incentive Research Foundation. Available at: www.incentivemotivate.com [Accessed 28 July 2010].

Shone, A. and Parry, B. (2014) *Successful Event Management: A Practical Guide* (4th edn), London: Cengage.

SITE (2020) Homepage. Available at: www.siteglobal.com [Accessed 10 March 2021].

Smart Meetings (2019) Incentive Travel Industry Index. October 4. Available at: www.smart meetings.com/magazine_article/lessons-from-the-biggest-incentive-travel-survey-ever [Accessed 10 March 2021].

Strafford, D., Crowther, P. and Schofield, P. (2018) Enlivenment and the Gruffalo: The Unfolding Story of Events in Destination Shopping Centres, *International Journal of Event and Festival Management*, 9 (2): DOI:10.1108/IJEFM-09–2017–0048.

The Supper Club (2021) About Us. Available at: www.thesupperclub.com/about-us [Accessed 11 March 2021].

Tattoo Jam (2016) Tattoo Jam 2016. Available at: www.tattoojam.com/ [Accessed 6 February 2017].

UFI (2021) The Global Exhibition Barometer. Available at: www.ufi.org/archive-research/the-global-exhibition-barometer-january-2021/ [Accessed 11 March 2021].

Vice (2014) Smirnoff Experience Festival Case Study. Available at: http://company.vice.com/en_us/casestudies/smirnoff-the-smirnoff-experience [Accessed 15 June 2016].

Visit Dubai (2021) What's on at the Dubai Shopping Festival. Available at: www.visitdubai.com/en/whats-on/dsf [Accessed 10 March 2021].

Weber, K. and Ladkin, A. (2003) The Convention Industry in Australia and the United Kingdom: Key Issues and Competitive Forces, *Journal of Travel Research*, 42: 125–132.

Wei, W. and Miao, L. (2017) Memorable Experiences in Customer – Customer Interactions (CCIs) at Conferences, *Event Management*, 21 (6): 771–787. DOI:10.3727/152599517X15073047237269.

World Travel Market (WTM) (2021) What's On. Available at www.wtm.com/africa/en-gb/whats-on.html [Accessed 10 March 2022].

Chapter 13

Cultural events and festivals

Contents

DOI: 10.4324/9781003102878-13

13.1 Aims

By the end of this chapter, students will be able to:

- define the different categories of cultural events and festivals
- explore key management issues for these types of events
- analyse the challenges involved in marketing cultural events and festivals
- discuss the ways in which cultural events and festivals can contribute to cultural and social change.

13.2 Introduction

Cultural events and festivals are major sectors of the events industry and are key drivers of the tourism and service economies in all the major developed economies and in most countries around the world. Cultural events are hugely diverse in nature, from a Beyoncé tour to the Venice Biennale and celebrations of identity and nationality. The calendar of festivals within just one country will inevitably be crowded with religious, seasonal and community festival events.

This chapter provides an overview of the cultural events and festivals sector. The aim is to introduce the reader to the variety of different events and festivals in this category and to draw their attention to some key management processes involved in producing this diverse group of special events.

13.3 Cultural events

The concept of 'culture' has always been problematic and difficult to define, when approached from a management perspective (Patel 2017). Some authors place cultural events under the more general category of 'special events' (Raj *et al.* 2017), while others include a separate category of 'cultural events' in their typologies of events, but separate these artistic events from other kinds of cultural expression, such as festivals of identity and community. Getz and Page (2016: 6) define cultural celebrations as 'solemn or joyous events that have cultural meaning', but this anthropological definition does not capture the aesthetic components of culture, packaged together by many authors as 'merely' entertainment events.

Sonder (2004) unites many of the kinds of events described in this chapter through the concept of 'entertainment', but elsewhere this term has been seen as separate, almost by definition, from the arts which make up so much of our cultural practices. The term 'cultural events' takes a more holistic view of human activity and those events which emphasise the cultural, as opposed to other, aspects of our lives.

Any definition of cultural events needs to differentiate these events from others that are more easily defined as business events, sports events or mega-events, for example, while also remaining sufficiently open to cover the broad range of events that we associate with the broad term of 'culture'.

13.3.1 Defining cultural events

Cultural events are associated with expressions of 'culture', but what does this term mean, if anything? The cultural economist Arvo Klamer (2002: 1) describes the diversities of culture and their significance:

> It may be a bridge, a piece of wood. Or a temple, a windmill, a painting, a piece of furniture, a mask, jewel, bead. It may even be a language, a ritual, or a practice. Whatever it is, it differs from other goods because people may consider it a symbol of something – a nation, a community, a tradition, a religion, a cultural episode.

To discuss the management of cultural events, it is necessary to elaborate on this list of cultural forms to produce one that resembles cultural forms as we experience them in the events marketplace; but even then the list is remarkably diverse. Looking at a range of such events internationally, there are events in which culture is understood anthropologically – in Raymond Williams' (2010) terminology, as 'a way of life' – as well as events that are better understood as expressions of an aesthetic culture (see Table 13.1).

Although this overview of the diversity of culture as a concept gives us a framework for identifying cultural events, if we are to move on to a consideration of their management, there is a need for a more 'greatly useful' definition that event managers can operationalise.

Taking into account these definitional issue in the use of the word culture, we can define cultural events as events that either present a particular expression of culture or aim to represent the cultural expressions of specific groups.

Table 13.1 Categorising cultural events

Anthropological		Aesthetic	
type	Example	type	Example
National cultural	King's Day, Netherlands	Arts	China Shanghai International Arts Festival, China
Religious	Holi, Sri Lanka	Music	Burning Man, USA
Ethnicity	Chinese New Year, Australia	Heritage	La Tomatina, Spain
Sexuality	Sarajevo Pride, Bosnia and Herzegovina		
Community	Notting Hill Carnival in London		

13.4 Festivals

Festivals are extremely common forms of cultural practice and, although many have long histories, there has been a huge growth in festivals taking place over the past two decades, as they have come to be seen as ways of showcasing cultures, attracting tourists, and generating revenue for performers and promoters. The International Festivals and Events Association estimates that there are between 4 and 5 million recurring festivals worldwide each year (IFEA 2015: The Power of Celebration). In the USA alone, there are more than 800 music festivals each year, attracting more than 32 million attendees (Time 2019). Around the world, there are now more than 500 major international film festivals, as well as thousands more that attract national, regional or local audiences (Jilani 2019).

Festivals are both a particular kind of cultural event, each with its own history and tradition, and a specific celebratory form, with structural elements that can be used within a range of cultural traditions. Sonder (2004: 18) groups together parades, fairs and festivals as 'particular types of themed events that may simultaneously contain historical, cultural, ceremonial, religious, patriotic and social themes'.

The term 'festival' is used by event organisers to describe a broad range of event forms – from short celebrations of a particular place or culture to events that extend over weeks and can involve vast numbers of venues and performers:

> Each January, Sydney Festival presents bold and memorable experiences that ignite, unite, and excite the city of Sydney.
>
> In 2021, we're building on our proud 44-year history of commissioning and presenting inspiring and ground-breaking new Australian art, with a program that celebrates the best work from our finest artists and companies.
>
> More than any other cultural event, Sydney Festival defines Sydney's personality, while audacious contemporary programming positions it at the forefront of arts practice in Australia and as one of the most wonderful arts festivals in the world.
>
> For over four decades we have presented international artists, commissioned works that have become Australian classics, opened new perspectives and created a buzz like no other.
>
> (Sydfest 2021)

> Clovelly Herring Festival always falls in November. It's the time of year when our historic village celebrates the coming of the great 'Silver Darlings', better known as Herring. We celebrate and promote this tasty, nutritious fish whilst supporting sustainable fishing. The village always depended on the harvest of herring, caught in superb condition for a short season off this coast. Records go back over 400 years and in 1749 there were about a hundred herring boats in the port. When fishing was good, 9000 herring could be landed at one time. Those days of massive catches are long gone. These days we have just two herring fishermen, both employing sustainable fishing methods using only drift nets and long lines.
>
> (Clovelly Herring Festival 2021)

Festivals can be divided into eight different types:

1 Multi-form professional arts festivals
2 Single-form professional arts festivals
3 Amateur arts festivals
4 Multi-genre arts festivals
5 Single-genre arts festivals
6 Seasonal festivals
7 Festivals connected to a specific place
8 Festivals connected to the expressions of specific communities

Getz (2013: 51) offers a simple, clear definition of festivals as 'themed, public celebrations', which he concedes does not 'do justice to the richness and diversity of meanings' attached to this kind of event. This difficulty stems from the historical and fundamental role that festivals have played in human culture – as celebratory, commemorative or ritualistic events. The first recorded festival took place in 534 BC in Greece in honour of the God Dionysus, and there are records of festivals playing important social and cultural roles from the twelfth century to the present day in Europe (Quinn 2005). Some writers even place the 'carnival-esque' experience of festivals at the heart of an understanding of how society manages itself and is governed. For theorists such as Bakhtin (1984), festivals offer a short period of time when we can rebel against, challenge and reimagine society, before we are obliged to return to an altered, but mainly preserved, social reality (Anderton 2018).

Because festivals and society are so intertwined, it can be very difficult to isolate the elements that define a 'festival', but all festivals share the following characteristics:

- themed content
- the presence of multiple individual events
- possibilities for participation
- extension in time and space
- celebratory or commemorative functions.

Each of these elements creates a set of management challenges that will be present to a greater or lesser degree in every festival.

CASE STUDY 13.1

Llum BCM: Barcelona's light festival

Location: Barcelona, Spain
Event type: Festival
Attendees: 200,000

Llum BCN is an annual three-day light festival held in Barcelona, Spain, during the Santa Eulàlia festivities in February. A series of light installations are set up within the city's 'Old Quarter' area to create new visual spectacles and to draw attention to the city's heritage and landmarks. These installations and artworks are designed by teachers and students from the city's schools of art, interior design, architecture and lighting, as well as featuring artwork by renowned international artists, and is led by the Instituto de Cultura de Barcelona.

Light festivals have become increasingly popular but are not a new phenomenon. In many countries, celebrations and festivals have incorporated fire, light shows and fireworks to add excitement and novelty to significant events. Additionally, some religious festivals have light as a key element, including Diwali and Loi Krathong. Modern light festivals can now draw on innovative technologies such as drones, projection mapping and lasers to create dramatic mass spectacles with media audiences, as well as more intimate illuminations of smaller destinations.

The festival

In 2020, Llum BCN featured 42 different installations from 23 artists from around the world. Many of the installations used virtual and augmented reality technology, as well as artificial intelligence applications, to create what organisers described as effects that would 'challenge your sense in a high-intensity sensorial experience'. Among the internationally renowned artists who took part were Luke Jerram (UK), United Visual Artists (UK), Kurt Hentschläger (Austria) and Catalonia's Antoni Arola, with their works being shown alongside 25 other pieces by artists and 17 by local schools of art, design and architecture.

Image 13.1 Museum of the Moon visual montage in front of the Glories Tower is illuminated for the Llum BCN 2020
Source: Getty Images

The festival is organised and funded by the City Council of Barcelona, primarily with the aim of engaging visitors and residents with the city, and promoting its cultural activities. The first edition of the festival consciously referenced the Monjuïc light fountains that were created by the artist Calas Buïgas for the Universal Exposition in 1929. This involved lighting up famous buildings such as the Sagrada Família, the Arc de Trimof and Casa Batlló. As the event has evolved and become more popular, the festival has added installations in patios, squares and streets in the Poblenou neighbourhood, encouraging visitors to explore areas of the city that they might otherwise ignore, through trails and tours. Since the first edition in 2012, visitor numbers have grown each year, reaching approximately 200,000 in 2020.

Who is the festival for?

Camprubí and Coromina (2019) carried out research to investigate the different motivations that locals and visitors had to attend the event, their attitudes towards the artworks and installations themselves, and whether they were likely to attend the festival again in the future. When public money is being spent on an event, residents, media and politicians frequently ask questions about the benefits for local residents. Attracting visitors to a neighbourhood at night-time can be unpopular, due to the additional noise and other inconveniences associated with events. Although visitors, especially tourists, will often stay locally and spend money in local businesses, if the local community for a festival is alienated, then the festival will not be sustainable in the long term.

In their research, Camprubí and Coromina (2019) found significant differences between residents and visitors who participated in their survey. Although all respondents said that one of their main motivations for attending the festival was to 'see new and different things', this motivation was particularly important for local residents, showing how the festival provides enjoyment for residents and gives them ways to experience their own city in new ways. Visitors, however, expressed higher levels of satisfaction with the event, in particular associated with their experience of specific installations, indicating that the mitigating the impacts of the festival on local residents may still need further attention. Residents were more likely to attend the festival again in the future, which is to be expected, but also shows the importance of engaging local stakeholders, who may also be repeat visitors for events, contributing to their long-term success.

Study activity

Many towns and cities around the world have developed light festivals in recent years. What recommendations would you make to event managers responsible for these events, to help them to balance the needs of residents and visitors?

The following sections explain specific cultural event and festival forms in detail and then analyse the particular management functions that are associated with them.

13.5 Types of cultural events and festivals

13.5.1 Music events and festivals

Music events are by far the largest element of the whole events sector. In the UK alone, more than 34 million visits are made to music concerts each year, generating around £1.1 billion (Business Live 2019; Statista 2021). They vary greatly in form and style, from individual performances in bars and community centres to multi-day touring music festivals. However, they can be categorised into four main types: the first two view music events from the perspective of the artist, while the second two take an organisational perspective.

13.5.1.1 Music concerts

Music concerts are one-off music events that attract an audience because of the presence of an individual performer or group or a small number of performers or groups appearing together.

13.5.1.2 Music tours

Tours involve repeated performances by an individual performer or group of performers, moving between different venues. Touring occurs at three different scales: regional, national and international. Regional touring is usually carried out by artists with low national profiles, or artists working within local musical scenes. National tours take place when an artist's profile has developed to a level where they are gaining national media exposure. International touring is usually commercially viable only for the most successful artists.

13.5.1.3 Music programmes

Performance venues seek to design programmes (see section 13.6 on programming, below) that will attract event attendees to a venue throughout the year. These programmes can involve a succession of events featuring individual artists, or longer-term residencies where one artist or group of artists become a regular feature of a particular venue.

13.5.1.4 Music festivals

Music festivals are a growing phenomenon; in the United States in 2019, there were more than 100 music festivals with over 10,000 attendees (Florida 2019). Over a quarter of all adults in the United Kingdom visit music festivals each year (Mintel 2020). Although other music genres also make use of the festival form (for example, the annual Beijing Music Festival in China and the Joy of Jazz festival in Johannesburg, South Africa), the rock and pop festival market is the most dynamic and attracts the largest audiences. These large events draw on a recent countercultural tradition in popular music and offer a packaged, multi-day experience that promises not only a procession of high-profile and credible musical entertainment but camping on-site and a recreation of the glory days of the Woodstock era. One of the aspects of event design that separates festivals from other music events is the provision of non-music attractions, such as catering, accommodation, secondary events and retailing, all of which must be present in order to generate an 'authentic' festival experience (Bowen and Daniels 2005).

This phenomenon is not limited to Europe. As the events market matures in other regions, a similar growth in the outdoor festival market is occurring. In Japan, the annual Summer Sonic Festival is held simultaneously in the two cities of Osaka and Chiba, with performers travelling between the two destinations. It was founded in the year 2000, and by 2019 was attracting more than 135,000 visitors.

13.5.2 Film events and festivals

Film events come in a number of forms, including screenings in cinemas or more unorthodox settings, promotional events, award shows and festivals. Screenings follow a standardised format that offers little scope for customisation by event managers, and promotional events can be best understood from a marketing perspective. This section will therefore concentrate on film festivals and the niche market for specialist screenings.

Film festivals can be analysed in two ways: the promotional services that they provide to the film industry; and the networking and development opportunities they provide to film professionals (see Table 13.2).

Film festivals vary enormously in size – from the Cannes Festival in France, which receives more than 200,000 attendees and generates €200 million of economic benefits for the Cote D'Azure area (Palais de Festivals 2018), to the Sundance Independent Film Festival in the US, with around 50,000 annual visitors, to small local and regional events.

The Panafrican Film and Television Festival of Ouagadougou (FESPACO) is Africa's largest and longest running film festival, which was founded in 1969 in the West African country of Burkina Faso. Screenings take place in the capital, Ouagadougou, as well as the regional cities Bobo Dioulasso and Ouahigouya. FESPACO only accepts entries for its bi-annual competition from African filmmakers, and which are predominantly produced in Africa. The festival promotes networking between African filmmakers and African audiovisual professionals and aims to promote African cinema to a worldwide audience. Like Cannes and the Oscars, FESPACO involves a prestigious awards ceremony in which the highest award, the Golden Stallion of Yennenga, goes to the best film entered each year.

During the Covid-19 pandemic, cinemas around the world were forced to close, and most film festivals were either cancelled, postponed, or moved online. In response to new requirements for social distancing, many countries saw the re-emergence of an old-fashioned type of film event, the drive-in cinema. Although drive-in cinema had remained popular to some degree in the USA, they had dropped out of fashion elsewhere with the arrival of multi-plex cinema venues. During July–September 2020, more than 40 drive-in cinema events were held in the United Kingdom, with venues offering socially distanced cinema experiences to household groups sat in their own cars. Many of these events attempted to enhance the experience

---

Table 13.2 Elements of a film festival

Promotional services	Development opportunities
Film screenings	Technical exhibits
Marketing support	Networking events
Awards	Educational activities

Image 13.2 People hold portraits of African film directors on the Place des Cineastes in Ouagadougou, Burkina Faso, during the FESPACO, the Panafrican Film and Television Festival of Ouagadougou
Source: Getty Images

by featuring roller-skating masked-staff serving pre-ordered drinks and food and by staging additional entertainment around the screening itself. Additionally, many events were set up in picturesque or important locations such as heritage properties and city-centre parks, to increase their appeal:

> 'For us, the main reason really was to reach as many people as possible', Alan Crofton, founder of @TheDriveIn, told Variety. 'We know most people in the UK won't have had the chance to experience a drive-in cinema before, and we wanted to give that opportunity to as many people as possible, regardless of where they live in the country. As a festival company, we're also used to touring and putting on shows across the UK and the rest of the world, and this model was best for supporting our extensive roster of freelance staff who live all over the country'.
>
> 'We've found the majority of audiences are really good at adhering to our social distancing measures', The Luna Cinema founder George Wood tells Variety. 'The beauty of the drive-in is that you can have a fantastic experience at the movies and always be safe within your own car. We've had some great responses from audience members who have been shielding and feel safe enough at our events to come out of their homes to have fun for the first time in months, which is lovely to hear'.
>
> (Ramachandran 2020)

13.5.3 Community festivals and events

A community-themed festival or event is a 'public themed celebration which can act as a catalyst for demonstrating community values and culture' (Jepson *et al.* 2008: 2). A community represented through this process could be distinguished by its:

- nationality
- ethnicity
- sexuality
- interest
- place.

Festivals play an important role in helping to create and support community identities through celebration, preservation and renewal of the cultural identities and practices of a group of people. Huang *et al.* (2010: 254) define community-based festivals (CBF) more specifically as 'essentially small scale, bottom up, and run by one or more volunteers for the benefit of the locality'.

Although the majority of CBFs certainly are low-profile, small-scale events, many festivals and cultural events that have developed within specific communities now attract large audiences and have national and sometimes even international profiles. In some cases, transnational communities formed through diasporas and other migrations have generated international networks of cultural events and festivals (Zou *et al.* 2021), such as the annual Chinese New Year celebrations, held in Chinatowns in most of the world's major cities.

CASE STUDY 13.2

Pride in Sarajevo

Location: Sarajevo, Bosnia and Herzegovina
Event type: Community festival
Attendees: 2000

Pride in Sarajevo is an example of a festival associated with a community of sexuality. Ammaturo (2015) explains that Gay Pride events, including marches, festivals and parades, are one very visible aspect of lesbian, gay, bisexual, transgender, queer, intersex, and asexual (LGBTQIA+) social movements that originated in the 1960s. Interpride, the international organisation for LGBTQIA+ festival events, has more than 400 member organisations, with a collective attendance at member events of more than 15 million people every year, across at least 950 pride events globally (Interpride 2017).

Pride in Sarajevo was held for the first time in 2019. The capital of Bosnia and Herzegovina was the most recent European destination to hold a Pride event, which was held despite protests from conservative religious groups in the country. Two thousand people marched from the Eternal Flame, a memorial commemorating victims of the Second World War, to a celebration outside the national parliament building.

Despite fears of violence and unrest, the parade passed peacefully and inaugurated what should become a new tradition for the city, with an annual event representing LGBTQIA+ communities in Sarajevo. During the event, organisers from different ethnic groups, in a country that features ongoing ethno-nationalist divides, carried a pink banner with the slogan 'Ima Izac' or 'I Want Out' in both Latin and Cyrillic scripts. Activists carried placards reading "Love is not a Privilege" and "Queer Resistance", waving rainbow flags and singing anti-fascist songs.

Image 13.3 LGBTQIA+ activists hold a banner reading 'Need to Get Out' and rainbow flags as they march through Sarajevo city centre, on 8 September 2019, during Bosnia-Herzegovina's first ever Gay Pride parade
Source: Getty Images

Over the more than 40 years of its existence, the event has had a range of titles, including 'Gay Pride' and 'London Mardi Gras'. There have also been a number of organisations involved in managing the event. London Pride began as an event that was organised by a loose collection of groups working together, but as it has grown it has become more professional, and taken on more standardised events management practices. From 2004 to 2012, a charity called 'London Pride' ran the event, and more recently the Mayor of London supported the creation of the Community Interest Company 'Pride in London' as organisers. This new organisation is entirely run by volunteers and is supported by a large number of private and public-sector partners.

13.5.4 Arts events and festivals

Arts events and festivals can focus on the performing arts, the visual arts, sonic art, or a combination of all three. They are the most common type of festival event.

The performing arts include, but are not limited to, dance, theatre and opera. Often magical entertainment, circus arts and comedy are included within this framework, sharing common elements of performance, venue type and consumer. Performing arts events can take place on a one-off basis, as tours, as serial events or in festival format.

Arts events that are in the fields of visual and sonic arts can include short-term exhibitions of art and opening events, as well as festivals. Longer-term exhibitions of artworks are covered by the substantial literature in the field of museum and gallery management. Axelsen and Arcodia (2005) suggest that these short-term cultural events are little understood within the events management literature, despite their prominence within the visual arts field, with gallery managers increasingly using them to attract visitors and promote sales of specific artists and works. They suggest that these events are worthy of further exploration within the field of events management for three main reasons:

- They offer another perspective on events management as a subject and as a set of management techniques that can be incorporated into the development of subject knowledge and good practice in the industry.
- The art market is becoming less producer-led and more consumer-led, in common with the wider cultural industries, so understanding the art event consumer helps art event managers to meet the needs of the art market.
- Boundaries between high and low art have become blurred and there is a growing market of event consumers for art forms that have traditionally been seen as elitist, such as the visual arts.

An example of this kind of short-term event is Soundwalk – an annual one-day event that brings together international sound artists in Long Beach, California. The 2013 Soundwalk involved 50 artists from around the world, who collaborated to create a set of temporary sound art installations: 'The evening operates under the concept of a one-night multi-sensory experience as conveyed through sound art that is situated in various indoor and outdoor spaces throughout the East Village Arts District in Downtown Long Beach' (Soundwalk 2015). The Soundwalk events showcase the work of an emerging group of sound artists and introduce members of the public to a new artistic practice:

> This year, FLOOD [the event organisers] will be exploring 'connectivity' by expanding both geographically and conceptually. The activation of 1st Street as a 'sound corridor' will connect the Arts District with Pine Avenue, thus offering both participants and attendees interesting new contexts in which to exhibit and to experience art set forth in sound.

It has been FLOOD's aim to raise awareness as well as engender an appreciation for alternative artistic practices by exposing audiences, along with the larger community, to aesthetic sensibilities and innovative approaches that exist outside those of the contemporary mainstream.

(Soundwalk 2015)

Serial events are unique to the performing arts. They involve repeated performances of the same event over an extended period and, in the case of contemporary mega-musicals, often simultaneously in several venues in different countries. The musical *The Lion King* has been seen by over 50 million people worldwide, grossing an estimated $1.68 billion at the box office in more than 13 countries. This is the serial reproduction of one two-and-a-half-hour-long performance.

In many instances, a variety of art forms are programmed together in 'combined arts festivals' (CAF) (Finkel 2013). The majority of these festivals are produced outside the commercial sector and are often produced and/or promoted by local authorities. In a study of CAF across the United Kingdom, Finkel explains that there is increasing local and regional competition between CAFs, as local authorities come to see them as key tools for enhancing destination image and boosting tourism.

13.5.5 Literary events and festivals

Literary events and festivals are a growing sector of the cultural events industry. They vary in size and scope, but include:

- commercial book launches
- book clubs and reading groups
- talks and readings given by authors
- literary festivals.

Commercial launch events are organised by book publishers and generally take place in bookshops for a small audience or at trade fairs. With more than 32 million books in print, and more than 50,000 new books being released for Amazon's Kindle reader alone every month, launches and other entrepreneurial strategies are vital for the success of new books (Friedman 2020). The largest trade fair, in Frankfurt, attracted 209,672 visitors when it launched a digital version of this successful event in October 2020, during the Covid-19 pandemic (Frankfuter Buchmesse 2021).

Book clubs and reading groups are small, locally organised events that are usually informal in nature. They began in the eighteenth century as informal venues for women's education when they were denied access to traditional educational institutions, and are now ubiquitous to the point where more than five million people in the USA alone are members of local book clubs (Thomas *et al.* 2020). They have also become a feature of mass media and celebrity culture, with celebrity endorsements allied to publishers' more traditional marketing efforts. The most successful of these has been Oprah Winfrey's Book Club, with *Time* magazine reporting:

It's the greatest force in publishing today, with the power to raise authors from the dead (Leo Tolstoy) or crucify them on the national stage (James Frey). The all-powerful Oprah's Book Club is not so much a club as a ruthlessly influential marketing vehicle, with the power to fundamentally alter best-seller lists, Amazon rankings and royalty payments. Sure, the 'club' has 2 million 'members' and a web site that provides a space for users to share thoughts on featured titles, read excerpts and get advice like, 'How to Read a Hard Book'. But in the 12 years Oprah's Book Club has existed, its significance has been – from the perspective of authors and editors, at least – not its sense of community, but its influence on sales, which has been known to increase a print run fivefold.

(Pickert 2008)

Despite the commercial success of endorsed reading groups such as Oprah's, at the level of the individual event these book clubs are locally organised and, while they may make use of centrally (often publisher-) produced reading notes and supplementary material, they tend to involve no more than a dozen people at any one time. Literary festivals, by contrast, can attract thousands of times more visitors and are being developed in a number of countries, capitalising on the maturation of the festival market. These festivals combine authors' talks, catering, accommodation, retail and secondary events within the traditional festival spatial and temporal arrangements of a bounded site over multiple days.

The Hay Festival of Literature and the Arts is a charitable organisation that has promoted the Hay-on-Wye literary festival since 1988. Beginning as a small event that aimed to build on the tradition of bookselling in a small town in Wales, in 2018 it sold more than 270,000 tickets for 800 events during the festival, attracting visitors from more than 14 countries (Access All Areas 2018). In that year, speakers included Chelsea Clinton and Rose McGowan, while previous headliners have included Archbishop Desmond Tutu and Boris Johnson, demonstrating that the original aims of promoting the book trade have widened to include a range of intellectual activities. The Hay Festival has also recently expanded internationally, to include parallel events in:

- Segovia, Spain
- Alhambra, Spain
- Cartagena, Colombia
- The Maldives
- Zacatecas, Mexico
- Nairobi, Kenya
- Beirut, Lebanon
- Arequipa, Peru

The festival in Peru shows how literary festivals, as one kind of cultural event, can be developed to address broader social issues as well as being successful commercial events in their own right:

This year, the festival grew by about 10% compared to the 2018 edition (which had 27,500 attendees), said Cristina Fuentes La Roche, director of the Hay Festival International. This growth is measured in the full capacity of all the educational and cultural activities programmed for the festival and the growth of the specific cultural activities for the child and young adult audience: there's Hay Festivalito and Hay Joven. In addition, this year, the authors also held discussions with prisoners in male and female prisons.

(Hay Festival Arequipa 2019: 14)

Study activity

Visit the website for the Hay Festivals around the world: www.hayfestival.com/festivals. Explore the programmes for the different events and answer the following questions:

- What are the various elements of the festivals that are consistent across different countries?
- Why do you think the Hay Festival has expanded internationally?
- What are the difficulties of expanding a cultural event into different countries?
- Who sponsors these events? Why do you think they want to be associated with them?

13.6 Programming cultural events and festivals

Although the idea of programming is used across the events industry, the term is used in a specific way for cultural events and festivals. In this instance, it describes the process of choosing and presenting a set of events that are joined together by venue, content or organisation. It is a central, but under-researched, concept for understanding the management of cultural event organisations and cultural event venues, such as theatres and concert halls (Cancellieri and Turrini 2016). Programming in this manner should be distinguished from the concept of developing a programme for an event, which involves assembling the elements of event design for a single event within a theme.

Decisions about what to programme within a venue, or a festival space, are influenced by diverse factors, including global and local demand, the level and type of funding available for specific elements of a programme, and the characteristics of the local community, including their openness to innovation or risk (Cancellieri and Turrini 2016). Castaner and Campos (2002) identify the factors involved in the programming decision-making process that event managers go through when designing a programme of cultural events. These can be divided into environmental and cultural factors that impact upon an organiser's ability to develop innovative programmes within a specified form.

13.6.1 Environmental factors

These can be divided into macro-, meso- and micro-level influences on the cultural organisation. Macro factors come from the external environment, such as changes in legislation, changes in society and the influence of other organisations. Micro factors are internal to the organisation and include its strengths and weaknesses, its level of available resources, and human resource issues. Meso factors refer to those influences that span the internal and external operating environments, such as relationships with particular funding bodies and sponsors, and organisations working in partnership (see Figure 13.1).

Figure 13.1 Determinants of cultural event programming

These environmental factors, taken together, form the practical horizons of what a cultural organisation will be able to programme within a venue or a festival.

13.6.2 Cultural factors

In order to understand the programming process fully, it is necessary to examine cultural factors, too. These factors are both internal and external to an organisation and relate to the cultural orientations of the audience and to the orientations of the cultural programmers themselves. The influence of inherently conservative audiences or programmers will produce 'safe' programmes that avoid risk in order to consolidate existing audiences. Meanwhile, audiences and programmers who are enthusiastic about cultural innovation will exert pressure that produces more innovative, creative programming, even though this carries the risk of alienating the existing audience.

Successful programming works through a creative tension between conservative and innovative approaches to programming decision-making, within a set of environmental constraints that are specific to every cultural organisation.

Allen *et al.*'s (2010) discussion of the factors influencing the development of a programme for a *single* event shows that the process of event design and the development of multiple-event programmes operate under a similar set of constraints. The authors explain that the programme for a single event depends on:

● the expectations of the audience
● the constraints of the venue and the infrastructure
● the culture of the client and the main sponsors
● the availability of elements of the staging and their relationship to each other
● the logistics
● the creative intent of the event team.

Cultural programmes can be expressed according to four main stylistic conventions, as shown in Table 13.3.

Assassi (2005) carried out a study of French theatres to determine the characteristics of performing arts programming decision-making and discovered four elements of this process, as shown in Figure 13.2.

The *reactive component* of programming relates to the box-office potential of a cultural event, expressed either as an attendance figure or as an income stream. The *relational component* is a measure of how far the programme is designed as a response to feedback from and interaction with cultural consumers. The *proactive component* describes how the programming

---

Table 13.3 Programming styles

Programming style	Example
Thematic	A concert season programmed in partnership with a scientific organisation, themed on the relationship between music and science
Temporal	A programme of outdoor theatre events during the summer in the grounds of a country estate
Disciplinary	A visual arts festival
Audience constituency	A festival of Kurdish music and poetry

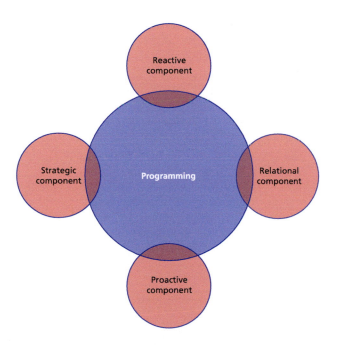

Figure 13.2 Components of programming
Source: Adapted from Assassi (2005)

decisions reflect the cultural objectives of the organisation. Finally, the *strategic component* refers to how far the programming decisions meet the broad strategic aims of the organisation.

According to this model, successful programming will be a mix of all four of these elements, with the split between the requirements of reactive and non-reactive elements determined by the financial situation and profit-driven motivation of the organisation involved.

Study activity

- Use the three models set out in this section to analyse the programming of a major national cultural venue or festival in your country.
- How useful do you find each model in understanding the programming decisions of the organisation?
- What information do you need to help you to carry out this analysis?
- What recommendations can you make for developing the programming strategy of your chosen organisation?

13.7 Marketing cultural events and festivals

Consumers are presented with an ever-increasing volume of marketing messages for cultural activities, due to the growth of the 'cultural industries' and the extension of the marketplace into their leisure time (Hesmondhalgh 2018). Cultural organisations are competing for consumers' attention, not only against other cultural organisations but with other 'agents of leisure', such as cinemas, leisure centres, digital broadcasters and shopping malls. In order to gain a competitive advantage, they now make use of sophisticated marketing techniques. This has been a relatively recent development, with the controversies over the commercialisation and commodification of culture now playing a less prominent role in cultural management discourse. New technologies, innovative funding regimes and the growth of cultural sponsorship have all helped to support a global cultural sector that is recognised by most developed nations as fundamental to their economic success and cultural identity. This diverse group of cultural producers within the 'cultural industries' (Hesmondhalgh 2018) make use of the full repertoire of marketing strategies and techniques that were explored in Chapter 7. However, when considering cultural events specifically, we can make use of two models that help event managers to develop both their marketing strategies and the cultural form in which they are working. These models are the concept of the 'cultural consumer' and the group of social marketing techniques known as 'audience development'.

13.7.1 The cultural events consumer

Kolb (2020) sets out four core challenges facing cultural organisations in the competition for consumers:

1 Cultural marketers can no longer assume that they know what the consumer wants from the cultural experience.
2 Consumers living in a multi-media, cross-cultural environment will want more combinations of art forms and new delivery methods.

3 Cultural marketers must target packaged events to specific market segments.
4 These packaged events must provide multiple benefits to meet consumer needs, while fitting within consumers' time and budget constraints.

Bearing in mind these constraints, Kolb goes on to suggest that, when faced with this level of uncertainty within an organisation and the cross-cultural, multi-media competencies and expectations of cultural event attendees, there is a need for a specific cultural segmentation model for cultural consumers. This model of the 'cultural consumer' can be used by cultural event managers to attract specific groups of attendees through the design and marketing processes. It first classifies the consumer in terms of their engagement with the cultural form or event (see Figure 13.3).

This model shows cultural consumers segmented into five groups, each of which is represented to a different degree for different cultural forms within a total population of cultural consumers. *Petty producers* have developed such a strong level of engagement with the culture that they have started to create it at an amateur level. They are looking for cultural experiences that allow them to participate in production or that offer opportunities for their advancement or development within their preferred cultural field.

Those within the *enthusiast* segment of the cultural consumer marketplace have an excellent knowledge of the cultural form that goes beyond mere attachment to a particular individual, group or venue. They are very knowledgeable about their chosen field and it is a significant element in their social and friendship networks. This group of event consumers will be attracted to cultural events and festivals that are innovative and have a clear relationship to the traditions associated with their cultural form.

Cultists are a heavily specialised segment of this market who have developed attachments to specific events, stars or groups. They are characterised by the lengths they will go to in order to indulge their interests, both financially and temporally. They will seek out events that are related to their particular interests and those that give them opportunities to meet like-minded consumers.

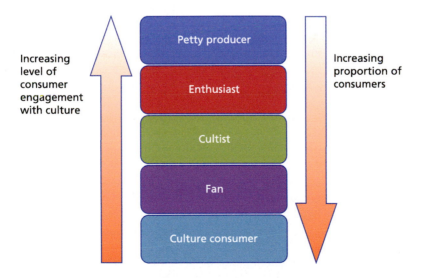

Figure 13.3 Cultural consumers
Source: Adapted from Kolb (2013)

Cultural events and festivals

A *fan* is similar to a cultist, but will devote less time and money to pursuing their interest. This allows fans to have multiple allegiances and to be more open to developing new cultural interests. They are attracted by the familiarity of the form or content of the event, or the connection between the event and another that they have attended in the past.

The majority of the population – the mass audience for cultural events and festivals – can be classified as *cultural consumers*. They do not have specialist cultural event interests, but consume culture as part of day-to-day life. For these consumers, factors such as convenience and cost are key elements in their decision-making processes, as are the effects of reference groups.

Kolb's model is important for understanding the marketing of cultural events and festivals as it shows how different kinds of cultural consumers have specific, event-related expectations and desires, which will influence their value to a cultural organisation in terms of income or programming choices. However, cultural organisations seek to develop both the cultural forms in which they work and the audiences for their work. This idea of 'audience development' is fundamental to understanding the relationship between the marketing goals of a cultural event and its broader cultural mission. Table 13.4 shows how this model can be applied, using the example of theatre events.

Table 13.4 Cultural consumer model applied to theatre events

Type of consumer	Example consumption activity	Value to the organisation
Petty producer	Begins to write and get involved in amateur theatre. Prepared to spend for 'important/exclusive' events.	Can generate new cultural workers and products. Audience for specific high-value events.
Enthusiast	Studies a course in theatre history. Prepared to travel widely and invest in their interest.	Part of valuable networks that can be accessed for marketing purposes. Potentially a large attendee group, but often dispersed. Market for high-value events.
Cultist	Attends all events featuring a specific film star.	A reliable audience with patterns of repeat attendance. Likely to consume cult-related products, such as exclusive events and signings, and to purchase related merchandise. Part of valuable networks of cultists.
Fan	Excited by music, theatre and productions starring certain TV or film personalities.	A large audience group that can be targeted using specific events or programming.
Cultural consumer	Will attend the theatre as part of an evening out or in response to a marketing campaign that emphasises entertainment, price and/or convenience.	This is the mass audience for all culture. Theatres will need to attract these people to develop sustainable audiences to support wider programming aims and ensure financial survival.

As the marketing manager of a boxpark-style venue with multiple small performance areas, food and retail offers in a large city, how would you go about attracting the various segments of the cultural marketplace – as defined in Kolb's model – for your events?

Use the following questions as a guide:

- Which segment(s) would you focus on and why?
- How would you effectively market your event to your chosen segment(s)?
- How would your chosen segment(s) influence the event design process?

13.7.2 Developing audiences for cultural events and festivals

Audience development is an umbrella term for techniques and approaches that are designed to increase audiences for cultural events. While these have much in common with general marketing approaches, cultural organisations employ them in the hope of achieving broader goals. (In this sense, they are a form of social marketing.) These goals include cultural, financial and social objectives, and the innovative aspect of audience development is combining these within the field of cultural management, as is shown in Figure 13.4.

These objectives relate to the internal and external relationships of a cultural organisation. Some of these relationships are grounded in the mission of the cultural organisation, such as a commitment to develop a particular cultural form, while others focus on external factors, such as the requirements of funding bodies or a relationship with the local community.

Audience development aims to break down barriers to access and deliver new audiences for cultural events by changing perceptions and behaviours of potential and existing event attendees. These changes will then lead to attendees:

- attending an unfamiliar cultural form
- attending more frequently
- attending new venues
- transforming from lapsed into regular attendees
- forming closer bonds with a cultural organisation
- becoming donors of time or money
- increasing their level of interaction within their social groups and the wider community.

Within cultural event and festival organisations, audience development is a cross-functional activity that requires the participation of the whole organisation (Cuenca-Amigo and Makua 2017). Successful audience development requires that cultural producers, marketers, educational professionals and strategists work together to align the activities of an event organisation with audience development plans. Table 13.5 gives an overview of the relationships between organisational goals and audience development activities. Kawashima (2006), having conducted a review of audience development practices in the cultural sector, shows the multiple benefits of pursuing such strategies:

- providing financial security
- increasing opportunities for cultural production and participation

Cultural events and festivals

- promoting individual development and fulfilment for audiences
- promoting social cohesion.

All of these outcomes are dependent on increasing *participation* in cultural events. McCarthy and Jinnet (2001), in a study of arts organisations in the United States, found three ways in which participation can be increased:

- *Diversifying participation* involves attracting event attendees who would not normally attend a cultural event. Such people will need to be convinced of the benefits of attending, so this form of developing participation is the most time and resource-intensive.
- *Broadening participation* involves attracting more people to an event, from a pool of likely cultural event attendees. To broaden participation successfully, it is important to widen the scope of your marketing activities, providing information about your programmes and events to those who are already interested in your type of cultural event but who have not previously attended. Marketing messages that emphasise price and convenience are also appropriate for this strategy.

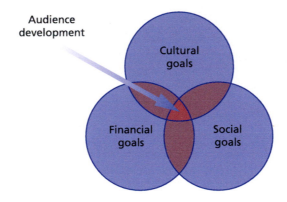

Figure 13.4 Audience development goals

Table 13.5 Audience development relationships and activities

Organisational goal	*Relationship to organisation*	*Outcomes*
Cultural	Internal	Enhancing understanding of a cultural form Building support for cultural innovation
	External	Developing dialogue with an audience
Financial	Internal	Increasing revenue Developing loyalty
	External	Meeting criteria of funding bodies
Social	Internal	Providing an educational experience
	External	Addressing issues of social exclusion Providing therapeutic benefits

Organising a variety of audience development techniques within these categories gives a useful overview of the diversity of audience development practices within the cultural sector (see Table 13.6).

Table 13.6 Audience development techniques

Participation strategy	Benefits to the organisation	Example techniques
Diversifying	Attracting new event attendees Developing new sources of revenue Generating support for cultural innovation	Producing new cultural forms: for example, staging performances of new musical forms or programming a season of films targeted at specific potential attendees
		Changing the environment, mood and/or tone of a venue or event Developing new customer service strategies
		Programming events that cross over cultural forms
Broadening	Increasing audience size Developing sustainable revenue streams Consolidating support for cultural innovation	Marketing development Pricing structure and incentives Communications Collaborative events with other providers
Deepening	Increasing audience loyalty Increasing audience spending Extending support for cultural innovation	Event interpretation: for example, pre-and post-event talks, access to rehearsals and/or venue tours Educational activity: for example, workshops, summer schools and/or master classes Increasing opportunities for feedback from and dialogue with event attendees

---

CASE STUDY 13.3

Audience Development in Dance

Location: Rambert Dance Company, UK
Venue type: Various theatres
Attendees: School groups

Rambert is Britain's oldest dance company. We gave our first performances in 1926. Our history dates even further back, to 1914, when Polish emigree and former Ballet Russes dancer Marie Rambert arrived in London fleeing the outbreak of the First World War . . .

Rambert today has the most far-reaching touring programme of any British contemporary dance company, presenting new, large scale works of the highest standards to audiences throughout the UK, complemented by equally extensive education, outreach and participation work.

(Rambert 2020)

Despite offering free workshops and other activities to schools in Wales and Scotland for a number of years, Rambert had found it very difficult to attract school group bookings for touring performances in the country. The company identified that dance was not being taught across all schools, and so developed a new technique for bringing these audiences to their contemporary dance performances.

Rambert decided to advertise all school tickets at £1, to generate positive PR for their Scottish tour, which was visiting the Theatre Royal, Glasgow; Festival Theatre, Edinburgh; and His Majesty's Theatre, Aberdeen. Along with this, the company offered workshops to schools for their students and, for the first time, free teacher training days for all schools who sent a group to the theatre. Rambert also approached the national arts agency (Creative Scotland) for the details of dance practitioners who were not based in schools, so that they could extend this offer to other settings where young people were encountering contemporary dance.

This approach to audience development was very successful, with all of the free teacher training days being fully booked, leading to an additional 150 tickets for performances being booked by school groups at the Theatre Royal and also at the Festival Theatre. Following this success in Scotland, Rambert carried out a similar campaign in Wales with similar success and are now targeting venues in England which struggle to bring in particular school groups.

Source: The Audience Agency (2020)

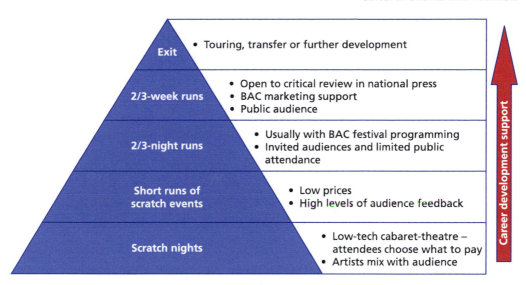

Figure 13.5 The BAC's Ladder of Development

13.8 The public role of cultural events and festivals

Cultural events and festivals are increasingly forming part of public sector strategy (see Chapter 11), usually linked to economic development through increased tourism, secondary spending or business development. Recently, they have also been promoted as vehicles for developing social capital and/or community cohesion through ideals of participation and the representation of excluded groups in the public sphere.

Hall and Rusher (2004) set out five perspectives from which the intersection of public policy and events can be studied:

- The political nature of the event policy-making process.
- Public participation in the event planning and policy process.
- The sources of power in event policy-making.
- The exercise of choice by public officials in complex policy environments.
- Perceptions as to the effectiveness of event policies.

Quinn (2005: 927) notes that there has been a 'reconceptualisation of the festival as a useful strategy for the contemporary city to adopt in the attempt to reposition and differentiate itself in an increasingly competitive world'. This new world for cities has been developed through new approaches to urban management that emphasise competitiveness and integration; structural changes in economic production that have seen Western cities deindustrialise and develop their service sectors, and the use of cultural industries to restructure wealth and job creation. All of this has taken place in a globalising system that has produced urban areas of incredible cultural diversity.

For example, the city of Manchester has seven designated 'pillar' events that together form a key part of the city's economic, tourism and community development strategies:

- Enchanted Evenings – combined arts festival
- Manchester Jazz Festival
- D.Percussion – a music festival
- Manchester Pride
- Manchester Literature Festival
- Manchester Food and Drink Festival
- Manchester 'Smile' Comedy Festival.

These events contribute at least £49 million to the city's economy through direct and indirect event expenditure by 505,000 attendees (Jura Consultants 2006).

The European Festival Association (EFA 2010) states that festivals:

- Inspire citizens through the arts, challenge and offer them occasions to broaden their horizons.
- Help deconstruct stereotypes.
- Promote a creative society that sustains and develops quality of life, social well-being and equal opportunities for all.
- Boost geographic, social and generational solidarity by bringing people together through inventive and participatory initiatives.

However, one should not view these positive economic and social effects as inevitable. Hosting cultural events and festivals can have both positive and negative impacts, so the event manager must work hard to maximise the former while minimising the latter. Moscardo (2008) provides a useful summary of the range of negative and positive impacts that event hosting can have on a location (see Table 13.7).

In Serbia, the EXIT Music Festival was held for the first time in 2000. This event demonstrates how the political and social potential of cultural festivals and events can be realised in a way that moves beyond the prevailing instrumental analyses of cultural events and festivals in the literature.

Table 13.7 Summary of event and festival impacts

Category	Positive	Negative
Economic	Direct income Multiplier effect Employment	Loss-making events Increased prices for locals Opportunity costs
Tourism	Enhanced destination image Extension of tourism season	Risk of reputation damage
Physical	New facilities and infrastructure Regeneration of rundown areas	Environmental damage Overcrowding Congestion
Socio-cultural	Social opportunities for locals Improved social networks	Commodification of culture Antisocial behaviour Dissatisfaction with event image
Psychological	Enhanced sense of community ExcitementPride	Conflict
Regional community development	Enhanced skills for volunteers and participants Support for other regional products and services	Conflict with other regional activities

Source: Moscardo (2008)

CASE STUDY 13.4

EXIT 2020

Location: Novi Sad, Serbia
Event type: Music festival
Attendees: 55,000 per day

The first EXIT festival was held in the summer of 2000 and was conceived as a protest against the Milošević regime in Serbia, which was seen as illegitimate and repressive by many of the country's citizens. The tag line of this first event was 'Exit from ten years of madness' – in reference to the government – and it was held to coincide with the presidential elections as a way of mobilising young people to become more involved in politics.

EXIT Festival was established in 2000 in University Park as a student movement for the fight for peace and freedom, both in Serbia and in the Balkans. Over the past 20 years, it has grown into one of the most eminent music festivals in the world, bringing to Novi Sad, its venue, as many as two Best European Festival titles won for 2013 and 2017. The Festival is organized at one of the largest medieval fortresses in Europe. Social responsibility remains one of the key aspects of the Festival through the work of the EXIT Foundation, whose social activism is focused on youth development and peace promotion, creative industries, environmental protection and destination branding.

(EXIT 2020)

After the overthrow of Milošević, the festival moved into the mainstream, and it has been funded and supported by a range of public bodies that see it as a key means of establishing national identity in the wake of two decades of conflict and of presenting a fresh destination image to the international tourism industry.

The festival today

The festival is held in the former fortress of Petrovaradin, a military fortification built in the seventeenth century and of immense cultural and symbolic significance as a relic of the former power of the region in European affairs. EXIT is now the largest music festival in South East Europe: in 2019 more than 225,000 people attended the four-day event. It takes place across 20 stages and features hundreds of music performers. In 2019, the line-up included the Cure, Greta van Fleet, the Chainsmokers, Carl Cox and Chase and Status.

In 2020, during the Covid-19 pandemic, the festival could not take place, in what was due to be its twentieth anniversary year. In response to this, the festival moved online, promoting the 'EXIT Life Stream', in partnership with the United Nations World Food Programme, so that the festival could continue to achieve its humanitarian goals during a year when all global festivals were forced to shut down. This online format played to more than four million people worldwide and featured live performances from the festival site, as well as streaming events featuring recorded shows from the festivals history, most of which was made available online for the first time.

As well as being a major event in the European festival circuit, comparable to Glastonbury in England and the Love Parade in Berlin, EXIT promotes peace, democracy, multiculturalism and human rights. This is a key element in the identity of the festival as a commercial brand and as an expression of contemporary Serbian culture and identity. The majority of attendees come from neighbouring former Yugoslavian states, and recent research has shown that most of them believe that EXIT has made a significant contribution to improving Serbia's image in the rest of the world.

Sources: EXIT (2020), Lukic-Krstanovic (2008), Zakic *et al.* (2009), Wise and Mulec (2015)

The EXIT festival shows how cultural events can have impacts that are more complicated than simply making an economic contribution to an area. Choose a music festival in your area and identify the range of impacts that are associated with it. Which of these do you think is the most significant and why?

Industry voice

Jianing RAO, General Manager, Jiangsu Culture Innovation Development Co., Ltd, Nanjing City, Jiangsu Province, China

Jiangsu Culture Innovation Development Co., Ltd was founded in 2012. The original purpose of founding the company was to further develop cultural exhibitions in an industry that was completely dominated and operated by the government at the time. The first exhibition operated by us was the former 'The China (Nanjing) Innocreative Cultural Fair', which now is known as China's first exhibition to integrate culture with technology, now called the China (Nanjing) Culture & Technology Integration Exhibition Achievement Fair (CTI).

Over the past nine years, I have operated nearly 20 exhibitions across the cultural industries in China and worked on many exhibitions events with related enterprises in my city. I have found that government-dominated exhibitions, even operated by the professional market-oriented teams, still have many operational problems. In terms of government-dominated exhibitions, it is like a magnet which is highly expected to attract industrial resources. And the two poles of the magnet are the government demands and market willingness. In the operation of exhibitions, these two poles are mutually exclusive, but they are expected to work together.

So, how can government-dominated cultural exhibitions be better operated? First of all, the level of the organisational structure of exhibitions, that is, the administrative level of the main organiser and the industry influence, is the essential factor. The higher the status of the organisers and the closer relationship they have with the events industry, the greater their influence, bringing easier recruitment work and more considerable income. For instance, if an exhibition is organised by national authorities, then the corresponding departments will more actively organise enterprises to participate in the exhibition. For the leading enterprises, the willingness to participate in the exhibition will be stronger and their investment will be more considerable, which is because this kind of exhibition is a report and display of their achievements towards the government, and this helps them to promote themselves. Secondly, satisfying the maximum demands of the market through an exhibition's professionalism plays an essential role in ensuring the exhibition's vitality. Although government-dominated exhibitions have the basis of administrative organising, the exhibitors' resources cannot support the long-term rising development of an exhibition. Essentially speaking, enterprises' basic purpose for participating in exhibitions is to explore customers, partners and capitals, receive orders and trade.

To analyze the industrial chain scientifically, it is very important to find out who is the true exhibitor, who are the true buyers, and then you will find out where the pain points and blind spots of the industry are. The exhibition's strong vitality can be ensured by finding the development trends of this industry, accurately selecting the subjects and continuously polishing from "extensive" to "vertical" development after the creation of a co-existent and strongly absorbing "magnet" of industrial resources.

As mentioned, my first cultural exhibition has transformed from a traditional cultural fair to China's "first exhibition" of integrating culture with technology. It was established on the basis of judging and seizing on the development directions of the national culture industry in 2016. With the release of Guidance and Suggestions on Further Propelling the Deep Integration of Culture and Technology, CTI has become the market leader in China for cultural exhibitions.

The transformation is also exploration. In 2019 and 2020, I selected the topic of 'immersive industry' for CTI, cultivated the Immersive Industry Development Forum, and began to focus on subdivisions. In 2021, the first immersive industrial park in China, merging industrial resources by the forum, was launched in Nanjing. It is believed that in the near future, events around cultural subdivisions will also appear at CTI. Through our research on the 14th Five-Year Plan for National Economic and Social Development, we finely adjusted the direction of the exhibition organisation of CTI itself. By focusing on the national strategy of 'cultural digitisation', we chose several cultural formats that were always popular, such as animation, film and TV, gaming and cultural tourism. By analysing industry chain relations and development trends, we positioned CTI as the most important platform of technological innovation and innovative solutions in the Chinese cultural industry. By targeting the audience in the middle and lower stream enterprises in the field above, we started to build a platform where technique and scenario are linked and traded so as to play a leading role besides its typical role of indicating the development trend.

We believe that the dual effect of guiding development trends and market demands could enable culture exhibitions win a better and higher prospect in the future.

13.9 Summary

This chapter has set out a framework within which one can identify a set of events and festivals that can be grouped together as 'cultural'. Bringing these events together is a response to the way in which the huge diversity of human cultural expressions has imploded under the pressures of globalisation and marketisation, forming the 'cultural industries' from which so many of our leisure and social experiences are drawn. Concepts such as the 'cultural consumer', 'audience development' and 'programming' unify the cultural events sector and help event managers to transfer knowledge between different events and festivals to produce successful events in an increasingly crowded, cultural marketplace.

Further reading

Jepson, A. and Clarke, A. (2015) *Managing and Developing Communities, Festivals and Events*, London: Palgrave Macmillan. Contains a range of case studies showing the social and cultural impacts of cultural events and festivals and the challenges involved in managing these types of events.

Kolb, B. (2020) *Marketing Strategy for the Cultural and Creative Industries* (2nd edn), London: Routledge. A very useful, practical book that covers marketing from planning to evaluation, with a specific focus on the cultural sector.

Video links

Blur singer Damon Albarn on playing to 'cows not crowds' at Glastonbury during COVID: www.youtube.com/watch?v=hU6lG4mAiDI

Edinburgh Fringe Festival: www.youtube.com/watch?v=RNY1bSAh72o

Opening of Shanghai International Arts Festival: www.youtube.com/watch?v=dG-6Aq-YyKU

Weblinks

Association of Festival Organisers: www.festivalorganisers.org/

InterPride: www.interpride.org/

Top Ten Chinese Film Festivals: www.china.org.cn/arts/2019-12/12/content_75506461_8.htm

References

Access All Areas (2018) Am-Hay-Zing Figures from Hay Festival 2018. Available at: https://accessaa.co.uk/am-hay-zing-figures-from-hay-festival-2018/ [Accessed 31 July 2022].

Allen, J., O'Toole, W., Harris, R. and McDonnell, I. (2010) *Festival and Special Event Management* (4th edn), Oxford: John Wiley and Sons.

Anderton, C. (2018) *Music Festivals in the UK: Beyond the Carnivalesque*, Abingdon: Routledge.

Assassi, I. (2005) The Influence of Theaters' Programming Strategy on Their Relations with Artistic Production Companies: An Analysis Based on the French Experience, paper presented at the 8th International Conference on Arts and Cultural Management, 3–6 July, Montreal, Canada.

The Audience Agency (2020) *Case Study: Rambert*. Available at: www.theaudienceagency.org/resources/case-in-point-rambert [Accessed 31 July 2022].

Axelsen, M. and Arcodia, C. (2005) Conceptualising Art Exhibitions as Special Events, *Journal of Convention and Event Tourism, 6* (3): 63–80.

Bakhtin, M. (1984) *Rabelais and his World*, Indianapolis: Indiana University Press.

Bowen, H. and Daniels, M. J. (2005) Does the Music Matter? Motivations for Attending a Music Festival, *Event Management, 9* (3): 155–164.

Business Live (2019) The Huge Impact of the UK Music Industry from Festivals to the Vinyl Revival. Available at: www.business-live.co.uk/opinion-analysis/huge-impact-uk-music-industry-17307700 [Accessed 31 July 2022].

Camprubí, R. and Coromina, L. (2019) Residents Versus Visitors at Light Festivals in Cities: The Case of Barcelona, *Journal of Policy Research in Tourism, Leisure and Events, 11* (3): 455–468.

Cancellieri, G. and Turrini, A. (2016). The Phantom of Modern Opera: How Economics and Politics Affect the Programming Strategies of Opera Houses, *International Journal of Arts Management, 18* (3): 25–36.

Castaner, X. and Campos, L. (2002) The Determinants of Artistic Innovation: Bringing in the Role of Organisations, *Journal of Cultural Economics*, 26: 29–52.

Clovelly Herring Festival (2021) Clovelly Herring Festival. Available at: www.clovelly.co.uk/events/clovelly-herring-festival-2-2/ [Accessed 31 July 2022].

Cuenca-Amigo, M. and Makua, A. (2017) Audience Development: A Cross-National Comparison. *Academia Revista Latinoamericana de Administración, 30* (2): 156–172.

EFA (2010) Home Page. Available at: http://www.open-the-door.eu/ [Accessed 10 May 2009].

EXIT (2020) Exit Festival. Available at: http://eng.exitfest.org/ [Accessed 9 May 2020].

Finkel, R. (2013) 11 Events and Political Agendas. In R. Finkel, D. McGillivvary and G. McPherson (eds) *Research Themes for Events*: 118–128, Wallingford: CABI.

Florida, R. (2019) The Rise, and Urbanization, of Big Music Festivals. Available at: www.bloomberg.com/news/articles/2019-08-13/the-rise-and-urbanization-of-big-music-festivals [Accessed 31 July 2022].

Frankfurter Buchmesse (2021) The 72nd Frankfurter Buchmesse – Special Edition in Facts & Figures. Available at: www.buchmesse.de/files/media/pdf/FBM_2021_FactsFigures_EN.pdf [Accessed 31 July 2022].

Friedman, J. (2020) *The Business of Being a Writer*, Chicago, IL: University of Chicago Press.

Getz, D. (2013) *Events Studies* (2nd edn), Oxford: Butterworth-Heinemann.

Getz, D. and Page, S. J. (2016) *Event Studies: Theory, Research and Policy for Planned Events* (3rd edn), Abingdon: Routledge.

Hall, C. M. and Rusher, K. (2004) Politics, Public Policy and the Destination, in I. Yeoman, M. Robertson, J. Ali-Knight, S. Drummond and U. McMahon-Beattie (eds), *Festival and Events Management: An International Arts and Culture Perspective*, Oxford: Butterworth-Heinemann.

Hay Festival Arequipa (2019) Arequipa 2019. Available at: https://cloud.hayfestival.com/arequipa/Hay-Festival-Arequipa-2019-Report.pdf [Accessed 31 July 2022].

Hesmondhalgh, D. (2018) *The Cultural Industries* (4th edn), London: Sage.

Huang, J., Li, M. and Cai, L. (2010) A Model of Community-based Festival Image, *International Journal of Hospitality Management, 29* (2): 254–260

IFEA (2015) The Power of Celebration. Available at: http://www.ifea.com/joomla1_5/index.php?option=com_contentandview=articleandid=180andItemid=306 [Accessed 10 May 2016].

Interpride (2017) Pride Radar 2016/17. Boston, MA: Interpride.

Jepson, A., Wiltshier, P. and Clarke, A. (2008) Community Festivals: Involvement and Inclusion, paper presented at the CHME International Research Conference, Strathclyde Business School, University of Strathclyde, 14–16 May, Glasgow.

Jilani (2019) Do Film Festivals Help or Hurt their Host Cities? Available at: www.the guardian.com/cities/2019/sep/11/do-film-festivals-help-or-hurt-their-host-cities-ven ice-sundance#:~:text=Film%20festivals%20have%20been%20around,%2C%20 niche%2C%20and%20intermittent%20ones [Accessed 31 July 2022].

Kawashima, N. (2006) Audience Development and Social Inclusion in Britain, *International Journal of Cultural Policy, 12* (1): 55–72.

Klamer, A. (2002) On the Economics of Arts and Culture. Available at: http://www.klmar.nl/art.htm [Accessed 26 July 2005].

Kolb, B. (2013) *Marketing for Cultural Organisations* (3rd edn), London: Thompson.

Kolb, B. (2020) *Marketing Strategy for the Cultural and Creative Industries* (2nd edn), London: Routledge.

Lukic-Krstanovic, M. (2008) The Festival Order: Music Stages of Power and Pleasure, *Issues in Ethnology and Anthropology, 3* (3): 129–143.

McCarthy, K. and Jinnet, K. (2001) *A New Framework for Building Participation in the Arts*, New York: RAND.

Mintel (2020) Raving Mad: UK Music Festival Attendance at Highest Level in Four Years. Available at: www.mintel.com/press-centre/leisure/raving-mad-uk-music-festival-attend ance-at-highest-level-in-four-years [Accessed 31 July 2022].

Palais de Festivals (2018) Cannes Tourism Press Pack. Available at: www.palaisdesfesti vals.com/uploads/brochures/Press-Pack-Cannes-Tourism-2018.pdf [Accessed 31 July 2022].

Patel, T. (2017) Multiparadigmatic Studies of Culture: Needs, Challenges, and Recommendations for Management Scholars, *European Management Review, 14* (1): 83–100.

Pickert, K. (2008) Oprah's Book Club. Available at: http://www.time.com/time/arts/article/0,8599,1844724,00.html [Accessed 19 May 2010].

Quinn, B. (2005) Arts Festivals and the City, *Urban Studies, 42* (5/6): 927–943.

Raj, R., Walters, P. and Rashid, T. (2017) *Events Management: Principles and Practice* (3rd edn), London: Sage.

Ramachandran, N. (2020) UK Drive-Ins Boom in Pandemic Era with 40 New Cinemas. Available at: https://variety.com/2020/film/news/uk-drive-in-cinemas-boom-40-venues-comscore-1234712174/ [Accessed 31 July 2022].

Rambert (2020) Our History. Available at: www.rambert.org.uk/about-us/our-history/ [Accessed 31 July 2022].

Sonder, M. (2004) *Event Entertainment and Production*, Hoboken: John Wiley and Sons.

Soundwalk (2015) Home Page. Available at: http://www.soundwalk.com/ [Accessed 9 May 2016].

Statista (2021) Music Concert and Festival Attendance in the United Kingdom (UK) from 2012 to 2019. Available at: www.statista.com/statistics/282032/music-concert-and-fes tival-attendance-in-the-uk-by-attendee-type/#:~:text=Attendance%20at%20music%20 concerts%20and,million%20attending%20festivals%20in%202019 [Accessed 31 July 2022].

Sydfest (2021) About Us. Available at: www.sydneyfestival.org.au/about-us [Accessed 31 July 2022].

Thomas, T. C., Pyle, M. A. and Handelman, J. M. (2020) Identification Incubators: Reflexivity in Consumer Book Clubs, *Consumption Markets & Culture, 23* (5): 456–480.

Time (2019) How Music Festivals Became a Massive Business in the 50 Years Since Woodstock. Available at: https://time.com/5651255/business-of-music-festivals/ [Accessed 31 July 2022].

Williams, R. (2010) *Keywords: A Vocabulary of Culture and Society*, London: Fontana Press.

Wise, N. and Mulec, I. (2015) Aesthetic Awareness and Spectacle: Communicated Images of Novi Sad (Serbia), the Exit Festival, and the Petrovaradin Fortress, *Tourism Review International*, 19 (4): 193–205.

Zakić, L., Ivkov-Džigurski, A. and Ćurčić, N. (2009). Interaction of Foreign Visitors of the EXIT Music Festival with Domestic Visitors and Local Population, *Geographica Pannonica*, 13 (3): 97–104.

Zou, Y., Meng, F. and Li, Q. (2021) Chinese Diaspora Tourists' Emotional Experiences and Ancestral Hometown Attachment, *Tourism Management Perspectives*, 37: 100768.

Chapter 14

Event impacts and sustainability

Contents

DOI: 10.4324/9781003102878-14

14.1 Aims

By the end of this chapter, students will be able to:

- understand the relationship between events and the Sustainable Development Goals
- evaluate the positive and negative impacts of a range of events
- analyse and design sustainable events
- discuss the principles of responsible events.

14.2 Introduction

This chapter will provide an overview of a range of perspectives on the impacts of events. Different kinds of impacts will be explored, using examples, and the varied ways of measuring these impacts will be discussed. The issue of event legacies will be introduced, along with a scale of event impacts, showing the important long-term and wide-ranging effects that are the hallmarks of a legacy scheme.

It is through the measurement of event impacts, across a range of domains, that we can evaluate the sustainability of an event and begin to understand the place of green events within the events industry. Event sustainability is the measure of the contribution made by event impacts to positive change in external fields, including the environment, social justice and economic justice. The United Nations have set out 17 Sustainable Development Goals (SDGs) intended to 'end poverty, protect the planet and improve the lives and prospects of everyone, everywhere' (United Nations 2015). Events can make a contribution to many of the SDGs and are both affected by and contribute to all of the issues that underlie them. Much research into events and sustainability has focused on events' environmental impacts to the neglect of their social and economic dimensions (Mair and Smith 2021), but this chapter will help you to understand the multidimensional ways in which events are connected to sustainable development.

14.3 Event impacts

Event impacts can be split into three categories, as shown in Figure 14.1.

Figure 14.1 Event impacts

Personal impacts are covered in more detail in Chapter 3. Suffice to say here that they can include (Getz 2007):

- Positive experiences, expressed as:

  - o perceptions that the event met or exceeded expectations
  - o satisfaction, happiness
  - o attitude change (towards the events, sponsors, causes, or events in general)
  - o fundamental personal change in terms of lifestyle, personality or values.

- Negative experiences, expressed as:

  - o perceptions of poor value-for-money
  - o no intent to repeat event experience
  - o lack of satisfaction
  - o failure to meet expectations.

Organisational impacts can include:

- Financial impacts – revenue generation, profit- and loss-making activity.
- Human resource impacts – recruitment and retention, motivation of staff, training opportunities.
- Impacts on organisational capacity – growth, skills development, client acquisition.
- Marketing impacts – profile-raising, word-of-mouth, media attention.

In this chapter, the focus will be on the *external impacts* of events and on the interactions between the events industry, the economy, the environment, society and culture.

14.3.1 Economic impacts of events

Economic impact assessments have been used to justify government support for events and in making decisions about investing in the events industry, including the construction of conference and exhibition venues as well as their supporting infrastructure, such as roads and hotels. For example, the stadium development company Oak View Group have been granted permission to build a new 23,500 capacity arena in the city of Manchester, UK, following a comprehensive economic impact study. It is forecast that the project will create 3,350 jobs during construction, and 1,000 permanent direct jobs once open. The arena will additionally support 1,400 jobs indirectly in the local economy and increase local spending by around £36 million per year (Oak View Group 2020).

Morgan and Condliffe (2006) set out the three steps necessary to develop a methodology for assessing the economic impacts of an event:

1 Define the geographical area under study – this could be the town, city, district, region or country where an event takes place.
2 Identify the industries from which to collect data to assess direct impacts. For example, for investments in infrastructure and venues, you will need to collect construction industry data, while assessment of tourism impacts will need data from the leisure and hospitality sectors.
3 Collect data on or estimate the direct impacts of the event on the industrial sectors that have been identified.

Within this third point, a range of different approaches can be used to measure economic impact. It is important to be able to distinguish between the economic activity within an area independent of the presence of an event and when that area is influenced by an event. For this reason, it is always important to have baseline data of economic activity so that changes can be measured. Three of the most frequently used methods of calculating economic impacts are explained below.

14.3.1.1 Multiplier effects

Multiplier calculations are the most frequently used method for evaluating the economic impacts of events. Multipliers capture the direct and indirect spending associated with events by calculating the money spent by attendees on attending the event itself *and* the extra spending in the economy that is facilitated by this initial injection. The extent to which the initial attendee spend generates additional spending is known as the multiplier effect. As Carlsen (2004: 247) explains, 'The size of the multiplier effects will be determined by the extent to which the economy can retain the additional event-related expenditure in the local economy'. This relates to the concept of 'leakage' – the movement of event-related expenditure outside the geographical area within which impacts are being assessed. For example, a percentage of the revenue generated by a touring performance by the Rolling Stones at the O2 Arena in London will flow out of the event hosting area and return to the Netherlands, where the band members are registered for tax purposes. This is a leakage of money from the event area to another area, so it cannot be included in the local economic impact of an event and must be subtracted from a multiplier calculation.

A model setting out the various aspects of a multiplier calculation is given in Figure 14.2. By calculating the spending under each of the three categories in this figure, the total spending

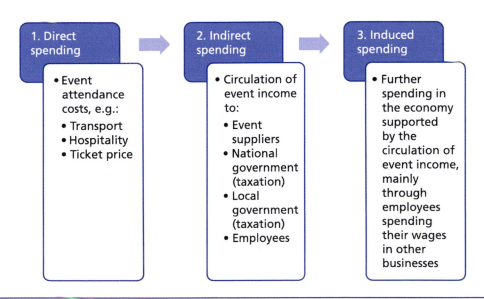

Figure 14.2 Aspects of multiplier calculations

generated by an event can be calculated. This can then be used to produce a figure that demonstrates the impact of event spending on the local economy.

There are two ways of calculating a multiplier:

Direct spending + Indirect spending/Direct spending = Multiplier

or

Direct spending + Indirect spending + Induced spending/Direct spending = Multiplier

The more commonly used first type does not include induced spending as this is usually difficult to estimate.

Hussain *et al.* (2017) carried out research to estimate the economic impact of business events in Malaysia. They collected spending data from more than 5,500 business event tourists visiting the country, who mostly attend conferences and exhibitions. These tourists were defined as people visiting Malaysia as conference delegates and exhibition buyers. Using a multiplier model known as the MGM (money generation model), an overall multiplier of 2.1 was observed, accounting for $2.96 billion of economic impact in the country. They also found that this economic activity supported (directly and indirectly) 325,437 jobs in the Malaysian economy.

14.3.1.2 Input – output analysis

Input – output modelling has a 'before and after' perspective on the economic impacts of events. The economic data used to carry out this form of analysis come from national-level statistical data that describe the economic relationships between various industrial sectors and regions. In the UK, these data are collected by the Office for National Statistics and are organised according to Standard Industrial Classification (SIC) codes, which categorise every business by industrial sector. The data show the contribution made by each industrial sector to the economy and give multiplier values that demonstrate how much an extra investment in any particular sector will contribute to the broader economy. By calculating the amount of income generated for each industrial sector by an event (for example, attendee spending on transport or hospitality), it is then possible to apply the multipliers given in the input – output table for that sector to calculate the value added to the economy by the event.

Tribe (2005) shows the direct relationship between a multiplier value and leakage in the economic impacts of an event (Table 14.1).

> ## Table 14.1 The multiplier – leakage relationship
> Source: Adapted from Tribe (2005: 271)

Value of multiplier	Leakages from the local economy	Impact of expenditure on the local economy
High	Low	High
Low	High	Low

CASE STUDY 14.1

The economic impact of the York Beer Festival

Location: York, United Kingdom
Event type: Cultural event
Attendees: 10,000
Website: https://yorkbeerfestival.camra.org.uk/faqs.html

The York Beer Festival (YBF) has taken place in York in the county of North Yorkshire, in the United Kingdom, since 1978. It initially attracted just 300 attendees and has grown steadily, moving around a number of small venues until it settled in its current venue, a field next door to the York Racecourse, known locally as The Knavesmire. It now attracts in excess of 10,000 visitors and takes places over four days. In 2019, if featured Europe's longest bar, at over 75 meters long, with over 550 beers and ciders available during the event. It is run entirely by volunteers, mostly associated with the Campaign for Real Ale (CAMRA), a charity which supports independent brewing and pubs in the UK.

Cabras *et al.* (2020) measure the economic impacts of the beer festival on the city of York. They used questionnaires to carry out a survey of festival attendees to estimate the total expenditure generated inside and outside of the event itself. They estimated that the York Beer Festival adds between £959,000 and £1.18m in economic activity to the city and that it directly creates between 14 and 18 jobs.

The method used to create these estimates of economic impact had four stages. Firstly, the total expenditure of each of 1,090 survey respondents was calculated. Secondly, correlations were identified between expenditure and different variables such as age groups and whether the visitors were local or non-local. Thirdly, multipliers were applied to the data to assess the total economic impact that could be generated by this expenditure. Finally, two different scenarios were created, modelling different assumptions about visitor spending.

To measure expenditure at the festival, the following formula was used:

$$\text{Tot\_exp}_i = \text{Fest\_exp}_i + \text{Acc\_exp}_i + \text{Meal\_exp}_i$$

where

Tot_expi = Estimated total expenditure, for respondent i.
Fest_expi = Estimated expenditure within YBF premises, for respondent i.
Acc_expi = Estimated expenditure on accommodation, for respondent i.
Meal_expi = Estimated expenditure on meals in the local town, for respondent i.

This measure of expenditure was then used to calculate the average expenditure by day per festival attendee, and this sum was then further modified in light of the number of overnight stays associated with the event, and spending on meals outside of the event venue itself.

Finally, multipliers were applied to the data, which related to the industries most closely associated with the beer festival – the manufacture of beverages, accommodation and event catering. Doing this allowed for the estimated overall economic impact of the event to be calculated.

14.3.1.3 Cost–benefit analysis

This method of analysis places values on the costs associated with staging an event and the benefits that it generates. These two values are then compared and the event is deemed viable if the benefits outweigh the costs. This is a very simple method of calculating the economic impacts of an event and is often used as a starting point for economic analysis in the planning stages. It can, however, be used in a more sophisticated way by including the tangible and intangible aspects of event costs and benefits. Carlsen (2004) provides a description of the tangible and intangible elements of a cost–benefit calculation, as outlined in Table 14.2.

The advantage of this method of analysis is that it allows for the incorporation of what economists call 'externalities'. These are aspects of the event that cannot be accounted for in direct economic terms; they appear in Carlsen's framework as the intangible costs and benefits. Traditionally, investment decisions have been made on the basis of return on investment (ROI) models which make calculations such as those given above. However, contemporary events management takes into account these externalities in the production of sustainable events. The next two sections look at two categories of externality in event planning: environmental impacts and socio-cultural impacts.

Table 14.2 Intangible costs and benefits of events
Source: Carlsen (2004: 253)

Intangible costs	Intangible benefits
Crowding and inconvenience	Enhanced community pride
Noise and visual pollution	Cultural renewal
Personal crime and property damage	Increased interest and investment in host destination
Resident exodus and tourist avoidance of event area	Enhanced commercial and residential property values

Intangible costs	Intangible benefits
Capital and construction costs	New facilities and venues
Wages and other employment costs	Employment for event employees
Additional essential services cost (e.g. police, sanitation, road maintenance)	Increased tourism expenditure before, during and after the event
Long-term event facilities maintenance	Positive media coverage and images

14.3.1.4 Social return on investment (SROI) models

SROI is a modelling technique that accounts for broader aspects of the value created by investment than those produced by standard accounting models (Boyle and Simms 2009). It shares much with 'triple bottom line' (TBL) and 'social accounting' methods in that it considers the social and cultural impacts of spending, and it is increasingly being promoted within the fields of social enterprise and public policy.

SROI is based on principles that emphasise the specificity of the local socio-economic context of investment, and it is concerned with measuring the sustainable creation of social value. It can measure the value of the social impacts created by an event and provides a monetised indicator of this value:

SROI = value of event impacts/value of event spending

The value of the impacts is calculated by focusing on four areas (adapted from Rotheroe and Richards 2007: 34):

1 *Stakeholder engagement* – Event stakeholder objectives are identified and made central to the process.
2 *Materiality* – Focusing the analysis of impacts on those areas determined as important to the event stakeholders, who will be both within and outside an event management organisation: for example, local residents and sponsors.
3 *Impact map* – Using a cause-and-effect chain from inputs through to outputs, outcomes and impacts. Develops a pathway to understand how the event causes changes in its external environment.
4 *Appreciation of deadweight* – Calculating the proportion of outcomes that would have occurred regardless of the presence of the event.

This approach to placing a financial value on event impacts has much in common with TBL accountancy practices. It places ecological and social impacts alongside financial information to report on event performance in three categories, rather than the traditionally dominant 'bottom line' of profit and loss. Hede (2008) discusses the TBL model as reflecting the three interests of event stakeholders:

● economic interests
● social interests
● environmental interests.

> **Table 14.3** Event stakeholders
> Source: Hede (2008)

Individual level	Organisational level
Residents	Community groups
Shareholders	Government
Tourists and attendees	Sponsors
Volunteers	Media
Event employees	Business

Hede identifies two overarching groups of event stakeholders whose interests should be taken into account in this reckoning of event impacts (see Table 14.3).

14.3.2 Environmental impacts of events

The environment, in its natural or physical aspects, is a core part of the event product. The staging of an event in a particular country, region or locality implies a set of relationships to the environment which are reciprocal in nature. The climate, landscape and setting of an event venue impact on the attractiveness and success of that event and are, in turn, acted on by the presence of the event.

In order to carry out an evaluation of the environmental impacts of an event, it is necessary to collect data in the following categories:

- Baseline environmental data for the location of the event, before the event takes place.
- The primary impacts of the event on the environment, such as the construction of facilities and infrastructure, waste management and the carbon footprint of the event itself.
- The secondary impacts of the event, such as congestion and pollution caused by travel to and from the venue and the use of accommodation by attendees.

No event will ever have zero environmental impacts, so it is incumbent upon event managers to develop management strategies that maximise positive impacts and minimise negative ones. Positive impacts can include the construction of zero-carbon facilities and the contribution that events can make to the physical improvement of town and cities. Negative environmental impacts associated with events include resource consumption, noise, the carbon footprint of the event itself and the travel associated with it.

David (2009) shows the energy consumption associated with the attendance of one consumer at an event, depending on their mode of travel (Table 14.4). For self-propelled travel, the energy needs are met through the consumption of foodstuffs, but for automated transport the energy comes from burning carbon in fuel. Making transportation associated with events more sustainable has significant impacts on all three traditional dimensions of sustainability: there is an economic impact on the organisers, who are responsible for providing or encouraging alternative forms of transport to private cars; there are social impacts for local residents linked to congestion and inconvenience, as well as the displacement of local residents from public transport in the area; and there are environmental impacts associated with pollution (Chirieleison and Scrucca 2017).

Getz (2007: 315) suggests a number of techniques that can be used to minimise the negative environmental impacts of events:

- *Impacts of event travel* – Support mass-transit travel solutions, concentrate multiple events in one location, stress small-scale events.
- *Investment in event infrastructure and venues* – Avoid sensitive areas, impose design standards, implement sustainable development practices.
- *Event activities* – Require green event practices, clean up after events, and educate visitors.

Table 14.4 Transport energy intensity
Source: David (2009)

Means of transport	Energy consumption per passenger kilometre (KJ)
Aircraft	6000
Train	2100
Coach	2100
Car with 1–4 passengers	1900–7800
Cyclist	120
Pedestrian	250

CASE STUDY 14.2

Using festivals to promote environmental sustainability

Location: Munich, Germany
Event type: Street festival
Attendees: 250,000–300,000
Website: www.streetlife-festival.de

The Streetlife Festival in Munich, Germany, is a mixture of a street festival of the kind that has become popular in many cities, with an environmental exhibition and a fair. The festival is held twice per year, at the start of the summer in May or June, and again at the end of the summer, in September. Munich is already well known for its famous Oktoberfest event, which draws tourist audiences from around the world, but Streetlife has a more local and regional focus.

The festival began in the year 2000, on European Car-Free Day, with the aim of promoting sustainable alternative forms of transport to local residents. Since then, it has grown every year and widened its focus to more broad sustainability issues affecting the city. In 2019, the festival attracted a quarter of a million people with a theme of the 'green city':

> Oh Munich, you green city! Granted, when you think of Munich, the green city might not be the first association. The Oktoberfest, Kaufingerstraße and busy underground trains and streets come to mind first. A picture shaped by asphalt, hardly a trace of green. Yet Munich has all sorts of green spaces to offer. And how great they are! The English Garden, for example, is one of the largest inner-city green spaces in the world. Furthermore, the Isar flows like a kind of blue-green lifeline across the city and allows it to bloom and flourish on the Flaucher. Lovingly designed parks and gardens extend in all directions – in short: the meadows are there, you just have to know where.
>
> For this reason 'Green City' is this year's motto of the Streetlife Festival. It is both a confession and an appeal. A commitment to the fact that we can perceive Munich as a liveable city with many poles of calm and an appeal to do this more often. Green spaces can be found. You can be used. You can be created. So come with us on a journey through the city and learn to see it with different eyes.
>
> Get to know Munich as a green city!
>
> (Streetlife Festival 2021)

The festival takes over two large public spaces, Leopoldstraße and the Ludwigstraße and mixes traditional aspects of festivals such as music stages and food stalls with exhibition-style booths and stands, as well as talks and presentations. There are eight separate music stages, showcasing diverse music from indie-rock to salsa and hip-hop, and the programming of the festival's spaces aims to bring together the hedonistic pleasures of attending a festival, with the organiser's education aims:

> Climate change and festival.
>
> Not necessarily the easiest combination. Isn't this about strolling, dancing, having fun? Definitely! And yet: If we want a good life in the future, we have to start together NOW. The Bavarian Climate Alliance shows how this could work with a large, green installation on Odeonsplatz.
>
> Let's go!
>
> (Streetlife Festival 2021)

The Streetlife Festival is organised by Green City EV, a non-profit organisation who were founded in 1990 with the aim of making the city of Munich greener and more livable, by reducing the use of private motorised transport and reducing pollution, including the emissions of gases that contribute to climate change. Green City EV has around 25 full-time employees, but additionally draws on the skills and effort of more than 2,000 volunteers to support its work. They organise more than 150 events and marketing campaigns every year with the aim of influencing politicians, businesses and residents. Streetlife is their largest event.

Image 14.1 Munich Streetlife Festival

Study activity

Do you think a festival format is appropriate for a serious educational cause? Look at the programmes of festivals from your country and consider how you could include pro-sustainability messages within the events. Can you identify any festivals where this is already happening?

14.3.3 Social impacts of events

There has been a relatively small amount of research into the social impacts of events, when compared with the wealth of studies on economic and environmental impacts. However, all events, not just cultural events, take place in social and cultural contexts that differ from event to event and location to location. Understanding the social implications of producing an event in a particular location is key to managing its impacts. Measurements of social impacts are usually constructed from resident perceptions of those impacts, rather than through an objective measure, due to the complexity of measuring subjective factors. Additionally, most social impact studies have been carried out into one-off events, or single occurrences of a serial event (Wallstam *et al.* 2020). This complexity makes it difficult for event managers to develop an objective social impact assessment methodology, and suggests that a conceptual approach is needed which identifies broad areas of impacts.

Whilst most measurements of social impacts on a community assess the negative implications of hosting an event, Ferdinand *et al.* (2016) point out that events also serve an important positive function in contemporary society; they mark significant life events and form part of the texture of daily life. The increasing demands of work, the isolating impacts of modern media and the changing of traditional family structures have all contributed to a reduction in opportunities for social interaction. Events at the community level, and those which involve communities in their planning and execution, can therefore fulfil important human needs for association and friendship.

Small (2007) conceptualises the social impacts of an event as shown in Figure 14.3.

- *Inconvenience* – This relates to the impact of hosting an event on the day-to-day lives of a community. It includes such factors as reduced parking availability, traffic congestion, increased queuing time in local shops, and extra noise and litter.
- *Community identity and cohesion* – This element is the extent to which an event increases feelings of togetherness and identity within a community. Events which are based on authentically local cultural practices, for example, will often increase residents' feelings of identity and cohesion.
- *Personal frustration* – This is the extent to which individual members of a community feel personally impacted by an event. Residents affected in this way feel that they are less important than event attendees during the event period and may therefore be resentful towards the event itself.
- *Entertainment and socialisation opportunities* – This identifies the extra opportunities for entertainment and social interaction that are available to residents due to the presence of an event. These opportunities can come from attending the event itself or from secondary effects in the community, such as increased numbers of tourists.
- *Community growth and development* – This element summarises the opportunities for skills development and other improving activities that become available to a community through hosting an event. This impact can be achieved through community involvement in the planning stages of an event as well as through participating in event-related activities, such as volunteering.
- *Behavioural consequences* – These are the new behaviours that can be introduced into a community through hosting an event. They can include increases in crime and vandalism, for example.

Figure 14.3 Small's social impact model
Source: Small (2007)

The social impacts of the Mangaung African Cultural Festival

Location: Bloemfontein, South Africa
Event type: Festival
Attendees: 140,000
Website: www.facebook.com/OfficialMacufe/

The Mangaung Cultural Festival (MACUFE) is one of Africa's largest cultural events and takes place every year in the city of Bloemfontein, in the Free State Province of South Africa. MACUFE is a ten-day long festival with a mixed cultural programme that focuses on African culture. The event includes performances such as live jazz, gospel choirs, stand-up comedy and fashion shows.

These take places in various venues across the city over the ten-day festival period. As well as cultural events like these, the festival also hosts sports events, including the Sparta Macufe football competition and an arts and crafts market. The festival was launched in 1997 with 30,000 attendees, but now attracts more than 140,000 visitors annually.

Ahead of its 2019 edition, the festival organisers explained that:

> MACUFE is to be the biggest, most culturally balanced showcase of African Arts and Culture in the world. . . True to its African identity a 1½ hours musical collaboration between South African and Congolese artists will be showcased during the festival.
>
> (Macufe 2019)

Scholtz *et al.* (2019) carried out research into the social impacts of MACUFE, in order to investigate the sustainability of the event from the perspectives of the residents of its host city of Bloemfontein. The city had launched the event in 1997 in part to attract more tourists to the area, which lacked significant tourist attractions, and to support local economic development, as well as to promote social cohesion in the area by celebrating African culture. Residents of the city were approached in public places near to the festival's venues, and asked to complete a questionnaire, and 452 residents were included in the survey.

Scholtz *et al.* (2019) identified four different factors that influenced residents' perceptions of the social impacts of the Mangaung Cultural Festival. The first factor was *community enhancement*. This included aspects of the festival's impacts such as increases in local pride, improvements to living standards in the area, improvements to the maintenance of local facilities and improvements in the image of the city. The second factor was *community degradation*. This factor related to issues such as noise, problem drinking and drug use, littering, local price inflation, disruptive behaviour and overcrowding. Thirdly, the factor of *tourism growth* was identified as an important influence on resident perceptions of social impacts. This factor included issues such as an increase in tourist numbers, increased visits from friends and family and extra revenue for local businesses. The final factor that was identified was *increased public spending and interaction*. This factor related to an increase in attention to the area from local government and included issues such as increases in funding for community activities, improvements to the appearance of the area, and increased participation in community activities.

The research found that *community degradation* was the most important factor influencing how residents felt about the social impacts of the festival, highlighting that the negative impacts of the festival were undermining its sustainability, from a social perspective, even though it continues to grow in terms of revenues and attendees. This has important implications for the future of the festival, because if local people stop supporting the event, this will lead to antagonism and resistance, and the eventual withdrawal of popular and political support for the event.

Study activity

Using Small's social impact model, analyse the information in Case Study 14.3. How can you categorise the negative social impacts according to Small's model and how could you develop strategies to achieve more positive outcomes?

14.4 Measuring impacts and evaluating events

To understand the impacts of an event fully, it is necessary to carry out an evaluation. This is a process of checking performance against a set of predefined criteria. It is the method by which you measure the success of an event and is the first stage of the planning process for the next event. Brown *et al.* (2015) give 11 reasons why evaluating events is necessary. It enables the event manager to:

- Justify the event
- Build legitimacy
- Assign value/worth as assets
- Aid in planning/design/marketing
- Solve problems
- Clarify logic and goals
- Improve management systems
- Improve competitiveness
- Stay 'on track'
- Be successful
- Determine outcomes/impacts

Evaluation should be an ongoing process that is built into the management of an event, and it should draw on a number of quantitative and qualitative sources of data. Some areas of evaluation require both kinds of data in order to arrive at a holistic understanding of a particular set of impacts. Evaluation has also been described in terms of its relationship to impact assessment, with Getz (2019) highlighting four areas where impact assessment and event evaluation share concerns:

1 Forecasting the impact of an event, often through a feasibility study.
2 Post-event impact assessment focusing on the achievement of targets and identification of impacts.
3 Strategic impact assessment, involving the forecasting of multiple impact scenarios, and the choices between them.
4 Retrospective assessment of impacts, allowing for the more broad or long-term impacts of events to be assessed.

We can see from Table 14.5 that evaluation requires the synthesis of information from three perspectives, and it is only by combining these three perspectives that a systematic evaluation can be conducted (see Figure 14.4).

Table 14.6 categorises sets of data into each of these three perspectives and suggests methodologies for collecting this information.

Table 14.5 Evaluation data sources
Source: Adapted from Shone and Parry (2010: 246)

Quantitative data	Qualitative data
Attendee statistics, including market segmentation data	Attendee perceptions
Sales figures	Interviews with attendees and staff
Financial reports and accounts	Management notes and commentary
Economic impact analysis	Social impact analysis
Environmental impact analysis	Environmental impact analysis
Social impact analysis	

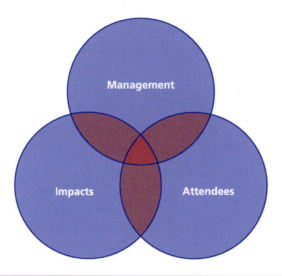

Figure 14.4 Perspectives in event evaluation

Table 14.6 Evaluation data sets

Evaluation perspective	Data sets	Suitable methodologies
Management	Financial information	Audit of financial records and accounts
	Attendee statistics, including market segmentation data	Analysis of booking data Attendee survey

Evaluation perspective	Data sets	Suitable methodologies
	Management notes and commentary	Analysis of meeting records and staff communications Interviews with management staff
	Staff perceptions of the event	Interviews with staff Staff surveys
Attendees	Attendee perceptions of the event	Interviews Surveys Analysis of social media related to the event
Impacts	Economic impacts	Quantitative economic impact analysis
	Environmental impacts	Quantitative and qualitative environmental impact analysis
	Social impacts	Quantitative and qualitative social impact analysis

14.5 Sustainable events

Driven by a combination of consumer demand and government regulation, as well as innovations from within the industry, the events industry has begun to focus much more on issues associated with sustainability. This has led to a proliferation of terms to describe this trend, but no universally accepted definition of what a sustainable event is. This lack of a definition can lead to difficulties in analysing these events, and problems for event managers who are searching for best practice to help them produce them. Some of the terms that are used to describe them include:

- Carbon neutral events
- Eco-events
- Eco-friendly events
- Green events
- Circular events
- Responsible events
- Sustainable events

Event managers have ethical and, increasingly, legal responsibilities to produce events that are 'socially, culturally and environmentally responsible' (Getz 2009: 70). They also have responsibilities to their colleagues and stakeholders that relate to the health of their own organisation. Getz (2009: 70) goes on to state, 'Sustainable events are those which maximise benefits in each of these categories while minimising negative impacts; sustainable events are those which can endure indefinitely without consuming or spoiling the resources upon which they depend, including the vital resource base of community goodwill and support'.

The most widely quoted definition of 'sustainability' was set out by the United Nations World Commission on Environment and Development after the Rio Earth Summit in 1992: 'Sustainable development is development that meets the needs of the present without compromising the ability of future generations to meet their own needs' (UNCED 1992: 1.1). This overarching definition is now applied to many aspects of human activity, including business, urban planning, policy development and, increasingly, events management. In recent years, growing acceptance of the probability of catastrophic climate change, as well as research into the social and cultural aspects of event impacts, has forced the events industry to reflect on its sustainability as a whole as well as the sustainability of individual events and event organisations. This reflection has prompted the development of new industry standards and awards, as well as the growth of a new kind of 'green event', defined by Laing and Frost (2010: 262) as an event that 'has a sustainability policy or incorporates sustainable practices into its management and operations'.

In tandem with this, however, concerns have arisen about 'greenwashing'. This terms describes a process where an event will be promoted using messages connected to sustainability, perhaps involving easy-to-obtain certification of sustainability 'standards', in order to attract attendees for whom considerations about the sustainability of events influence their choices about which events to attend (Anderton, 2018). This is an issue which is particularly noticeable in the music festivals sector, where promoters compete aggressively to attract young audiences, who are notably environment conscious. This is a real challenge for music festivals, where the nature of the events, involving high travel intensities, waste problems and internationally mobile artists creates significant tensions in terms of designing and promoting sustainable events (Brennan *et al.* 2019). Of course, many events in other sectors present problems for sustainable development, especially in terms of carbon emissions. The United Nations Sustainable Development Goal 13, which calls for urgent action to tackle climate change, has a clear focus on reducing emissions associated with transport, but Dornier (2021) found that French event agencies faced barriers to supporting this goal, not least their tendency to organise events that involved flights.

Since 1992, the media, governments, interest groups and citizens have increasingly focused on issues of sustainability, and in particular on those issues associated with the environment and climate change. In these cases, most attention has been paid to the issue of resource use, especially the depletion of natural resources and the use of fossil fuels in transport and industry. To achieve the targets set by the Intergovernmental Panel on Climate Change, we need to reduce our global carbon emissions by 85% by 2050, compared to 1990 levels. However, between 1990 and 2019, annual global carbon emissions in fact rose substantially, from 22 billion tons, to 36 billion tons (Our World in Data, 2020). This pessimistic outlook for the global climate places a moral obligation on all citizens to act in a sustainable way, in order to allow future generations to live their lives in similarly favourable conditions to our own.

Although there is no international consensus on the relative national contributions to sustainable development and climate change reduction that should be made by each country, most governments have national policies on sustainable development. These policies relate to areas of government activity that directly impact on events management, such as transport policy, infrastructure development, energy and taxation. For instance, following the Stern Review of Climate Change Economics for the UK Treasury in 2006, the UK government passed a Climate Change Act that requires all businesses to report on their carbon emissions and sets new targets for businesses and local authorities in respect of their waste management (DECC 2008).

In addition to governments, two other external forces are driving the events industry towards greater sustainability: sponsors and consumers. Companies with a commitment to sustainability will seek to sponsor events that support this commitment and help them to broadcast it to a wider audience. The growth of corporate social responsibility (CSR) within corporations, and pressure from lobby groups, has meant that many large organisations now see sustainability as a core part of their brand and insist that this is reflected in the events they sponsor. CSR within the events industry itself, however, is still an emerging issue, with Richardson (2019) identifying very low levels of awareness of this concept with event organisers themselves. Changing consumer preferences also have a direct impact on event management, with potential customers refusing to attend some events because of a perceived lack of sustainability.

CASE STUDY 14.4

The challenges of holding sustainable events within historic buildings

Location: London, UK
Event type: Various
Attendees: Various

As historic buildings around the world struggle to conserve their built heritage, at the same time as securing their financial futures, more and more have turned to events as a way of generating new revenue. These buildings are not always lucky enough to be able to rely on generous benefactors, or owners, and public funding for heritage is often unreliable and hard to obtain. Supplementary sources of income from tourism, retail, hospitality and events can provide independent income that enables many of these buildings to survive.

Using events to generate revenue, however, presents the managers of these buildings with new challenges. Holding events leads to wear and tear and sometimes the venues need costly adaptations to be able to host events, including the installation of technology, accessibility measures and catering facilities. Additionally, the venues' stakeholders are often very conservative, and may not support frequent commercial activity in heritage settings, which they can see as conflicting with the 'values' of the properties. Despite these difficulties, managed correctly, events can make a contribution to the sustainable management of historic venues.

Turner and Kennell (2018) carried out a study in London, in the United Kingdom, to capture the perspectives of event managers and key stakeholders of historic venues. London is the centre of the UK's events industry and has a high number of historic sites and buildings, many of which present attractive venues for event organisers in the city. The research found that:

- Event managers within historic buildings took a very broad view of sustainability, in which financial considerations were only seen as one part, and as a means to support the long-term sustainability of the buildings.
- The social aspects of events were seen as vital for the social sustainability of the buildings, in contributing to the goals of making heritage accessible and available for communities to learn from.

Historic buildings face some very specific challenges in holding sustainable events, including: reliance on external suppliers for catering and technology, increasing the transport associated with the event; problems with installing and operating reliable Wi-Fi, making it hard to make events paperless; problems with energy efficiency due to poor building insulation, temperature and humidity requirements, and regulations that prevent a lot of physical improvements to the fabric of the buildings.

Study activity

Research the availability of event venues within historic buildings in your town or city. What kinds of events do these venues host? Do they make claims about sustainability in their marketing materials, or on their websites? Using the knowledge from Case Study 14.4, what recommendations could you make to event managers in these venues, to help them to produce more sustainable events?

14.6 Responsible events

As discussions of sustainable development and sustainable business have developed over the last 30 years, there has been a gradual realisation that sustainability cannot be achieved in any field through regulations and prohibitions. Although it is the role of governments to pass laws for the public good, and to take a long-term view on the development of society, approaches to sustainability that have relied on government action and the regulation of businesses have failed to generate sustainable development in any advanced economy. New thinking on sustainability emphasises the role of citizens and consumers in generating 'bottom-up' pressure on governments and companies to act more sustainably, and advocates for a more 'responsible' attitude towards sustainability see it as a goal to be achieved in partnership, and through education and dialogue, rather than through legislation (Musgrave 2011).

The 'responsibility' approach emphasises that it is people who are at the heart of sustainable development and that only by firstly educating, and then including, everyone within aspirations to become more sustainable can sustainable development be achieved. This means moving the focus towards inclusion, fairness, and the day-to-day aspects of taking individual and collective responsibility. In events terms, this places the responsibility on event organisers to include staff, customers and stakeholders in their sustainability efforts in a meaningful way, rather than setting out strategies and targets and waiting to see if they are achieved. Of course, for this to be successful, event attendees must also become 'responsible consumers' (Kumar and Dholakia 2020), who make decisions about which events to attend, and how to spend their money when they are there, in line with sustainable development principles. As many of the examples in this chapter have shown, events offer many opportunities for encouraging and promoting responsible consumption through the messages that they transmit, the practices that they endorse or require and the decisions that they make about their own supply chains and impacts.

Marvell (2018: 2) provides a definition of responsible events:

> Responsible events is not the same thing as sustainable events. Sustainability is the goal, a goal which can only be achieved by people taking responsibility, together with others, to achieve it. Responsible events is about taking responsibility for making events sustainable, it is about what people do to address the many specific challenges we face.

CASE STUDY 14.5

Guidelines for creating responsible sports events

Organisation: Council for Responsible Sport, USA
Event type: Sports
Attendees: Various

The Council for Responsible Sport is a not-for-profit organisation in the USA, whose member organisations have all adopted a specific framework for the evaluation of their events as 'responsible'. The mission of the organisation is:

> to provide objective, independent verification of the socially and environmentally responsible work event organisers are doing and to actively support event organisers who strive to make a difference in their communities.

Sports event organisations can apply to be certified through the 'certify framework', which is based on a set of Responsible Sports Standards. An evaluation of the organisation's work against these standards is carried out by an independent, third-party evaluator.

The council has produced guidelines for creating 'radically responsible' sports events, which are based on the following ten principles:

1 Simplify. Eliminate the unnecessary.
2 Vote with your purchases for a clean planet and wellbeing for all.
3 Get circular. Divert waste material from the landfill.
4 Be climate accountable. Measure and offset carbon emissions.
5 Power your event with clean energy. Support the transition to renewable sources of electricity.
6 Be more inclusive. Offer ways to help disadvantaged people overcome barriers to participation.
7 Collaborate to create a positive and lasting local impact.

8   Get organised. Prioritise, allocate capacity and measure performance.
9   Unify efforts under a comprehensive sustainability plan.
10   Integrate communications to build awareness.

The council explains that:

> The ten radically responsible things events do proposed here are based on ten years of observation and evaluation of many of the leading socially and environmentally aware events in the US and beyond by the Council for Responsible Sport and the many events that have embraced it. The word radical stems from the Latin for 'root', indicating getting down to the bottom of things. Radically responsible events, then, are committed to re-thinking their very structures in order to best align with what they most value about their communities and places.
>
> Source: Council for Responsible Sport (2019)

Study activity

Review the principles of 'radically responsible events' in Case Study 14.5. To what extent do you think these reflect a new understanding of responsibility in sustainable development?

Using these principles, carry out an evaluation of a local sport event in your town or city. Make use of the event's website and media reports about the event to find evidence of whether the event could be described as responsible using these criteria. What recommendations can you then make to the organisers to enhance the sustainability of their event in the future?

Industry voice

Jarno Stegeman, International Consultant in Sustainable Events, www.eventtutor.com

You can approach your event concept as if it is a story. There are certain components that make a story work. In the case of sustainable event management, you should include the following:

Audience

What does your audience expect of your event when they buy a ticket? What do they expect when they walk onto your event site? The event experience, or the event story, really comes to life when the tickets have been received (Yes! I'm going to this event!). The question then is: what do you tell your audience? How do you want them to perceive your event?

Picture the scene: an abandoned festival site littered with plastic cups, used napkins floating in the air, bins overflowing, and plastic water bottles sticking half-emerged out of the ground. You might think that that must have been a pretty awesome event! But I hope that from an event manager's point of view you look at this and come to the conclusion that your waste management plan wasn't really working. That what you had in mind, a clean event site, has not been achieved.

I work for A Greener Festival, a non-profit organisation dedicated to improving the sustainability of events, tours, venues, festivals and all live sector contributors (aGreenerFestival.com 2021).

In my role as assessor, I visited the 90,000-capacity Bonnaroo Music & Arts Festival in Tennessee, USA. Throughout the weekend the festival site was clean. Plenty of bins were scattered (in all the right places) around the site and behind these bins were volunteers. Trash talkers they were called, directing you to the correct bin every time you wanted to throw something away.

After each main stage performance an army of volunteers would clean the site. I interviewed a volunteer who picked up cigarette butts from the field. When I asked her why she did it she answered: 'We're all here to have a fantastic experience and I want to leave the site the way it was before we came here'. The expectations for the Bonnaroo experience were set by the organisation and the audience bought into it. So much so, the audience were happy to help.

Marketing communication

A marketing and communication strategy for an event plays a huge part in this. How you come across to your potential audience says a lot about who you are as an event, or as an event organisation. Is it just about creating a fun experience or are you willing to educate your audience on sustainability matters?

The ethos of The DoLaB, the organisation behind the Lightning in a Bottle (LIB) festival in California, USA, is all about inspiring individuals and creating a better society. Sustainable event management is very much at the core of their events and they clearly communicate this to their audience. The DoLaB is vocal about their initiatives and how their 25,000 LIB-fans can help them. The result is an incredible clean event site and a festival with fantastic environmental and social sustainability credentials.

Location

With your event concept in mind, you 'shop around' for event locations. Sometimes the concept comes first and sometimes the location comes first. Either way, you want to make sure that there is a natural fit between your event concept and your chosen location.

I was lucky enough to assess the sustainability efforts of Symbiosis Gathering, which took place at Woodward Reservoir in California, USA. It was a transformational festival, a festival where the audience could learn about personal development, ethics, a better society, healthy lifestyles, creativity and life itself.

Some participants had signed up for Permaculture classes, which started prior to the opening of the festival. Permaculture is about learning agricultural skills to become self-sufficient in a sustainable way. A location was needed where allotments could be created. Not every location allows you to organise such an event but from a sustainable development point of view, sharing knowledge, it really ticks a lot of boxes.

Stakeholders

And then there are the stakeholders. The main thing an event organiser should remember is that 'you are in the driving seat', you decide what goes on at your event. To make that decision easier you should consider implementing an environmental management system (EMS). This EMS allows you to work on your environmental policy. It is your environmental policy in which you stipulate what you expect from your stakeholders.

To clarify, an EMS is a set of procedures and practices that enable an event organisation to reduce its environmental impacts and increase its efficiency.

An environmental policy is the commitment from the organisation to work in accordance with government regulations and advice with regards to the environment.

An event organisation's environmental policy is based on an environmental review (basically a risk assessment of your event and the impact it has on the environment), applicable legislation, significant aspects such as new technology, funding and grants, and the organisation's objectives and targets (what does the organisation want to achieve with its sustainable policies?).

So, it is the organisation that decides what goes on at an event and it stipulates this in its environmental policy. Shambhala Music Festival in Canada is an example of this. The organisation has made a conscious decision not to have any corporate sponsors. A few years ago, Shambhala Festival in the UK (not the same organisation) decided to make their festival meat and fish free. In doing so both festivals sent a clear message to their audience about who they are and what they want to achieve by working with their chosen stakeholders.

My two cents. . .

Before you start implementing a sustainability strategy you need to ask yourself what you, your organisation and your event stand for. What is your story? How does sustainability sit within that story? Is it an integral part of the organisation's management and strategy or is it seen as an afterthought, an expense?

Once you have honest answers for that, you can set aims and objectives for your organisation and for your event. You can start writing your sustainable event story. Implementing sustainable ideas takes time. Think through what you want to do and be creative. Because if anything, sustainable event management really allows you to write a creative story!

14.7 Summary

In this chapter, a range of perspectives on the impacts of events has been covered. First, three different techniques for calculating economic impacts were explained. Second, the environmental impacts of events were explored. Finally, the social impacts of events were identified. In each of these sections, a case study was included to help readers see how these concepts can be applied in practice, while study activities gave readers the opportunity to develop their own expertise in these areas. The sections on sustainability and responsible events put these individual impacts into a broader context.

The events industry, like all other industrial sectors, will have to change and adapt as the consequences of Covid and climate crises play out over the next ten years. It is clear that the event managers of the future will have to possess skills in impact assessment and will need to be able to apply these in an environment of increasing ecological and social change.

Further reading

Holmes, K., Hughes, M. and Carlsen, J. (2015) *Events and Sustainability*, London: Routledge. A thorough overview of a range of issues associated with sustainability and events management, with international case studies for each chapter.

Pernecky, T. and Lück, M. (eds) (2017) *Events, Society and Sustainability: Critical and Contemporary Approaches*, London: Routledge. An edited collection bringing together multiple critical perspectives on the relationship between events and sustainability.

Serpahin, H. and Nolan, E. (eds) (2020) *Green Events and Green Tourism: An International Guide to Good Practice*, London: Routledge. An edited collection with a more practical focus, that includes international best practice examples from music and arts festivals and sports events.

Video links

'A Greener Festival': Making Greener Festivals: www.youtube.com/watch?v=wUTyDANxwZc
Economic Impact of the Cannes Film Festivals: www.youtube.com/watch?v=Geabrx2modg
EURO 2016: A Fun, Friendly and Responsible Event: www.youtube.com/watch?v=4zd1CgDWlS0

Weblinks

A Greener Festival: www.agreenerfestival.com/

The Economic Impacts of Premier League Football: www.premierleague.com/this-is-pl/the-premier-league/686502

The United Nations Sustainable Development Goals: https://sdgs.un.org/goals

References

Anderton, C. (2018) *Music Festivals in the UK: Beyond the Carnivalesque*, Abingdon: Routledge.

Boyle, D. and Simms, A. (2009) *The New Economics: A Bigger Picture*, London: Earthscan.

Brennan, M., Scott, J. C., Connelly, A. and Lawrence, G. (2019) Do music festival communities address environmental sustainability and how? A Scottish case study, *Popular Music*, 38 (2): 252–275.

Brown, S., Getz, D., Pettersson, R. and Wallstam, M. (2015) Event Evaluation: Definitions, Concepts and a State of the Art Review, *International Journal of Event and Festival Management*, 6 (2): 135–157.

Cabras, I., Lorusso, M. and Waehning, N. (2020) Measuring the Economic Contribution of Beer Festivals on Local Economies: The Case of York, United Kingdom, *International Journal of Tourism Research*, 22 (6): 739–750.

Carlsen, J. (2004) The Economics and Evaluation of Festivals and Events, in I. Yeoman, M. Robertson, J. Ali-Knight, S. Dummond and U. McMahon-Beattie (eds), *Festival and Events Management: An International Arts and Culture Perspective*, Oxford: Butterworth-Heinemann.

Chirieleison, C. and Scrucca, L. (2017) Event Sustainability and Transportation Policy: A Model-Based Cluster Analysis for a Cross-comparison of Hallmark Events, *Tourism Management Perspectives*, 24: 72–85.

Council for Responsible Sport (2019) *A Practical Guide for Hosting Radically Responsible Events*, Portland, OR: Council for Responsible Sport.

David, L. (2009) Environmental Impacts of Events, in R. Raj and J. Musgrave (eds), *Event Management and Sustainability*, Oxford: CABI.

Department for Energy and Climate Change (DECC) (2008) Climate Change Act 2008. Available at: http://www.legislation.gov.uk/ukpga/2008/27/contents [Accessed 1 November 2010].

Dornier, R. (2021) The Sustainability of French Event Companies: An Exploratory Study, *Worldwide Hospitality and Tourism Themes*, 13 (1): 22–23.

Ferdinand, N., Shaw, S. J. and Forsberg, E. (2017) Understanding International Events. In N. Ferdinand and P. Kitchen (eds) *Event Management: An International Approach* (2nd edn): 5–35, London: Sage.

Getz, D. (2007) *Events Studies*, Oxford: Butterworth-Heinemann.

Getz, D. (2019) Event Evaluation and Impact Assessment: Five Challenges. In J. Ambrecht, E. Lundberg and T. Andersson (eds) *A Research Agenda for Event Management*: 48–65, Cheltenham: Edward Elgar Publishing.

Hede, A.-M. (2008) Managing Special Events in the New Era of the Triple Bottom Line, *Event Management*, 11: 13–22.

Hussain, K., Kumar, J., Kannan, S. and Nor, M. M. (2017) Investigating the Size and Economic Value of the Business Tourist Market in Malaysia, *Event Management*, 21 (4): 497–514.

Kumar, B. and Dholakia, N. (2020) Firms Enabling Responsible Consumption: A Netnographic Approach, *Marketing Intelligence & Planning*. DOI:10.1108/MIP-09–2018–0387.

Laing, J. and Frost, W. (2010) How Green Was My Festival: Exploring Challenges and Opportunities Associated with Staging Green Events, *International Journal of Hospitality Management*, 29: 261–267.

Macufe (2019) About. Available at: www.facebook.com/OfficialMacufe/about/?ref=page_internal [Accessed 31 July 2022].

Mair, J. and Smith, A. (2021) Events and Sustainability: Why Making Events More Sustainable Is Not Enough, *Journal of Sustainable Tourism*. DOI:10.1080/09669582.2021.1942480.

Marvell, A. (2018) Student Experiences of Facilitating Knowledge Exchange: Developing an Understanding of Responsible Events Through Blog Writing, *Journal of Hospitality, Leisure, Sport & Tourism Education*, 23: 1–9.

Morgan, A. and Condliffe, S. (2006) Measuring the Economic Impacts of Convention Centre and Event Tourism: A Discussion of the Key Issues, *Journal of Convention and Event Tourism*, 8 (4): 81–100.

Musgrave, J. (2011) Moving Towards Responsible Events Management, *Worldwide Hospitality and Tourism Themes*, 3 (3): 258.

Oak View Group (2020) Economic Impact and Market Assessment. Available at: https://cooplive.com/wp-content/uploads/2020/06/Economic-Impact-and-Market-Assessment-Factsheet.pdf [Accessed 31 July 2022].

Our Word in Data (2020) CO_2 Emissions. Available at: https://ourworldindata.org/co2-emissions?country= [Accessed 31 July 2022].

Richardson, N. (2019) Corporate Social Responsibility or Sustainability in Music Festivals, *International Journal of Organizational Analysis*, 27 (5): 1257–1273.

Rotheroe, N. and Richards, A. (2007) Social Return on Investment and Social Enterprise: Transparent Accountability for Sustainable Development, *Social Enterprise Journal*, 3 (1): 31–48.

Scholtz, M., Viviers, P. A. and Maputsoe, L. (2019) Understanding the Residents' Social Impact Perceptions of an African Cultural Festival: The Case of Macufe, *Journal of Tourism and Cultural Change*, 17 (2): 166–185.

Shone, A. and Parry, B. (2010) *Successful Event Management: A Practical Handbook* (3rd edn), Andover: Cengage.

Small, K. (2007) Social Dimensions of Community Festivals: An Application of Factor Analysis in the Development of the Social Impact Perception (SIP) Scale, *Event Management*, 11: 45–55.

Streetlife Festival (2020) Streetlife Festival. Available at: www.streetlife-festival.de/ [Accessed 31 July 2022].

Tribe, J. (2005) *The Economics of Recreation, Leisure and Tourism* (3rd edn), Oxford: Butterworth-Heinemann.

Turner, Z. and Kennell, J. (2018) The Role of Sustainable Events in the Management of Historic Buildings, *Sustainability*, 10 (11): 3884.

UNCED (United Nations Commission on Environment and Development) (1992) Our Common Future. Available at: http://www.un-documents.net/ocf-02.htm [Accessed 1 November 2010].

United Nations (2015) Transforming Our World: The 2030 Agenda for Sustainable Development: Preamble and Declaration. Available at: https://sustainabledevelopment.un.org/post2015/transformingourworld [Accessed 31 July 2022].

Wallstam, M., Ioannides, D. and Pettersson, R. (2020) Evaluating the Social Impacts of Events: In Search of Unified Indicators for Effective Policymaking, *Journal of Policy Research in Tourism, Leisure and Events*, 12 (2): 122–141.

Chapter 15

Events and the media

Contents

DOI: 10.4324/9781003102878-15

15.1 Aims

By the end of this chapter, students will be able to:

- define event media
- understand the role of the media in modern events
- identify what is required to manage media coverage of events
- predict the challenges inherent in modern coverage of events.

15.2 Introduction

This chapter focuses on media coverage as a mediated reality between those directly involved in an event and its wider stakeholders. Media coverage has been responsible for revitalising certain events and even re-engineering how events are organised and delivered. Media coverage not only increases sponsorship exposure among a much wider audience but significantly shapes international perceptions of events, resulting in important new challenges to their planning, management, delivery and legacies. In some cases, it can overshadow the main event objectives, and even 'hijack' the impact of their planned outcomes. However, many of the challenges that event planners face in obtaining media coverage, whatever the size of the event, can be overcome, and an attempt to understand how the media operates might well contribute to a more successful event. Given the proliferation in the number of available media outlets, understanding the media has never been more important, or more challenging. However, this also presents many more opportunities for event managers.

Event managers face an increasingly challenging global media environment, irrespective of geographical location, and they cannot ignore the importance of being effective managers of the media. Like it or not, the media plays an important role in our lives generally and we have no option but to work closely with the media, and to learn how they operate. There has been a proliferation of media training courses, many of them run by former journalists and broadcasters. The increased fragmentation of the media in general means that there are many more points of contact for event planners to consider. They must also be proficient with social media platforms, such as Facebook, Instagram, Twitter and YouTube, which present fresh opportunities and challenges. They must bear in mind that the media have the potential to make or break an event, so they should understand how to make best use of this influence, while at the same time ensuring that it does not destroy the reputation of an event.

The media, while very powerful and hungry for stories, works in a particular way, so an understanding of its rituals and procedures should lead to a much stronger mutual working relationship. It is therefore vital to understand all aspects of the media, its key players and the roles they occupy. The event team should make informing the media an important part of its overall tasks, in an attempt to maintain interest in the run-up to an event and during its staging, and should even consider employing a media specialist if the budget allows. There should also be a plan to deal with any stories that might damage the reputation and standing of the event, with crisis management built into the overall event planning process.

15.3 What is the media?

The media is defined as any communication medium that is designed and managed by an owner with the aim of informing or entertaining an audience (Katz 2019). Also referred to as the mass media, it is a form of communication that operates on a large scale, reaching and involving most people in society. Originally, the written word was the most effective way of communicating with an audience, but this was superseded by the arrival of radio and television. Distinctions were then made between print and electronic media. However, the introduction of web-based technology has led to many print newspapers being replaced by web versions (Katz 2019). Many newspapers globally have closed and many more are now facing closure as their sales plummet. Those that have embraced new technology are thriving and the immediacy of the web means that they often require more copy since they constantly update their stories.

There is much discussion about what the media is, and the elements shown in Table 15.1 (adapted from Katz 2019) are somewhat different from those itemised by McQuail (2002), who suggests that the media consists of newspapers, magazines, film, radio, television and recorded music. To this, we must add social media, such as Facebook, Instagram, Pin and Twitter, which offer opportunities to events managers to pass information on to their stakeholders, as will be discussed in more detail later in this chapter.

Newspapers and TV stations, in particular, invest heavily in their websites, as they are important platforms which require a constant supply of stories and regular updating. For many people, the media fills a large part of their social and leisure time, so the stories and images relayed are highly influential. It is the role of the media to convey information and entertainment to a variety of audiences, ranging from individuals to companies and other organisations (Katz 2019). While the media is not always seen as a positive force in advanced societies, and it is often considered too powerful, it cannot be ignored. It communicates with millions of people, as shown in the 2010 World Cup (Van Niekerk and Getz 2019), and it has the potential to change their attitudes towards specific events. It is worth considering the various components of the media in order to establish which represents the best choice when looking to communicate with an event audience. It is not uncommon for the media to take a positive approach to an event, and this message can be powerful and far-reaching.

15.3.1 Television

Television is possibly the most powerful of all media, given the size of the audience it can reach and the fact that it is viewed on demand not only on television sets, but also on portable devices and mobile phones. Some television stations are owned by the state, and as a general rule they do not attract advertising revenue, whereas others are owned by private companies and usually generate income from advertising and sponsorship. The majority of these stations are

---

Table 15.1 Components of the media
Source: Adapted from Katz (2019)

Print media	Electronic media	Social media
Newspapers	Television	Facebook
Magazines	Radio	Twitter
Outdoor billboards	Internet	Blogs
Direct mail	Podcasts	Instagram

viewed predominantly in their countries of origin, so they usually target the domestic market, although some programmes are viewed in more than one country.

Satellite television companies are generally multi-country and tend to specialise in specific areas, such as music, news and sports. Event managers send information to television news programmes or specialist programmes in order to publicise their events. In some cases, they might secure a television interview, although this is advisable only if they are competent and feel confident that they will be able to hold their own with the interviewer (Baines *et al.* 2005).

It is perhaps harder to gain publicity on television than in any other media, but that should not put off the ambitious event manager, as the sheer size of the audience means that the event may well receive a significant and instant boost if it *is* covered on TV. Where an event receives coverage in the media, it is possible to track increased 'hits' on their website and social media channels.

15.3.2 Radio

The number of private radio stations has grown significantly where the advancement of technology means that it is much easier and possibly cheaper to set up new radio channels. Most countries also have national radio stations that are usually aimed at specific target markets. A private commercial station tends to look for news items to fit into its hourly bulletins, with local stations concentrating on local events. Event managers should look to establish links with their local stations, and even target specific programmes or presenters, as they offer a targeted audience and can deliver instant news. This is especially useful if attendees need to be given last-minute information, for instance about traffic delays or congestion near the event.

15.3.3 Newspapers

There are significant differences in the availability of national and local newspapers, depending on the country. For instance, in the USA, there are many regional newspapers; whereas in the UK, national tabloids enjoy much wider circulations than local newspapers. All newspapers attempt to inform and entertain their readers through print and photographs. While they generate some revenue through direct sales, their main income comes from advertising, so they cannot afford to offend the companies and organisations that buy advertising space. Online newspapers update their stories frequently and have a greater need for new stories.

15.3.4 Magazines

It is important to recognise the two broad categories of magazine: consumer magazines, aimed predominantly at individuals; and trade magazines, which are read mainly by people who work in a particular business area. Event managers tend to make use of both categories to promote their events: for instance, details of a music festival might appear in both *NME* and in trade magazines aimed at the catering industry. All magazines produce reader data and media packs on their websites to encourage companies to buy advertising space, and these are useful for the event manager to check whether the attendee profile of their event matches that of some of the magazine readers.

15.3.5 Social networking sites

The proliferation of social media opportunities presents a number of challenges for event managers and it is imperative to be an innovator and embrace social media. Social networking sites – such as Facebook, LinkedIn, Instagram and Twitter – offer important ways of communicating with stakeholder groups and are now essential. According to the Sports Business Group report in 2015, Manchester United FC had just over 4 million Twitter followers, whereas Real Madrid and FC Barcelona had 14.4 million and 13.8 million. By March 2021 this had increased to 22.4 million for Manchester United. However, Real Madrid has a staggering 95.8 million Instagram followers and Barcelona 94.3 million. These sites bring together like-minded people and allow them to maintain dialogue with family, friends or business associates. Companies are increasingly using these sites to build contact lists of people who are interested in particular events or products. Glastonbury Festival also has around 580,000 Twitter followers and 700,000 followers on its official Facebook page. These sorts of figures are very attractive to sponsors and advertisers, and while they generate additional income, these outlets are also important for conveying messages to key stakeholders.

15.4 The role of the media in events management

When considering the media and events management, we must first look at the media's impact on society as a whole. A news story has the potential to reach millions of people within a very short period of time. A video on a social network site can reach millions in just a few days. Such is the power of the media that political groups are increasingly using it to inform the public of their activities. In terms of events management, the media plays a significant role in informing stakeholder groups about the importance of events, while at the same time making some events the focus of their stories. The 2010 Commonwealth Games in Delhi were dominated by media stories of poor facilities and problems with stadium management, even though, in reality, this was a relatively successful event in a developing country. The event organisers could have been more prepared to deal with the media and create more positive content to share with the world's media.

It might be argued that event managers are in competition with each other in pursuit of media coverage to increase interest in, or encourage people to attend, their events. The fact is that the events industry needs the media to help make events more prominent and increase awareness levels. With heightened awareness, there is a greater chance of enhanced ticket sales. With the increase in satellite communication, the media is able to transfer information about events instantly all around the world to media partners in other countries. Bowdin *et al.* (2010) even suggest that some events may be created for media consumption, and that a TV audience may dwarf the number of attendees. They then suggest that 'integration of the event with the media provides greater exposure to the event' (Bowdin *et al.* 2010: 638), which means that if the event organisers treat the media as potential partners, the latter will be more likely to be supportive.

The goal of developing relationships with the media is, therefore, to generate publicity, which Kitchen (1997: 7) states is 'information from an outside source used by the news media based on its news value or information perceived by the media as relevant to its audiences'. When the media endorses information in this way, it improves the event's relationship with its target audience. Even murderous regimes have understood the importance of utilising the power of the media: for instance, in 1978, the Argentinian military dictatorship hired a leading US public relations agency to improve its public image in the run-up to the FIFA World Cup.

15.4.1 Media events

A media event is either planned specifically to appeal to the media or simply receives extensive coverage because various media outlets feel it will be of interest to their audiences. While it is difficult to manufacture a media event, recognising when this happens is critical and might even form part of an overall plan for dealing with the media. These events are usually significant, sometimes on a global scale. They have been called 'a unique media genre that results when television's visual and narrative power taps into public fascination with a story that transcends daily experience' (Rivenburgh 2002: 32). People feel compelled to watch such an event, and in many cases broadcasters will adjust their schedules in order to cover it and audiences will adjust theirs in order to see it. One example is when a national sports team progresses into the final of a major tournament. Even though the rights to broadcast the match might be owned by one key media supplier, others will still cover the story in depth.

15.4.2 Media rights

Media companies often pay a premium to secure the rights for a particular event and compete with their rivals to secure these exclusive rights. The value of these broadcasting agreements is based on the amount of interest that such events generate among a television audience (which, for many major events, is likely to be a global audience). In the case of a major music festival, the media company that pays for exclusive broadcasting coverage will also invest heavily in promoting its involvement in the event and producing additional programmes in order to maximise the return on their investment. For instance, it might make a programme about setting up the event or one that shows its history. This programme might then hold a competition in which audience members can win tickets for the event or meet performers. This means that event organisers must be open to collaboration and see these extra events as important for improving awareness.

When a media company pays for exclusivity, it is important that the event manager does not breach the conditions of their agreement and allow rival broadcasters too much access. So, for instance, they should be careful not to leak stories to rival media groups or even answer every question that they receive about the event.

In order to improve the ratings for its main coverage of an event, a television company might include features in its main news programming. This reflects the importance of the event to the broadcasting organisation, rather than its importance to a wider audience, but it can serve to increase the event's popularity.

Study activity

For the following day-long events, suggest news stories that you think will be covered by the media. You should focus on participants, sponsors, attendees and spectators, and should suggest which media outlets might be interested in the stories.

1 A local music festival, with 50 acts, whose aim is to promote multiculturalism in the community.
2 An international trade fair for food and drink companies, with at least 40 countries represented.
3 A 5-kilometre fun run in fancy dress to raise money for a charity of your choice.

15.5 The media and links to stakeholders

Table 15.2 identifies stakeholder groups that are important to event managers. Each of these stakeholders can influence the outcome of an event, so the event manager must attempt to communicate with all of them. As it is difficult and resource-intensive for the event manager to contact such a wide range of stakeholders individually, they can provide information to the media in the hope that this will then be shared with the wider stakeholder group. While the media is listed as just one of a number of stakeholder groups in the table, it is a crucial resource for event managers as it is used to influence all of the other groups. Event managers must also be aware of the credibility of the media outlets that they use and ensure that the media audience is not too different from their own target audience. Arts events are very careful about their choice of media partners as they have to protect the image of their events.

Event organisers have access to a range of communication tools with which they can reach the most important stakeholder groups. It may well be impossible to communicate directly with all of the stakeholder groups listed in Table 15.2, perhaps due to budget or time constraints, so it is essential to prioritise them on the basis of their importance to the event. For large groups (such as attendees), media with a broad reach (such as television and newspapers) may be most effective, and these media might also communicate a message to other stakeholder groups.

However, event managers need to ensure that they always communicate with particular stakeholder groups in the most appropriate way, which means tailoring messages to specific audiences. For instance, it is probably advisable to contact government departments personally – through letters and an invitation for face-to-face meetings. Many media organisations – especially local radio stations and newspapers – are increasingly reliant on receiving news rather than using their own journalists to find it, so they are more likely to reproduce press releases. One way of engaging the media with a new event or a mass participation event is to invite members of the media to take part in the event. Journalists who are offered a place in a celebrity golf or football day or are invited to take part in a festival or carnival are more likely to cover the event, which will usually lead to more media coverage.

Table 15.2 Stakeholder groups and communication tools

Stakeholder groups	Communication tools
Attendees at the event (past, present or future)	Television, social media, radio
Event suppliers/agents	Newspapers
Community (location of event)	Magazines
Media	Specialist publications
Financial community/investors	Website
Sponsors	Social media (Facebook, Twitter, etc.)
National/local government	Personal letters
Employees/volunteers	Meetings
Potential employees/volunteers	Newsletter
Opinion leaders or formers	Direct mail and social media

What are the key messages that an event organiser should be trying to get across to their stakeholders? For an event of your choice, identify the most important stakeholders and show which messages you should target at each stakeholder group, and which media you should use. Present this in a table format.

CASE STUDY 15.1

Working effectively with the media: All or Nothing and Hard Knocks – when the media moves in to cover the event

Such is the interest in sport, there is a growing the number of 'fly-on-the-wall' documentaries, which are likely to also become a feature of other events, such as music and cultural events in the future. Since the introduction of the Hard Knocks programme, and more recently the All or Nothing programme on television and streaming platforms, it has become apparent that the media are now prepared to pay significant amounts of money to cover the day-to-day running of sports clubs. Investing these large sums of money gives media companies the rights to use this behind-the-scenes material in television programmes and as part of their own publicity. These programmes have featured clubs in Brazil, Germany, England, the USA and New Zealand, with more planned in the future. This coincides with a proliferation of in-house coverage of events and a number of club channels, where skilled content creators offer a variety of stories about their events.

The question for the event management team is whether they should allow this level of access to their events, and what the potential advantages and disadvantages of this coverage are. That is assuming that their event is deemed worth covering by media companies. Will this level of publicity increase awareness of an event and make more people want to attend or engage more with the event? Will this coverage resonate with their existing followers and encourage them to continue attending in the future? These are important questions for the event manager to address with the brand managers, as there is risk of the brand being damaged. This is a growth area and one that should be considered carefully.

15.5.1 Working with journalists

Many event managers do not have experience of working closely with journalists. However, along with many other people, they may have preconceived ideas of what journalists are like. Many commentators talk of a new breed of journalist who could not be more different from the traditional reporter, who was forever in pursuit of a lead, knocking on doors and interviewing members of the public. These new journalists spend most of their time at their desks, trawling the internet and looking at Twitter leads to find the latest information that they need for their stories. This phenomenon presents new opportunities for any event organiser who is willing to provide the media with consistently good copy. Given the value of achieving widespread media coverage for events, event managers should do everything in their power to make the journalist's job as easy as possible by supplying them with high-quality material, and in some cases, aiming to be a friend of the press. Once a journalist starts to trust a particular source of information, he or she is likely to keep going back for more stories.

Since newspapers are still often produced both digitally and in print, there is an even greater demand for stories. Events are perfectly equipped to meet this demand, and frequently provide great news stories that are usually well received by the journalists' audiences. Developing effective long-term relationships with the media should, therefore, be the goal of every event manager.

15.5.2 Working with the media at an event

Given the importance of the media to the event organisers, it is vital to ensure that their needs are catered for at events. It is important to designate specific media areas where the reporters can produce the material that is needed for their particular medium. This usually entails setting up a press room with refreshments and perhaps even offering administrative support – all of which should make it easier for the journalists to write their (hopefully favourable) copy. Elsewhere, the media should be provided with photo opportunities and press passes that enable them to move around the venue with ease. A key feature of new stadiums is their investment in the media, with a main press area and even space for the many photographers who attend an event. Good Wi-Fi access is a must for the media at your event.

15.6 Media management

Getz and Fairley (2004) considered the management of media at four different sporting events in Australia. Their paper contained interesting observations about the means employed by event organisers to develop their relationships with the media, and these can serve as guidelines for other event managers:

1 Employ a media relations officer to feed stories to the media and create media interest.
2 Advertise in local magazines or newspapers, and especially in special interest magazines, to promote the event.
3 Develop an event website to provide information to the media and other stakeholders.
4 Host media-familiarising tours of the event.
5 Organise media events to involve the media more closely with the event.

6 Monitor all media coverage, possibly through an agency.
7 Keep sponsors regularly informed of media coverage.
8 Employ a professional camera operator to capture images.
9 Create video 'postcards' and stories to send to the media.
10 Employ a photographer to develop digital images to send to the media.
11 Develop long-term media relationships.

This is a crucial checklist for event managers and highlights areas where new skills or additional resources might be required because a number of these options may stretch the budgets of smaller events. It is important to recruit the right people for these tasks, since dealing with the media demands considerable experience and understanding of how the system works. Employing a media relations officer will probably represent a new cost for the event, but hiring such a specialist, like as a former journalist – someone who is comfortable dealing with the media and knows how to create stories – should show a return on the investment. There might even be an experienced media person who might volunteer for this role, in return for access to the event.

> ## Study activity
>
> How would you suggest an event manager might maximise coverage of their event in the media? Use Getz and Fairley's framework to help develop your answers.

15.6.1 Creating news stories

It is important to understand the relationship between the media and advertisers when submitting information to the former. Advertising revenue usually represents the largest income stream for a media organisation, especially a small-scale one, so placing an advert for an event in the local paper will not only provide information for the target audience but will help to build up a close, mutually beneficial relationship with the newspaper as well. Some publications also feature 'advertorials' – combined adverts and news stories. These are a useful way of increasing the column inches devoted to an event. After all, the newspaper's editor might decide that an event is worth only four lines and no photo on an inside page, rather than the front-page splash that the event organiser had expected. Nevertheless, an experienced media relations officer should understand that any amount of coverage is valuable and should also know how to measure its impact.

There will be several opportunities to work closely with the media during larger events, including tours to the venue to give journalists more insight into the event. The media also now make extensive use of websites to gather information, so setting one up should be a priority for any event manager. Obviously, the website should be carefully managed to ensure that it releases only the appropriate information to the media and other stakeholders.

The event organiser must collect and monitor data about all the media coverage that has been generated, either by members of the media themselves or through press releases. While this research can be carried out by the event team itself, it might be better managed by a specialist agency that has the resources to monitor global media coverage as well as local stories. Remember that an event such as the annual Nuremberg Toy Fair can receive media attention in around 100 different countries and it would be difficult to monitor global coverage from their base in Germany. It is also important for sponsors to be kept informed of any coverage that they have received, since sponsorship deals can sometimes be improved on the basis of early positive coverage.

To reiterate a valid point: event organisers should try to help the media as much as possible. For instance, an event is much more likely to receive a favourable write-up if the journalist is sent a pin-sharp digital image rather than a poor-quality photo (Getz and Fairley 2004). Video 'postcards' and stories are also useful tools for publicising an event. Some event managers might think that the media should incur the costs of producing such material, as they will be using it to fill their pages or their news bulletins. However, the initial outlay will be recouped many times over if the material forms the basis of a five-minute segment on a local news programme or a half-page feature in a newspaper.

The event manager should strive to produce media kits and press packs that give more information than a simple press release, and they should present it in a format that the media can use immediately (Shone and Parry 2019). This means employing people who can provide good content and who understand the media business.

15.6.2 Media and sponsorship

As we saw in Chapter 7, sponsorship is an important element in events management. While media organisations sometimes sponsor events and promote their links to them, they are not always willing to promote other event sponsors in their coverage. They will usually mention a title sponsor – if the event officially carries the name of that sponsor – but at other times they will instruct their camera operators to avoid showing a sponsor's name, particularly during interviews that take place with sponsors' names and logos in the background. Consequently, many sponsors' logos are only partially shown or are out of focus during TV coverage of events.

Why do the broadcasters go to such lengths to keep the sponsors' names out of shot? The answer is simply that they are trying to protect their own advertisers (if they are a commercial station) or are trying to prevent sponsors from gaining free air time and name awareness (if they are state-owned). When the NFL cover events in London, the stadium managers have to cover any location outside the stadium that might feature the name of a sponsor from a previous event. Nevertheless, sponsors will pay heavily for events that receive wide media coverage, as these give them golden opportunities to expose their names to a large audience.

There is clearly a link between the media and sponsorship, and the event manager must be aware of its importance. The aim of the event manager should be to gain widespread media coverage for their event and then to use that coverage to leverage better sponsorship deals. Having secured these deals, they should work with the sponsors to devise a plan for maximum media presence during the event. Of course, television coverage of an event like a music festival might also generate more interest in the event itself and encourage viewers to attend the following year.

Study activity

Pick three different events and look for the media packs that the event organisers prepare for the media. What do these media packs tell you about the event organiser?

If you are advising an event organiser about developing a media pack, what would you put in this pack, if you have a limited budget? Consider the importance of influencers and bloggers and how you will work with them.

You might want to consider the Press Center section on the website produced for the Nuremberg Toy Fair in Germany: www.spielwarenmesse.de/en/press/press-center

15.6.3 Media and logistics

One important consideration for an event manager is the area that is assigned to the media, because, as Bowdin *et al.* (2010) suggest, their presence might well be disruptive. This is particularly true when the arena has limited space, as is the case at many sporting events. How much space will be needed for technical support staff, and where will they stay if they need to be present at the event for more than one day? At mega-events, such as the Olympics, as many as 8,000 journalists might cover an event with only 2,000 participants (Horne 2007).

CASE STUDY 15.2

NBA and European football television contracts: Facebook and Amazon join the party

Many sporting events receive significant income through the sale of media rights. In most cases, the largest figure comes from television rights. Clearly, many events make for excellent television programmes that generate high viewing figures, so media companies are prepared to pay much more than the event organisers could possibly generate in ticket sales. Such is the value of these media deals that the broadcasters wield significant influence over the event organisers and even dictate when some events take place. For instance, Monday night football games – which are now so common in television schedules around the world – were initiated by media companies looking to fill a previously little-watched slot.

Many events are now timed to suit the largest global TV audiences, rather than the live attendees or even the local TV audience. This has certainly had an impact: several studies have shown that attendance at the event itself usually falls when a game is shown live on television (Borland and Macdonald 2003; Forrest *et al.* 2006; Buraimo *et al.* 2010).

The figures in Table 15.3 show that the television rights for the NBA were around $500,000 a year in 1980, but this has now risen to beyond $1 billion per year. This deal allows media companies to televise all of the games, and to show live action on internet channels or through mobile technology. It is around 20% higher than the previous deal and four times higher than the deal struck in 2001. It was unclear if the value of these deals would continue to rise or if media companies had reached their limits, but the latest round has shown another significant increase.

In 2008, the new TV deal for the English Premier Football League began. It was worth £1.7 billion over three years, covered 138 live matches, and was granted to Sky and Setanta, although the latter went bankrupt not long after the deal had been signed. While this deal is the highest for any football league in the world, it is still dwarfed by those negotiated by American sports. However, the new deal is now worth about £5.1 billion over three years, which puts it at a similar level to sports in the USA.

Table 15.3 NBA cable television contracts
Source: Inside Hoops (2011)

Year	Broadcaster(s)	Value of contract
1979–80 to 1981–82	USA	$1.5 million/3 years
1982–83 to 1983–84	USA/ESPN	$11 million/2 years
1984–85 to 1985–86	TBS	$20 million/2 years
1986–87 to 1987–88	TBS	$25 million/2 years
1988–89 to 1989–90	TBS/TNT	$50 million/2 years
1990–91 to 1993–94	TNT	$275 million/4 years
1994–95 to 1997–98	TNT/TBS	$397 million/4 years
1998–99 to 2001–02	TNT/TBS	$840 million/4 years
2002–03 to 2007–08	TNT	$2.2 billion/6 years
2008–09 to 2015–16	ABC/ESPN/TNT	$7.4 billion/8 years
2016–17 to 2025–26	ESPN/Turner	$2.6 billion annually

Like the NBA, the Premier League negotiates deals on behalf of all the clubs in the league. However, Spanish football clubs negotiate their own deals. This means that the two biggest clubs – Real Madrid and FC Barcelona – account for 43% of all football TV revenue in Spain, with the remaining 57% split between the other 16 clubs in the top division. This has recently been challenged by the Spanish government who feel that the revenue should be split more equitably, and are attempting to pass legislation.

Perhaps the key question, given the annual increase in payments for media rights, is just how high media companies might be prepared to go to secure exclusive rights to these major sporting events in the future. The fact that the media are now prepared to pay such huge amounts suggests that rights used to be sold far too cheaply, to the benefit of the media companies and the detriment of the clubs, so the price might well continue to rise. On the other hand, if TV deals have now peaked and start to decline, this will obviously have a significant impact on sporting events organisers, who have perhaps become too reliant on the media to finance their events. Certainly, organisers should not underestimate the importance of negotiating media deals and should have a clear idea of the value of their product to the media. The entry of major international brands such as Facebook and Amazon into the sports broadcasting market has increased the number of potential outlets, and added extra competition in the market. This has shown how valuable these new brands believe that the media coverage is, in that it will help them to raise awareness of their own brands in the global market, while others are also monitoring the success of these new deals. Amazon and Facebook have significant turnover and billions of customers between them. They see sport as part of their overall communications packages, and can also sell advertising and sponsorship on the back of these deals. To what extent they are prepared to be part of any future deals, and how much they are prepared to pay, will determine the future of media rights. There is an expectation that they will be able to outbid companies such as Sky, and the upcoming new deals will be very interesting for event managers.

Specialist press areas are created for many major events. In the case of major sporting events, such as the FIFA World Cup Final, journalists tend to occupy areas that are converted back to seating areas for spectators once the main event has concluded. In the case of the London Olympics the Media Centre was housed in the Orbit, a huge tower that was converted into a visitor centre after the Olympic Games with panoramic views across London.

15.7 The impact of media coverage on events

Media coverage – be it positive or negative – invariably has some impact on an event. Getz *et al.* (2007) found that many festival organisers in Australia and Sweden believed that the media had more impact than any other group of stakeholders. They also learned that the local media in Sweden was the most effective means of changing people's perception of a music festival (from negative to positive). The importance of generating goodwill for an event through the media is also a priority when local government has pledged its financial support to an event and needs positive feedback from the local community. In this case, communication with the community is almost entirely facilitated through media coverage. Event managers are turning to services offered by organisations such as www.eventimpacts.com to work out the impact of coverage on their events.

15.7.1 Valuing media coverage

Carlsen *et al.* (2001) highlight frequent criticism of the Australian government by rival political parties and the media, who often claim that events have lost money and have had negative rather than positive impacts. By contrast, positive media coverage can certainly contribute to the success of an event, and there are a number of ways of evaluating this. Such evaluation will help the event planner to understand the impact of media coverage and will provide data that can then be used for setting objectives in future event plans.

Perhaps the most commonly held view is that any story about an event in the media is free publicity and therefore promotes the event (Dwyer *et al.* 2001). The simplest way to evaluate this impact is to time the length of the report (if it is broadcast media) or to calculate the number of column inches (if the story appears in print). However, this technique has its critics, and it is certainly the crudest way of evaluating impact. The number of tweets about an event can also be measured, as well as visits to a website, and these present further evaluation tools for event managers.

Cutlip et al. (2005) suggest that the first stage in assessing impact should be to compare the number of messages sent to the media with how many of those messages subsequently appear in print or on TV (Broom 2012). The next stage uses general viewing or readership figures to calculate how many people were likely to have seen the messages. Finally, more targeted research is undertaken to ascertain how the messages influenced people's attitudes to the event.

McNamara (2005) suggests that various forms of research – surveys, interviews and focus groups – should be carried out before, during and after an event to assess its impact. However, perhaps the most frequently used method for evaluating coverage in the media is advertising equivalency (see Chapter 7 for details of this technique). This is of limited use, though, because it does not take into account the quality of the coverage and the extent to which it reaches the event's target group and stakeholders. Coverage in a specialist publication about music festivals with a readership of only 20,000 might impact on many more potential attendees than an article in a regional newspaper with a readership of 100,000. Here, it is vital to understand who the key event stakeholders are and how they might best be reached through the media.

Brassington and Pettitt (2013) suggest that media coverage should be monitored for its 'tone'. While this is a subjective way of measuring coverage, the main emphasis is on trying to gauge whether the coverage is 'favourable' and/or 'prominent'. The most effective means of testing the impact of this type of coverage is to undertake attitude research before and after an event to monitor any changes in attitude. A clear example of attitude measurement was the IPSOS survey (IPSOS 2010), which showed that Londoners' attitudes to hosting the 2012 Olympic Games had changed: by July 2010, 73% were in favour, compared with 69% four years earlier.

A study by Solves *et al.* (2018), in their work on the coverage of the Paralympic Games by the Spanish media, found that there was an increase in coverage of an additional 3,070 lines of news, 79 extra news items and 129 photos of the London Paralympic Games compared to the Beijing Games four years earlier in 2008. This is perhaps a clear indication of the value of media coverage of an event in the media.

15.7.2 Working with the events media

Anyone writing press or media releases must remember that the media are only interested in news stories: that is, any story that editors or producers believe will be of interest to their audiences. This is frustrating for event managers. Their primary goal might be to inform potential attendees of the start date for a festival, but the media will only be interested in a quirky detail relating to a group of volunteers or the venue. While this generates some publicity for the event, it does not contain the main message that the organisers wish to get across. It is also important to understand that there is never enough space to cover every aspect of every story, and the media are usually inundated with stories that they generate themselves or have been given via press releases.

Media coverage is very competitive, and a newspaper might not publish an article on an event if its leading competitor has already broken the story. Increasingly there is competition between different events for media coverage, as acknowledged by Polo and Gonzalez (2019) in their work on Spanish film festivals. The quality of information sent to the media may also result in a story not being published or broadcast. Unfortunately, many press releases are simply not newsworthy as they tend to read more like adverts for the event. If we consider trying to generate coverage for a music festival, then the story might not necessarily be the festival itself, but the fact that one of the groups consists of a group of high-profile actors. The story of the festival should flow naturally from this story, but the main emphasis will remain on the group. The fact that you have reduced the event's carbon footprint might not be considered newsworthy by a major newspaper, but a specialist publication might find it fascinating. The event manager must therefore understand the priorities and interests of various media in order to increase the chances of the story being covered and reaching the target audience.

15.7.3 How to write a news or press release

A news release is sent to TV and radio stations, while press releases provide information for newspapers and magazines and social media groups. It is important to follow certain principles when sending information to the media. The event manager should research all of the specialist publications that are likely to feature events, and should consider their exact requirements and the main points of contact.

The event team should be familiar with how a newsroom operates. A local radio station that broadcasts a news bulletin every hour usually employs only a handful of staff, so they are highly unlikely to answer phones minutes before the bulletin goes out on air. The newsroom is a busy, hectic place as deadlines approach, and, as ever, event managers should do everything in their power to make the journalists' lives easier. They should not pressurise editors to cover their stories, because in the media – in contrast to other business sectors – persistence usually does not pay off and it can create the wrong impression. If the editorial team do not think a story should be covered, then that is the end of the road for that story – at least until the next opportunity to publicise it arises.

If an event manager manages to secure coverage on radio or television, obviously they should make every effort to comply with the broadcaster's wishes. For instance, if a radio station wants to conduct an interview on its breakfast show and asks the event manager to be at the studio by 6am, it would be unwise for the event manager to ask if this could be changed to 8am. Attempting to dictate the schedule to a programme editor in this way will often result in the item being dropped altogether, meaning that the event manager loses precious free publicity as well as the opportunity to communicate information to key stakeholders.

Holden and Wilde (2007) devised a template that is generally suitable for press and news releases (but always make sure that you follow publications' and broadcasters' individual guidelines for press releases, if they have them):

Today's date

This allows the department receiving the press/news release to assess its newsworthiness. Never send out a release that was dated some time ago.

For immediate release

It goes without saying that you have sent this at the right time for it to be used. If the story is not ready to be released, do not send it.

Heading or headline

Your target publications will probably be better at writing headlines than you are, so anything you write here is likely to be changed, but it is still worth putting down something. Practise writing headlines of fewer than ten words, and *always* include the most important and interesting points.

First paragraph

Remember that the rest of the press release might not be used (or even read), so it is important that the main facts of the story are included in the first paragraph. It might read like a summary of the rest of the press release.

You should include the 5Ws: who, what, why, when and where:

- **Who** is the story about? (In this case the event, the team and/or the participants.)
- **What** are you going to do?
- **Why** are you going to do this?
- **When** will it happen? (It is important to provide dates and times.)
- **Where** will this event take place? (If the release is about an event that has already taken place, make this clear.)

Subsequent paragraphs

These expand on the basic information given in the first paragraph. However, try to limit the whole text to about one side of A4. If the publication/broadcaster needs more information, the editorial team will contact you. Remember that good communication is possible in very few words.

Include quotations

Try to include a quotation in the release. This could come from a participant at the event or from a member of the management team, but you should always ensure that the journalists who receive the press release are in no doubt about who is being quoted.

'Ends'
Centre this word at the end of the press release so that the journalist can see where it finishes.

Notes for editors
Here you can include some additional background information for the editor. You might re-emphasise the name of the event or its website address at this point.

Contact details
Make sure that the journalists can get hold of you easily if they need to follow up on the story. Ensure that your phone is always switched on: if an editor needs to check something and is unable to get hold of you, the chances are that they will drop the story. Include details of your website and politely suggest that the editor can find additional information there.

Photographs
Digital technology has made it much easier for everyone to produce professional-looking photographs. It is often worth including a photograph, but only if it is appropriate for your press release. Check with each publication which format they prefer. A recurring criticism is that photographs do not have sufficiently high resolution for print purposes. Remember that if the story is interesting, the publication might well send its own photographer to get a picture.

15.7.4 Avoiding problems with press and news releases

Compiling and sending out a press/news release is time consuming, so it is important to get it right. The following points should help the event manager to avoid some common mistakes when producing and distributing their releases.

15.7.4.1 An advert disguised as a release

It is natural for an event manager to want to advertise their event in the media, especially if they believe they can do so for a fraction of the cost of buying conventional advertising space. Consequently, the news release is often seen as a way of gaining maximum publicity for very little outlay. However, editorial staff will immediately throw such obviously self-serving releases straight in the bin or send the file to trash. The key to a successful release is to create a story that will be of interest to the publication's target audience while still containing a clear link to and information about the event itself.

15.7.4.2 Poorly constructed media releases

Event managers sometimes send out releases that contain mistakes, miss the publication's or broadcaster's deadline, or lack key information. Journalists are busy people, and they always have alternative stories to cover, so they will not accept these errors. Again, the release will be discarded.

15.7.4.3 Contact details are missing or incorrect

A significant amount of work goes into producing press and news releases, so it would be a terrible shame if all your effort succeeded in arousing the interest of an editorial team, only for them to be unable to get hold of you to follow up the story. Journalists work to tight deadlines, so if they cannot contact you easily and quickly, they will move on to something else.

15.7.4.4 The story has been used elsewhere

In an attempt to gain maximum coverage, many see it as standard practice to send the release to as many media contacts as possible. However, it is important to remember that some major publications will not cover a story that has already featured in the pages of a rival as it loses any feel of exclusivity and ceases to be a new story.

15.7.5 Holding a press conference

A press conference enables the event planner to assemble important members of the press, television and newspapers and facilitates a two-way flow of information. Imagine all of the most important media people in one place, all fighting to ask the key question before relaying the answer back to their readers, listeners or viewers. They will generate interest in the event and awareness levels will rise dramatically. It is a straightforward process and merely requires a venue that can comfortably accommodate all of the invited journalists, with a stage area for the event representatives. Increasingly there is an expectation that press conferences should be held online, which increases the chance of attracting overseas media coverage, and creating the right image is important, with the use of back-drops that promote the event brand.

However, we should not underestimate the amount of time that will need to be devoted to organising such an event, nor the skills and time required to answer all of the journalists' questions at the conference itself. Also, remember such conferences do impose costs on the media companies that agree to attend – they will have to dispatch camera crews, technicians and recording equipment, as well as their reporters – so it is vital not to waste their time with a poor presentation. If the ultimate goal is to persuade the general public that you are staging an important and professionally run event, then the first people you have to convince are the reporters. Thus, you should only ever arrange a press conference when you have something important to say – something that cannot be communicated in a press release.

You must also be realistic and objective about the importance of your event before arranging a press conference. They are usually worthwhile only for big, significant events. The media are likely to attend only if they believe they are going to come away with a major news story that will be of interest to their readers and viewers – so holding a press conference simply to announce the dates of an annual festival, for instance, will generally be a waste of time.

In some cases, such as when an event has received negative publicity, the event team might be desperate to call a press conference to give their side of the story. But you should always remember that you can never force the media to attend, so the story you have to tell must be of interest to them too.

15.8 Crisis management for event managers

The one thing that any event manager dreads is that something happens at their event that impacts on the safety of spectators and participants. While in most cases events run without problems, we must be aware of the damage to our reputation should a serious incident occur without a contingency for dealing with it. Crisis management (CM) planning begins with identifying crises – or 'known knowns' (Regester 2008; Horne 2007) – that might impact on an event. The next stage is to prepare a response, which will enable the event team to be ready for action should the worst happen. Crises will obviously be of interest to the media, and to other stakeholders, so the CM plan must contain key media outlets' contact details and draft press releases that, with some modifications, could be used immediately. These crisis communication plans will enable the event manager to 'deal with the media in a demanding situation' (Jefkins 1994: 52) and will hopefully prevent that 'demanding situation' from becoming a major controversy. If there is crowd disorder at a music festival, the event organisers should immediately inform the media that procedures are in place to deal with the situation and avoid injury to attendees. Of course, crowd disorder at a major festival is a great news story for the media, so they will not ignore it, but they cannot be allowed to think that it has occurred because of the organisers' negligence, as that could have disastrous consequences for the event owners. Feeding key information to the media might kill off the story before it has a chance to develop, and it also allows the event organisers to communicate with a wider audience to show that their event is professionally managed.

Regester (2008) suggests that an event organiser who reacts positively and decisively to a crisis situation might even be viewed in a more positive light once it is over. The message is quite simple for all event managers: make yourself accessible to the media and give your side of the story, as this will reduce the risk of journalists going to other sources for their information.

Study activity

There are crowd problems at the entrance to your event and ten people have been injured and taken to hospital. Thankfully, they are not seriously injured, but the press has taken an interest in the story and they are trying to blame your organisation for the incident. Some journalists are suggesting that you could have done more to prevent the overcrowding and a rumour is circulating that excessive drinking might have exacerbated the problem. The reputation of your event is clearly at stake, and you need to show that you are a responsible event organiser.

Produce a 100-word report in the form of a press release to show that you took all possible steps to prevent the overcrowding and address all of the accusations that are being made against you.

Case Study 15.3 illustrates the changing demands of the media and why it is important to develop effective relationships with them, as well as recognising new forms of media such as social media, blogging and influencers. Given the reach of influencers and the growth in their numbers, their impact is significant, and can inform the same stakeholders as the event itself. It is important to provide them with information and regular updates and for event staff to be aware of their needs. This case also highlights how an event can become popular with the media and one that they look forward to as much as the event attendees.

CASE STUDY 15.3

Welcoming bloggers and influencers: Spielwarenmesse: The Nuremberg Toy Fair Press Centre

Location: Nuremberg, Germany
Event type: Large B2B event
Attendees: 70,000 visitors from 136 countries and 2,800 exhibitors from 70 countries

The Spielwarenmesse is a global event for the manufacturers in the toy industry, which takes over the town of Nuremberg in southern Germany for one week every year. It is a business-to-business (B2B) event, which allows manufacturers to showcase their products and services to retailers from around 140 different countries. For the organisers, this presents a challenge to ensure that they take advantage of the opportunity to publicise their event in so many different countries. In order to do this, they must offer access to the media from these countries and have invested in their press centre to help the media before, during and after the event. Not only do they cater to the press, but they also offer their services to bloggers and influencers who they have identified as a key source of publicity for their event. They have developed a relationship with bloggers and influencers and encourage them to seek information.

They have a physical space at the venue where the media are given access to working space, Wi-Fi, refreshments and any additional information that they require. While this represents a significant cost, it also demonstrates the importance of the media, and the role that they have played in turning this into one of the leading events in the world. Clearly, as a specialist market, there are a number of important outlets, such as ToyNews, the Toy Retailers Association and Toy World, however as the main focus of the fair is toys, there is also considerable interest from the media in general.

On their dedicated media webpages, the media are able to register to receive regular updates, download official pictures of the event, and the information is available in different languages. This also includes helping foreign journalists to find accommodation near to the venue and information about the local area, to make the stay of the media as enjoyable as possible. Their treatment of the media is important and they employ dedicated staff to work with them and to seek new opportunities to develop new relationships. The media appreciate this level of service and this possibly contributes to the positive publicity received for the exhibition. While this is a business event, and the toy industry is worth many billions of dollars, the main focus of the exhibition is toys, and so it is important to emphasise the fun side of the event and to present the media who attend with the opportunity to experience the toys and witness the 120 new products that are launched at the fair every year.

Industry voice

Richard Clarke, content, digital marketing and communications consultant

Richard Clarke has unique, global experience in the sports industry. He was responsible for editorial strategy across all media at Arsenal Football Club in London from 2002 to 2015 before moving to Major League Soccer in the USA to run the content and communications departments for the Colorado Rapids. Since returning to England, he has consulted for the Premier League, Bundesliga, UEFA, USA Swimming and Dugout. Richard has also enjoyed two-year spells as consultant Content Director with the Indonesian Football League and then the Pro League in the United Arab Emirates.

Richard started his career in sports journalism and has reported for most of the major English newspapers at one time or another. He hosts the Sports Content Strategy podcast, blogs at MrRichardClarke.com and writes a column for *The Cricket Paper*. His first book, *Last-Wicket Stand*, was published in 2020.

Tell us a little about the events that you have covered and how you have worked with the media

Arsene Wenger's tenure at Arsenal saw the Premier League develop into a broadcasting behemoth and the club grow into a global brand with diverse revenue streams. At that time, it was estimated that every game with Manchester United was seen by around a billion people around the world. So, in terms of size and scale, they must be among the biggest events I covered annually. The departure from Highbury was a year-long celebration but the last game was an intricately planned event which was broadcast globally. I distinctly recall the surreal feeling of running down the tunnel and onto the pitch to interview Wenger and the team at the end of the game. Less than a week later, we lost to Barcelona in the Champions League final in Paris, perhaps the biggest single event I have covered from the press box.

I like to think Arsenal were one of the pioneers in the area of club media. Our reach and engagement soared in the late noughties, a time before the social media companies began asserting their authority via algorithms. However, this led to numerous clashes with traditional media who were protective of their access. There is no-one so insecure as a journalist in danger of losing their exclusive and, even now, club media is still looked down upon by its mainstream cousins. However, in truth, it was no laughing matter on either side. The newspaper industry utterly misjudged the impact of digital. Its business models failed to see the danger and it was stuck trolling out the same old 'lines' for far too long. Sky were the first to shake up this lethargy but I like to think club media nudged the process too given we were digital-first long before anyone else.

When you are running events, what advice would you give to people to help them to maximise media coverage?

In terms of club media, it's simple – understand what your audience wants and how they want to consume your content. Then ask yourself where you can fit into that content mix and what niches you can 'own'.

My plan for Tim Howard's return to Major League Soccer covered all the usual bases in terms of general media but, at club level, I wanted to tell a different story. So I devised a seven part mini-documentary concentrating on different facets of his story. It involved covering his every move – sending our producers to US national team games to interview team-mates, calling in favours from friends at Everton, West Ham, Manchester United and Arsenal to tell the story of his Premier League years. His deal was announced in unison across numerous media – MLS, national television, Tim's management team and the Colorado Rapids – on the day we were playing in Washington DC. I remember racing out of a car to get some video of Tim standing outside the White House that day. He had been called the "Secretary of Defense" after his heroics at the previous World Cup so those shots had resonance and, as the club, we were the only ones able to get them. We also conducted a Facebook Live interview with fans at the team hotel after his announcement. The social media platform was promoting this format heavily that year and so the content reached 3m people. That was huge for a small franchise like the Rapids. Choosing the most advantageous social media platform is critical when you have limited resources. In the Indonesian League, I steered our strategy towards Instagram after researching social media demographics in the country. As a result, the official account went from 0 to 1 million followers in 12 months, quicker than Manchester United.

What do you think has been your most successful event in terms of media coverage received? What did you do to get this coverage?

When Arsenal announced the transfer of Mesut Ozil we made sure our stylised graphic and hashtag were prominent. As he signed while on international duty, there was no press conference or photoshoot so our artwork was used all around the world. In terms of global reach, this was probably the most significant event. However, this is a century ago in the dog years of social media and transfer announcements have developed significantly since then. One innovation we brought in at Arsenal was the 'goodbye interview' when a major player left. The last question of which was always a direct thank you to the fans with the player looking straight down the lens of the camera. Thierry Henry's thank you was so emotional and heartfelt that content creators clipped if off, added a stirring backing track and put it on YouTube. In the modern sense, this must be deemed a success. However, as a complete event, the Howard announcement with its live streamed press conference, full media round at the stadium, Facebook Live, mini-documentary and full media 'carwash' around

New York must take the prize. We even did a Twitter chat with fans as we drove around Manhattan going from *Good Morning America* in Times Square to CNN, Reuters and the *New York Times*. Howard was among the best-known US soccer players at the time so we had to serve national media. But at the club level, we commercialised it too by putting the mini-documentary on Facebook so we could track viewers and advertise to that interested, local audience with a bespoke ticket offer.

How does social media affect the media coverage of events?

It has a huge effect now. In fact, I'd argue it is now the most important channel given how most of the audience, especially the one that appeals to broadcasters and commercial partners, gets their news. It is something I have had to learn. Remember, I was appointed as Arsenal's first website editor in 2002. That is before Twitter, Facebook, YouTube and Instagram existed. It was my job to work out what the club could do with these so-called 'new media' platforms. One of the main claims of my career is that when I left the club, Arsenal were the third most followed sports team in the world on Twitter and the fifth most followed on Facebook. And, as journalists loved reminding the club at the time, we managed to get there without the boost of having won a trophy.

While newspapers have declined in terms of sales, their influence is still strong and they often set the agenda for other media. To use modern parlance, they are a key influencer. But we are starting to see media voices emerge from YouTube channels and social media. They look and talk differently but that is because they are appealing to a different audience. For me, a clever media professional understands the importance of different messengers for different messages.

How can an event manager get the most out of the media when promoting their events?

Firstly, get the basics right. The media need to know the who, what, why, when and where of the event, especially if it is a press conference. Get that out early and make it crystal clear. Also, you need to know how they are going to cover it, what their deadlines or pressures are and how you can help them be successful. Offering fast, stable internet or policing the use of key broadcast positions could be the difference between your story going top or fourth in that evening's sports news bulletin. If you are club media like I have been, you will want content that creates reach, engagement and positive sentiment. Major events are occasions to consider the commercial side of the club too. Clear pictures of partners' logos can make a difference when it is time to renew and you may need a favour from the money men at a later point in the year.

Oh and tea, coffee and decent biscuits never fail to foster good relationships.

15.9 Summary

The events industry must understand the importance of the media and the need to develop very strong relationships with media companies. The media thrive on the news stories that events present to them, which they need in order to keep their audiences entertained. Event managers and the media are entering a new area where greater emphasis is being placed on developing mutually beneficial relationships. The fragmentation of the media, and digital media, such as Facebook, Instagram, TikTok and Twitter, also means that the event manager has to work hard to understand the diverse needs of the media, and to develop new skills for working within it.

New television deals for leading sporting events are driving these events forward, and they now provide the largest revenue streams for many individual sports clubs. The case studies in this chapter have shown how the media have been largely successful in developing top-quality events by providing income for those events in return for media coverage. Obviously, event managers need to keep abreast of current deals, and they should keep a careful eye on how they develop in the future.

The media's role is changing at a rapid rate, so event managers must be prepared to devote time, energy and money to developing their relationships with the press and broadcasters. They must have a good understanding of how publicity is generated, and must be able to calculate the value of the extra awareness that this creates. Finally, they should develop an appreciation of how media organisations work, which will enable them to send out the most appropriate information at the right time.

Review questions

1. Why is global media coverage important for event managers?
2. Why is it important to supply the media with regular content about an event?
3. Why is television coverage considered to be the most important media outlet for event managers?
4. Why are media events important for event managers?
5. Why does the value of media rights increase for some sporting events?
6. How can sporting event organisers make their events more attractive to participants?
7. How does an event manager communicate with different stakeholders?
8. How can you classify event attendees?
9. Why is media coverage important for event sponsors?
10. What are the key areas to be covered in a press release?

Further reading

Getz, D., Andersson, T. and Larson, M. (2007) Festival Stakeholder Roles: Concepts and Case Studies, *Events Management*, *10*: 103–122. This article considers the role of stakeholders at festivals. It is one of the leading papers in this research area.

Pedersen, P. M., Laucella, P. C., Kian, E. and Geurin, A. N. (2020) *Strategic Sport Communication* (3rd edn), Champaign, IL: Human Kinetics.

Tench, R. and Waddington, S. (2020) *Exploring Public Relations and Management Communication* (5th edn), Harlow: Pearson.

Video links

Broadcasting and the Olympics: www.olympic.org/broadcasters

The Hillsborough Stadium Disaster: www.theguardian.com/uk-news/video/2016/apr/26/hillsborough-inquiry-anatomy-of-a-disaster-video

Media Centres for Major Sporting Events: https://architectureofthegames.net/tag/media-centre/

Media Coverage of Glastonbury Music Festival 2020: https://cstonline.net/live-forever-glastonbury-2020-television-time-memory-and-nostalgia-by-leanne-weston/

Rules for Press Releases: https://neilpatel.com/blog/ironclad-rules-for-press/

Weblinks

AIPS – International Sports Press Association: www.aipsmedia.com/index.html?page=artdetail&art=23043

Digital Transformation in the Events Industry: https://fleek.marketing/digital-technology/digital-transformation-in-the-events-industry

Fifty Event Management Experts and Influencers: www.socialtables.com/blog/social-media/event-management-experts-to-follow/

How to Manage Crowds at Events – Crisis Management: https://billetto.co.uk/blog/how-to-manage-crowds-at-events/

Social Media for Events – A Guide on How to Use Social Media for Events: www.eventmanagerblog.com/social-media-events

References

Baines, P., Egan, J. and Jefkins, F. (2005) *Public Relations: Contemporary Issues and Techniques*, Oxford: Elsevier.

Borland, J. and Macdonald, R. (2003) Demand for Sport, *Oxford Review of Economic Policy*, 19 (4): 478–502.

Bowdin, G., Allen, J., O'Toole, W., Harris, R. and McDonnell, I. (2010) *Events Management* (3rd edn), Oxford: Butterworth-Heinemann.

Brassington, F. and Pettitt, S. (2013) *Principles of Marketing* (3rd edn), Harlow: Pearson.

Broom, G. M. and Bey-Ling Sha (2012) *Cutlip and Center's Effective Public Relations* (11th edn), Harlow: Pearson.

Buraimo, B., Paramio, J. L. and Campos, C. (2010) The Impact of Televised Football on Stadium Attendances in English and Spanish League Football, *Soccer and Society*, 11 (4): 461–474.

Carlsen, J., Getz, D. and Soutar, G. (2001) Event Evaluation Research, *Events Management*, 6: 247–257.

Cutlip, S. M., Center, A. and Broom, G. M. (2005) *Effective Public Relations* (9th ed), Englewood Cliffs, NJ: Prentice Hall.

Dwyer, L., Mellor, R., Mistilis, N. and Mules, T. (2001) A Framework for Assessing 'Tangible' and 'Intangible' Impacts of Events and Conventions, *Events Management*, 6: 175–189.

Forrest, D., Simmons, R. and Buraimo, B. (2006) Broadcaster and Audience Demand for Premier League Football. In C. Jeanrenaud and S. Késenne (eds) *The Economics of Sport and Media*: 93–105, Gloucester: Edward Elgar.

Getz, D. and Fairley, S. (2004) Media Management at Sport Events for Destination Promotion: Case Studies and Concepts, *Events Management, 8*: 127–139.

Holden, P. and Wilde, N. (2007) *Marketing and PR*, London: A&C Black.

Horne, J. (2007) The Four 'Knowns' of Sports Mega-Events, *Leisure Studies, 26 (1)*: 81–96.

Inside Hoops (2011) NBA TV Contracts. Available at: www.insidehoops.com/nba-tv-con tracts.shtml [Accessed 6 March 2021].

IPSOS (2010) Survey. Available at: www.ipsos-mori.com/Assets/Docs/Polls/olympics-2012-sur vey-for-bbc-london-july-2010-topline.pdf [Accessed 1 June 2011].

Jefkins, F. (1994) *Public Relations*, London: Macdonald & Evans.

Katz, H. (2019) *The Media Handbook: A Complete Guide to Advertising, Media Selection, Planning, Research and Buying* (7th edn), Abingdon: Routledge.

Kitchen, P. J. (1997) Integrated Marketing Communications in US Advertising Agencies: An Exploratory Study, *Journal of Advertising Research*, September – October: 7–16.

McNamara, J. (2005) *Public Relations Handbook*, Sydney: Archipelago Press.

McQuail, D. (2002) *McQuail's Mass Communication Theory*, London: Sage.

Polo, M. P. and Gonzalez, J. V. (2019) Public Relations and Events: The Organization of Festivals as a Tool for Cultural Promotion, *International Review of Communication and Marketing Mix, 2*: 2.

Regester, M. (2008) *Risk Issues and Crisis Management in Public Relations*, London: Kogan Page.

Rivenburgh, N. (2002) The Olympic Games: Twenty-First Century Challenges as a Global Media Event, *Sport in Society, 5 (3)*: 32–50.

Shone, A. and Parry, B. (2019) *Successful Event Management: A Practical Handbook* (5th edn), Andover: Cengage Learning.

Solves, J., Pappous, I., Rius, I. and Kohe, G. (2018) Framing the Paralympic Games: A Mixed-Methods Analysis of Spanish Media Coverage of the Beijing 2008 and London 2012 Paralympic Games, *Communication and Sport, 7 (6)*: 729–751.

Van Niekerk, M. and Getz, D. (2019) *Event Stakeholders: Theory and Methods for Event Managers and Tourism*, Oxford: Goodfellow Publishers.

Index

Page numbers in *italics* refer figures; *cs* indicates case studies.